Computer Concepts
Third Edition—Illustrated
Introductory Enhanced

June Jamrich Parsons ♦ Dan Oja

COURSE TECHNOLOGY

THOMSON LEARNING

Australia • Canada • Mexico • Singapore • Spain • United Kingdom • United States

COURSE TECHNOLOGY

™

THOMSON LEARNING

Computer Concepts, Third Edition—Illustrated Introductory Enhanced

is published by Course Technology.

Contributing Author:
Rachel Biheller Bunin

Development Editor:
Pamela Conrad

Managing Editor:
Nicole Jones Pinard

Product Manager:
Emily Heberlein

Production Editor:
Anne Valsangiacomo

Associate Product Manager:
Emeline Elliot

Editorial Assistant:
Christina Kling Garrett

Interior Designer:
Joseph Lee, Blackfish Design

Photo and Video Researcher:
Abby Reip

Video Editor:
Jeanne Busemeyer, Hyde Park
Publishing Service

Composition:
GEX Publishing Services

Animations:
Planet Interactive

What's New to the *Enhanced* Third Edition of Illustrated Computer Concepts?

We've kept the same page-for-page content and the same multimedia CD-ROM as the Third Edition, but added two additional units to the book:

Unit I: Trends in Technology

Covering the most recent developments in computer software and hardware, this unit contains 8 new lessons and all new end-of-unit exercises to add to your course.

Bonus Unit: Issues and Up-to-Dates

Including additional exercises for Units A-H, this unit provides additional options for reinforcement and the latest information on developments relating to each unit. Eight new Issues articles and eight new Up-to-Date exercises relate to each of the eight existing units, and challenge students to expand their knowledge. Assign these exercises at the end of each unit, or assign the exercises at the end of the course. Refer to the footer of each page for easy reference back to the unit the exercises correspond to.

Other features of the Enhanced Edition

- ▶ The Instructor's Resource Kit includes TWO testing platforms, Course Test Manager and ExamView (see the Instructor's Resource Kit page for more information).
- ▶ The Instructor's Resource Kit includes all-new material for the two new units.
- ▶ The Student Online Companion includes all-new links for students to explore when working on the new units. It will also include the Buyer's Guide Appendix online!

What Distance Learning options are available with the Enhanced Edition?

MyCourse.com
Need a quick, simple tool to help you manage your course? Try MyCourse.com, the easiest to use, most flexible syllabus and content management tool available. MyCourse.com offers you brand new content, including Topic Reviews, Extra Case Projects, and Quizzes, to accompany this book.

WebCT
Course Technology and WebCT have partnered to provide you with the highest quality online resources and Web-based tools for your class. Course Technology offers content for this book to help you create your WebCT class, such as a suggested Syllabus, Lecture Notes, Practice Test questions, and more.

Blackboard
Course Technology and Blackboard have also partnered to provide you with the highest quality online resources and Web-based tools for your class. Course Technology offers content for this book to help you create your Blackboard class, such as a suggested Syllabus, Lecture Notes, Practice Test questions, and more.

Preface

Welcome to *Computer Concepts, Third Edition —Illustrated Introductory* **Enhanced**, the text that provides a fast-paced and engaging introduction to today's most cutting-edge computer concepts. No other book gets your students up to speed faster! In addition, this book provides numerous opportunities to use technology to enhance learning—CD Connections, CourseLabs, and InfoWeb links all provide students with added help, information, and practice in the concepts they encounter in the book. Icons throughout the book indicate when a Course Lab or InfoWeb is featured for a lesson, and when a CD Connection will bring the ideas illustrated in the text to life. The two new units for the Enhanced edition provide even more computer concepts, and extra exercises for reinforcement and additional exploration.

About this Book

What makes the information in this book so easy to access and digest? It's quite simple. Each concept is presented on two facing pages, with the main points discussed on the left page and large, dramatic illustrations presented on the right. Students can learn all they need to know about a particular topic without having to turn the page! This unique design makes information extremely accessible and easy to absorb, and makes a great reference for after the course is over. The modular structure of the book also allows for great flexibility; you can cover the units in any order you choose, and you can skip lessons if you like.

The sample lesson shown here highlights the standard elements and features that appear in the two-page lessons.

A single concept is presented in a two-page "information display" to help students absorb information quickly and easily.

Easy-to-follow introductions to every lesson focus on a single concept to help students get the point quickly.

Details provide additional key information on the main concept.

Defining the CPU

Digital computers represent data by using a series of electrical signals; data can be held in memory or transported over the data bus. But a computer does more than store and transport data. It processes data, performs arithmetic, sorts lists, formats documents, and so on. The computer processes data in the CPU.

DETAILS
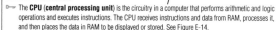
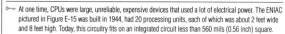

- The **CPU** (**central processing unit**) is the circuitry in a computer that performs arithmetic and logic operations and executes instructions. The CPU receives instructions and data from RAM, processes it, and then places the data in RAM to be displayed or stored. See Figure E-14.

- At one time, CPUs were large, unreliable, expensive devices that used a lot of electrical power. The ENIAC pictured in Figure E-15 was built in 1944, had 20 processing units, each of which was about 2 feet wide and 8 feet high. Today, this circuitry fits on an integrated circuit less than 560 mils (0.56 inch) square.

- The CPU on a mainframe usually consists of one or more integrated circuits and circuit boards. In a microcomputer, the CPU is a single integrated circuit called a **microprocessor**. The microprocessors in today's microcomputers might be housed in a large SEC, as shown in Figure E-16, or in a smaller square PGA.

- Most of today's PCs are designed around microprocessors manufactured by Intel or AMD. Intel created the first processor for the first IBM PC. Computers that contain Intel processors are more expensive than computers that contain "work-alike" processors from other manufacturers. Intel also produces a budget processor called a Celeron, which has slightly less sophisticated architecture than the Pentium models.

- Companies such as Cyrix and AMD produce "work-alike" processors. Computers with such processors are generally less expensive than an equivalent computer with an Intel processor.

- Macintosh computers use a 68000-series or PowerPC microprocessor. Until 1994, Macintosh computers contained a 68000-series microprocessor manufactured by Motorola. More recent models, called Power Macs, contain a PowerPC microprocessor that implements RISC architecture to provide relatively fast performance at a low cost. You'll learn more about RISC in a later lesson.

FYI Disk cache and RAM cache are not identical. Disk cache works with data between the disk and memory. RAM cache works with data between RAM and the CPU.

E-12 ► COMPUTER CONCEPTS

Time-saving QuickTips, Trouble comments, and FYI points provide students with helpful information to round out the lesson information.

Icons in the margins indicate that an interactive lab or InfoWeb is featured for that lesson.

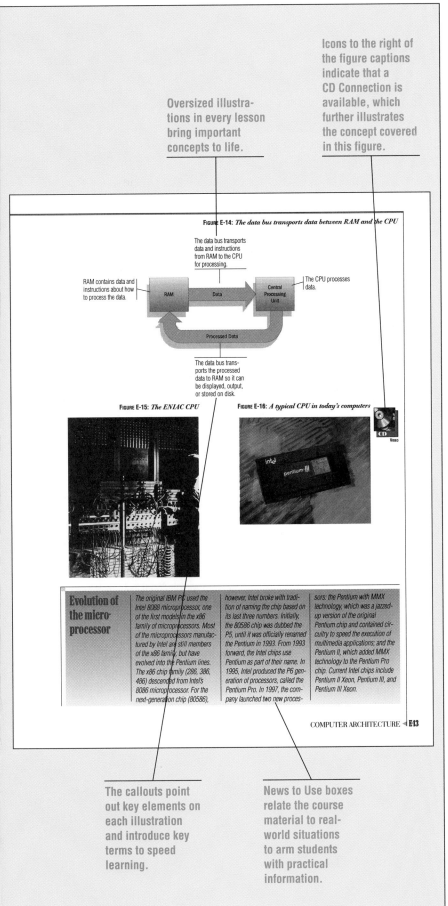

Oversized illustrations in every lesson bring important concepts to life.

Icons to the right of the figure captions indicate that a CD Connection is available, which further illustrates the concept covered in this figure.

FIGURE E-14: *The data bus transports data between RAM and the CPU*

The data bus transports data and instructions from RAM to the CPU for processing.

RAM contains data and instructions about how to process the data.

The CPU processes data.

RAM → Data → Central Processing Unit

Processed Data

The data bus transports the processed data to RAM so it can be displayed, output, or stored on disk.

FIGURE E-15: *The ENIAC CPU*

FIGURE E-16: *A typical CPU in today's computers*

Evolution of the microprocessor

The original IBM PC used the Intel 8088 microprocessor, one of the first models in the x86 family of microprocessors. Most of the microprocessors manufactured by Intel are still members of the x86 family, but have evolved into the Pentium lines. The x86 chip family (286, 386, 486) descended from Intel's 8086 microprocessor. For the next-generation chip (80586), however, Intel broke with tradition of naming the chip based on its last three numbers. Initially, the 80586 chip was dubbed the P5, until it was officially renamed the Pentium in 1993. From 1993 forward, the Intel chips use Pentium as part of their name. In 1995, Intel produced the P6 generation of processors, called the Pentium Pro. In 1997, the company launched two new proces- sors: the Pentium with MMX technology, which was a jazzed- up version of the original Pentium chip and contained cir- cuitry to speed the execution of multimedia applications; and the Pentium II, which added MMX technology to the Pentium Pro chip. Current Intel chips include Pentium II Xeon, Pentium III, and Pentium III Xeon.

COMPUTER ARCHITECTURE **E13**

The callouts point out key elements on each illustration and introduce key terms to speed learning.

News to Use boxes relate the course material to real- world situations to arm students with practical information.

Additional Features

The two-page lesson format featured in this book provides students with a power- ful learning experience. Additionally, this book contains the following features:

- **Outstanding Assessment and Reinforcement**— Every unit concludes with a wide variety of assess- ment exercises to test students' understanding and reinforce the material covered. End of Unit Exercises check students' knowledge of the key points in the unit. Independent Challenges provide assignments that enable students to explore on their own to develop critical thinking skills. Lab Assignments let students work further with the interactive Course Labs featured with this text.

  In addition, there are several other end of unit exercises to further enhance the content: The *Issues* section draws content from the unit to get students involved in expanding their knowl- edge, the *Study Tips* go into further detail, a *Visual Workshop* encourages independent think- ing, and an *Icon Grid* details all the CD elements in the units.

  The Bonus Unit contains additional Issues articles for each unit, and an Up-to-Date exercise for each unit, requiring students to research and compare information they find to information presented in the book.

- **Practical tips for today's computer user**—This book arms students with useful information they can apply at home or on the job.

- A **Buyer's Guide Appendix** provides real-world advice to help students purchase their own computers, software, and Internet services.

- **World Wide Web exposure**—To embrace the power of the information superhighway, this book provides opportunities for exploring the World Wide Web. InfoWebs on the student CD and Student Online Companion offer students the chance to explore the Internet for further informa- tion on topics covered in the book. Web Work Independent Challenge assignments at the end of each unit also encourage students to use the Web as a resource to get information. These exercises are labeled with a Web Work icon.

◀ **V**

Instructor's Resource Kit

The Instructor's Resource Kit (IRK) is Course Technology's way of putting the resources and information needed to teach and learn effectively into your hands. With an integrated array of teaching and learning tools that offer you and your students a broad range of technology-based instructional options, we believe this kit represents the highest quality and most cutting edge resources available to instructors today. Many of these resources are available at www.course.com. The resources available with this book are:

▶ **Course Labs: Bring Concepts to Life**—Computer skills and concepts come to life with the Illustrated Course Labs—highly interactive tutorials that combine illustrations, animations, digital images and simulations. These Labs guide students step by step, present them with Quick Check questions for reinforcement, allow them to explore on their own, and provide printed feedback.

▶ **Electronic Instructor's Manual: Help is only a Few Keystrokes Away**—This enhanced Instructor's Manual offers an outline for each unit, lecture notes, solutions to end-of-unit material, and numerous teaching tips. The Electronic Instructor's Manual can be found on the IRK CD-ROM, or at www.course.com.

▶ **Course Test Manager: Testing and Practice Online or On Paper**—Course Test Manager is a powerful testing and assessment package that enables instructors to create and print tests from testbanks designed specifically for Course Technology titles. In addition, instructors with access to a networked computer lab can administer, grade, and track tests on-line. Students can also take online practice tests, which generate customized study guides that indicate where in the text students can find more information on each question.

▶ **ExamView**—ExamView is a powerful testing software package that allows instructors to create and administer printed, computer (LAN-based), and Internet exams. ExamView includes hundreds of questions that correspond to the topics covered in this text, enabling students to generate detailed study guides that include page references for further review. The computer-based and Internet testing components allow students to take exams at their computers, and also save the instructor time by grading each exam automatically.

▶ **PowerPoint Presentations**—Presentations have been created for each unit (except the Bonus Unit of Exercises) to assist instructors in classroom lectures or to make available to students. The presentations are available on the IRK CD.

▶ **Course Student Online Companion**—Available at www.course.com, this book features its own Student Online Companion where students can go to gain access to Web sites that will help them complete the Web Work Independent Challenges. These links are updated on a regular basis.

About The Technology

CD Connections

CD Connections reveal videos, animations, screen tours, and other treasures to enhance learning and retention of key concepts. CD Connection icons that appear to the right of figure captions and within News to Use boxes indicate when viewing a CD Connection will bring an illustration or explanation to life.

InfoWebs

InfoWebs connect you to Web links, film, video, TV, print, and electronic resources. InfoWebs stay up-to-date and solve the problem of constantly changing URLs. If you have Internet access, you can click on an InfoWeb and be linked directly to resources on the Internet using your browser of choice.

Course Labs

Concepts come to life with the Labs—highly interactive tutorials that combine illustrations, animations, digital images, and simulations. Course Labs guide you step-by-step through a topic, present you with Quick Checks, let you explore on your own, test comprehension, and provide printed feedback. Lab assignments are included at the end of each relevant unit. A Course Lab icon on the left page of a lesson indicates that a Course Lab is featured for that particular concept.

Credits

Author Acknowledgements

We offer heartfelt thanks to all of the members of the Illustrated team for contributing their vision, talent, and skills to make this book a reality. A special thanks to Pamela Conrad, the Developmental Editor, for her insight, superior skill, and devotion through all the editions of this book. Whether you are a student or an instructor, we thank you for using our book and hope that you find it to be a valuable educational tool.

Brief Contents

Contents

UNIT D Computer Files and Data Storage   D-1

UNIT G The Internet   G-1

UNIT H   Data Security and Control   H-1

UNIT I   Trends in Technology   I-1

BONUS Bonus Issues and Up-To-Dates   1

APPENDIX A Buyers Guide   1

Computers: Essential Concepts

In this unit you will be introduced to computer systems—specifically, microcomputer systems. You will learn which computer components are necessary for communication between people and computers. You will also learn about user interfaces typically found on today's computer systems and ways to respond to what you see on the computer screen. The unit concludes with a discussion about resources and how you can get help as you learn how to interact with a specific computer system or software package.

Defining computers

Computers have been called "mind tools" because they enhance our ability to perform tasks that require mental activity. Computers are adept at performing activities such as making calculations quickly, sorting large lists, and searching through vast information libraries. Although people can perform all of these activities, a computer can often accomplish them much more quickly and more accurately. Our ability to use a computer makes us more productive. The key to making effective use of the computer as a tool is to know what a computer does, how it works, and how to use it. This book defines a **computer** as a device that accepts input, processes data, stores data, and produces output. A computer is actually part of a computer system. This lesson identifies the basic elements of a computer system.

DETAILS

- A **computer system** includes hardware, peripheral devices, and software. Refer to Figure A-1 for a picture of a basic computer system.

- **Hardware** includes the electronic and mechanical devices that process data. The computer itself is part of the computer system hardware. In addition to the computer, the term "hardware" refers to components called peripheral devices.

- **Peripheral devices** expand the computer's input, output, and storage capabilities.

- An **input device** is a peripheral device used to gather and translate input into a form that the computer can process. As a computer user, you will probably use the keyboard as your main input device.

- An **output device** is a peripheral device that displays, prints, or transmits the results of processing from the computer memory. As a computer user, you will probably use the monitor as your main output device.

- The computer hardware in and of itself does not provide a particularly useful mind tool. A computer requires a set of instructions, called **software** or a **computer program**, which tells the computer how to perform a particular task. Software sets up a computer to do a particular task by telling the computer how to interact with the user and how to process the user's data.

- The distinction between a computer and a computer system is that a computer does not include peripheral devices, but a computer system does. Many people, when they say "computer," actually mean "computer system."

Why does a computer need software?

A computer without software is like a tape player without tapes or a CD player without CDs. Without software, a computer is just a useless gadget that does not let you do much more than turn it on and off. Fortunately, software is available for an astonishing number of tasks, including producing resumes, managing a small business, helping you study for the Graduate Record Examination, teaching you Spanish, helping you plan your diet, composing music, and taking you on an adventure through a dangerous labyrinth.

INFOWEB
COMPUTER
TERMINOLOGY

The primary output device on a micro-computer is the **monitor**—a display device that forms an image by converting electrical signals from the computer into points of colored light on the screen.

A **floppy disk drive** is a storage device that writes data on floppy disks. A typical micro-computer system has a 3½-inch floppy disk drive that stores as many as 1.44 million characters of data on one floppy disk. A light indicates when the floppy disk drive is in use. This is a warning not to remove your disk until the light goes out.

The **system unit** is the case or box that contains the power supply, storage devices, and the circuit board with the computer's main processor and memory.

A **CD-ROM drive** and **DVD drive** are storage devices that use laser technology to read data from optical disks.

Floppy disks are popular micro-computer storage media. **Storage media** are physical materials that provide long-term storage for computer data.

CD-ROM and **DVD disks** look similar. Typically, both contain information when you purchase them and do not allow you to add or change the information they contain.

Most computers are equipped with a **keyboard** as the primary input device. A computer keyboard includes the letter and number keys, as well as several keys that control computer-specific tasks.

A **hard disk drive** can store billions of character on a non-removable disk platter. A hard drive is mounted inside the system unit; an external light indicates when the hard disk drive is in use.

A **mouse** is an input device that you use to manipulate objects on the screen.

Exploring computer functions

A basic computer system is defined as a device that accepts input, processes data, stores data, and produces output. To understand a basic computer system, it is important to look more closely at the functions it performs. Figure A-2 illustrates the fundamental computer functions and components that help the computer accomplish each function.

DETAILS

- A computer accepts input. Computer **input** is whatever is put into a computer system. Input can be supplied by a person, by the environment, or by another computer. Examples of the kinds of input a computer can process include the words and symbols in a document, numbers for a calculation, instructions for completing a process, pictures, audio signals from a microphone, and temperatures from a thermostat. *Input* is also used as a verb meaning "to feed information into a computer."

- A computer processes data. **Data** refers to the symbols that represent facts and ideas. Computers manipulate data in many ways, and we call this manipulation "processing." In the context of computers, then, we can define a **process** as a systematic series of actions a computer uses to manipulate data. Some ways a computer can process data include performing calculations, sorting lists of words or numbers, modifying documents and pictures according to user instructions, and drawing graphs. A computer processes data in a device called the **central processing unit (CPU)**.

- A computer stores data. A computer must store data so it is available for processing. The places a computer puts data are referred to as **storage**. Most computers have more than one location for storing data. The place where the computer stores data depends on how the data is being used. The computer puts data in one place while it is waiting to be processed and in another place when the data is not needed for immediate processing. **Memory** is an area that holds data waiting to be processed. Storage is the area where data can be left on a permanent basis while it is not needed for processing.

- A computer produces output. Computer **output** is the result produced by a computer. Examples of computer output include reports, documents, music, graphs, and pictures. *Output* is also used as a verb meaning "to produce output."

John von Neumann

When the photo in Figure A-3 was published in 1947, the caption read, "Dr. John von Neumann stands in front of a new Electronic 'Brain,' the fastest computing machine for its degree of precision yet made. The machine, which can do 2,000 multiplications in one second and add or subtract 100,000 times in the same period, was displayed today for the first time at the Institute for Advanced Study. Its fabulous memory can store 1,024 numbers of 12 decimal places each. Dr. von Neumann was one of the designers of the wonder machine." Dr. von Neumann wrote one of the first reports specifically defining the components of a computer and describing their functions.

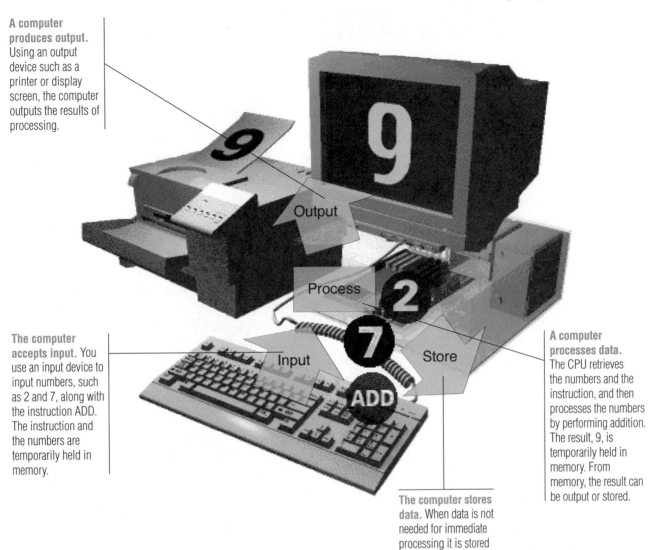

A computer produces output. Using an output device such as a printer or display screen, the computer outputs the results of processing.

Output

Process

Input

Store

ADD

The computer accepts input. You use an input device to input numbers, such as 2 and 7, along with the instruction ADD. The instruction and the numbers are temporarily held in memory.

A computer processes data. The CPU retrieves the numbers and the instruction, and then processes the numbers by performing addition. The result, 9, is temporarily held in memory. From memory, the result can be output or stored.

The computer stores data. When data is not needed for immediate processing it is stored on disk or tape.

FIGURE A-3: *John von Neumann*

JOHN VON NEUMANN

Categorizing computers

Traditionally, computers have been classified into four categories that provide some indication of their processing capabilities or "power": microcomputers, minicomputers, mainframes, and supercomputers. A computer is categorized based on its technology, function, physical size, performance, and cost. Because the criteria for these categories evolve as technology advances, the lines that divide the computer categories shift. Computer sales literature often includes how the manufacturer classifies the computer.

DETAILS

- **Microcomputers**, also known as personal computers (PCs), are the computers you typically find in homes and small businesses. The microcomputer you use might be a stand-alone unit, or it might be connected to other computers so you can share data and software with other users. Even when your computer is connected to others, however, it will generally carry out only your processing tasks. A microcomputer processor performs about 500 million operations per second. Microcomputers come in many shapes and sizes. Refer to Figure A-4 for an example of one microcomputer.

- **Minicomputers** are somewhat larger than microcomputers and are generally used in business and industry for specific tasks, such as processing payroll. One minicomputer can carry out the processing tasks for many users. If you are using a minicomputer system, you use a terminal to input your processing requests and view the results. A **terminal** is a device used for input and output, but not for processing. Your terminal transmits your processing request to the minicomputer. The minicomputer sends back results to your terminal when the processing is complete. The minicomputer system with several terminals shown in Figure A-5 is fairly typical.

- **Mainframes** are large, fast, and fairly expensive computers, generally used by business or government to provide centralized storage, processing, and management for large amounts of data and to provide that data on demand to many users. Mainframes remain the computer of choice in situations where reliability, data security, and centralized control are necessary. Mainframes can service more users than a minicomputer. Users who input processing requests using a terminal. To process large amounts of data, mainframes process billions of instructions per second and often include more than one processing unit. One processing unit might direct overall operations, a second might handle communication with all the users requesting data, and a third processing unit might find the data requested by users. A typical mainframe computer is shown in Figure A-6.

- **Supercomputers** are the largest, fastest, and most expensive type of computer. Unlike minicomputers and mainframes, supercomputers are not designed to optimize processing for multiple users. Instead, supercomputers use their significant processing power to solve very difficult problems such as predicting the weather, molecular modeling, and high-performance animation, as shown in Figure A-7. A supercomputer can process one trillion instructions per second.

Computer networks

A **computer network** is a collection of computers and other devices connected to share data, hardware, and software. A network can connect microcomputers, minicomputers, and mainframes. A network has advantages for an organization and must be secure to protect the data it stores. Networks are cost-effective. For example, if a group of users shares a printer on a network, the organization saves money because it does not have to purchase a printer for every user. Network users can send messages to others on the network and retrieve data from a centralized storage device. The world's largest computer network, the Internet, provides connections for millions of computers all over the globe. The Internet provides many information services, the most popular is the World Wide Web, often referred to as the Web. Computer sites all over the world store data of various sorts, such as weather maps, census data, product information, course syllabi, music, and images.

FIGURE A-4: *Typical microcomputer*

▼ A **desktop microcomputer** fits on a desk and runs on power from an electrical wall outlet. The display screen is usually placed on top of the horizontal desktop case.

FIGURE A-5: *Typical minicomputer*

▲ A typical microcomputer handles processing tasks for multiple users. Terminals act as each user's main input and output device. The terminal has a keyboard for input and a display screen for output, but does not process the user's data.

◄ This minicomputer stores data for all users in one centralized location.

FIGURE A-6: *Typical mainframe*

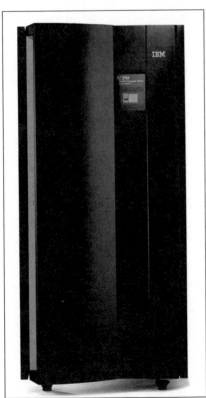

▲ The closet-sized system unit for an IBM S/390 G5 mainframe computer contains the processing unit, memory, and circuitry to support multiple terminals.

FIGURE A-7: *Animated dinosaur*

▲ When creating the animated dinosaur skeleton for a McDonald's commercial, processing each frame might have required one hour of computer time on a very fast microcomputer. At 24 frames per second, it would take 24 hours to complete one second of animation. The animators at Synchromics used the supercomputer at the Maui High Performance Computing Center to reduce this time from 24 hours to 2 hours.

Examining microcomputers

Microcomputers, minicomputers, mainframes, and supercomputers all input, process, and store data. This book focuses on microcomputers, because they are a part of most people's daily lives. Individuals are most likely to use this type of computer. Although hundreds of companies manufacture microcomputers, only a small number of microcomputer designs or **platforms** exist. Today, two major microcomputer platforms are used: IBM-compatibles and Macintosh-compatibles. Because the vast majority of the microcomputers in use today are IBM-compatible, the examples in this book focus on the IBM platform.

DETAILS

- **IBM-compatible computers**, also referred to as **PCs**, are based on the architecture of the first IBM microcomputers, which were built with standard off-the-shelf components. IBM still manufactures a full line of PCs. IBM-compatible computers are manufactured by many companies including Compaq, Dell, and Gateway. Figure A-8 shows a typical IBM-compatible computer. The software designed for PCs is usually called **Windows software** and, therefore, the PC platform is sometimes referred to as the Windows platform.

- **Mac platform**, the second major microcomputer platform, is based on the Macintosh computer. **Macs** are based on proprietary Macintosh computer architecture, which is manufactured almost exclusively by Apple Computer, Inc. Figure A-9 shows a Power Mac G4 Macintosh computer.

- Computers that operate in essentially the same way are said to be **compatible**. Two computers are compatible if they can communicate with each other, share the same software, share data, and use the same peripheral devices. Not all microcomputers are compatible with each other. The IBM platform and the Macintosh platform are not regarded as compatible because they cannot use the same hardware devices or programs without hardware and software specially designed to translate between them. Therefore, sharing data between these two platforms is inconvenient, but not impossible.

- Microcomputers come in a variety of shapes, sizes, and colors. Microcomputers can range in size from palm-top models like the PalmPilot to notebooks to desktop models. Figure A-10 shows some of the various sizes available. The Macintosh iMac, a desktop microcomputer, even comes in a variety of colors.

Hardware product life cycle

Microcomputers and related products are changing rapidly. Ideas for new products are everywhere; users express their needs for improved features, engineers produce more efficient designs, scholars publish new theories, and competitors announce new products. As a consumer, you should be wary of making purchasing decisions based on product announcements. A product announcement can precede the actual product by several years. New microcomputers and their products offer the latest features and often sell for a premium price. When a product is first introduced, the hardware manufacturer usually establishes a list price slightly higher than its previous generation of products.

▲ Some desktop microcomputers feature a vertically oriented tower case, which typically allows more room for expansion than a horizontal case. The tower unit can be placed on the floor to save desk space.

FIGURE A-9: *Mac platform microcomputer*

FIGURE A-10: *Microcomputer packaging*

▼ A **notebook computer**, sometimes called a "laptop," is small and light, giving it the advantage of portability that standard desktop computers do not have. A notebook computer can run on power from an electrical outlet or batteries.

▼ A **desktop microcomputer** fits on a desk and runs on power from an electrical wall outlet. The display screen is usually placed on top of the horizontal desktop case.

▲ A **personal digital assistant** (PDA), or "palm-top" computer achieves even more portability than a notebook computer by shrinking or eliminating some standard components, such as the keyboard. On a keyboardless PDA, a touch-sensitive screen accepts characters drawn with your finger. PDAs easily connect to desktop computers to exchange and update information.

Introducing peripheral devices

Microcomputer, minicomputer, mainframe, and supercomputer systems all include peripheral devices, which are used to input, output, and store data. This lesson discusses the hardware peripheral components you are likely to use on a typical microcomputer system.

DETAILS

☞ What are peripheral devices? **Peripheral devices** are equipment used with a computer to enhance its functionality. They are hardware components that are "outside" of, or in addition to, the computer. For example, a printer is a popular peripheral device used with microcomputers, minicomputers, and mainframe computers. The keyboard, monitor, mouse, and disk drive for your microcomputer are also peripheral devices, even though they were included with your basic computer system. Figure A-11 shows some popular peripheral devices used with microcomputers.

☞ Why use peripheral devices? Peripheral devices allow you to expand and modify your basic computer system. For example, you might purchase a computer that includes a mouse, but you might want to modify your system by purchasing a trackball to use instead of the mouse. You might want to expand your computer's capabilities by adding a scanner so that you can input photographs. If you're an artist, you might want to add a graphics tablet, so you can sketch pictures using a pencil-like stylus. A peripheral device called a modem connects your computer to the telephone system so that you can access information stored on other computers. A modem is a required peripheral if you want to connect to the Internet.

☞ How are peripheral devices installed? Most microcomputer peripheral devices are designed for installation by users who don't have technical expertise. When you buy a peripheral device it usually comes with installation instructions and specially designed software. You should carefully follow the instructions to install the device. The instructions will also explain how to install any software that might be necessary to use the peripheral device. When installing peripherals on a PC, Windows lets the system do all the installing and configuring of additional peripheral devices by identifying the new device and setting it up to work with your computer system. Always make sure that the computer is turned off before you attempt to connect a peripheral device so you don't damage your computer system.

Pointing devices

Pointing devices such as a mouse, a trackball, and a light-pen help you to manipulate objects and select menu options. The most popular pointing device is the mouse. The mouse is used to input data and to manipulate objects displayed on the screen. A pointer on the screen shows the movement of the mouse. Virtually every computer is equipped with a mouse.

◀ Monitors come in many shapes and sizes, including this flat panel liquid crystal display (LCD).

▶ A color ink-jet printer creates characters and graphics by spraying ink onto paper.

◀ A computer projection device produces a large display of the information shown on the computer screen.

▶ A laser printer uses the same technology as a photocopier to produce professional-quality text and graphics.

◀ A scanner converts a page of text or images into an electronic format that the computer can display, print, and store.

▶ A dot matrix printer creates characters and graphics by printing a fine pattern of dots using a 9-pin or 24-pin print mechanism.

◀ A digital camera records an image, then special digitizing hardware and software convert the image into a signal that a computer can store and transmit.

▶ A multifunction device like this combination printer, scanner, fax, and answering machine provides an alternative to purchasing several separate devices.

◀ A trackball and a joystick are pointing devices that you might use as an alternative to a mouse.

▶ A graphics tablet accepts input from a pressure-sensitive stylus, converting pen strokes into images on the screen.

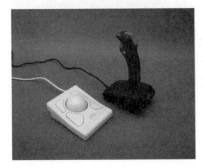

Examining keyboards

Most computers are equipped with a keyboard as the primary input device. A computer keyboard includes keys or buttons with letters and numbers as well as several keys with special characters and special words to control computer-specific tasks. Virtually every computer user interface requires you to use a keyboard. Although you don't have to be a great typist to use a computer effectively, you should be familiar with the computer keyboard and its special keys. Figure A-12 shows the location of the keys on a standard computer keyboard.

KEYBOARD AND
TYPING TUTOR

DETAILS

- You use the keys to input commands, respond to prompts, and type the text of documents. A cursor or an insertion point indicates where the characters you type will appear. The **cursor** appears on the screen as a flashing underline. The **insertion point** appears on the screen as a flashing vertical bar. You can change the location of the cursor or insertion point using the arrow keys or the mouse.

- The **numeric keypad** provides you with a calculator-style input device for numbers and arithmetic symbols. You can type numbers using either the set of number keys at the top of the keyboard or the keys on the numeric keypad. Notice that some keys on the numeric keypad contain two symbols. When the Num Lock key is activated, the numeric keypad will produce numbers. When the Num Lock key is not activated, the keys on the numeric keypad move the cursor in the direction indicated by the arrows on the keys.

  The Num Lock key is an example of a toggle key. A **toggle key** switches back and forth between two modes. The Caps Lock key is also a toggle key. When you press the Caps Lock key, you switch or "toggle" into uppercase mode. When you press the Caps Lock key again you toggle back into lowercase mode.

- **Function keys**, those keys numbered F1 through F12, are located either at the top or along the side of your keyboard. They were added to computer keyboards to help you initiate commands. For example, with many software packages, you press the [F1] key to get help. The problem with function keys is that they are not standardized. In one program, you might press [F7] to save a document; but in another program, you might press [F5] to perform the same task.

- **Modifier keys**, the [Ctrl] (Control), [Alt], and [Shift] keys are located at the periphery of the typing keypad. There are 12 function keys, but you usually need more than 12 commands to control software. Therefore, you can use the [Ctrl], [Alt], and [Shift] keys in conjunction with the function keys to expand the repertoire of available commands. The [Alt] and [Ctrl] modifier keys also work in conjunction with the letter keys. Instead of using the mouse, you might use the [Alt] or [Ctrl] keys in combination with letter keys to access menu options. Such combinations are called **keyboard shortcuts**. If you see Alt+F1, [Alt F1], Alt-F1, or Alt F1 on the screen or in an instruction manual, it means to hold down the [Alt] key and press [F1] at the same time. You might see similar notations for using the [Ctrl] or [Shift] keys. In many Windows programs, [Ctrl]+X works as a keyboard shortcut to cut a selection and place it on the Clipboard, [Ctrl]+V works as a keyboard shortcut to paste the contents of the Clipboard at the insertion point, and [Ctrl]+[C] works as a keyboard shortcut to copy selected contents so that you can paste that information at the insertion point.

The **Esc** or "escape" key cancels an operation.

Function keys execute commands, such as saving a document. The command associated with each function key depends on the software you are using.

Each time you press the **Backspace** key, one character to the left of the insertion point is deleted.

The **Print Screen** key either prints the contents of the screen or stores a copy of your screen in memory that you can manipulate or print with graphics software.

The function of the **Scroll Lock** key depends on the software you are using. This key is rarely used with today's software.

Indicator lights show you the status of each toggle key: Num Lock, Caps Lock, and Scroll Lock. The Power light indicates whether the computer is on or off.

The **Insert** key toggles between insert mode and typeover mode.

The **Num Lock** key is a toggle key that switches between number keys and arrow keys on the numeric keypad.

The **Caps Lock** key capitalizes all the letters you type when it is engaged, but does not produce the top symbol on keys that contain two symbols.

You hold down the **Ctrl** or the **Alt** key while you press another key. The result of Ctrl key or Alt key combinations depends on the software you are using.

You hold down the **Shift** key while you press another key. The Shift key capitalizes letters and produces the top symbol on keys that contain two symbols.

The **Home** key takes you to the beginning of a line or the beginning of a document, depending on the software you are using.

The **arrow** keys move the insertion point.

The **End** key takes you to the end of the line or the end of a document, depending on the software you are using.

The **Page Up** key displays the previous screen of information. The **Page Down** key displays the next screen of information.

Alternative keyboard designs

In addition to the standard keyboard, innovative alternatives are becoming available. For example, some keyboards come with Internet hot keys. These keyboards have special keys that let you instantly access favorite Internet activities such as e-mailing, shopping, or searching the Web. Another alternative is an ergonomically designed keyboard, such as the one shown in Figure A-13, which may prevent computer, stress-related wrist injuries.

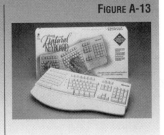

Examining monitors

The primary output device on a microcomputer is the monitor. A **monitor** is a display device that converts the electrical signals from the computer into points of light on a screen to form an image. A monitor is a required output device for just about every computer-user interface. A computer display system consists of a monitor and a graphics card, also called a **video display adapter** or **video card**. A **graphics card** is an expansion card that controls the signals that the computer sends to the monitor. The monitor displays results, prompts, menus, and graphical objects. Monitors are manufactured with different features that determine whether they can display color and graphics.

**DISPLAYS
SYSTEMS**

DETAILS

▭— Monochrome monitors, which were the first microcomputer monitors and which still remain in use as displays on many terminals, are character-based. A **character-based display** divides the screen into a grid of rectangles. The set of characters that the screen can display is not modifiable; therefore, it is not possible to display different sizes or styles of characters. Character-based displays are technically classified as monochrome displays because they use only one color to display text on a black background.

▭— Color monitors are more commonly used with microcomputers. Factors that influence the quality of a color monitor include screen size, dot pitch, and maximum resolution.

- **Screen size** is the measurement in inches from one corner of the screen diagonally across to the opposite corner. Typical monitor screen sizes include 13", 15", 17", 19", and 21". The 13" and 15" monitors are considered "small," whereas the 17", 19", and 21" monitors are considered large. With a large monitor, you can switch to a higher resolution to fit more on the screen, and the text will remain reasonably large. On most monitors, the viewable image does not stretch to the edge of the screen, instead, a black border makes the image smaller than, for example, the 15" size specified. Many computer vendors now include a measurement for the **viewable image size (vis)**, as shown in Figure A-14.

- A **graphics display** or **bitmap display** divides the screen into a matrix of small dots called **pixels**. Any characters or graphics that the computer displays on the screen must be constructed of dot patterns within the screen matrix. **Dot pitch** is a measure of image clarity: a smaller dot pitch means a crisper image. Technically, dot pitch is the distance in millimeters between like-colored pixels.

- The more dots your screen displays in the matrix, the higher the **resolution**. The specifications for a monitor include its **maximum resolution**—the maximum number of pixels it can display. Figure A-15 illustrates how resolution affects the image you see on your screen. Standard resolutions include 640 x 480, 800 x 600, 1024 x 768, 1280 x 1024, and 1600 x 1200. It is important to realize that both the graphics card and the monitor determine the maximum resolution you can use. If your graphics card supports 1600 x 1200 resolution, but your monitor supports only 1280 x 1024, the maximum resolution you can use will be 1280 x 1024.

▭— For many years, CRT monitors were standard on desktop computer displays. **CRT (cathode ray tube)** technology uses a gunlike mechanism to spray the screen with dots of color. This inexpensive and dependable technology is similar to that used in most television sets. **LCD (Liquid Crystal Display)** technology offers an alternative to CRT monitors. LCD displays produce an image by manipulating light within a layer of liquid crystal cells. Modern LCD technology is compact and lightweight, and it provides a stable, easy-to-read display. LCD displays are standard on notebook computers but have also become available for desktop computers, as shown in Figure A-16.

FYI

Video display adapters can use special graphics chips called accelerated video adapters to increase the speed at which images are displayed.

► Most of today's PCs feature a color monitor that displays text amd graphics within a matrix of pixels. The more pixels in the matrix, the higher the resolution, and the smoother, more realistic the image.

FIGURE A-15: *Comparing screen resolution*

◄ The upper screen shows a simulation of a computer display set at 1024 x 768 resolution. Notice the size of characters and other screen objects.

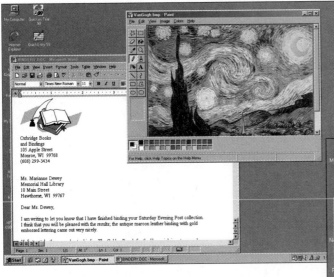

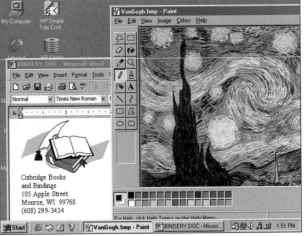

► This screen is set at 640 x 480 resolution. Characters and icons appear larger, but the screen-based desktop appears to be a smaller work area with the higher resolution.

FIGURE A-16: *Flat panel LCD monitor*

◄ A flat panel LCD monitor provides good image quality and requires only a small amount of desk space.

Examining printers

After monitors, printers are the second most common peripheral output device for many computer systems. This is because if you want to have a hard copy (paper copy) of your output, you need a printer. The four most important factors to consider when comparing printers are resolution, color capability, speed, and cost. Several types of printers are available: laser printers, ink-jet printers, and dot matrix printers. This lesson looks at each type of printer in more detail.

DETAILS

InfoWeb
PRINTERS

☞ **Laser printers**, see Figure A-17, use the same technology as duplicating machines. A laser charges a pattern of particles on a drum, which picks up a powdery black substance called **toner**. The toner is transferred onto paper that rolls past the drum.

In the past, the high price of laser printers limited their use to businesses and large organizations. They have decreased in price and are now affordable for individuals. Personal laser printers produce 6 to 8 pages per minute (ppm) at a resolution of 600 dots per inch (dpi). Professional models print at 15–25 ppm and at 1,200 dpi.

Color laser printers work by reprinting each page for each primary color. For each reprint, the paper must be precisely positioned so each color is in exactly the right spot. This requirement dramatically increases the complexity of the print mechanism and the amount of time required to print each page. Operating costs include replacement toner cartridges and print drums.

Laser printers accept print commands from a PC, but use their own language to construct a page before printing. **Printer Control Language (PCL)** is the most widely used, but some printers also use **PostScript**, the language preferred by professionals.

☞ **Ink-jet printers**, see Figure A-18, produce characters and graphics by spraying ink onto paper. The print head is a matrix of fine spray nozzles. Patterns are formed by activating selected nozzles. Ink-jet printers typically form a character in a 20 x 20 matrix. They use CMYK color, which requires only cyan (blue), magenta (pink), yellow, and black inks to produce a printout that appears to have thousands of colors. Color ink-jet printers have excellent resolution, ranging from 600 dpi to 1,440 dpi, and they print at a respectable rate of 5 ppm. Ink-jet printers provide low-cost, high-quality print on plain paper.

☞ **Dot matrix printers**, see Figure A-19, create letters and graphics by striking an inked ribbon with a column of small wires called *pins*. Also called "impact printers," they can print multipart forms and were the technology of choice when computers first appeared in the late 1970s. By activating some wires in the column, but not activating others, the printer creates patterns for letters and numbers. The more pins in the column, the better the print quality. Therefore, a 24-pin dot matrix printer is capable of better-quality output than a 9-pin printer. With a maximum resolution of 140 dpi, such printers produce low-quality output.

For dot matrix printers, speed is measured in characters per second (cps). A fast dot matrix printer can print at a rate of 455 cps or 5 ppm. Dot matrix printers are used primarily for back office applications that demand low operating cost and dependability, but not high print quality.

Making the most of limited desk space

If your home office has limited desk space, you can buy a device that combines equipment such as a fax machine, telephone, answering machine, copier, printer, and scanner. Multifunction printers use either laser or ink-jet technology to take the place of a variety of printing and communication devices. See Figure A-20.

FIGURE A-20

CD
VIDEO

◀ Laser printers use the same technology as duplicating machines. A laser charges a pattern of particles on a drum, which picks up a powdery black substance called toner. The toner is transferred onto paper that rolls past the drum.

InfoWeb

▶ An ink-jet printer produces characters and graphics by spraying ink onto paper. The print head is a matrix of fine spray nozzles. Patterns are formed by activating selected nozzles. An ink-jet printer typically forms a character in a 20 x 20 matrix, producing a high quality printout.

CD
ANIMATION

◀ The print head in a dot matrix printer contains a row of fine wires that strike the ribbon and paper to produce a matrix of dots that form characters or graphical images.

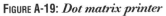

Communicating with computers: prompts, wizards, and command-line interfaces

To use the computer effectively, you must communicate with it; you must tell the computer what tasks to perform, and you must accurately interpret the information the computer provides to you. The means by which people and computers communicate is referred to as the **user interface**. A good user interface makes a computer easy to use, intuitive, and unobtrusive. Through the user interface, the computer accepts your input and presents you with output. This output provides you with the results of processing, confirms the completion of the processing, or indicates that data was stored. Three means of communicating with computers are prompts, wizards, and command lines.

DETAILS

○━ A **prompt** is a message displayed by the computer that asks for input from the user. Some prompts, such as "Enter your name:," are helpful and easy to understand, even for beginners. Other prompts, like A:\>, are less helpful. You respond to a computer prompt by entering the requested information or by following the instruction.

A sequence of prompts is sometimes used to develop a user interface called a **prompted dialog**. In a prompted dialog, a sort of conversation takes place between the computer and user. Prompted dialogs are rarely found in microcomputer software packages.

○━ Current microcomputer software tends to use wizards instead of prompted dialogs. A **wizard** is a sequence of screens that direct you through multistep software tasks such as creating a graph, a list of business contacts, or a fax cover sheet. Wizards, like the one shown in Figure A-21, use graphics and dialog boxes (discussed in the next lesson) to help explain the prompts and allow users to back up and change their responses.

○━ A **command** is an instruction that you input to tell the computer to carry out a task. An interface that requires the user to type in commands is referred to as a **command-line user interface**. Each word in a command results in a specific action by the computer. Learning to use a command-line user interface is not easy, however. You must memorize the command words and know what they mean. These interfaces are typical of first-generation computers, sometimes referred to as DOS machines.

The commands you input must conform to a specific syntax. **Syntax** specifies the sequence and punctuation for command words, parameters, and switches. **Parameters** specify exactly how you want the command to be carried out. If you misspell a command word, leave out required punctuation, or type the command words out of order, you will get an **error message** or **syntax error**. When you get an error message or syntax error, you must figure out what is wrong with the command and retype it correctly. If you forget the correct command word or punctuation, or if you find yourself using an unfamiliar command-line user interface, you may be able to find help right on the computer. Look for Help on the menu bar, or press [F1].

When you use a command-line user interface, the prompt C:\> means the computer is ready to work with the hard disk drive. In the command line C:\>dir/ON, *dir* is the command to display the contents of drive C, and the parameter *ON* specifies that the directory display the list in order by name.

CD
SCREENTOUR

The Business Card Wizard helps you create business cards that you can print on a laser printer.

The wizard prompts you at each step. First, you enter the information you want printed on the card.

Business Card Wizard Step 1 of 3

About

Type the information you would like your business card to contain.

Name: Sandra B. Philips

Position: Systems Analyst

Company: Consultant Services Group

Address: One Main Street

City, State, Zip: Cambridge, MA 04141

Telephone: 817-552-1234

Fax:

e-mail: sphilips@scg.com

Cancel   < Back   Next >   Finish

Next you decide what style you'd like for your business card. The wizard lets you move forward or backward to change your responses until the business card is set up to your satisfaction.

Business Card Wizard Step 2 of 3

Select the style for your business card.

Style
- Classic
- Contemporary
- Casual

Logo

Sandra B. Philips
Systems Analyst

Consultant Services Group
One Main Street
Cambridge, MA 04141

Phone: 817-552-1234

e-mail: sphilips@scg.com

Cancel   < Back   Next >   Finish

Is the user interface hardware or software?

The user interface is a combination of software and hardware. The software that controls the user interface defines its characteristics. For example, software controls whether you accomplish tasks by manipulating graphical objects or by typing commands. Software interface elements include prompts, wizards, menus, dialog boxes, and graphical objects. The hardware controls the way you physically manipulate the computer to establish communication—for example, whether you use a keyboard, mouse, or your voice to input commands. After you have a general understanding of user interfaces, you will be able to figure out quickly how to make the computer do what you want it to do.

Communicating with computers: menus and dialog boxes

Menus and dialog boxes were developed in response to the difficulties many people experienced when trying to remember the command words and syntax for command-line user interfaces. Menus and dialog boxes are popular because when you use them, you do not have to remember command words. You simply choose the command you want from a menu or enter information in a dialog box specific to the task you want the computer to complete.

DETAILS

- A **menu** displays a list of commands or options. Each line of the menu is a command and is referred to as a **menu option** or a **menu item**. Figure A-22 shows you how to use a menu.

  You might wonder how a menu can present all the commands that you want to input. Obviously, there are many possibilities for combining command words, so there could be hundreds of menu options. Two methods are generally used to present a reasonably sized list of menu options. One method uses a sub-menu. The other method uses a dialog box.

- A **hierarchy** is an organization of things that are ranked one above the other. For example, a business might show the hierarchy of its employees on an organizational chart. A **submenu**, as its name implies, means that menus are arranged in a hierarchical structure. After you make a selection from one menu, a submenu appears, and you can make additional choices by selecting an option from it.

- Instead of leading to a submenu, some menu options lead to a dialog box. A **dialog box** displays the options associated with a command. Although a dialog box appears in conjunction with a menu, it is really a different type of user interface element. It combines the characteristics of both menus and prompts. You fill in the dialog box to indicate how you want the command to be carried out, as shown in Figure A-23.

  Dialog box controls let you specify settings and other command parameters. Figure A-24 explains how to use some common dialog box controls.

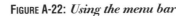

FIGURE A-22: *Using the menu bar*

SCREENTOUR

Most of today's software includes a menu bar with a list of titles such as File, Edit, and View. Clicking a menu title displays the menu.

A menu displays a list of menu options. You can select an option by using the mouse.

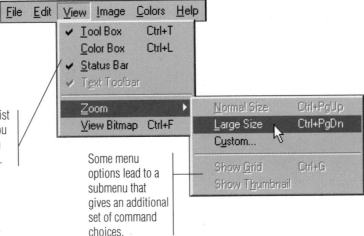

Some menu options lead to a submenu that gives an additional set of command choices.

FIGURE A-23: *Using a dialog box*

SCREENTOUR

The Print option displays three dots to indicate that it leads to a dialog box.

When you select Print, the Print dialog box opens. The dialog box prompts you to enter specifications about how the computer should carry out the print task.

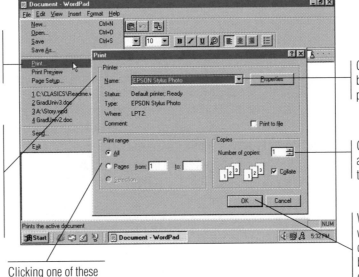

Clicking this arrow button displays a list of printers you can use.

Clicking one of these arrow buttons changes the number of copies.

When you are satisfied with the print specifications, click the OK button. Otherwise, click the Cancel button to discard your specifications.

Clicking one of these buttons specifies how much of the document to print.

FIGURE A-24: *Dialog box controls*

Round **option buttons**, sometimes called "radio buttons", allow you to select one of the options. Square **check boxes** allow you to select any or all of the options.

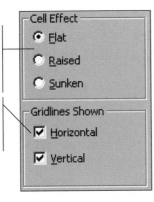

Drop-down lists display options when you click the arrow button.

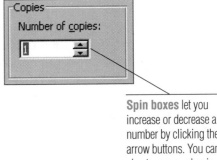

Spin boxes let you increase or decrease a number by clicking the arrow buttons. You can also type a number in the box.

Working with GUIs

Graphical user interfaces or GUIs (pronounced "gooies") are found on most of today's microcomputers. GUIs are based on the philosophy that people can use computers intuitively—that is, with minimal training, people can manipulate on-screen objects that represent tasks or commands.

USER
INTERFACE

USING A MOUSE

DETAILS

- **Graphical objects** are key elements of GUIs. A graphical object is a small picture on the screen that you can manipulate using a mouse or other input device. Each graphical object represents a computer task, a command, or a real-world object. You show the computer what you want it to do by manipulating the object instead of entering commands or selecting menu options. Graphical objects include icons, buttons, and windows, as explained in Figure A-25.

  For example, you manipulate on-screen objects when you delete a document using Windows. The documents you create are represented by icons that look like sheets of paper. A Recycle Bin represents the place where you put documents that you no longer want. Suppose you used your computer to write a report named "Sport Statistics," but you no longer need to store the report on your computer system. You use the mouse to drag the Sport Statistics icon to the Recycle Bin and erase the report from your computer system, as explained in Figure A-26.

  - Most graphical user interfaces are based on a metaphor in which computer components are represented by real-world objects. For example, a user interface using a desktop metaphor might represent documents as file folders and storage as a filing cabinet.
  - Graphical user interfaces often contain menus and prompts in addition to graphical objects because graphical user interface designers have found it difficult to design icons and tools for every possible task, command, and option you might want to perform.

- Pointing devices such as a mouse, a trackball, or a lightpen help you manipulate GUIs. The most popular pointing device is the mouse. A pointer on the screen shows the movement of the mouse. Figure A-27 shows you how to hold and use a mouse.

  - A **pointer**—usually shaped like an arrow—moves on the screen in a way that corresponds to how you move the mouse on a hard surface like your desk. When you drag an object, but your mouse runs into an obstacle on your desk or you come to the end of the **mouse pad**, just pick up the mouse, move it to a clear space, and continue dragging.
  - You **click** the mouse by pressing the left mouse button a single time to select an object on the monitor.
  - You **double-click** by clicking the mouse twice in rapid succession. Some operations require you to double-click.
  - You can use the mouse to **drag** objects from one screen location to another by clicking the object, holding down the mouse button, and moving the mouse to the new location for the object. When the object is in its new location, you release the mouse button.

Most software has a left-handed mouse option to switch the functions of the mouse buttons. If you are left-handed, you can hold the mouse in your left hand and click the right mouse button.

▶ A **window** usually contains a specific piece of work. For example, a window might contain a document you are typing or a picture you are drawing. You can think of windows as work areas, analogous to different documents and books that you might have open on your desk. Just as you switch between the documents and books you have on your desk, you can switch between windows on the computer screen to work on different tasks.

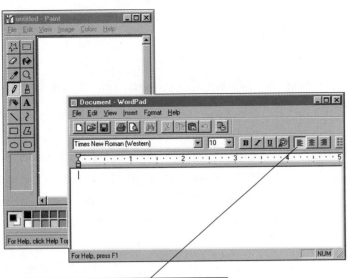

An **icon** is a small picture that represents an object. When you select an icon, you indicate to the computer that you want to manipulate the object.

A selected icon is highlighted. The My Computer icon on the right is selected, so it is highlighted with dark blue.

A **button** helps you make a selection. When you select a button, its appearance changes to indicate that it has been activated.

The Align Left button is selected here, and it appears to be pushed in. Buttons are sometimes referred to as "tools."

SCREENTOUR

▶ Graphical objects called icons often represent real things, such as documents. By manipulating an icon, you manipulate the thing it represents.

1. The Sport Statistics document is no longer needed.

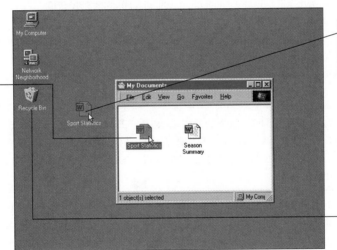

2. Using the mouse you can drag the Sport Statistics document icon to the Recycle Bin.

3. Once it is placed in the Recycle Bin, the document will no longer appear in the My Documents window. Periodically, you can empty the Recycle Bin to delete its contents permanently.

VIDEO

▶ Using a mouse is an important computing skill.

A pointer on the screen, usually shaped like an arrow, moves as you move the mouse. To select an object, use the mouse to position the pointer on the object, then click the left mouse button.

To hold the mouse, rest the palm of your right hand on the mouse so your index finger is positioned over the left mouse button. Lightly grasp the mouse using your thumb and ring finger. Move the mouse right, left, forward and back to move the pointer on your screen.

Using resources

Part of learning about computer systems is learning how to use them. Individuals have different learning styles. Some people enjoy discovery learning, whereas others prefer structured lectures. As you learn to use your computer system, you can find resources to match your learning style. If, when you use your computer system, you have difficulty, you can find "how to" information about installing computer hardware and using computer software in a variety of resources. These resources might be printed materials such as books or manuals, they might be courses that you take, or they might even be available directly on your computer screen. To use these resources effectively, you need to know that they exist, you need to know where to find them, and you need to develop some strategies for applying the information they contain.

DETAILS

○→ **Reference manuals** are usually printed books or online resources that describe each feature of a hardware device or software package. Reference manuals are usually included with the hardware or software that you buy. You can also find independent publishers who produce reference manuals for popular hardware and software. Most often, reference manuals are printed documents, but a recent trend is to provide computer-based reference manuals.

A reference manual is typically organized by features, rather than in the lesson format used by tutorials. Use a reference manual to find out whether a feature exists or how to use it. When consulting a reference manual, you should first check the table of contents or index to locate the information you need, then turn to the appropriate section and read it carefully.

○→ Another approach to learning how to use computers is to take a course. Courses are available from schools, manufacturers, and private training firms. They might last from several hours to several months. Courses about software packages tend to be laboratory-based, with an instructor leading you through the steps.

○→ A **telephone support** line is a service offered over the phone by a hardware manufacturer or software publisher to customers who have questions about how to use a software or hardware product. Sometimes these phone calls are toll-free; sometimes they are not. You might also pay a fee for the time it takes the support person to answer your question.

○→ The term "online" refers to resources that are immediately available on your computer screen. Reference information is frequently available as **online Help**, accessible from a Help menu, a button on the toolbar, or by typing **Help** at a command-line prompt. Figure A-28 shows the Office Assistant available through online Help for the Microsoft Office 2000 software.

○→ A **tutorial** is a guided, step-by-step learning experience. Usually this learning experience teaches you the generic skills you need to use specific hardware or software.

Tutorials might be produced by the publisher of the software you want to learn to use or by independent publishers. Tutorials come in a variety of forms, as listed in Figure A-29, to match your learning style.

QUICK TIP

If you run into a problem and are pressed for time, the best course of action might be to ask an expert or a friend who knows a lot about computers.

QUICK TIP

Public libraries, bookstores, and newsstands have computer trade magazines that provide interesting articles and current, pertinent tips about computers. The information in these magazines is often presented in non-technical, easy-to-use language.

► Online Help provides information about the features of a software application.

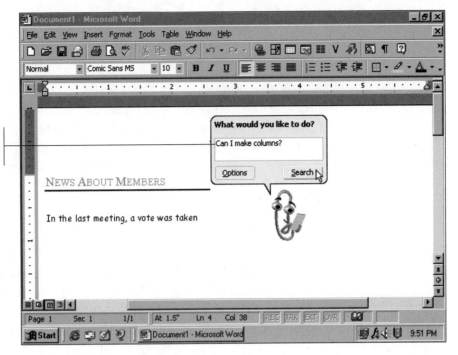

The Office Assistant responds to questions that you type.

LEARNING STYLES

RESOURCE		DESCRIPTION
Printed tutorial		Provides printed step-by-step instructions. To use a printed tutorial, you read how to do a step, then you try to do it on the computer.
Computer-based tutorial		Provides a simulation of the hardware or software and displays tutorial instructions in boxes or windows on the screen. Computer-based tutorials have an advantage over their printed counterparts because they can demonstrate procedures using computer animation. In the last few years, computer-based tutorials have become much more widespread.
Audio tutorial		Verbally walks you through the steps of the tutorial. An advantage to this type of tutorial is that you do not have to read instructions. You do have to stop the tutorial and rewind, however, if you do not hear or understand the instructions. You might like audio tutorials if you easily retain information presented in lectures.
Video tutorial		Visually illustrates how the software or hardware works. Some video tutorials are designed so that you watch them, take notes, then try the steps on the computer later. Other video tutorials are designed to be used while you are sitting at the computer. As with audio tutorials, you can stop and rewind video tutorials if you miss something.

Science fiction usually depicts computers as intelligent devices. In the film *2001*, HAL certainly seemed to think for himself. But are thinking machines just the stuff of science fiction? In 1950, the well-respected British mathematician Alan Turing wrote, "I believe that at the end of the century the use of words and general educated opinion will have altered so much that one will be able to speak of machines thinking without expecting to be contradicted." Can computers think? This subject has inspired a debate that has raged among computer scientists and philosophers for more than half a decade.

Putting aside for a moment the question of whether computers can think, consider how you "know" that other people can think. How can you tell if a person is able to think? You can't "get inside" someone's mind to find out first-hand. Instead, you probably use logic something like: "I am a person and I can think. Therefore, other people must be able to think, too." This logic seems correct, but you can't apply it to entities that are not people. You could not use it, for example, to determine if an extra-terrestrial being can think, or if computers can think. So, do you have an alternative way of assessing whether someone or something can think? You might be able to tell by observing behavior. If, for example, a person or an extra-terrestrial behaves in an intelligent way, you would assume that he or she can think. Is it possible to use behavior as the criteria for determining whether a computer can think? In fact, just this strategy was proposed by Alan Turing.

Turing described a "test" of machine intelligence. The Turing test, as it is now called, is somewhat like a TV game show. It pits a contestant against two backstage opponents, one a computer and one a human. The contestant asks questions to try to identify the computer. Turing suggested that if the computer could not be identified, then it was acting just as intelligently as the human. A computer that can behave as intelligently as a human must, therefore, be intelligent and must be able to think.

ARTIFICIAL INTELLIGENCE

Since 1950, designing a computer that can pass the Turing test has become the holy grail for a field of research known as artificial intelligence. **Artificial Intelligence** (AI) refers to the ability of computers to solve problems and perform tasks that were once thought to be uniquely human. AI researchers have produced computers that can move and manipulate robotic limbs, respond to human speech, diagnose diseases, translate documents from one language to another, play chess at the grand master level, and learn new tasks. So far, however, no computer has passed the Turing test.

Even if a computer can eventually pass the Turing test, not everyone would agree that it can think. Philosopher John Searle, for example, attempted to refute the Turing test using the now famous Chinese-Room Thought Experiment. Suppose you are an English-speaking person who cannot understand written or spoken Chinese. You are locked in a room and given a stack of papers containing Chinese writing. You receive other papers containing a set of simple rules, written in English, that tell you how to manipulate Chinese characters. Next, someone slides a sheet of paper under the door of your room and you see that it contains Chinese writing. Using the simple set of rules, you squiggle something on the sheet of paper and return it to the person on the other side of the door.

It happens that the person outside of the room speaks and reads Chinese. The paper you received under the door actually contained a question in Chinese. By following your set of English rules, the squiggle that you wrote on the paper turned out to be the correct answer to the question. So, your written response makes it look like you can communicate in Chinese, even though you can't understand a word of it.

Searle suggests that a similar process occurs in a computer. Rather than using intelligence, the computer mindlessly manipulates symbols. Searle contends that even if a computer passed the Turing test, it would have no understanding of the conversation it was having with humans—rather, it would simply be processing symbols, while appearing to answer the questions of the game show contestant.

Does Searle's Chinese-Room Thought Experiment effectively refute the possibility that computers can think? Consider this—could the person in the Chinese room manipulate the symbols without using any intelligence? The answer seems to be "No." Therefore, you might conclude that a computer requires intelligence to pass the Turing test or to perform any sort of processing task.

Despite many years of debate, the question "Can computers think?" has yet to be answered, but the debate has spurred fruitful AI research and produced technologies that improve the way we live. AI has not, however, fulfilled the prophesies of science fiction or Turing's expectation that by the year 2000 computers would generally be considered thinking machines.

EXPAND THE IDEAS

1. What do you think: Can computers think? Research media archives. Find several examples of articles, documentaries, or news stories on computers and intelligence in society. Write a summary of each article or media piece. Analyze your findings—was the media voice consistent? Why or why not?

2. How would you define thinking? Work in small groups to brainstorm a definition. Use the group definitions to compile a class definition. Could the group/class agree on a definition? Why or why not?

3. Is human intelligence different from machine intelligence? Write a one-page paper supporting your position and include specific examples.

4. Would a computer that could beat chess champion Gary Kasparov also pass the Turing text? Write a one-page paper supporting your position and include specific examples.

5. Which of the applications that you use requires the computer to do more "thinking?" Which requires less "thinking?" Work in small groups. Compile your findings into a multimedia presentation.

6. List films that have explored the issue of a computer that thinks. Write a one-page paper describing these films and what conclusions they may have drawn.

End of Unit Exercises

STUDY TIPS

1. At the top of a sheet of paper, write "Definition of the term computer," then make a list of important words, names, and phrases that are related to your list.

2. Use lines to divide a sheet of paper into four equal sections. In the upper-left corner, write "microcomputer." Write "minicomputer" in the upper-right corner, "mainframe" in the lower-left corner, and "supercomputer" in the lower-right corner. Place words, phrases, and definitions in each section that describe and differentiate each type of computer.

3. List as many peripheral devices as you can, without referring to this book. Indicate whether each is an input device, an output device, or both. Refer to Figure A-11 and review any devices you omitted.

4. Make a list of the user interface elements covered in this chapter. Write at least three terms or phrases associated with each. For example, user interface element: prompt. Associated terms and phrases: (a) prompted dialog, (b) wizards, and (c) can be ambiguous or confusing.

5. Make a list of information resources that might help you install hardware and learn to use software. Write a one-sentence description of each resource.

6. Write a paragraph that explains the difference between a spin arrow, drop-down list, and a menu in a dialog box.

FILL IN THE BEST ANSWER

1. Systematic actions that a computer uses to manipulate data are called _____.

2. A(n) _____ is a storage device that uses laser technology to read data from a disk.

3. A case or box that contains the power supply, storage devices, and circuit boards is the _____.

4. _____ is a measure of the number of dots your screen displays.

5. The category of computer that describes the fastest, largest, most capable computer used for advanced scientific calculations is the _____.

6. A(n) _____ is a sequence of screens that directs you through a multistep software task.

7. A(n) _____ resembles a microcomputer but does not have any processing capability.

8. A(n) _____ is a pointing device used to input data.

9. A(n) _____ is a tiny square or dot that divides a screen.

10. The symbols processed by a computer are known as _____.

11. The four functions performed by a computer are _____, _____, _____, and _____.

12. The computer puts data temporarily in _____ while the data is waiting to be processed.

13. A(n) _____ is a device generally devoted to carrying out the processing tasks of only one user.

14. An IBM computer is _____ with a Compaq computer because it operates in essentially the same way.

15. A computer _____ allows you to access data from a centralized storage device.

16. If your organization wants to provide processing for more than 200 users and reliability, security, and centralized control are necessary, a(n) _____ computer would best meet your needs.

17. If you type a command, but leave out a required space, you have made a(n) _____ error.

18. Instead of leading to a submenu, some menu options lead to a(n) _____, which displays the options associated with a command.

19. Most microcomputers are equipped with a(n) _____ as the primary input device and a(n) _____ as the primary output device.

20. You can use the _____ key and the _____ key in conjunction with letter keys instead of using the mouse to control menus.

21. A(n) _____, such as "Enter your name:," is one way that a computer can tell the user what to do.

22. Instead of prompted dialogs, today's software tends to use _____ to direct a user through multistep software tasks, such as creating a graph or creating a fax cover sheet.

23. Most _____ are based on a metaphor in which computer components are represented by real-world objects, such as a desktop metaphor in which documents are represented by folder icons.

INDEPENDENT CHALLENGE 1

It is important that you familiarize yourself with the type of computer you are using. You may need to consult the computer resource person at your school or the manual that came with your computer to answer the following questions.

To complete this independent challenge:

1. Identify the components of your computer.

    a. With what type of computer are you working?

    b. What kind of system unit case do you have?

    c. How much memory does the computer have?

    d. What peripheral devices are connected to your computer?

2. Draw a sketch of a computer system in your computer lab, home, or office and do the following:

    a. Title the sketch appropriately—for example, "My Computer at Home."

    b. List its brand name and model number.

    c. Label the following parts, if applicable: monitor, screen, hard drive light, 3.5" disk drive, power switch, power light, CD-ROM drive, mouse, printer, printer (type), system unit, keyboard, other peripheral devices.

INDEPENDENT CHALLENGE 2

Computer magazines contain advertisements for a variety of microcomputers. Such advertisements provide a wealth of information about the products. You can learn a lot about the computers available and current trends in technology by just reviewing the current literature in these magazines.

To complete this independent challenge:

1. Find and photocopy an advertisement from a computer magazine for each of the following items:

    Desktop computer
    Tower computer
    Notebook computer
    PDA

2. Label each component for each computer pictured in the advertisements.

3. Indicate whether each component is an input device, an output device, a processing device, or a storage device.

4. Compare the computers based on the advertisement information. Answer questions such as the following:

    How are the units similar?
    How are they different?

5. In what situations would you be more likely to use one type of computer than another type of computer?

INDEPENDENT CHALLENGE 3

Do this project only if your school has a computer network for student use. You may need to obtain a user ID and password before you can access the network. Learn how to log in. Your school might offer a short tutorial that teaches you how to use the network, or your instructor might provide a demonstration.

To complete this independent challenge:

Write a one-page to two-page step-by-step tutorial on how to log into the network. Your tutorial should include the following:

1. A title

2. An introductory paragraph explaining where the network is located, who can access it, and how students can get a user ID and password

3. Numbered steps to log into the network (if your lab policy requires that you turn on the computer each time you log in, you should include instructions for doing this in your tutorial)

4. Numbered steps for logging out of the network

INDEPENDENT CHALLENGE 4

You encounter a user interface each time you turn on your computer and start an application. You should be familiar with the different elements that are available in the various applications that you use.

To complete this independent challenge:

1. Start your computer.

2. List three icons on your desktop.

3. Start your word processor.

4. List the first three options on the menu bar.

5. Open the Print dialog box, list three elements inside the dialog box, then cancel out of the dialog box.

6. Locate a toolbar. List at least five buttons.

7. Start your Internet browser.

8. List the first three options on the menu bar.

9. Open the Print dialog box, list three elements inside the dialog box, then cancel out of the dialog box.

10. Locate a toolbar. List at least five buttons.

11. Compare and contrast the different buttons on the two applications.

12. Start a third application, such as a graphics package or another type of application.

13. List the first three options on the menu bar.

14. Open the Print dialog box, list three elements inside the dialog box, then cancel out of the dialog box.

15. Locate a toolbar. List at least five buttons.

16. Summarize your findings. Exit all open applications.

INDEPENDENT CHALLENGE 5

Do this project only if your school provides you with acess to the Internet. The Internet is a worldwide computer network that provides access to a phenomenal variety of information. The Internet can be useful right from the start of this course. Several of the end-of–unit projects refer you to information resources on the Internet. If you would like to use the Interent for these projects, this is a good time to get started.

To complete this independent challenge:

1. Connect to the Internet.

2. Point your browser to a search engine. Popular search engines include *www.Yahoo.com*, *www.altavista.com*, and *www.lycos.com*.

3. Use the search engine to find information about various computer manufacturers.

4. Locate a computer system and determine the components available.

5. Print out two pages from manufacturers' Web sites. Popular manufacturers include IBM, Dell, Gateway, and Apple.

6. Take notes about the Web sites you visit along the way.

7. Print out a Web page that includes graphics. Did you have to pick from a list on a Web site? Notice common graphical elements on Web sites, and list them.

8. Disconnect from the Internet.

USER INTERFACE LAB

The Course Labs are designed to help you master some of the key computer concepts and skills presented in each unit of text. If you are using your school's lab computers, your instructor or technical support person should have installed the Labs software for you. If you want to use the Labs on your home computer, see the information in the Preface of this book.

Each lab has two parts: Steps and Explore. Use the Steps first to learn and review concepts. Read the information on each page and complete the numbered steps. As you work through the lab, you will be asked to answer QuickCheck questions about what you have learned. At the end of the lab, you will see a report that scores your answers to the QuickChecks. If your instructor wants you to turn in this report, click the Print button on the QuickCheck Report screen.

When you have completed the Steps, you can click the Explore button to complete the Lab Assignments. You can also use Explore to practice the skills you learned and to explore concepts on your own.

You have learned that the hardware and software for a user interface determine how you interact and communicate with the computer. In the

User Interfaces lab, you will try five user interfaces to accomplish the same task—creating a graph.

1. Click the Steps button to find out how each interface works. As you work through the Steps, answer all of the QuickCheck questions. When you complete the Steps, you will see a report that summarizes your performance on the QuickChecks. Follow the directions on the screen to print the QuickCheck Report.

2. In Explore, use each interface to make a 3-D pie graph using data set 1. Title your graphs "Cycle City Sales." Use the percent style to show the percentage accounted for by each slice of the pie. Print each of the five graphs (one for each interface).

3. In Explore, select one of the user interfaces. Write a step-by-step set of instructions for how to produce a line graph using data set 2. This line graph should show lines and symbols, and have the title "Widget Production."

4. Using the user interface terminology you learned in this lab and in this chapter, write a description of each of the interfaces you used in the lab. Then, suppose you work for a software publisher and you are going to create a software package for producing line, bar, column, and pie graphs. Which user interface would you use for the software? Why?

USING A MOUSE LAB

A mouse is a standard input device on most of today's computers. You need to know how to use a mouse to manipulate graphical user interfaces and to use the rest of the labs.

1. The Steps for the Using a Mouse lab show you how to click, double-click, and drag objects using the mouse. Click the Steps button and begin the Steps. As you work through the Steps, answer all of the QuickCheck questions that appear. When you complete the Steps, you will see a report that summarizes your performance on the QuickChecks. Follow the directions on the screen to print the QuickCheck Report.

2. In Explore, demonstrate your ability to use a mouse and to control a Windows program by creating a poster. To create a poster for an upcoming sports event, select a graphic, type the poster caption, then select a font, font styles, and a border. Print your completed poster.

KEYBOARD AND TYPING TUTOR LAB

To become an effective computer user, you must be familiar with your primary input device—the keyboard.

1. The Steps for the Keyboard and Typing Tutor lab provide you with a structured introduction to the keyboard layout and the functions of special computer keys. Click the Steps button and begin the Steps. As you work through the Steps, answer all of the QuickCheck questions that appear. When you complete the Steps, you will see a report that summarizes your performance on the QuickChecks. Follow the directions on the screen to print the QuickCheck Report.

2. In Explore, start the typing tutor, which helps you develop your typing skills. Take the typing test and print out your results.

3. In Explore, try to improve your typing speed by 10 words per minute. For example, if you currently type 20 words per minute, your goal would be 30 words per minute. Practice each typing lesson until you see a message that indicates you can proceed to the next lesson. Create a Practice Record as shown here to keep track of how much you practice. When you have reached your goal, print out the results of a typing test to verify your results.

Practice Record for (Name): _____

Start Date: _____ Start Typing Speed: _____ wpm

End Date: _____ End Typing Speed: _____ wpm

Lesson #: _____ Date Practiced/Time Practiced:

_____

The following table lists various supplemental elements that are available for this unit.

LESSON	COMPONENT AND TITLE	LESSON	COMPONENT AND TITLE
Defining computers	COMPUTERS TERMINOLOGY	**Communicating with computers: prompts, wizards and command-line interfaces**	SCREENTOUR
Exploring computer functions	JOHN VON NEUMANN	**Communicating with computers: menus and dialog boxes**	SCREENTOUR SCREENTOUR
Categorizing computers	MICROCOMPUTERS MINICOMPUTERS MAINFRAME COMPUTERS SUPERCOMPUTERS VIDEO	**Working with GUIs**	USER INTERFACE USING A MOUSE SCREENTOUR VIDEO
Examining keyboards	KEYBOARD AND TYPING TUTOR	**Uses resources**	SCREENTOUR LEARNING STYLES
Examining monitors	DISPLAY SYSTEMS	**Can Computers Think?**	ARTIFICIAL INTELLIGENCE
Examining printers	PRINTERS VIDEO ANIMATION		

VISUAL WORKSHOP

The image is a dialog box from Microsoft Word, a word processing program. Included in this screen are many graphic elements. List as many as you can find and determine what each one does in this dialog box.

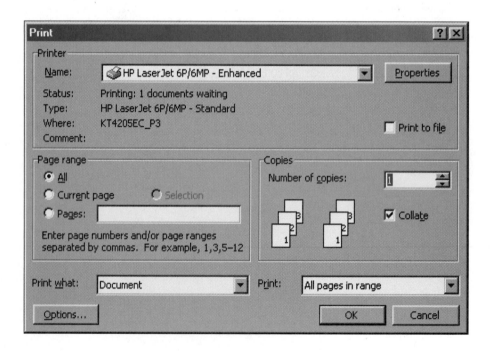

Software and Multimedia

The computer is the most successful and versatile machine in history. A computer's versatility is made possible by software. The introduction of reliable, reasonably priced software and hardware designed for microcomputers ushered in a new era of computing. In this unit, you will learn how a computer uses software. You will learn the difference between system software and application software and you will explore the copyright laws that attempt to protect software from unauthorized use. You will learn about multimedia computing, which includes digital sound, images, and animation. Finally, the unit concludes with an overview of how to purchase and install software as well as an introduction to marketing channels.

Understanding computer software basics

Computer software determines what a computer can do. In a sense, it transforms a computer from one kind of machine to another—from a drafting station to a typesetting machine, from a flight simulator to a calculator, from a filing system to a music studio, and so on. The distinction between software, programs, and data is important. This lesson defines the terms *computer program, data,* and *software.*

DETAILS

○━ A **computer program** is a set of detailed, step-by-step instructions that tell a computer how to solve a problem or carry out a task. The steps in a computer program are written in a language that the computer can interpret or "understand." As you read through the simple computer program in Figure B-1, notice the number of steps required to perform a relatively simple calculation. At one time, computer users had to invest in the time and expense of writing many of their own programs. Today, people rarely write computer programs for their personal computers, preferring to select from thousands of commercially written programs.

○━ **Data** is the words, numbers, and graphics that describe people, events, things, and ideas. Data can be included in the software, like the data for a dictionary in a word processing program, or the text and images in a CD-ROM encyclopedia. Data, such as numbers you provide to create a graph, can also be added to files by using a computer program.

○━ **Software** is a basic part of a computer system, but the term has more than one definition. In the early days of the computer industry, it became popular to use the term "software" for all nonhardware components of a computer. In this context, software referred to computer programs and to the data used by the programs. Today, the term "software" is more typically used to describe a commercial product, as shown in Figure B-2, which might include more than a single program as well as data.

In this textbook, software is defined as instructions and associated data, stored in electronic format, that direct the computer to accomplish a task. Using this definition, computer software may include more than one computer program if those programs work together to carry out a task. Also using this definition, software can include data, but data alone is not software. For example, word processing software might include the data for a dictionary or a thesaurus of words and their synonyms, but the data you create using a word processor is not referred to as software. "Software" is a plural noun, so there is no such thing as "softwares" or "one software." Use the term "software package" when referring to a particular example of software.

| Distinguishing system software from application software | Because there are so many software titles, categorizing software as either system software or application software is useful. System software helps the computer carry out its basic operating tasks. Application software helps the computer user carry out a task. | System software and application software are further divided into subcategories. Use Figure B-3 to help you understand the differences between system software and application software. |

This computer program converts feet and inches to centimeters.

1. The first section of the program states that there are 12 inches in 1 foot and 2.54 centimeters in 1 inch.

2. The var, or variable, section lists the factors in the problem that might change each time you use the program.

3. When you use the program, it asks you to enter the length you want to convert.

```
program Conversion(input,output);
const
    inchesPerFoot = 12;
    centimetersPerInch = 2.54;
var
    feet, inches, lengthInInches: integer;
    centimeters: real;
begin
    write('What is the length in feet and inches?');
    readln(feet, inches);
    lengthInInches :=inchesPerFoot * feet + inches;
    centimeters :=centimetersPerInch * lengthInInches;
    writeln('The length in centimeters is ', centimeters:1:2)
end.
```

4. The program converts the length you entered into inches.

5. Next, the program converts the inches into centimeters.

6. Finally, the program displays the length in centimeters.

FIGURE **B-2**: *A commercial software package*

A commercial software package typically contains a reference manual and floppy disks, a CD-ROM, or a DVD.

FIGURE **B-3**: *Software categories*

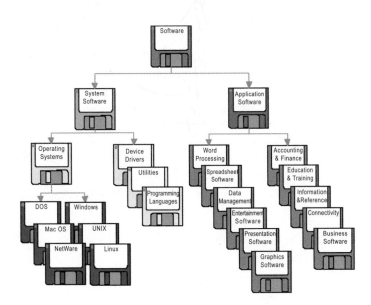

Examining software copyrights and licensing

Just because you can copy software doesn't make it legal to do so. Like books and films, most computer software is protected by a copyright. A **copyright** is a form of legal protection that grants the copyright owner exclusive rights to copy the software, to distribute or sell the software, and to modify the software. When you purchase the software, you do not become the owner of the copyright. Your purchase allows you to use the software on your computer, but you cannot give away or sell the software.

DETAILS

- ☞ The **Copyright Act**—Figure B-4 excerpts sections 106 and 117 of the 1980 U.S. Copyright Act—states under what circumstances you can and cannot legally copy copyrighted software. The restrictions stated by the Copyright Act apply only to the programs and data included as part of the original software. The data you enter—the documents, files, and graphics you create—can be copied without restriction.

- ☞ Copyrighted materials, such as software, display a **copyright notice** that contains the word "copyright" or the **copyright © symbol**, the year of the publication, and the name of the copyright holder. When you start a computer program, the copyright notice usually appears on the first screen. It is also usually printed in the reference manual.

- ☞ A **software license** is a legal contract that defines the ways in which you may use a computer program. It indicates whether you are buying or licensing the software, how many copies you can make, whether you can rent it, whether you can sell it, and whether a warranty exists. For microcomputer software, you will find the license on the outside of the package, on a separate card inside the package, or in the reference manual. Mainframe software licenses are usually a separate legal document negotiated between the software publisher and a corporate buyer. Table B-1 describes the different licenses that are available.

SHAREWARE

- ☞ **Shareware** is copyrighted software marketed under a "try before you buy" policy. It usually includes a license that allows you to use the software for a trial period. If you want to continue to use the shareware, you must become a registered user by sending in a registration fee. When you become a registered user, you are granted a license to use the software beyond the trial period. You might also receive a free copy of the latest version of the software or printed documentation for the program. These shared copies provide a low-cost marketing and distribution channel. Unfortunately, the registration fee relies on the honor system, so many shareware authors collect only a fraction of the money they deserve for their programming efforts.

- ☞ **Public domain software** is owned by the public rather than by the author. Sometimes an author abandons all rights to a particular title and places it in the public domain, making the program available without restriction. Public domain software may be freely copied, distributed, and even resold. The primary restriction on public domain software is that you cannot apply for a copyright on it.

- ☞ **Software pirates** are people who illegally copy, distribute, or modify software. These illegal copies are referred to as **pirated software**.

InfoWeb
COPYRIGHT

Only the copyright owner can reproduce, sell, or distribute the copyrighted software.

Section 106. Exclusive Rights in Copyrighted Works
Subject to sections 107 through 118, the owner of copyright under this title has the exclusive rights to do and to authorize any of the following:

(1) to reproduce the copyrighted work in copies or phonorecords;
(2) to prepare derivative works based upon the copyrighted work;
(3) to distribute copies or phonorecords of the copyrighted work to the public by sale or other transfer of ownership, or by rental, lease, or lending…

It is legal to copy the software from the distribution disks to the hard disk of your computer.

Section 117. Right to Copy or Adapt Computer Programs in Limited Circumstances
Notwithstanding the provisions of section 106, it is not an infringement for the owner of a copy of a computer program to make or authorize the making of another copy or adaptation of the computer program provided:

It is legal to make an extra copy of the software in case the copy you are using becomes damaged.

1. that such a new copy or adaptation is created as an essential step in the utilization of the computer program in conjunction with a machine that is used in no other manner; or

If you give away or sell the software, you cannot legally keep a copy.

2. that such new copy or adaptation is for archival purposes only and that all archival copies are destroyed in the event that continued possession of the computer program should cease to be rightful. Any exact copies prepared in accordance with the provisions of this section may be leased, sold, or otherwise transferred, along with the copy from which such copies were prepared, only as part of the lease, sale, or other transfer of all rights in the program. Adaptations so prepared may be transferred only with the authorization of the copyright owner.

You cannot legally sell or give away modified copies of the software without permission.

TABLE B-1: *License Agreements*

TYPE OF LICENSE	DESCRIPTION
Shrink wrap license	When you purchase computer software, the disks, CD-ROM, or DVD in the package are usually sealed in an envelope or plastic shrink wrapping; opening the wrapping signifies your agreement to the terms of the software license; shrink wrap licensing is one of the most frequently used methods for providing legal protection for computer software.
Single-user license	Limits the use of the software to one user at a time. Most commercial software is distributed under a single-user license.
Multiple-user license	Allows more than one person to use a particular software package. This type of license is useful in cases where users each have their own personalized version of the software. It is generally priced per user, but the price for each user is typically less than the price of a single-user license.
Concurrent-use license	Allows a certain number of copies of the software to be used at the same time. For example, if an organization with a computer network has a concurrent-use license for five copies of a word processor, at any one time up to five employees may use the software. Concurrent-use licenses are usually priced in increments.
Site license	Generally allows the software to be used on any and all computers at a specific location—such as within a corporate office building or on a university campus. A site license is priced at a flat rate, for example, $5,000 per site.

Defining operating systems

System software performs tasks essential to the efficient functioning of computer hardware. Operating systems are a subcategory of system software. An **operating system** (OS) is the software that controls the computer's use of its hardware resources such as memory and disk storage space. An operating system works like an air traffic controller to coordinate the activities within the computer. It directs the fundamental operations of a computer, such as displaying information on the screen, storing data on disks, sending data to the printer, see Figure B-5, interpreting commands entered by users, and communicating with peripheral devices.

InfoWeb
OPERATING
SYSTEMS

DETAILS

☞ The operating system is the master controller and sets the standard for all application software that a computer runs. Figure B-6 helps you envision the relationships among your computer hardware, the operating system, and application software.

☞ The operating system provides **external services** that help users start programs, manage stored data, and maintain security. You, as the computer user, control these external functions. The operating system also provides **internal services**. That is, it works behind the scenes while the application software is running to perform tasks essential to the efficient functioning of the computer system. These internal services are not generally under your control, but instead are controlled by the operating system itself.

☞ **Control basic input and output:** An operating system controls the flow of data into and out of the computer, as well as to and from peripheral devices. It routes input to areas of the computer for processing and routes output to the screen, a printer, or any other output device you request.

☞ **Ensure adequate space:** An operating system ensures that adequate space is available for each program that is running and makes sure that each processor quickly performs each program instruction. If you want to run two or more programs at a time—a process called **multitasking**—the operating system ensures that each program has adequate space and time to run.

☞ **Allocate system resources:** An operating system allocates system resources so that programs run smoothly. A system resource is part of a computer system, such as a disk drive, memory, printer, or processor time that can be used by a computer program.

☞ **Manage storage space:** An operating system keeps track of the data stored on disks and CD-ROMs. Think of your disks as filing cabinets, your data as papers stored in file folders, and the operating system as the filing clerk. The filing clerk takes care of filing a folder when you finish using it. When you need something from your filing cabinet, you ask the filing clerk to get it. The filing clerk knows where to find the folder.

☞ **Detect equipment failure:** An operating system monitors the status of critical computer components to detect failures that affect processing. When you turn on your computer, the operating system checks each of the electronic components and takes a quick inventory of the storage devices. For example, if an electrical component inside your computer fails, the operating system displays a message identifying the problem and does not let you continue with the computing session until the problem is fixed.

☞ **Maintain security:** An operating system helps maintain the security of the data on the computer system. For example, it might not allow you to access the computer system unless you have a user ID and a password.

You "see" the operating system each time you turn on your computer.

1. The user tells the word processing application to print the document.

2. The word processing application signals the operating system that a document must be sent to the printer.

3. The operating system sends the document to the printer.

FIGURE B-6: *The operating system interacts with application software and computer hardware*

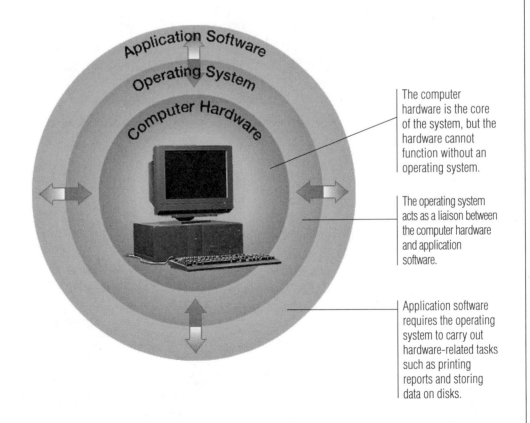

The computer hardware is the core of the system, but the hardware cannot function without an operating system.

The operating system acts as a liaison between the computer hardware and application software.

Application software requires the operating system to carry out hardware-related tasks such as printing reports and storing data on disks.

Examining Windows operating systems

Microsoft Windows is the most popular operating system for today's microcomputers because it supports a vast array of application software and peripheral devices. If you purchase a microcomputer, the operating system is usually preinstalled on the hard disk and ready to use. If you purchase a new PC, it will most likely have the latest version of Windows preinstalled on its hard disk.

DETAILS

- Microsoft Corporation took a more graphical approach to operating systems when it released Windows. The first versions of the Windows operating system—Windows 1.0, 2.0, and 3.0—did not generate much interest among computer users. Windows 3.1, introduced in 1992, really established Windows as the PC microcomputer operating system of choice. It provided icons, buttons, and other onscreen controls that could be manipulated by a mouse or other pointing device as well as menus to issue commands. All applications that ran under Windows had a consistent look, so it was easy to use new programs. Beginning with Windows 3.1, you could run more than one program at a time—a service called multitasking—in separate "windows" on the screen and easily transfer data between them.

- In 1995, Microsoft introduced Windows 95, which offered better operating efficiency than Windows 3.1. In addition to programs designed for Windows 95, it could run software designed for Windows 3.1 and DOS. In 1998, Microsoft introduced Windows 98 to add enhanced Internet features. Windows 95 and Windows 98 feature a similar user interface. See Figure B-7.

  Windows 95 and 98 provide some basic networking capabilities, making them suitable operating systems for homes and businesses. They are classified as desktop operating systems and would not be found on a minicomputer, mainframe, or supercomputer.

- **Windows NT Workstation** and **Windows 2000 Professional** are workstation versions of the Windows operating systems. A **workstation** is a high-performance, single-user microcomputer that would typically be used for advanced or high-end computing tasks such as professional video editing, scientific visualization, and computer-aided design.

  Windows 2000 Professional is designed for the desktop but does support small networks. Its differentiating features include increased security, greater reliability, and ability to support specialized software applications designed for high-performance workstations. It cannot, however, run some software or support all of the peripheral devices designed for Windows 98.

- Windows NT Workstation and Windows 2000 Professional have essentially the same interface as Windows 98. See Figure B-8.

- Microsoft Windows NT Server and Windows 2000 Server are operating systems for servers, which are computers that provide centralized storage and communications services for local area networks and Internet sites. They are similar in appearance to Windows NT Workstation and Windows 2000 Professional but provide additional features for managing the flow of data on large networks and Web sites.

Desktop and server operating systems

Operating systems are classified into two categories: server operating systems and desktop operating systems. See Figure B-9. The server—also called network—operating system is designed for computers that provide centralized storage facilities and communications capabilities for networks and Web sites. Desktop—also called client—operating systems are designed for single-user microcomputers.

FIGURE B-7: *Windows 95 and 98 have similar features*

Two different programs can run in two separate windows.

Icons represent computer hardware components and software.

The taskbar indicates which programs are running.

The Start button provides access to a menu of programs, documents, and utilities.

FIGURE B-8: *Microsoft Windows 2000 Professional*

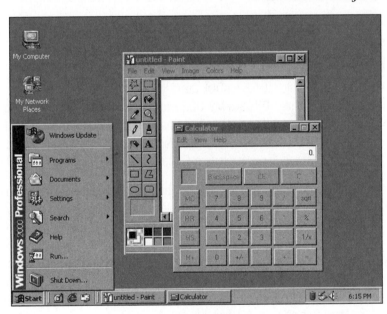

FIGURE B-9: *Network workstations and server operating systems*

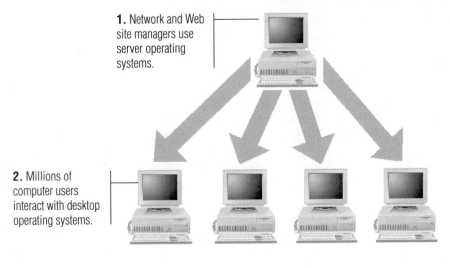

1. Network and Web site managers use server operating systems.

2. Millions of computer users interact with desktop operating systems.

Examining other operating systems

You might be familiar with the names of the most popular microcomputer operating systems: Microsoft Windows, DOS, and Mac OS. You are less likely to be familiar with the names of minicomputer and mainframe operating systems, such as UNIX, VMS, and MVS, or server operating systems, such as Novell NetWare and Linux. Operating systems for microcomputers, minicomputers, and mainframe computers perform many similar tasks. How can you tell which operating system your computer uses? Many microcomputer users can recognize an operating system by looking at the first screen that appears when they turn the computer on or by recognizing the operating system prompt. Reviewing commonly used operating systems, in addition to Windows, will help you recognize these operating systems if you encounter them in the future.

DETAILS

- **DOS:** DOS, which stands for Disk Operating System, is marketed under the trade names PC-DOS and MS-DOS. Both PC-DOS and MS-DOS were developed primarily by Microsoft Corporation and are essentially the same operating system. It was the operating system for the original IBM PC, which shipped in 1982. It was the first operating system used by many in the computer industry and had a stark, difficult-to-use command-line user interface. Figure B-10 shows the first version of DOS.

- **Mac OS:** In 1984, Apple Computer introduced the revolutionary Apple Lisa computer, which defined a new direction in operating system user interfaces. It included a graphical user interface with menus and icons. Lisa was not a commercial success, but the next product—the Macintosh computer—has been very successful. The graphical Macintosh operating system, shown in Figure B-11 and referred to as Mac OS, was a major factor. Mac OS has evolved through many versions in which features have been modified and added, including multitasking capabilities and support for small networks. Apple's iMac computer, introduced in 1998, features Mac OS. The software that is compatible with Mac OS is usually referred to as Macintosh software. Although Macintosh and iMac users can select from a large pool of Macintosh software, fewer software titles are available for Mac OS than for Windows. Special emulation hardware and software make it possible to run some Windows software on a Macintosh computer, but performance is not optimal. For that reason, most Mac OS users stay with Macintosh software.

- **UNIX:** UNIX is an operating system that was developed by AT&T's Bell Laboratories in 1969 and is one of the foundation technologies for networks and Web servers. Although UNIX was originally designed for minicomputers, it is now available for microcomputers and mainframes and provides an appropriate operating system for servers and high-performance workstations. Many versions of UNIX exist, such as AIX from IBM, XENIX from Microsoft, and ULTRIX from Digital Equipment Corporation.

- **Linux:** A variation of UNIX, Linux has recently gained prominence as a server operating system for microcomputers and minicomputers. It is available as freeware and provides a secure and stable operating environment. Early versions of Linux (and UNIX) featured a difficult command-line user interface. Add-ons for the operating system now make it possible to "paste" on a graphic user interface so the user can ignore the old-fashioned and cumbersome command-line interface. See Figure B-12.

The C:\> DOS prompt is a distinguishing feature of MS-DOS and PC-DOS.

```
Microsoft (R)
(C) Copyright Microsoft Corp 1981-1998

C:\>_
```

FIGURE B-11: *Mac OS*

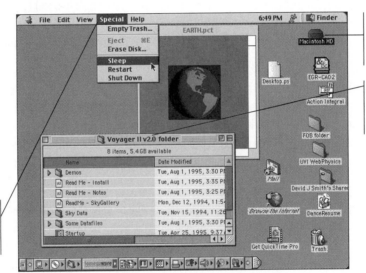

Icons represent computer hardware components and software.

Two different programs can run in two separate windows.

Menus and other on-screen objects are manipulated by using a mouse.

FIGURE B-12: *Linux*

The Linux operating system, popular with network and Web site managers, typically sports a graphical user interface.

Two or more programs can run in separate windows.

The taskbar and menus look much like the Windows interface.

Reviewing utilities, drivers, and programming languages

In addition to the operating system, other system software is available. Utilities software, device driver software, and programming language software are all system software. In addition to your operating system software, you may at times need one or more of these other types of system software.

DETAILS

- **Utilities** software is designed to augment the operating system by providing a way for a computer user to control the allocation and use of hardware resources. Some utilities software that is included with the operating system performs tasks such as preparing disks to hold data, providing information about the files on a disk, and copying data from one disk to another. Additional utilities software can be purchased separately from software publishers and vendors. For example, Norton Utilities, published by Symantec, is a popular utilities software. (See Figure B-13.) It can perform tasks such as retrieving data from damaged disks, securing data by encrypting it, and troubleshooting problems with a computer's disk drives.

- **Device driver** software helps the computer control a peripheral device. When you purchase a new peripheral device, the installation instructions that come with the device usually tell you how to install both the device (hardware) and the necessary device drivers (software). Once the device and device driver(s) are installed correctly, the computer uses it "behind the scenes" to communicate with the device. If you have followed the instructions for installing a new device driver but the device doesn't work correctly, check with the manufacturer to see if an updated device driver is available.

- **Computer programming language** software is needed if you want to write programs that run on your computer. Computer programming language software allows a user to write programs using English-like instructions. These instructions are translated by the programming language into a format that the computer can interpret and process. Most computer users don't need to write programs; therefore, most computer systems do not include preinstalled programming language software. If you want to write programs, you must purchase programming language software. Some of the most popular programming languages are BASIC, Visual Basic, C, C++, COBOL, and Java.

Formatting disks

One important task performed by an operating system utility is formatting a disk. Each disk must be formatted before you can store data on it. Think of formatting as creating the electronic equivalent of storage shelves. Before you can put things on shelves, you must assemble the shelves. In a similar way, before you can store data on a disk, you must make sure the disk is formatted. Your computer's operating system provides basic utilities for formatting disks. Although you can buy preformatted disks, you still might need a disk format utility if you are going to use a disk that has not been preformatted or was formatted for a different type of computer. Figure B-14 shows how to use the format utility for Windows.

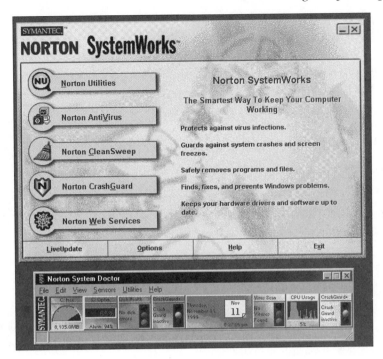

2. Click the floppy disk drive icon in the My Computer window.

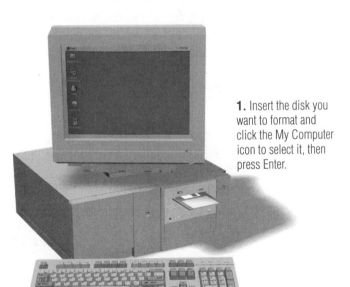

1. Insert the disk you want to format and click the My Computer icon to select it, then press Enter.

3. Click File on the menu bar, then click Format to open the Format window.

4. Make sure the Capacity box matches the size of the disk you want to format, then click the Start button.

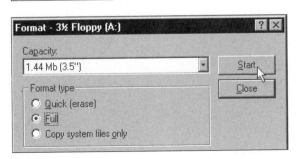

Introducing application software

Computers use application software to help you accomplish a specific task. You can use a computer to accomplish a variety of tasks, such as producing documents, performing calculations, creating graphics, managing financial resources, composing music, playing games, and maintaining files of information. Application software packages are often simply referred to as "applications."

APPLICATION SOFTWARE

DETAILS

☛ Application software is categorized in broad terms as productivity, office suite, groupware, and business software. There is some overlap within these categories. For example, an office suite can include productivity and groupware software. The lines between categories are not clearly defined, but the categories help chunk the vast array of software into manageable concepts.

- **Productivity** software is designed to help you work more effectively. Used by individuals, businesses, and organizations, the most popular types of productivity software include word processing, spreadsheet, and data management software.
- **Office suite** software refers to a number of applications that are packaged together and sold as a unit. A typical office suite includes software you would use to write documents, work with numbers, create graphics, and track data.
- **Groupware** software provides a way for more than one person to collaborate on a project. It facilitates group document production, scheduling, and communication. Often, it maintains a pool of data that can be shared by members of a workgroup.
- **Business software** helps organizations efficiently accomplish routine tasks. It is often classified into

two categories: horizontal market software and vertical market software. **Horizontal market software** is any generic software package that can be used by many different kinds of businesses, such as payroll software. **Vertical market software** is designed for specialized tasks in a specific market or business, such as software designed to estimate the cost of labor and materials for a new building and provide a bid for the price of the finished building.

☛ Application software is also categorized by how it is used. Document production software, for example, helps you create, edit, and publish documents. Connectivity software connects your computer to the Internet, to other computers, and to networks. Once again, the names of these functional categories are not used consistently because it is difficult to categorize the extensive array of application software. You may find discrepancies in how software is categorized when you shop for software in superstores, on the Internet, and at local software retailers. It is important to understand the basic framework, however, for these categories. Table B-2 organizes the applications into categories that you may find useful.

Understanding the difference between versions and revisions

Software publishers produce computer software. A newly released software product can be a new **version** (also called a "release") with significant enhancements or a **revision** designed to add minor enhancements and eliminate additional bugs found in the current version. The original version is typically called version 1.0. Revisions are often made available to current owners of the software at little or no cost and are released with little publicity. A revision number is separated from the version number with a period. Soon after a new version of a software product is released, the software publisher usually stops selling and reduces technical support for the earlier version—so it is a good idea to upgrade.

TABLE B-2: *Categorizing application software*

APPLICATION	USE TO	APPLICATION	USE TO
Software Category: Document Production		**Software Category: Data Management**	
Word processing	Write and spell check documents such as reports, letters, and marketing materials	**File management**	Work with simple lists of information such as holiday card addresses; information used by file management software is stored in **flat files**, which are similar to index cards
Desktop publishing	Enhance the format and appearance of documents such as newsletters, brochures, newspapers, magazines, and books through sophisticated graphic design features	**Database**	Manage a **database**, which is a collection of related files, to store, find, organize, update, and report information stored in more than one file; most frequently used by businesses, government, and educational institutions
Web authoring	Design and develop Web pages that you can publish on the Internet		
Software Category: Graphics		**Software Category: Connectivity**	
Graphics	Create, edit, and manipulate images	**Communications**	Dial your connection; built into most microcomputer operating systems, often classified as a system utility
Paint	Create and edit bitmap images; bitmaps are stored as a series of colored dots	**Browsers**	View Web pages and navigate links on the Internet
Photo editing	Enhance and manipulate photographs by modifying contrast, brightness, cropping, and removing red-eye	**Remote control**	Establish a connection between two computers, such as one in your home and one in your office; use the keyboard of one to control the other
Vector graphics	Create diagrams, corporate logos, and schematics	**E-mail**	Send and receive e-mail messages over the Internet; manage your computer mailbox
3-D graphics	Represent a three-dimensional object by covering a wire frame with surface color and texture		
Software Category: Presentation		**Software Category: Education and Training**	
Presentation	Combine text, graphics, graphs, animation, and sound into a series of electronic slides	**Education, exam prep, edutainment**	Learn and practice new skills and languages; prepare for standardized tests; play while learning
Software Category: Spreadsheet and Statistical		**Software Category: Accounting and Finance**	
Spreadsheet	Perform calculations based on numbers and formulas; transform data into graphs; examine investments;	**Personal**	Help track monetary transactions, bank accounts, credit card transactions, and bills as well as monitor investments; also balance checkbooks; track budgets support **online banking**, which is a way to use your computer and modem to download transactions directly from your bank
Statistical	Analyze large sets of data to discover relationships and patterns; summarize survey and experiment results, and test scores to help visualize and explore trends	**Small business**	Track invoices, accounts, customer data, purchasing history, payroll, and inventory functions
Mathematical modeling	Solve a wide range of math, science, and engineering problems		
Software Category: Information and Reference		**Software Category: Entertainment**	
Information and reference	Access information on a wide array of topics, such as general encyclopedias, medical references, map software, cookbooks, and telephone books	**Action, adventure, roleplaying**	Play games such as simulations, toys, and leisure fun; often feature 3-D graphics to play and interact with the environment. Duke Nukem, Doom Diablo, Tomb Raider, Sim City, Nascar Racing. Stand-alone: Nintendo, Sony Playstation

Understanding multimedia computing

Before computers, multimedia required a different machine for every type of medium. Multimedia means "one medium" that is digital. Computer technology is controlling many of the technologies and media that are used for multimedia presentations, such as slides, videotapes, audiotapes, records, CD-ROMs, and photos. Advances in computer technology have made it possible to combine text, photo images, speech, music, animated sequences, and video into a single interactive computer presentation.

InfoWeb
MULTIMEDIA

Lab
MULTIMEDIA

DETAILS

○━ The term **multimedia** is defined as an integrated collection of computer-based text, graphics, sound, animation, photo images, and video.

○━ To display realistic graphic and video, your computer system must have a high-resolution monitor and a CD-ROM drive. Figure B-15 shows a computer well equipped for multimedia.

○━ Multimedia was once considered a software category. That is no longer true, however, because digital media have now found their way into many different types of application software. For example, if your computer system is equipped with sound, some word processors will read your documents aloud. A popular office suite features an animated assistant to help you as you work. Computer games include fast-action animation and sound effects. Multimedia encyclopedias contain articles and pictures on a wide range of topics and provide a rich selection of text, graphics, sound, animation, and video. Most multimedia applications are shipped on a CD-ROM because the graphics, sound, and video require large amounts of storage space.

○━ Using multimedia requires sound and graphics capabilities. A speedy processor and a CD-ROM drive or DVD drive are also desirable. Ten years ago, multimedia components were costly extras. Today, however, multimedia components are standard equipment.

- **Sound card:** A sound card gives a computer the capability to record and play sound files as well as video soundtracks. Housed within the system unit, a sound card contains connectors that project from the back of the computer so you can attach speakers, headphones, and a microphone. Expensive sound cards include circuitry for special audio effects, such as 3-D sound.
- **Graphics card:** The computer graphics card takes signals from the processor and uses them to paint an image on the screen. It is installed inside the system unit and provides a connection for the monitor's data cable. To display videos, it must repaint every pixel on the screen 15 times per second. Accelerated graphics cards have circuitry that optimizes these tasks.
- **Processor:** Multimedia has become so popular that many of today's computers have a special multimedia processor with 3DNOW or MMX technology. These processors speed up sound and video. Only specially written software, however, can take advantage of the special multimedia features on these processors.
- **CD-ROM and DVD drives:** A CD-ROM drive allows your computer to access audio and software CD-ROMs. A DVD drive allows you to watch feature-length movies on your computer using DVDs that you can rent at a local video store. A DVD drive can access multimedia data from CD-ROMs as well.

The process of converting videos into a format that can be stored on a computer disk is called digitizing.

You can use the inexpensive headphones from your portable CD player, but remember that better-quality headphones produce clearer sound.

A sound card provides a connection for speakers, headphones, and a microphone. High-performance sound cards support special audio effects such as 3-D sound.

DVD drives work with CD-ROMs as well as DVDs. Many computer manufacturers are now equipping computers with DVD drives to provide access to both CD-ROM and DVD formats.

A basic computer microphone is suitable for voice recording and dictation. For recording instrumental music and vocals, higher-quality results can be achieved with a professional microphone.

Inexpensive speakers provide basic radio-quality sound. A top-quality speaker system with subwoofer boosts the bass sound and screens out background noise.

A faster processor provides better multimedia quality, but the newest, fastest processors are always the most expensive.

Understanding the sound system

With the proliferation of multimedia applications, a sound system has become an essential piece of computing equipment. A basic computer sound system includes a sound card and speakers or earphones. If you plan to record sounds, your computer system will also need to be equipped with a microphone. If your computer system is equipped with a sound system, you can play sounds that are part of videos and multimedia applications, as well as record sounds, using your computer.

SOUND SYSTEMS

DETAILS

○── A **sound card** converts digital data in a sound file into analog signals for instrumental, vocal, and spoken sounds. A sound card lets you make your own recordings by converting analog signals into digitized sound files that you can store on disk. In a desktop computer, a sound card usually resides in an expansion slot, as shown in Figure B-16. The sound card circuitry for a notebook computer is often built into the motherboard, and the speakers are built into the case. Companies other than those who manufacture computers typically manufacture sound cards. Sound Blaster, one of the first sound cards designed for PCs, has become the de facto standard. Most sound cards feature Sound Blaster compatibility and wavetable synthesis.

○── **Wavetable synthesis** creates music by playing digitized sound samples of actual instruments. These sound samples are stored in the card or loaded into main RAM each time your computer boots. The size of the wavetable affects sound quality—the larger the wavetable, the more realistic the sound. Numbers such as 64, 128, and 512 in the sound card specifications usually indicate the size of the wavetable.

○── Speakers can be built into the computer system or they can be stand-alones. Stand-alone speakers plug into the sound card via the expansion slot. The sound card outputs sound to the speakers or earphones. Higher-quality speakers provide richer sound and enhanced volume.

○── Sound recordings are easy to digitize using a basic microphone and software that's included with the Windows operating system. See Figure B-17. You can digitally record a narration, vocal segment, or music clip, and then store it on disk.

○── Sound or audio data can be represented in two very different ways: as a waveform or as MIDI music. **Waveform** audio is a digital representation of sound. To record sound digitally, samples of the sound waveform are collected at periodic intervals and stored as numeric data.

○── The **sampling rate** refers to the number of times per second the sound is measured during the recording process. The sampling rate is expressed in hertz (Hz). Higher sampling rates increase the quality of the sound recording but require more storage space than lower sampling rates.

○── **MIDI (Musical Instrument Digital Interface)** files contain instructions that MIDI instruments and sound cards use to recreate or synthesize sounds. This music notation system allows computers to communicate with music synthesizers. MIDI files store and recreate musical instrument sounds, but not voice sounds. The computer encodes the music as a sequence and stores it as a file with a .mid, .cmf, or .rol filename extension. MIDI files are much more compact than waveform files. Three minutes of MIDI music requires only 10 KB of storage space, whereas three minutes of waveform music requires 15 MB.

FIGURE B-17: *Using Sound Recorder software*

SCREENTOUR

To use the Sound Recorder software, click the Record button, then speak into the microphone. Click the Stop button when you're finished recording. Use the Save option on the File menu to store the recording on disk.

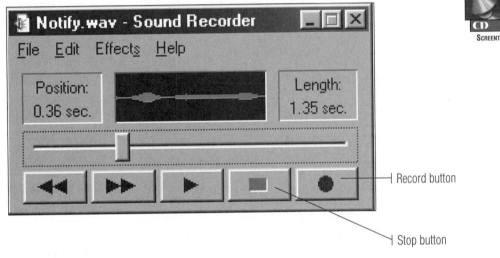

Record button

Stop button

More about waveforms

SCREENTOUR

Music, voice, and sound can all be recorded as waveforms. The waveform files you record, store, or download on your computer generally have .wav, .mod, .au, or .voc filename extensions. To record or playback waveform files, you need music software. Using music software, such as the Windows Sound Recorder, you can see the sound wave as you listen to the sound.

FIGURE B-18: *Sound wave*

Understanding digital images and animation

In addition to sound, images are an essential component of multimedia. Photos and other static images are often referred to as "still images" to distinguish them from videos and animation. Digital photos are digitized real objects. Digital animation and video encompass a number of technologies, including those that produce theater-quality special effects, DVD movies, and desktops videos. Still images must be converted into a format that can be used in multimedia.

Lab
PHOTO EDITING

DETAILS

- A **scanner** converts still images from paper format to digital format. Figure B-19 shows a typical scanner. A scanner converts a printed image into a bitmap graphic by essentially dividing it into a fine gridwork of cells and assigning a digital value to the color in each cell. These values are then stored by your computer and can be manipulated with graphics software, added to documents, and incorporated into multimedia projects. Scanners are inexpensive to purchase and easy to use.

- A **digital camera** provides an alternative way to digitize still images. Traditionally, you captured a still image by taking a photo with a camera, having the film processed, and then digitizing the photo with a scanner. Today, a digital camera makes it possible to take a photo in digital format. You can transfer the digital image directly to your computer.

  When you take a photo with a digital camera, the image that enters the camera lens is divided into a fine gridwork of cells. The digital color values for each cell in an image is saved on a storage device within the camera. Different cameras use different types of storage, including standard floppy disks and small flash memory cards like the one shown in Figure B-20. To transfer the image from a floppy disk, you place the disk in the floppy disk drive of your computer. To transfer the image from a flash memory module, you transfer the image data over a cable that runs between the camera and the computer.

- Once you've digitized the image, you will probably want to make additional adjustments to it. Software, such as a photo editing application, allows you to make adjustments to digitized images, such as removing red-eye.

- In addition to digitized still images, multimedia includes video and animation. **Digital video** is based on footage of real objects. **Digital animation** is typically created "from scratch" by an artist with the help of a computer. Computer-generated special effects are created one frame at a time using powerful microcomputers, workstations, mainframes, and even supercomputers with a process similar to rendering images from a 3-D wireframe.

  The first computer-generated graphics sequence was the spectacular transformation of the Genesis effect in the 1983 film *The Wrath of Khan*. The film *Toy Story* was the first feature film created entirely with digital animation. The quality of computer-generated special effects has become so good that it is difficult to identify them on the screen.

- **Desktop video** refers to images that are captured by a digital video camera or that have been converted into digital format from a videotape. Desktop videos—popular additions to many multimedia projects such as encyclopedias, computer-based training lessons, and Web sites—are constructed using a microcomputer. Unfortunately, today's microcomputers have storage and processing speed limitations that prevent the quality of desktop videos from reaching the standard of DVD movies.

  Desktop videos typically display at only 15 frames per second and appear in a small window on the screen compared with DVD movies, which display at 30 frames per second and appear in a full window. Figure B-21 shows Adobe Premier, a video editing software.

FIGURE B-19: *Using a scanner*

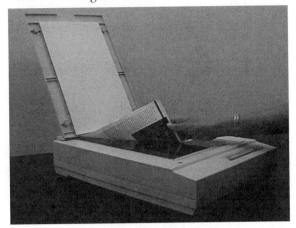

To use a scanner, place a document or photo face down on the glass surface, then close the cover. Activate your scanning software, check the scan settings, then initiate the scan.

FIGURE B-20: *A digital camera*

VIDEO

This digital camera saves as many as 32 images on the small flash memory card pictured in front of the camera.

FIGURE B-21: *Video editing software*

CD

SCREENTOUR

After you capture video footage from a camera or video tape, you can use video editing software to assemble the video and add a soundtrack.

1. Arrange your video clips in any sequence.

2. Add a soundtrack.

3. Preview your video.

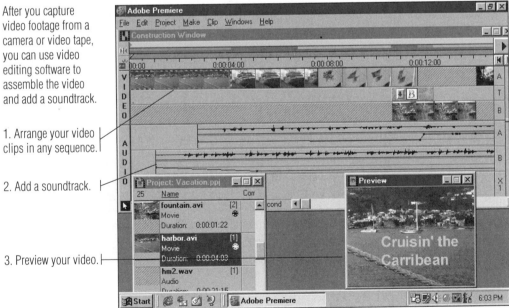

Should I get a CD drive or a DVD drive?

Virtually every computer on the market today comes equipped with a CD-ROM or a DVD-ROM drive. CD-ROM drives typically are part of less expensive computer systems, whereas DVD-ROM drives are more likely to be included with more expensive systems. Most experts recommend a DVD-ROM drive because it reads CD_ROM, CD-R, CD_RW, DVD-ROM, and DVD movie formats. A CD-ROM drive cannot read DVD-ROM or DVD movie formats.

Purchasing and installing software

Many microcomputers are sold with preinstalled system and application software, but eventually most computer users want to install additional software. Figure B-22 shows you how the **setup program** guides you through required steps to install Windows application software.

DETAILS

- Before you install software, you must make sure that the software is compatible with your computer system. To be compatible, the software must be written for the type of computer you use and for the operating system that is installed on your computer. For example, Microsoft Word is available for both PCs and Apple Macintosh computers, but these applications are separate versions of the software. You cannot use the Macintosh version of Microsoft Word on your PC, and vice versa. Once you know the software is compatible with the type of computer you use, you must make sure the software will work with your operating system.

- **System requirements** specify the operating system type and the minimum hardware capacity needed for a software product to work correctly. You must make sure that your computer meets or exceeds the system requirements specified for the software. The system requirements are usually listed on the outside of the software package and might also be explained in detail in the software reference manual.

- **Software distribution** refers to how computer software is usually shipped. Most computer software today is shipped on CD-ROMs because one CD-ROM is more convenient and more cost-effective than 20 or 30 distribution disks. Some older software, however, may come on 3.5-inch disks, called **distribution disks**. Instead of using software directly from the distribution media, you usually install the software on your hard disk. You don't copy all multimedia elements to your hard disk, however, so as to save space. You will need the CD-ROM or distribution disks when you use software installed in this manner.

- **Installation** is the process of copying programs and data files for the software to the hard disk of your computer. When you install non-multimedia applications such as word processing or accounting software, the computer copies all program modules from the distribution medium so that you do not need to insert the CD-ROM or disk every time you use the program. For multimedia applications, the procedure might be different. You generally copy only a small startup program to your hard disk, leaving most of the multimedia images, videos, and sounds on the CD-ROM.

Downward compatibility

Operating systems go through numerous versions. A higher version number indicates a more recent version. Operating systems are usually downwardly compatible, which means that you can use

application software designed for an earlier version of the operating system, but not software designed for a later version. For example, if Windows 98 is installed on your computer, you can generally use software

designed for earlier versions of Windows, such as Windows 3.1. On the other hand, your software might not work correctly if it requires Windows 98 but you have Windows 3.1 on your computer.

1. A setup program guides you through the steps required to install Windows application software. Insert the setup disk, CD-ROM, or DVD and start the setup program.

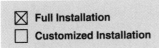

2. Select the installation option that best meets your needs. During a full installation, the setup program copies all files and data from the distribution medium to the hard disk of your computer system. A full installation provides you with access to all features of the software.

During a customized installation, the setup program displays a list of software features for your selection. After you select the features you want, the setup program copies only the selected program and data files to your hard disk. A customized installation can save space on your hard disk.

3. If the software includes multiple disks or CD-ROMs, insert each one in the specified drive when the setup program tells you to do so.

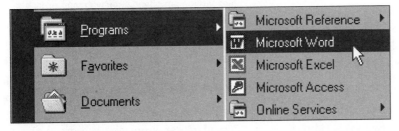

4. When the setup program has finished, start the program you have just installed to make sure that it works.

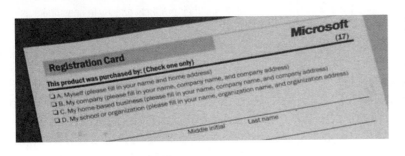

5. Fill out the registration card and send it in. When you send in the card, you become a registered user. The perks of being a registered user vary with each software publisher, but they might include receiving free technical support, product information, or discounts on new versions of the software.

Understanding marketing

Before you purchase hardware or software, it is important to understand the computer industry marketing structure, including marketing tiers, marketing channels, and marketing terminology. As many consumers point out, "No one pays list price for software." Having a good understanding of marketing structures is important as you expand your hardware and build your software library.

DETAILS

▸ Since 1981, hundreds of companies have produced personal computers. Industry analysts classify these companies into three **marketing tiers** or categories.

- The top tier consists of large companies that have been in the computer business for many years and have an identifiable share of total computer sales. These companies include IBM, Apple, Compaq, Dell, and Hewlett-Packard. They offer the most expensive computers because they have higher overhead costs, their management is often paid higher salaries, and they devote substantial financial resources to research and development.

- The second tier includes newer companies with high sales volume but somewhat less financial resources than companies in the first tier. The computers they offer are less expensive than top-tier company computers, even though they may use the same components in their PCs. They have minimized operating costs and often contract out the repair and warranty work.

- The third tier consists of smaller startup companies that sell primarily through mail order. Their computers are the least expensive. Sometimes they pass along low operating costs, but the inexpensive computers are often of poorer quality and may not be supported by the company.

▸ Computer hardware and software are sold by **marketing outlets** or **marketing channels**. These channels include computer retail stores, mail order/Internet outlets, value-added resellers, and manufacturer direct sales. See Figure B-23.

- **Computer retail stores** are either small local shops or nationwide chains that specialize in the sale of microcomputer software and hardware. They purchase computer products from a manufacturer or distribution center and then sell the products to consumers. Employees are often knowledgeable about a variety of computer products and can help you select a hardware or software product to fit your needs. Many computer retail stores also offer classes and training sessions, answer questions, provide technical support, and repair hardware products. A computer retail store is often the best source of supply for buyers who are likely to need assistance after the sale, such as beginning computer users or those with complex computer systems, such as networks. But computer retail stores can be a fairly expensive channel for hardware and software. Their prices reflect the cost of purchasing merchandise from a distributor, maintaining a retail storefront, and hiring technically qualified staff.

- **Mail-order suppliers** take orders by mail or telephone and ship the product directly to consumers. Mail-order suppliers generally offer low prices but provide limited service and support. A mail-order supplier is often the best source of products for buyers who are unlikely to need support or who can troubleshoot problems with the help of a technical support person on the telephone. Experienced computer users who can install components, set up their software, and do their own troubleshooting are often happy with mail-order suppliers.

- **Value-added resellers (VARs)** combine commercially available products with specialty hardware or software to create a computer system designed to meet the needs of a specific industry. Although VARs charge for their expertise, they are often the only source for a system that really meets the needs of a specific industry.

- **Manufacturer direct** refers to hardware manufacturers that sell their products directly to consumers using a sales force or mail order to distribute directly to individual consumers. The sales force usually targets large corporate or educational customers, where large volume sales can cover costs and commissions. These manufacturers can sell their products directly to consumers for a lower price than when they sell them through retailers, but they cannot generally offer the same level of support and assistance as a local retailer.

▶ Manufacturers produce products and ship them to VARs, distribution centers, computer centers, computer retailers, and mail-order suppliers. Some manufacturers ship products directly to customers.

▶ Distribution centers stock products from many different manufacturers and then sell the products to retailers.

▶ Computer retailers stock products from several manufacturers and sell these products to customers.

▶ VARs generally modify products or assemble them into complete hardware and software solutions that are targeted at specific businesses.

▶ Mail-order suppliers specialize in taking phone orders and shipping products to customers using U.S. mail or courier services.

Marketing terminology

The **introductory** price is the price listed when a new software product becomes available. The publisher often offers the software at a special price that is designed to entice customers. Even after the introductory price expires, most vendors offer sizable discounts. The average discounted price is referred to as the **street price**. The **version upgrade price** is the price that is made available to previous owners of a software package. If you supply proof to the vendor that you own the earlier version, you can get the new version at a discount. A **competitive upgrade** is a special price offered to consumers who switch from one company's software product to the new version of the competitor's product.

Software is easy to steal. You don't have to walk out of a CompUSA store with a Microsoft Office 2000 box under your shirt. You can simply borrow your friend's CD-ROM and install a copy of the program on your computer's hard disk. It seems so simple that it couldn't be illegal. But it is.

In many countries, including the United States, software pirates are subject to criminal prosecution. And yet, piracy continues to grow. According to the Software and Information Industry Association (SIIA), a leading anti-piracy watchdog, revenue losses from business software piracy typically exceed $12 billion per year. This figure reveals only a part of the piracy problem—it does not include losses from rampant game and educational software piracy.

A small, but vocal minority of software users believe that data and software should be freely distributed. Richard Stallman writes in the GNU (which stands for "Gnu's Not UNIX") Manifesto, "I consider that the golden rule requires that if I like a program I must share it with other people who like it. Software sellers want to divide users and conquer them, making each user agree not to share with others. I refuse to break solidarity with other users in this way. I cannot in good conscience sign a nondisclosure agreement or a software license agreement."

Is software piracy really damaging? Who cares if you use Microsoft Office without paying for it? Software piracy is damaging because it has a negative effect on the economy. Software production is the third-largest industry in the United States, employing more than 2 million people and growing at a phenomenal rate of 5.8 percent per year. This industry, however, is losing an estimated $32 million every day, which translates to 130,000 lost jobs and $1 billion in lost tax revenues.

Decreases in software revenues can have a direct effect on consumers, too. When software publishers have to cut corners, they tend to reduce customer service and technical support. As a result, you, as the consumer get put on hold when you call for technical support, you find fewer free technical support sites, and you encounter customer support personnel who are only moderately knowledgeable about their products. The bottom line—software piracy negatively affects customer service.

As an alternative to cutting support costs, some software publishers might build the cost of software piracy into the price of the software. The unfortunate result is that those who legitimately license and purchase software pay an inflated price.

Software piracy is a global problem. Although the United States accounts for the highest dollar amount of software piracy, approximately two-thirds of the piracy occurs outside the United States. The countries with the highest piracy rates include China, Japan, Korea, Germany, France, Brazil, Italy, Canada, and the United Kingdom. Piracy is a problem in other countries, too. By some estimates, a very large percent of all business software used in Bulgaria, Indonesia, Russia, and Vietnam is pirated.

ANTI-PIRACY

As a justification of high piracy rates, some observers point out that people in many countries simply might not be able to afford software that is priced for the U.S. market. This argument would make sense in China, where the average annual income is equivalent to about $3,500, and in Korea, where the average income is only $900. A Korean who legitimately purchases Microsoft Office for $250 would be spending more than one-quarter of his or her annual income. Most of the countries with a high incidence of software piracy, however, have strong economies and respectable per capita incomes. To further discredit the theory that piracy stems from poverty, India—which has a fairly large computer-user community, but a per capita income of only $1,600—is not among the top ten countries with high rates of software piracy.

If economic factors do not account for the pervasiveness of software piracy, what does? Some analysts suggest that people need more education about software copyrights and the economic implications of piracy. Other analysts believe that copyright enforcement needs to be increased by supporting and implementing more vigorous efforts to identify and prosecute pirates.

EXPAND THE IDEAS

1. Do you believe software piracy is a serious issue? Write a one-page paper supporting your position. Be sure to include your resources.

2. How do you think software publishers can control piracy in the United States? Abroad? Work with a small group. Brainstorm, and then research your ideas. Compile your ideas into a poster presentation.

3. What laws currently address software piracy? How are these laws enforced? What punishment do you think is acceptable for software piracy? Work in small groups. Compile your findings into a multimedia presentation.

4. How have the media treated software piracy? Research media archives. Find several examples of articles, documentaries, or news stories on software piracy. Write a summary of each article or media piece. Analyze your findings—was the media voice consistent? Why or why not?

End of Unit Exercises

STUDY TIPS

Study Tips help you organize and consolidate the information in a unit by making lists, outlines, charts, and sketches. You can use paper and pencil or word processing software to complete most of the Study Tips activities.

1. Under U.S. copyright law, what are the two major rights granted to the copyright holder? What are the three rights granted to the user of copyrighted materials?

2. Explain the difference between internal and external operating system services.

3. Complete the following "legal" matrix to clarify the difference between copyrighted software, licensed software, shareware, and public domain software.

	COPYRIGHTED SOFTWARE	LICENSED SOFTWARE	SHAREWARE	PUBLIC DOMAIN SOFTWARE
Legal to make a backup copy?				
Legal to sell a copy?				
Legal to give a copy to a friend?				
Protected by copyright?				

4. Make a two-column list of multimedia equipment. In the first column, list the computer components that enable a computer to play multimedia. In the second column, list the devices that enable you to create multimedia.

5. In your own words, explain the concept of downward compatibility and give an example using specific operating system versions and application software.

6. Make a list of the application software covered in this unit that you have used or are familiar with. *Hint:* Begin your list with word processing software and desktop publishing software. Give examples of what you might create with each application or how you might use each application.

7. Explain, in a detailed list, the steps you would follow to install a software package that was distributed on a CD-ROM.

FILL IN THE BEST ANSWER

1. _____ software helps the computer carry out its basic operating tasks; _____ software helps the computer user carry out a task.

2. The set of instructions that tell a computer how to convert inches to centimeters is called a computer _____.

3. The _____ is the software that controls the computer's use of resources.

4. The DOS, Windows, and Mac OS operating systems are typically used on _____ systems.

5. Examples of _____ software include word processing, desktop publishing, and Web authoring software.

6. Multimedia applications combine media such as _____, _____, _____, _____, _____, and _____.

7. If you use a computer to write a report, the report is considered software. True or False? _____

8. To use a computer effectively, you need to be a computer programmer. True or False? _____

9. A(n) _____ license would be useful in a situation where each network user needs a personalized version of the software.

10. A(n) _____ license generally allows software to be used on any and all computers at a specific location.

11. The "try before you buy" policy refers to _____ licenses.

12. UNIX and Linux are server operating systems, whereas Windows 98 is a(n) _____ operating system.

13. A freeware operating system called _____ is gaining popularity for network and Web site servers.

14. _____ software helps the computer accomplish such tasks as preparing a disk for data, providing information about the files on a disk, and copying data from one disk to another.

15. Install a(n) _____ to tell the computer how to use a new peripheral device.

16. A(n) _____ allows you to write computer programs using English-like instructions.

17. If you purchase a software _____, you will get several applications in one package.

18. _____ software provides sophisticated features for producing professional-quality newspapers, magazines, and books.

19. _____ software is used to dial and connect to the Internet.

20. _____ refers to the number of times per second the sound is measured during the recording process.

21. _____ creates music by playing digitized sound samples of actual instruments.

22. A(n) _____ file stores information in records similar to index cards, whereas a(n) _____ is a collection of related files.

23. A(n) _____ provides an alternative way to digitize still images, whereas a(n) _____ digitizes printed images.

24. _____ software manages your computer mailbox.

INDEPENDENT CHALLENGE 1

To digitize still images, you would typically need to add a digital camera or a scanner to your computer system. For this project, use your library and Web resources to research information about digital cameras and scanners.

To complete this independent challenge:

1. Research and find the manufacturers and model numbers for three digital cameras. Write a comparison of the features, strengths, and weaknesses of each model. If you were in the market for a digital camera, which camera would you purchase and why?

2. Research and find the manufacturers and model numbers for three scanners. Write a comparison of the features, strengths, and weaknesses of each model. If you were in the market for a scanner, which scanner would you purchase and why?

3. Look for information about the quality of the images produced by the digital cameras you researched in Step 1 and the scanners you researched in Step 2. Determine whether it is better to scan a photo that you have taken with a conventional high-quality 35mm camera or to take the photo directly with a digital camera. Write a one-page analysis of your findings.

INDEPENDENT CHALLENGE 2

In this unit, you learned how to identify microcomputer operating systems by looking at the main screen and prompt. In this independent challenge, you will explore more about the operating system in your school computer lab. If you have more than one lab or if your computer uses more than one operating system, your instructor should tell you which one to use for this independent challenge.

To complete this independent challenge:

1. Find out which operating system is used in your school computer lab. Be sure you find out the type and version. You can obtain this information online from one of the computers. If you see a command-line user interface, try typing **ver** and then pressing **Enter**. If you see a graphical user interface, try clicking the Apple menu or clicking the Help menu, then selecting About.

2. Once you know the operating system used in your school lab, use the operating system reference manual and library resources to answer the following questions:

   a. Which operating system and version is used in your school lab?

   b. Which company publishes the operating system software?

   c. When was the first version of this operating system introduced?

   d. Does this operating system have a command-line user interface or a graphical user interface?

   e. Does this operating system support multitasking?

   f. Do you need a password to use the computers in your school lab? Even if you do not need to use a password, does the operating system provide some way to secure access to the computers?

   g. How much does the publisher of this operating system usually charge for upgrades if you are a registered user?

INDEPENDENT CHALLENGE 3

There are so many software packages that it is difficult to get an idea of what's available unless you take a look through current computer magazines and software catalogs. This independent challenge has two parts. Do either one part or both parts depending on your instructor's assignment. Step 1 helps you discover the breadth of available software applications. Step 2 helps you research an application or operating system in more depth. You will be able to find the information for this independent challenge in computer magazines in your library. If you have access to the Internet, use your favorite search engine to locate software retailers—there are many of them.

To complete this independent challenge:

1. Find an ad for a computer vendor that sells a large variety of software. Jot down the name of the vendor and note where you found the ad. List the categories that the vendor uses to classify software and the number of software packages in each category.

2. Select one type of software: operating system, utilities, document production, graphics, presentation, electronic mail, desktop publishing, spreadsheet, database, accounting, or Web authoring.

   a. Read a comparison review of software packages for the type of software you select.

   b. Try to locate and photocopy ads for each of the products in the review. Look through the software vendor ads to find the best price for each product.

   c. Write a one-page or two-page summary explaining your purchase recommendation.

INDEPENDENT CHALLENGE 4

When you use a software package, it is important to understand the legal restrictions on its use. You would be able to make decisions on how you can use the software legally based on the license.

To complete this independent challenge:

1. Locate at least two commercial software packages that have license agreements either written on the box or inside the package on the documentation.

2. On a separate piece of paper:

   a. Identify the software to which each license corresponds.

   b. Is it a shrink-wrap license? Why or why not?

   c. After you pay your computer dealer for the program covered by each license, who owns the program?

   d. Can you legally have one copy of the program at work and another copy of the program on your computer at home if you use the software in only one place at a time?

   e. Can you legally sell the software?

   f. Under what conditions can you legally transfer possession of the program to someone else?

   g. If you were the owner of a software store, could you legally rent the program to customers if you were sure they didn't keep a copy after the rental period was over?

   h. Can you legally install this software on one computer but give more than one user access to it?

   i. If you use this program for an important business decision and you later find out that a mistake in the program caused you to lose $500,000, what legal recourse is provided by the license?

INDEPENDENT CHALLENGE 5

Folk wisdom tells us to use the appropriate tool for a job. This idea holds true for software tools, too. In this independent challenge, you decide what software tool is most appropriate for a task. You can do this project on your own or discuss it in a small group.

To complete this independent challenge:

For each of the scenarios that follow, decide which software tool (for example, word processing) would accomplish the task most effectively.

   a. You want to keep track of your monthly expenses and try to figure out ways to save some money.

   b. As the leader of an international team of researchers studying migration patterns of Canadian geese, you want all team members to communicate their findings to each other quickly.

   c. You are the office manager for a department of a Fortune 500 company and one of your responsibilities is to arrange meetings and schedule facilities for the employees in your department.

   d. As a partner in a law firm, you need to draft and modify legal briefs.

   e. You are in charge of a fund-raising campaign and you need to track the names, addresses, phone numbers, and donations made by contributors.

   f. You are going to design and produce the printed program for a community theater play listing the actors, director, lighting specialists, and so on.

   g. A sales manager for a cosmetics company wants to motivate the sales force by graphically showing the increases in consumer spending in each of the past five years.

   h. The marketing specialist for a new software company wants to send out announcements to 150 computer magazines.

   i. The owners of five golf courses in Jackson County want to design a promotional brochure that can be distributed to tourists in restaurants and hotels.

j. The owner of a small business wants to keep track of ongoing income and expenses and print out monthly profit and loss statements.

k. The superintendent of a local school system wants to prepare a press release explaining why student test scores were 5 percent below the national average.

l. A contractor wants to calculate his cost for materials needed to build a new community center.

m. A college student wants to send out customized letters addressed to 20 prospective employers.

n. The parents of three children want to decide whether they should invest money for their children's education in the stock market or whether they should buy into their state's prepaid tuition plan.

o. The director of fund-raising for a large nonprofit organization wants to keep a list of prospective donors.

LAB: MULTIMEDIA

Multimedia brings together text, graphics, sound, animation, video, and photo images. In this lab, you will learn how to apply multimedia and then have the chance to see what it might be like to design some aspects of multimedia projects.

1. Click the Steps button to learn about multimedia development. As you proceed through the Steps, answer the QuickCheck questions. When you complete the Steps, you will see a report that summarizes your performance on the QuickChecks. Follow the directions on the screen to print the QuickCheck Report.

2. In Explore, browse through the STS-79 Multimedia Mission Log. How many videos are included in the Multimedia Mission Log? The image on the Mission Profile page is a vector drawing. What happens when you enlarge it?

3. Suppose you were hired as a designer for a multimedia series targeting fourth- and fifth-grade students. Describe the changes you would make to the Multimedia Mission Log so that it would be suitable for these students. Also, include a sketch showing a screen from your revised design.

4. When you view the Multimedia Mission Log on your computer, do you see the palette flash? Why or why not? If you see the palette flash, list the images that flash.

5. Multimedia can be effectively applied to projects such as encyclopedias, atlases, and animated storybooks; to computer-based training for foreign languages, first aid, or software applications; for games and sports simulations; for business presentations; for personal albums, scrapbooks, and baby books; for product catalogs and Web pages.

Suppose you were hired to create one of these projects. Write a one-paragraph description of the project you would develop. Describe some of the multimedia elements you would include. For each element, indicate its source and whether you would need to obtain permission for its use. Finally, sketch a screen or two showing your completed project.

LAB: PHOTO EDITING

A digital camera or scanner produces digital still photos that you can include in multimedia projects and e-mail. But digital photos—like their film and paper counterparts—are not necessarily "perfect." They are sometimes out of focus, too bright, too dark, or poorly framed. The good news is that fixing a digital photo is relatively simple. To alter a digital image, you can use generalized bitmap graphics software or specialized photo editing software. In this lab, you will have the opportunity to use both types of software to compare features and ease of use.

1. Click the Steps button to learn about photo editing software. As you proceed through the Steps, answer the QuickCheck questions. After you complete the Steps, you will see a QuickCheck Report. Follow the instructions on the screen to print this report.

2. When you click the Explore button, Microsoft Paint opens and displays a photo called Dog.bmp. You can continue the Explore activities using Paint, or you can save Dog.bmp on a disk, close Paint, and proceed using the photo editing software of your choice.

3. Using Microsoft Paint or the photo editing software of your choice, try to complete the list of editing tasks below. The number of tasks that you can complete will depend on the software that you have elected to use.

   Crop the photo so that you see only the dog and the toys.

   Remove the "green" eye.

   Change the bear's nose from red to black.

   Remove the small scar from the dog's forehead.

   Smooth or despeckle the photo.

   Decrease the brightness until you can see the details of the white bear's fur.

4. Save your revised photo and print it out. Use a color printer if one is available; otherwise, use a back-and-white printer.

5. On the back of your printout, indicate which software you used and list the photo editing tasks that you were able to complete.

LESSON	MEDIA ELEMENT	LESSON	MEDIA ELEMENT
Examining software copyrights and licensing	COPYRIGHT SHAREWARE	Understanding the sound system	SCREENTOUR SOUND SYSTEMS
Defining operating systems	OPERATING SYSTEMS	Understanding digital images and animation	PHOTO EDITING VIDEO SCREENTOUR
Reviewing utilities, drivers, and programming languages	SCREENTOUR	Purchasing and installing software	VIDEO
Introducing application software	APPLICATION SOFTWARE SCREENTOUR 3-D GRAPHICS PRESENTATIONS SCREENTOUR MONEY MANAGEMENT SCREENTOUR WEB BROWSERS GAMES GALORE	Issue: Are Copyrights Fair?	ANTI-PIRACY
Understanding multimedia computing	MULTIMEDIA MULTIMEDIA		

VISUAL WORKSHOP

In the multimedia computer system pictured, identify each of the lettered components and how they would contribute and perform as you work using a program, which includes text, sound, graphics, animation, and video information.

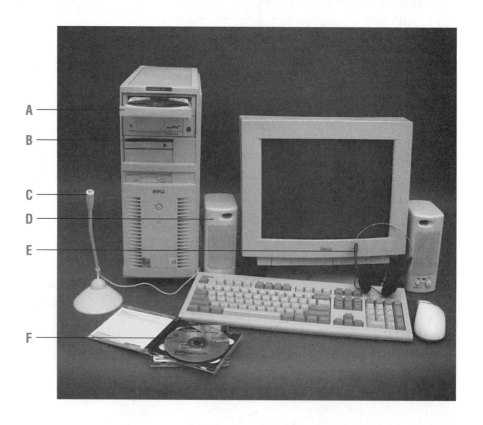

Productivity Software

Today, it seems as if most everyone uses computers. Document production software makes it possible to create professional-looking documents. Spreadsheet software makes it relatively painless for novices to set up complex numerical calculations. Database software makes it possible for computer users to organize their information. This chapter looks at how these productivity software tools affect the computing you do today and how they have affected our society.

Introducing document production software

Documents are an integral part of our society and culture and an important component of our everyday lives. There are historical documents such as the Declaration of Independence and the U.S. Constitution, literary documents such as *Gone with the Wind* and *War and Peace*, popular fictional books, weekly magazines, daily newspapers, legal contracts, and personal correspondence. Initially, documents were handwritten and then hand-copied. See Figure C-1. As literacy has increased throughout the world, however, the tools of document production have changed.

DETAILS

- **Document production software** includes word processing software, desktop publishing software, and the software that helps you create e-mail and hypertext documents for the Internet's World Wide Web. Document production software makes it easy to let your ideas flow and correct typing and spelling errors because it handles many writing tasks automatically. Figure C-2 describes reasons to use a computer for writing.

- Typing was once a specialized skill practiced mainly by women in secretarial positions. Now, typing or "keyboarding" is a skill possessed to some degree by a sizable percentage of the population in highly literate nations. The pervasiveness of this skill stems from the popularity of computerized document production. Although there are advantages to being a good keyboarder, you don't need to be an expert typist to create documents. Document production software includes features that can help you create error-free documents. If you want to improve your keyboarding skills, typing tutor software can increase your typing speed and accuracy.

- Steps in creating a document using a word processor:
  - Type the text.
  - Edit the document until you are satisfied with the content and writing style.
  - Format and print the document.
  - For highly designed documents, transfer your document to desktop publishing software to complete the format and layout before printing.

- **Word wrap** determines how the text will flow from line to line by automatically moving words to the next line as you reach the right margin. Imagine that the sentences in your document are ribbons of text. Word wrap bends the ribbons. Changing the margin size just means bending the ribbon in different places. Even after you have typed an entire document, adjusting the size of your right, left, top, and bottom margins is a simple task. The lines will break automatically, readjusting for the new margins.

- Sections of your document are referred to as **blocks** or **text blocks**. You can easily insert text, cut sections of text, and move entire paragraphs or pages to improve the structure and logical flow of a document. The action of deleting or moving a text block is sometimes referred to as a **block operation**.

- Some writers find that the limited amount of text displayed on the screen prevents them from getting a good look at the overall flow of ideas throughout the document. The outline feature helps you develop a document as a hierarchy of headings and subheadings. When you create a hierarchical document, you "tag" each heading to identify whether it starts a chapter, section, subsection, or whatever organizational structure you determine. To get an overall view of the document, use the outline feature to show only the levels within sections.

FIGURE C-1: *Technology has had a significant effect on document production*

VIDEO

LITERACY

FIGURE C-2: *Good reasons to use a computer for your writing*

TYPING

Good reasons to use a computer for your writing

- You want to improve the technical aspects of your writing, such as spelling, grammar, and writing style.
- When you proofread your work, you see sections that you know you can improve.
- You have good ideas, but bad handwriting.
- You're a perfectionist.
- You're not a good typist and can't afford to hire one.
- You want to post your documents on the Web or e-mail them to friends or colleagues.

Improving the quality of writing

Critics have implied that instead of helping writers, computers have somehow lowered literary standards. In fact, people–not computers–create documents. When used skillfully, computerized document production tools can help you improve the quality of your writing. With such tools, it is easy to edit the first draft of your document to refine its overall structure, and then zero in to make detailed improvements to your sentence structure and word usage. Indeed, once you have taken care of the overall structure of your document, you can turn to the details of spelling, grammar, and word usage.

WORD PROCESSING

IMPROVE YOUR WRITING

DETAILS

- A document with spelling and grammar errors reflects poorly on the writer. An **in-line spell checker** checks the spelling of each word as you type. A spell checker looks through your entire document any time you activate it. See Figure C-3.

  - A **spell checker** works by looking for each word from your document in a list called a **dictionary**. If the word from your document is in the dictionary, the spell checker considers the word correctly spelled. If the word is not in the dictionary, the word is identified as misspelled.
  - As you type, an in-line spell checker marks errors with a colored background or wavy underline. You can backspace and correct the error manually, or you can click the misspelled word and then select from a list of correctly spelled options.

- A **grammar checker** is a feature of most word processors that coaches you on correct sentence structure and word usage. Think of a grammar checker as an assistant that will proofread your document, point out potential trouble spots, and suggest alternatives. Refer to Figure C-4. A grammar checker will not change your document for you. Instead, it highlights possible problems, suggests alternative words or phrases, and gives you the option of making changes.

- The online **thesaurus** helps you find descriptive words to clarify and enliven your writing. A thesaurus will find synonyms and antonyms for a highlighted word in a document.

- The **search** feature is used to hunt for all occurrences of any problem word. For each occurrence, you can decide to leave it or revise it. **Search and replace** is useful if you want to substitute one word or phrase for another. For example, after you finish the first draft of a short story, you might change a character's name by using search and replace to change every occurrence of "Rachel" to "Emily."

FYI

Document production software tools, such as spell and grammar checkers, cannot guarantee error-free documents—you must read your work.

FIGURE **C-3**: *A word processor's spell checker*

SCREENTOUR

The spell checker finds a misspelled word and highlights it.

The spell checker offers some correctly spelled options. You can select one of the options to replace the misspelling.

You can use these buttons to tell the spell checker how to handle the highlighted word.

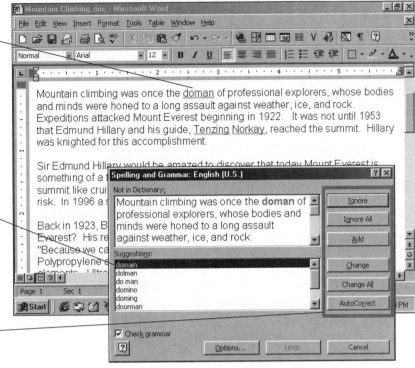

FIGURE **C-4**: *A word processor's grammar checker*

SCREENTOUR

GRAMMAR

The grammar checker highlights the sentence it is currently checking.

The problem is indicated in green.

A suggestion for improvement.

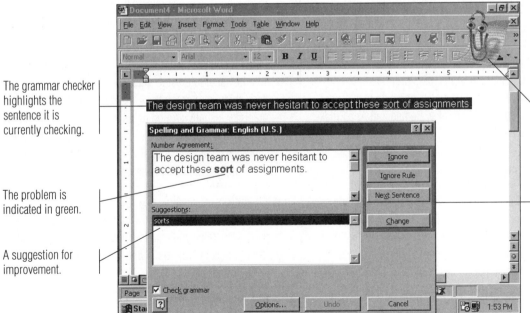

If requested, the Office Assistant explains the basis for the grammar checker's suggestion.

You can use these buttons to tell the grammar checker how to handle the highlighted grammar problem.

Formatting documents

Before the printing press, documents were hand-copied. Many of the hand-copied documents, called illuminated manuscripts, were works of art in addition to being a means of communicating information. Today, modern printing techniques make it cost-effective to produce beautiful documents that are available in libraries, bookstores, and newsstands to everyone. Document production software includes formatting tools such as document templates, wizards, fonts, styles, borders, and clip art, which make it possible for individuals to produce professionally formatted and illustrated documents.

DETAILS

- A **document template** is a preformatted document into which you type your text. In a document template, format settings such as margins, line spacing, heading fonts, and type size have all been set up for you. Figure C-5 shows some of the document templates typically available with today's word processing software.

- Some software goes a step further than templates, by furnishing **document wizards** that not only provide you with a document format, but also take you step-by-step through the process of entering the text for a wide variety of documents. For example, to create an entry-level résumé, you might find it easy to use a résumé wizard like the one shown in Figure C-6.

- A **font** is a typeface or style of lettering. See Figure C-7. Typesetters and artists design fonts. Your document production software generally supplies you with many fonts. Typeset fonts, such as Times New Roman and Arial, make your document look formal and professionally produced. Research studies show that sans-serif fonts are easier to read on the computer screen.

- You can manipulate the appearance of your document by adjusting the line spacing, margins, indents, tabs, and borders. Larger margins and double-spacing generate white space, make your document appear less dense, and make your document seem easier to read. The margins for most papers and reports should be set at 1 inch or 1.5 inches. Most word processors automatically set the line spacing at an appropriate distance for the font size.

- **Justification** defines how the letters and words are spaced across each line. Typeset documents can be fully justified so that the text is aligned evenly on both the right margin and the left margin.

- **Columns** enhance readability and tables organize data. In document production terminology, columns generally mean newspaper-style layout of paragraphs of text. **Tables** arrange data in a grid of rows and columns. Tables are more appropriate than columns for numeric data and for lists of information.

- When you summarize or list information, or even when you type your answers to homework questions, your points will stand out if you use **hanging indents**, bulleted lists, or numbered lists. The details on this textbook page are an example of a bulleted list with hanging indents. Generally, the number in a hanging indent is positioned at the left margin, and the text is aligned under the tab stop.

- To add visual interest to your documents, incorporate borders, rules, and graphics. A **border** is a box around text or graphics, usually around a title, heading, or table. A **rule** is a line, usually positioned under text. Rules can be horizontal, vertical, or diagonal. The thinnest rule is one pixel thick and is called a hairline rule.

- A **frame** is an invisible box that can contain text or graphics. You can position a frame anywhere on the page. Generally, you can flow text around the frame and layer frames one on top of another to achieve complex layout effects.

- **Graphics** are pictures and illustrations. **Clip art** collections provide hundreds of graphic images that you have permission to use in noncommercial works. You can also find graphics on the Internet. With the right equipment, you can also scan pictures from books and magazines. Be sure that you check for permission before you borrow any graphic for your documents.

FIGURE C-5: *Document templates*

Template categories include letters and faxes, memos, reports, and Web pages.

Within each category, you can choose from several templates.

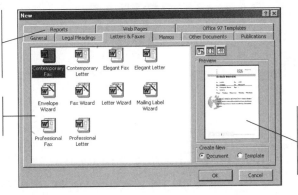

A Preview window displays an example of a document created using the selected template.

FIGURE C-6: *Document wizards*

SCREENTOUR

The Résumé Wizard prompts you to enter your name, address, and phone number, which it uses to create the heading for your résumé.

You can select the type of information you want to include in the body of your résumé.

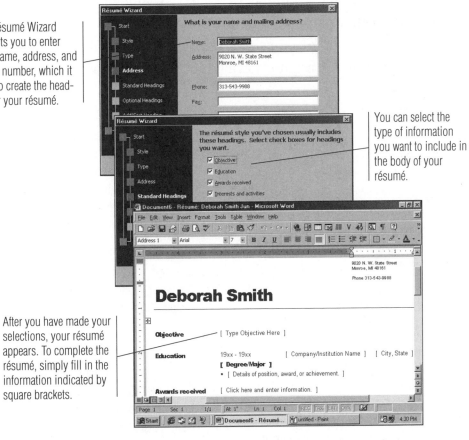

After you have made your selections, your résumé appears. To complete the résumé, simply fill in the information indicated by square brackets.

FIGURE C-7: *Fonts and kerning*

InfoWeb

FONTS

FONT TREATMENT	DESCRIPTION	EXAMPLE
Serif	A serif font has embellishments called "serifs" on the ends of the lines that form the characters.	Look at this!
Sans serif	A sans-serif font lacks serifs.	Look at this!
Kerned	A kerned font provides a wider space for wide letters, such as the "w," but reduces the amount of space allotted to narrow letters, such as "t."	wwwww ttttt
Monospaced	Each character in a monospaced font takes up the same amount of space.	wwwww ttttt

Examining electronic publishing

Printing with movable type existed in Asia as early as 1000 A.D. This technology did not exist in Europe, however, until Johann Gutenberg demonstrated his movable-type printing press in 1448. Printing eventually replaced hand-copying as a means of producing documents. Nevertheless, like many other technological innovations, the printing press had to overcome initial resistance from some segments of society. To alleviate fears of the movable type process, Gutenberg and other early printers produced Bibles and other religious documents. The change from hand-copying to machine printing had a massive effect on Western culture and civilization by making information available to all who could read.

PUBLISHING

DETAILS

- Thomas Paine harnessed the power of the printed word in 1776 when he sold 500,000 copies of a 50-page pamphlet, *Common Sense*. This document asserted that it was just common sense for the American colonies to become independent from Great Britain. Six months later, the Declaration of Independence was signed. Thomas Paine and his compatriot, Thomas Jefferson, envisioned a free press as the cornerstone of a free society. They hoped that publishing would spread ideas, foster dialogues among diverse interest groups, and help to establish a common social agenda.

- Early expectations were that computerized document production would make it easy for individuals, not just publishing companies, to produce professional-quality books and pamphlets. Word processors have made it possible for individuals to create more documents, such as newsletters and manuscripts.

- The expedient development of a worldwide data communications network has opened up opportunities for electronic publishing. Electronic documents are easy to send, store, and manipulate. They might even bring us closer to the global democracy that Thomas Paine envisioned. Today, virtually anyone can post a document on the World Wide Web, send an e-mail message, or participate in online discussion groups. Political pamphlets and position papers can be linked to popular sites. For individuals, organizations, and special-interest groups that cannot afford to produce paper publications, the Internet provides a low-cost means of distributing ideas and other information. See Figure C-8. The power of the printed word seems to be evolving into the power of the electronically published word.

- The Internet provides a powerful communications channel for disseminating many kinds of information. A single e-mail letter can be sent to hundreds of recipients and forwarded from those recipients to hundreds more.

- To create pages for the World Wide Web, you must convert your document into a Web-compatible format such as HTML (Hypertext Markup Language). Many word processors and desktop publishers will automatically generate an HTML-formatted document from any document you have entered and stored. When you create a Web page, your goal should be to combine and format basic Web elements effectively to create a visual display that enhances the content of your page. Figure C-9 shows the basic elements of a Web page. Saving a document as an HTML file does not place it on the Web for public access, however. You must transfer your HTML file to a Web site. For details on how to publish your Web pages, you can consult the Webmaster at your school, office, or local Internet service provider (ISP).

FIGURE C-8: *Disseminating ideas on the Web*

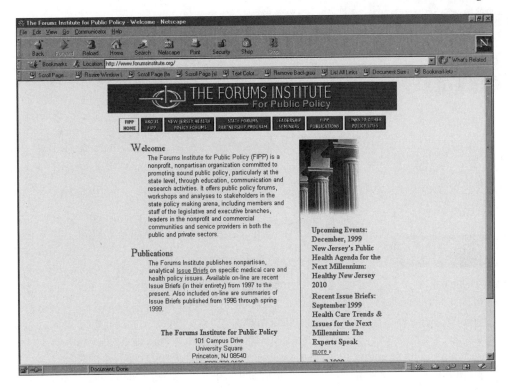

FIGURE C-9: *Web page elements*

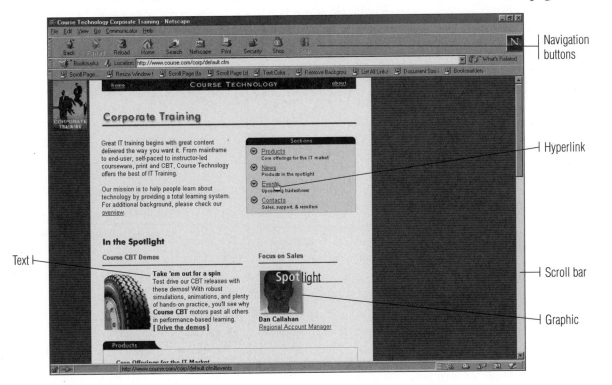

Navigation buttons

Hyperlink

Text

Scroll bar

Graphic

Automating document production

Computers are highly talented when it comes to tackling repetitive tasks such as counting, numbering, searching, and duplicating. Document production automates many of the repetitive tasks associated with document production, which in turn saves time and increases productivity.

Who wrote it?

DETAILS

- As you edit a document and change its format, you might remove or insert large sections of text, reducing or expanding the page count. Or you might decide to double-space the document, doubling the page count. **Automatic page numbering**, sometimes called **pagination**, means that the computer numbers and renumbers the pages as you edit and format your document.

- Page numbers are often included in a header or footer. A **header** is text that automatically appears in the top margin of every page. A **footer** is text that appears in the bottom margin of every page. Headers and footers help identify the document and make your documents look more like published works, which often have a header, a footer, or both on each page. The footer in this book includes the book and unit titles as well as page numbers.

- If it's important to determine the number of words in a document, your computer can count the words with the automatic word count feature of your document production software. Another use for a computer's ability to count words is for literary analysis. A **concordance** is an alphabetized list of words in a document and the frequency with which each word appears. Concordance has been used to determine authorship of historical and contemporary documents by comparing the frequencies of words used in a document by an unknown author with the frequencies of words used in a document of known authorship.

- **Mail merge** automates the process of producing customized documents such as letters and advertising flyers. Figure C-10 explains how it works.

- Most grammar checkers have built-in **readability formulas** that count the number of words in each sentence and the number of syllables per word. Most writers aim for a seventh- or eighth-grade reading level in documents intended for the general public. As you write, you can use readability formulas to target your writing to your audience. The longer your sentences and words, the higher the reading level required to understand your writing.

- Scholarly documents often require **footnotes** that contain citations for works mentioned in the text, as shown in Figure C-11. As you revise your text, the footnotes need to stay associated with their source in the text and must be numbered sequentially. Your document production software includes footnoting facilities that can position and number the footnotes even if you move blocks of text. Some software can gather citations at the end of a document, creating endnotes, and printing the endnotes in order of their appearance in the document or in alphabetical order. In addition, some word processors have wizards that help you enter your citations in the correct format depending on whether the citation is a book or a magazine article.

- Many people have come to expect that all documents—not just those created by professional publishers—have indexes and tables of contents. Most document production software will automatically generate an **index** and **table of contents**, and then automatically update them as you edit your document.

- **Boilerplate** text refers to information that remains constant from one document to the next. Law offices frequently use boilerplate text to draw up legal documents for wills, divorces, trusts, and so on.

FIGURE C-10: *Mail merge*

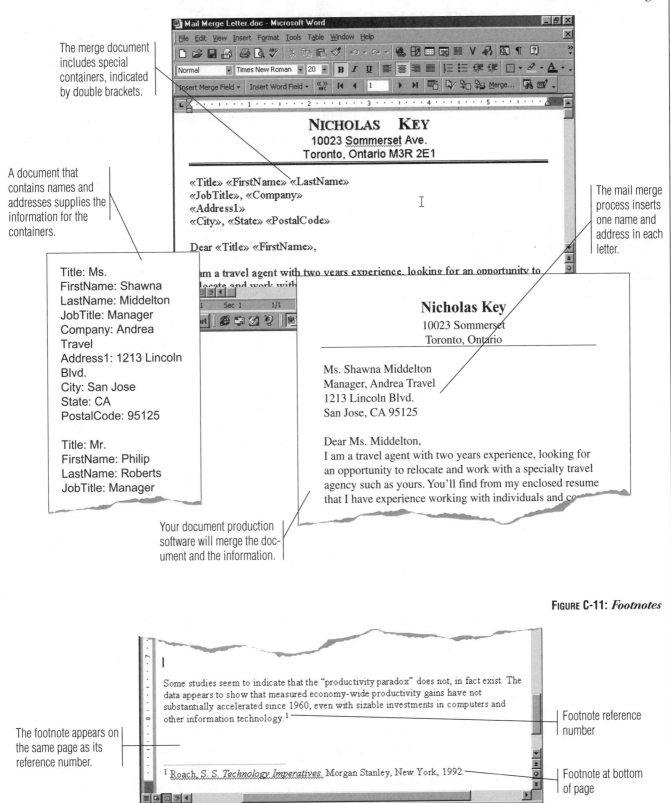

The merge document includes special containers, indicated by double brackets.

A document that contains names and addresses supplies the information for the containers.

The mail merge process inserts one name and address in each letter.

Your document production software will merge the document and the information.

Title: Ms.
FirstName: Shawna
LastName: Middelton
JobTitle: Manager
Company: Andrea Travel
Address1: 1213 Lincoln Blvd.
City: San Jose
State: CA
PostalCode: 95125

Title: Mr.
FirstName: Philip
LastName: Roberts
JobTitle: Manager

NICHOLAS KEY
10023 Sommerset Ave.
Toronto, Ontario M3R 2E1

«Title» «FirstName» «LastName»
«JobTitle», «Company»
«Address1»
«City», «State» «PostalCode»

Dear «Title» «FirstName»,

am a travel agent with two years experience, looking for an opportunity to locate and work with

Nicholas Key
10023 Sommerset
Toronto, Ontario

Ms. Shawna Middelton
Manager, Andrea Travel
1213 Lincoln Blvd.
San Jose, CA 95125

Dear Ms. Middelton,
I am a travel agent with two years experience, looking for an opportunity to relocate and work with a specialty travel agency such as yours. You'll find from my enclosed resume that I have experience working with individuals and co

FIGURE C-11: *Footnotes*

The footnote appears on the same page as its reference number.

Some studies seem to indicate that the "productivity paradox" does not, in fact exist. The data appears to show that measured economy-wide productivity gains have not substantially accelerated since 1960, even with sizable investments in computers and other information technology.[1]

[1] Roach, S. S. *Technology Imperatives.* Morgan Stanley, New York, 1992.

Footnote reference number

Footnote at bottom of page

Introducing spreadsheets

The United States is one of the most technologically based societies on earth. Therefore, it is somewhat surprising to find that some people are afraid to balance their checkbooks, calculate their tax returns, work out expense budgets, or decide what to do about financing their retirement. Entrepreneurs have devised a number of tools to ease the burden of making such calculations. To date, the most ambitious of these tools is the computerized spreadsheet.

DETAILS

- A **spreadsheet** is a numerical model or representation of a real situation. For example, your checkbook register is a sort of spreadsheet because it is a numerical representation of the cash flowing in and out of your bank account. Figure C-12 shows a typical checkbook.

- One expert describes spreadsheets as "intuitive, natural, usable tools for financial analysis, business and mathematical modeling, decision making, simulation, and problem solving." Figure C-13 shows a spreadsheet set up to reconcile a simple checkbook.

- A handheld calculator might be useful for simple calculations, but it becomes less convenient as you deal with more numbers and as your calculations become more complex. The major disadvantage of most calculators is that the numbers you entered are stored, but you can't see them. You can't verify if they're accurate. Also, it is difficult to change the numbers you have entered without redoing the entire calculation. By contrast, if you use spreadsheet software, all of your numbers are visible on the screen, and they are easy to change. You can print your results as a nicely formatted report, you can convert your numbers into a graph, and you can save your work and revise it later. You can easily incorporate your calculations and results into other electronic documents, post them as Web pages, and e-mail them to your colleagues.

- You use spreadsheet software to create an on-screen spreadsheet called a worksheet. A **worksheet** is based on a grid of columns and rows. Each **column** is lettered and each **row** is numbered. The intersection of a column and row is called a **cell**. Each cell has a unique cell address—its cell reference, which is derived from its column and row location. For example, the upper-left cell in a worksheet is cell A1 because it is in column A of row 1. Figure C-14 shows a simple worksheet.

- A cell can contain a number, text, or a formula. A **number** is a value that you want to use in a calculation. **Text** is used for the worksheet title, for labels that identify the numbers, and for numbers used as text, such as Social Security numbers. A **formula** tells the computer how to use the contents of cells in calculations. You can use formulas to add, subtract, multiply, and divide numbers.

- Building a worksheet from scratch requires thought and planning so that you end up with an accurate and well-organized worksheet. When you create your own worksheets, use these guidelines:

  - Visualize your worksheet: Determine the main purpose of the worksheet; list the information available to solve the problem; make a list of the calculations you'll need; picture the rows and columns needed.
  - Enter data: Enter numbers and labels in the cells, then enter the formulas; enter descriptive labels in adjoining cells to the left of data; include a title.
  - Format the worksheet: To improve readability, increase font sizes, boldface key labels, and use colors and graphs to emphasize key data.
  - Test the worksheet: Ask yourself, "Do the results make sense?" Check for typos and verify your data.
  - Save and print the worksheet.

FIGURE C-12: *A checkbook is a manual spreadsheet*

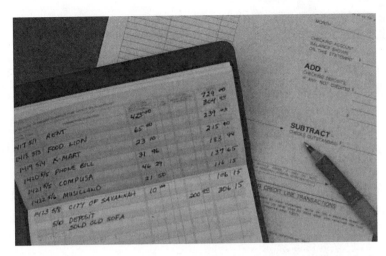

FIGURE C-13: *Spreadsheet software used to maintain a checkbook*

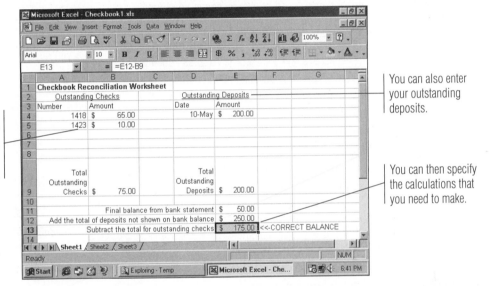

Following the instructions on your bank statement, you can enter your outstanding checks.

You can also enter your outstanding deposits.

You can then specify the calculations that you need to make.

FIGURE C-14: *A typical worksheet*

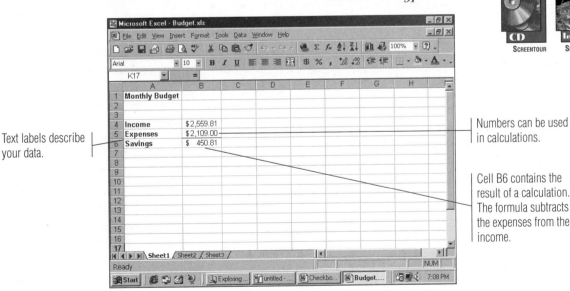

Text labels describe your data.

Numbers can be used in calculations.

Cell B6 contains the result of a calculation. The formula subtracts the expenses from the income.

Understanding spreadsheet basics

The value of spreadsheet software comes from the way it handles the numbers and formulas in a worksheet. Think of the worksheet as having two layers—the layer you see and a hidden layer underneath. The hidden layer can hold formulas, but the results of these formulas appear on the visible layer. Figure C-15 shows how this structure works.

SPREADSHEET
ERRORS

DETAILS

- Whenever you add or change something in a cell, the spreadsheet recalculates all of the formulas. Thus the results displayed on your worksheet always reflect the current figures contained in the cells. Formulas can include numbers and references to other cells. This feature is what gives a spreadsheet such flexibility. If you have a formula that says "subtract the contents of cell B5 from the contents of B4," it doesn't matter what those cells contain. Modifying the text, numbers, and formulas in a worksheet is easy. When you enter new numbers in a worksheet, the computer automatically recalculates all formulas, keeping the results up-to-date.

- A **function** is a predefined formula. Spreadsheet software has built-in functions to calculate hundreds of functions for mathematical, financial, date, and statistical calculations.

- You can also modify the structure of a worksheet by inserting and deleting rows and columns, or moving the contents of cells to other cells.

  - Unless you specify otherwise, a cell reference is a **relative reference**—that is, a reference that can change from B4 to B3, for example, if the data in column B moves up one row. The spreadsheet software attempts to adjust your formulas so that the cell references they contain remain accurate, and you do not have to revise all formulas on your worksheet, as shown in Figure C-16.
  - If the formula shouldn't change when you change the structure of a worksheet, you

can define any reference in a formula as an **absolute reference**. An absolute reference never changes when you insert rows or columns or when you copy or move formulas.

- Spreadsheet software seems to be able to anticipate what you want it to do.
  - Spreadsheet software is able to distinguish text data from numerical data. If you enter a phone number or a Social Security number in a cell, the data should be treated as text, not as a mathematical formula.
  - Spreadsheet software contains many handy shortcuts to help simplify the process of creating, editing, and formatting a worksheet.
  - Fill operations continue a series you have started. Type "January" in one cell and "February" in the next cell, and then use a fill operation, and the spreadsheet will automatically enter the rest of the months in the next 10 cells. Figure C-17 shows an example of a fill operation.

- Testing, called **auditing** in spreadsheet jargon, is an important step in creating worksheets. To test a worksheet, you can enter some test data for which you already know the result. Most spreadsheet software includes auditing features to help you find references to empty cells, cells not referenced, formulas that reference themselves and cause a never-ending calculating loop, or values that fall outside specified limits for certain calculations.

You are responsible for the accuracy of spreadsheets you create. Don't rely on your worksheet until you test it.

FIGURE C-15: *Formulas work behind the scenes*

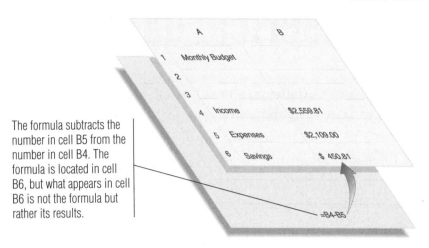

The formula subtracts the number in cell B5 from the number in cell B4. The formula is located in cell B6, but what appears in cell B6 is not the formula but rather its results.

=B4-B5

FIGURE C-16: *Formulas adjust when you insert, move, or delete cells*

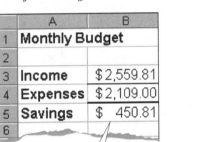

= B4-B5

A formula in cell B6 calculates savings based on numbers in cells B4 and B5.

= B3-B4

The spreadsheet software automatically changes the formula to reflect the new location of the Income and Expenses numbers.

FIGURE C-17: *Fill operations*

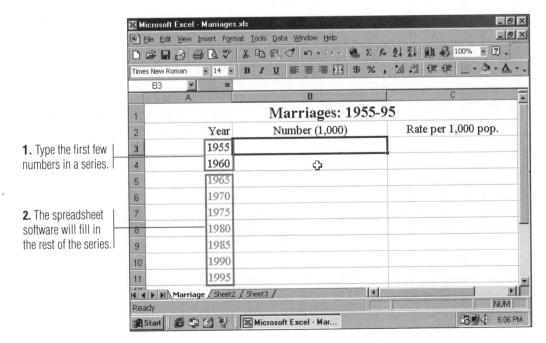

1. Type the first few numbers in a series.

2. The spreadsheet software will fill in the rest of the series.

Presenting numerical data

As the business world embraced spreadsheets, sharing them with colleagues, employees, and customers became important. A spreadsheet works well for recording and graphing data, for making calculations, and for constructing numerical models of the real world. Today, business meetings have an element of theater as computer projection devices display full-screen, full-color, beautifully formatted worksheets.

LIES

DETAILS

☞ A worksheet **template** is a worksheet form created by professionals who have done all of the formatting and formulas for you. If you decide to use a template, you simply select the one you want and then fill it in with your numbers. One popular spreadsheet program offers templates for tasks such as the following: tracking a household budget, deciding on the best car-lease option, calculating monthly loan payments, recording business expenses while you travel, and tracking the time you work on various projects.

☞ Spreadsheet software is characterized by its ability to easily create professional-looking graphs and charts. Graphs provide a quick summary or overview of a set of data. Trends that might be difficult to detect in columns of figures come into focus when skillfully graphed. When you design graphs, you have a responsibility to your audience to create a visual representation of the truth. Although you might not intentionally design a graph to "lie," it is all too easy to design a graph that implies something other than the truth.

☞ Spreadsheet software provides you with formatting options to improve the appearance of your worksheet. See Figure C-18. Worksheets that you intend to print might be formatted differently than worksheets that you intend to view only on the screen. Using a larger font for the title and italicizing or boldfacing important numbers

and their labels add to the professional appeal of the worksheet. You might consider omitting the grid between rows and columns. Figure C-19 provides some tips for improving the readability of a worksheet.

☞ Worksheets that will be projected in presentations often require a format different from that used in printed worksheets. Worksheets for presentations must be legible when displayed by a projection device. For this reason, you might consider using a larger type size—one that can be easily viewed from the back of the room. Scrolling is usually not desirable in a presentation situation, so try to fit the worksheet on one screen. A **workbook** can contain several worksheets if you need to present multiple charts and graphs.

☞ The use of color will help to highlight important data on the worksheet. If you are also planning to print your worksheet in black and white, select your colors carefully. Colors appear in shades of gray on a black-and-white printout. A dark shade of gray can obscure labels and numbers. Figure C-20 provides some examples of worksheets formatted for presentations.

☞ **Spreadsheet modeling** means setting up numbers in a worksheet to describe a real-world situation. The process of setting up a model and experimenting with different numbers is often referred to as **what-if analysis**.

How did it all begin?

A Harvard Business School student, Dan Bricklin, invented computerized spreadsheet software in 1978. Many computer historians believe that his software, called VisiCalc, not only launched a new genre of computer software, but also put a rocket under the fledg-ling microcomputer industry and launched the Digital Age. Before VisiCalc became available, consumers couldn't think of much use for a personal computer. VisiCalc provided business people with a handy tool for making calculations without visiting a statistician or accountant. It contained the basic elements of today's electronic spreadsheets—a screen-based grid of rows and columns, predefined functions, automatic calculations, formatting options, and rudimentary "intelligence" for copying and replicating formulas.

FIGURE C-18: *Formatting a worksheet*

Every worksheet should have a title.

Documentation helps you keep track of revisions and explains how the sheet was created, in case someone else needs to revise it.

Data is usually organized in vertical columns.

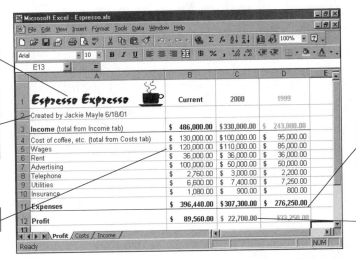

Lines called "cell borders" help divide the worksheet into sections.

You can use bold, italics, and colors to highlight important data.

FIGURE C-19: *Make it look like a typeset document*

A large font emphasizes the title.

Cell grid lines have been removed for a more professional look.

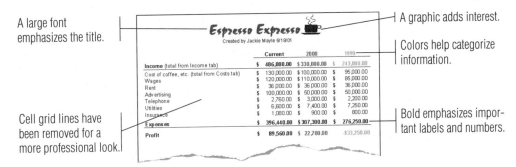

A graphic adds interest.

Colors help categorize information.

Bold emphasizes important labels and numbers.

FIGURE C-20: *Spreadsheets for presentations*

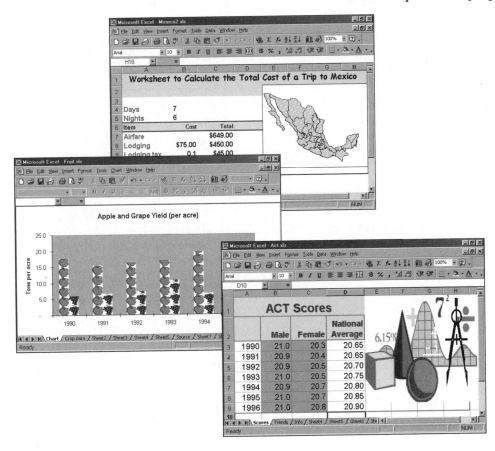

Introducing databases

Sometime in the middle of this century, our industrial society began to evolve into an information society. The way we live has changed in many ways. We interact more frequently with information, we enter careers connected to information management, we increasingly attach a cash value to information, we tend to depend on information, and we are becoming aware of the potential problems that can occur when information is misused. Understanding and using databases is an important skill for living in the Information Age.

DATABASES

DETAILS

○━ Although a technical definition of the term "database" exists, it is largely ignored in popular usage. The broad, nontechnical definition of a **database**—as a collection of information stored on one or more computers—is how the term is used in this book. In this lesson, the focus is on software that is designed to search for information in databases, rather than on database management software that's designed to create and manipulate data. The overwhelming majority of the times you encounter databases, you will be looking for information, rather than creating or adding information.

○━ The Information Age has been fueled by an explosion of data that is collected and generated by individuals, corporations, and government agencies. Some experts estimate that the amount of data doubles every year. This data is stored in an enormous number of databases, most of them computerized. In the course of an ordinary day, you're likely to interact with more than one of these databases, such as a library card catalog, your bank's database of checking and savings account balances, CD-ROM encyclopedias, the computer's directory of files, and your e-mail address book. You might also have experience interacting with collections of information accessed via the Internet, such as Web sites devoted to hip-hop music, the stock market, the job market, or travel.

○━ Databases come in two types: structured databases and freeform databases. A **structured database** (also called a structured data file) is a file of information organized in a uniform format of records and fields. Figure C-21 shows an example of a record from a structured database for a library card catalog. Structured databases typically store data that describes a collection of similar entities. Examples include a medical database, which stores data for a collection of patients; an inventory database, which stores data for a collection of items stocked on store and warehouse shelves; and a library card catalog, which stores information about the books in the collection. In a structured database, data is stored in a series of records. Each record contains the same field names, such as "Title" and "Author." The data in each field, such as "Harry Potter and the Sorcerer's Stone" and "J. K. Rowlings," depends on the entity that the record describes.

○━ A **freeform database** is a loosely structured collection of information, usually stored as documents, rather than as records. You might consider the collection of word processing documents stored on your computer to be a freeform database of your own writing. A CD-ROM containing documents and videos of the Civil War would be another example. The World Wide Web, with its millions of documents stored worldwide, is another example of a freeform database. Whether stored on your hard disk, a CD-ROM, or the Internet, freeform databases have the potential to contain varied and useful information for you as a student or as a career professional. Popular search engines, such as those used on the Web, can help you sort through the available data to find the information you want. See Figure C-22.

FIGURE C-21: *A structured database*

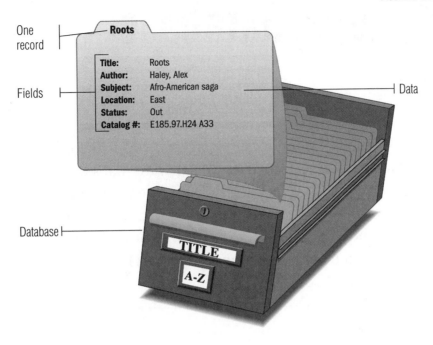

One record

Fields

Data

Database

FIGURE C-22: *Search the Web—a freeform database*

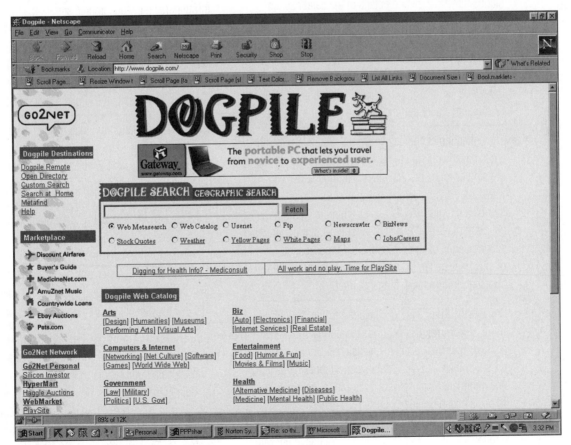

Understanding database searches

You will probably look for information more often than you will create or add information to a database. This lesson focuses on software that's designed to search for information in databases, rather than on database management software that's designed to create and manipulate databases. Different databases inevitably use different data access software. Consequently, becoming an effective information gatherer in the Information Age requires you to be flexible and willing to learn different searching procedures for different data access software.

InfoWeb
INFORMATION CAREERS

InfoWeb
SEARCH ENGINES

DETAILS

Data access software is the interface you use to search for information in a database. You tell the data access software what you're looking for, and it attempts to find it. The data access software understands the structure and details of the database, so you don't need to worry about those points. Depending on your data access software, you might enter your search specifications using a menu, a hypertext index, a keyword search engine, a QBE (Query by Example), a QL (Query Language) or SQL (Structured Query Language), or a natural language.

The collection of choices you're given to interact with a database is referred to as a **menu**. Database menus are similar to the menus you use in most other software. They can be screen-based or audio-based. Menus are typically arranged as a hierarchy, so that after you make a choice at the first level of the menu, a second series of choices appears. Screen-based menus have become a popular format for providing access to information via the Internet.

Some screen-based menus include a feature called a **hypertext index** that links you to information and categories, such as education, entertainment, and business. For instance, AltaVista's hypertext index helps you find information on the Web, as shown in Figure C-23. To use a hypertext index, you select a general category, which leads you to a list of subtopics. You then continue through a series of lists until you get to a document with the information you are seeking.

A **keyword search engine**, as shown in Figure C-24, lets you access data by keyword, instead of by topic or through a menu of subject categories. Keyword search engines are especially popular for searching through the many documents stored in a freeform database such as the World Wide Web. To use a keyword search engine, you simply type in a word and the search engine locates related information. Almost every search engine lets you enter topics, define expert searches, and specify the strength of the match.

When the information in a database needs to be accessed quickly, it is usually stored as a structured database. Because of the structure, a computer can generally locate data in a structured database faster than it can locate information in a freeform database. Unfortunately, the structures of structured databases can cause a problem for users who might not know the format for the records in a particular database. One way to help users search structured databases is by providing a **QBE** (Query by Example) user interface like the one shown in Figure C-25.

A **query language** is a set of command words that you can use to direct the computer to create databases, locate information, sort records, and change the data in those records. To use a query language, you need to know the command words and the grammar or syntax that will let you construct valid query sentences. For example, the **SQL** (Structured Query Language) command word to find records is "select."

FIGURE C-23: *AltaVista's hypertext index*

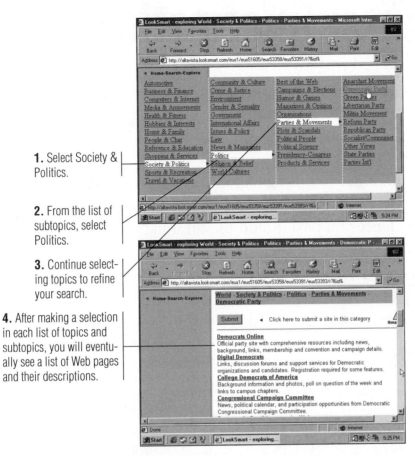

1. Select Society & Politics.

2. From the list of subtopics, select Politics.

3. Continue selecting topics to refine your search.

4. After making a selection in each list of topics and subtopics, you will eventually see a list of Web pages and their descriptions.

FIGURE C-24: *Keyword search*

Enter your search topic here, then click the "Go Get It!" button to begin the search.

FIGURE C-25: *Query by Example*

When you use a QBE interface, you see a blank record on the screen.

Enter examples of what you want the computer to find. In this case, the user is looking for a book published in 1993 or later that includes "Economics" in the title.

Using database information

The power of information comes not only from finding it, but also from using it. In an information-rich society, finding information that is astonishing, amusing, and informative is not difficult. Finding information that is bizarre, offensive, destructive, and confidential is not difficult either. Keep in mind that the information you seek, collect, and disperse reflects your values and ethics. Laws and regulations on the publication and use of information in electronic form have not really kept up with the technology. It is up to you to "use it, but don't abuse it." Once you have found the information in a database, you can use it in a number of ways.

DETAILS

☞ Print it: When you find information in a structured database, you can generally print out a single record or a list of selected records. For example, after searching on any particular topic, you can print out a list of article titles that match your topic and the journals in which they appear. You can also print out information that you find in a freeform database.

   Information that you find in databases can be copied to a document or worksheet. Figure C-26 shows how to copy information from a Web page—which is part of the Web's freeform database. The ability to copy information is especially useful with the information you find in freeform databases because you often want the information from just one section of one document.

☞ Export it: You might find some data that you want to analyze or graph using spreadsheet software. Many databases automatically **export data** by transforming it into a format that's acceptable to your spreadsheet software. If your database does not have this capability, your spreadsheet software might be able to **import data** by reading the database data and translating it into a worksheet.

☞ Save it: When you find a group of records in a structured database that you want to work with later, your database software might provide you with an option to save the records as a file on a hard or floppy disk. You should be aware that you might need the same database software that was originally used to enter and create records so as to work with the records later. You might therefore have to use export or copy options instead. If you find data on the Web, the software you are using to access the information usually provides you with a way to save it on your own computer.

☞ Transmit it: Today, you are plugged into a "global village" where e-mail arrives in just minutes or seconds after it was sent and where you can "chat" online with people from all over the world. You can electronically distribute the information you collect. Figure C-27 shows an easy way to insert information into e-mail messages.

Search with Natural Languages

Advances in artificial intelligence have led to some progress in the ability of computers to understand queries formulated in a natural language such as English, French, or Japanese. To make such natural-language queries, you don't need to learn an esoteric query language. Instead, you just enter questions such as "What Byzantine statues are in the museum collection?" Computers still have some interpretation difficulties arising from ambiguities in human languages, so the use of natural-language query software is not yet widespread.

FIGURE C-26: *Copy and paste text and graphics*

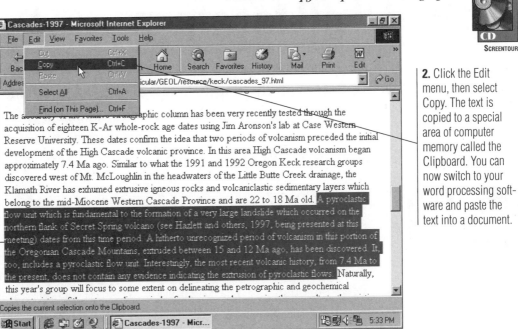

2. Click the Edit menu, then select Copy. The text is copied to a special area of computer memory called the Clipboard. You can now switch to your word processing software and paste the text into a document.

1. Highlight the text you want to copy.

FIGURE C-27: *E-mail a Web page*

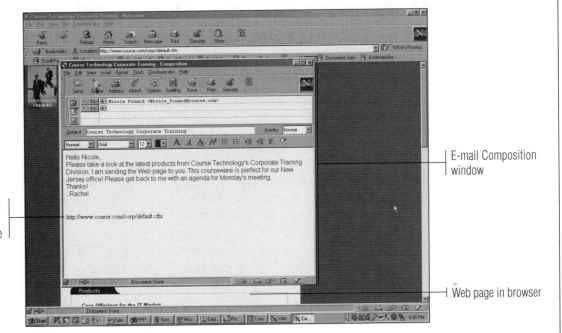

E-mail Composition window

Web page URL that is being sent with the e-mail message

Web page in browser

Putting it all together

You shouldn't leave this unit with the impression that you use only one software tool per project. It is true that word processing, spreadsheet, and database software tools all have their own strengths. Nevertheless, you can be more productive if you use the tools together. Table C-1 provides an overview of how to integrate your applications.

ONLINE CARD CATALOGS

INTERNET CITATIONS

DETAILS

☞ Choose your topic, then browse your library and the Internet to find sources of information. The trend today is to use a computer to search a variety of databases. From your home or office, you can look through millions of Web documents and search through the card catalogs of many libraries.

☞ You might want to photocopy articles, check out relevant books, and save any information you find on the Web. Make sure that you keep track of where you obtain your information—including information that you gather from the Internet. Every document on the World Wide Web has a unique address called a **uniform resource locator** (URL). Most Web browser software has a setting that allows you to include the URL on any Web pages you send to your printer. See Figure C-28. If you note the URL for every bit of information you gather, you will be able to give credit to the authors in your final report.

☞ Make sure that as part of your information-gathering activities, you have a way to distinguish which information you copy verbatim, which information you paraphrased, and which information is in your own words. For example, you might simply put quotes around the material that you copied verbatim. Be sure to cite the source.

☞ Begin a new document in your word processing software by typing in your main point. Next create an outline of items that will support your main point. Use the outlining feature of your word processor to type in the headings and subheadings for your report. Work on your document until you're satisfied, and then run a spell and grammar checker. Always proofread your work.

☞ Before you finalize the content of your paper, decide whether some sections would be clearer if you include a graph or illustration. You can use spreadsheet software to create graphs for data you have gathered. You can use graphics software to access or modify images for your report. Use copy and paste commands to insert the graphs or images.

☞ When you're happy with the content of your document, save it on disk. Make an extra copy of your work on a different disk, just to be safe. You might also want to print your paper, even though you have not formatted it yet. If you lose your electronic copies, you can still reconstruct it from the printout.

☞ If you have not been provided with style guidelines from your instructor or boss, you should follow a standard style manual, such as *The Chicago Manual of Style*, *Publication Manual of the American Psychological Association*, or *Turabian's Student Guide for Writing College Papers*. These manuals tell you how large to make your margins, what to include in headers and footers, how to label graphs and illustrations, how to format your footnotes or endnotes correctly, and so forth. Use the formatting features of your word processing software to follow the style guidelines.

☞ Enhance your report with visual aids, such as handouts or computer-generated slides created with presentation software. See Figure C-29.

☞ Create speaker notes using your word processing software or insert the notes directly in your presentation using the appropriate feature in your presentation software.

FIGURE C-28: *URL on a Web page and on a printed page*

URL on
Web page

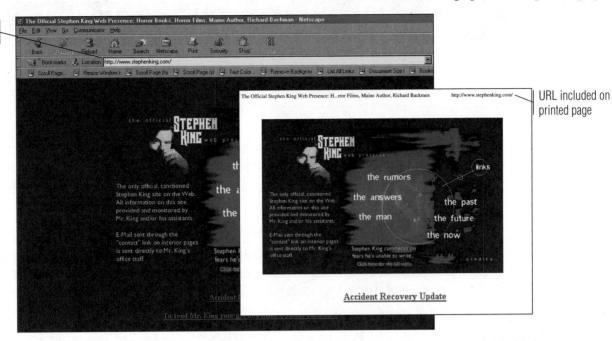

URL included on
printed page

FIGURE C-29: *Using presentation software
to enhance a presentation*

TABLE C-1: *Putting it all together*

WHAT TO USE	WHEN
Database and data access software	To search the World Wide Web and other databases for resources and data To collect and organize information such as a database of resources
Word processing software	To create an outline To write a rough draft To improve the quality of your writing using tools such as a spell checker, a grammar checker, and a thesaurus
Spreadsheet software	To analyze data To add graphics and charts To represent data in your report
Presentation software	To present your report to a large audience To make handouts of your report
Communication software	To publish your report electronically To broaden your research—for example, by using e-mail to contact resources

Word processing, spreadsheet, and database software have been called "productivity software" because they are supposed to increase the amount of work that a person can produce. It seems to be a sensible supposition. Computers increase productivity, right? Without computers, life would certainly be different. For example, we take it for granted that we can make as many telephone calls as we want. However, futurist Paul Saffo points out that if telephone companies still used human operators instead of computer switching, they would have to employ more than one-third of the U.S. population to handle the volume of telephone calls for a typical day. Without computers, phone usage would be severely restricted.

Computers are everywhere and common sense seems to indicate that they should increase productivity. They help us sift through mountains of data on the Internet much more easily than we could search through the stacks of a large research library. They help us communicate via e-mail much faster than old-fashioned ground mail. They let us plan and budget far more effectively with spreadsheet software than with a calculator.

PRODUCTIVITY PARADOX

Unfortunately, as Nobel Prize-winning economist Robert Solow has said, we see computers everywhere except in the productivity statistics. According to the U.S. Bureau of Labor Statistics, during the 1950s and 1960s, the U.S. economy posted a 3 percent annual increase in productivity. To measure productivity, you count how many units a person, group, or machine can make in a given period of time. In the past 30 years, however, productivity growth has slowed to about 1 percent per year. These statistics are curious because the slowdown in productivity coincides with the introduction of microcomputers and their massive deployment in homes and businesses. Despite the personal computer "revolution" and the billions of dollars that have been invested in computer technology, productivity actually appears to have decreased. Economists have coined the phrase **productivity paradox** to describe this discrepancy between increasing technology deployment and decreasing productivity.

What could possibly account for the productivity paradox? Some experts suggest that we need to look no further than our own desktops to discover how computers might actually reduce productivity. The "dither factor," for example, encourages us to tinker with every sentence that we type, revising it over and over in a quest for literary perfection. A document that might take us only 30 minutes to scribble out by hand, could end up taking three hours on the computer.

The "futz factor" kicks in when we run into a software bug or a hardware problem. In the past, only technicians had to worry about mechanical and electronic problems. Now those problems face every person who works with a PC. A few years ago, a survey by SBT Accounting Systems of San Rafael, California, showed that the typical computer user in a business setting wastes 5.1 hours per week on PCs.

The "game factor" can also have a negative effect on productivity. How many times have you been sidetracked by an interesting Web site, a chat room, or a computer game? A study by Forrester Research showed that 20 percent of employees' time on the Internet at work didn't involve their jobs. Employers, who quickly translated this statistic into overpaid wages and lost income, became alarmed. And yet, intuition told these employers that removing computers from the workplace would be even more counterproductive. Is there another perspective to the productivity paradox?

Some experts have suggested that, although productivity might be a valid measure of success in an industrialized society, it might not be as important in an information or service society such as the United States, the European Union, Australia, and Canada. As mentioned earlier, productivity measures how many units a person, group, or machine can make in a given period of time. Increasing productivity means increasing the number of units. But does this increase translate into better customer service, better product quality, or faster availability? Perhaps measuring units leads the statisticians to miss more important measures of success and effectiveness.

The growth of the U.S. economy seems to indicate that some positive factor is at work. Whether it is technology or some other yet-to-be-identified factor is a question that challenges economists. Businesses and individuals are also interested in the economics of prosperity. If productivity is a measure of economic success, prosperity and employment opportunities might be expected to increase as productivity increases. If computers can't provide a productivity boost, what other aspect of the economy can?

EXPAND THE IDEAS

1. Have computers increased the quantity of work that you produce? Write a one-page paper supporting your position and include specific examples.

2. Have computers increased the quality of work that you produce? Write a one-page paper supporting your position and include specific examples.

3. Can you think of an incident when a computer made you less productive? Can you think of a scenario where this might be true for someone you know? Work in small groups. Compile your findings into a short skit presentation.

4. Do you believe computers have had a beneficial effect on your country's economy? What sectors or industries have been more affected than others? Research media archives. Find several examples of articles, documentaries, or news stories on the effects of computers on society. Write a summary of each article or media piece. Analyze your findings. Was the media voice consistent? Why or why not?

End of Unit Exercises

STUDY TIPS

Study Tips help you organize and consolidate the information in a unit by making lists, outlines, charts, and sketches. You can use paper and pencil or word processing software to complete most of the Study Tips activities.

1. Make a list of the document production features discussed in this chapter.

2. Describe the steps in the writing process recommended in this chapter.

3. Write one or two paragraphs describing how a spreadsheet works.

4. Think of two aspects of your daily life that a spreadsheet might help you to organize. Describe how you might use a spreadsheet to help you with these tasks or situations.

5. Explain each of the following spreadsheet items: a number, a formula, a function, and a cell reference.

6. Explain the difference between a structured database and a freeform database.

7. List and describe at least three search procedures that you might use to locate information in a database.

8. Describe how you might use productivity software—word processing, spreadsheet, and database—to put together a report or compete a project.

FILL IN THE BEST ANSWER

1. A feature of word processing software called _____ takes care of where to break lines of text.

2. A(n) _____ provides preset formats for a document, whereas a(n) _____ is a feature that coaches you step-by-step through the process of entering text into a document.

3. One of the most significant effects of computerized document production has been to encourage _____ publishing.

4. Web pages, which are documents posted on the World Wide Web, are in _____ format.

5. _____ has been used to establish the authorship of historical and contemporary documents.

6. In a spreadsheet grid, each _____ is lettered and each _____ is numbered.

7. B3 and B4 are called cell _____.

8. Most spreadsheet software includes hundreds of predefined formulas called _____ for mathematical, financial, and statistical calculations.

9. The process of setting up a model and experimenting with different numbers is often referred to as _____ analysis.

10. In popular terminology, a(n) _____ is a collection of information stored on one or more computers.

11. A(n) _____ database is a file of information organized in a uniform format of records and fields, whereas a(n) _____ database is a loosely structured collection of information.

12. Menus, keyword searches, Query by Example, Query Language, and natural language are all methods used to _____ information in a database.

13. When using a(n) _____ user interface to search a database, you use a blank record to enter examples of the data you want the computer to find.

14. A(n) _____, such as SQL, consists of a set of command words that you can use to direct the computer to create databases, locate information, sort records, and change the data in those records.

15. When you cite a World Wide Web page, you should include its _____ as part of your paper or report.

16. When you first type a document, it is best not to get distracted by how the final product will look. Instead, you should concentrate on expressing your ideas. True or False? _____

17. Spreadsheet software never adjusts formulas when you insert or delete cells. True or False? _____

18. The spreadsheet software publisher is responsible for the validity of the figures and formulas in your worksheets. True or False? _____

INDEPENDENT CHALLENGE 1

One of the most commonly used document production software applications is word processing. You should have a good understanding as to why this tool is so valuable in our society today. Use your word processor to create a report that covers these important concepts.

To complete this independent challenge:

1. List the features of word processing software that make it easy for you to enter the text of your documents.

2. Make a list of editing tasks that word processing software can help you accomplish.

3. Explain the difference between a document template, a font, a style, and a document wizard.

4. Explain the difference between serif and sans serif as they apply to fonts.

5. In document production terminology, what is the difference between a column and a table?

6. Conclude your report with your reaction to this statement: "Word processing has improved the quality of writing in our society today."

INDEPENDENT CHALLENGE 2

Spreadsheet software is a widely used numerical analysis tool. Your neighbor just bought a new computer and is deciding which applications to install on the computer. At the request of your neighbor, you decide to put together a report explaining the benefits of spreadsheet software.

To complete this independent challenge:

1. Write one or two paragraphs describing how a spreadsheet works to someone who has never seen one or used one.

2. Explain the difference between the following spreadsheet terms: a number, a formula, a function, and a cell reference.

3. Make a list of five careers, and then write a brief description of a spreadsheet application that would be useful in each.

4. Make a list of tips for formatting worksheets. Divide your tips into three categories: on-screen, printed, and projected.

5. Explain what happens to the cell references in a formula when you copy that formula to a different column. How does this issue relate to absolute references?

6. What does it mean to audit a spreadsheet? Describe techniques for auditing a worksheet.

INDEPENDENT CHALLENGE 3

A new neighbor just bought a modem and subscribed to a local Internet service provider. He wants to begin doing research for a report. Become the resident database expert for this person, and write a report that he can use to help him learn about databases and the Web.

To complete this independent challenge:

1. Explain the difference between a structured database and a freeform database.

2. List and describe at least three search procedures that you might use to locate information in a database.

3. Describe three ways in which you can use search results.

4. List three different databases that you encounter each day.

5. Describe the types of information gathering that you do each day and detail the techniques you use to gather information.

6. List different search engines available on the Web and note their differences.

7. Explain how you can use search results. Include a few ideas on what responsibilities you have as you use the information you find.

INDEPENDENT CHALLENGE 4

Although close to 80 percent of the population for most industrialized countries has completed high school, journalists supposedly write for an audience with only an eighth-grade reading level. Is this true? To find out, you can use your word processing software to discover the reading level of typical articles in popular magazines and newspapers.

To complete this independent challenge:

1. Locate two articles you think are typical of the writing style for the magazines or newspapers you read.

2. Using your word processor, enter at least 10 sentences from the first article.

3. Use your word processor's spell checker, grammar checker, and reading-level feature to check what you typed.

4. Print the passage. On the printout, note any spelling errors, grammar errors and the reading-level statistics you obtained from your word processor.

5. Do the same with the second article. Submit both of your printouts to your instructor. Be sure to include full bibliographical data on both articles.

Using a search engine is becoming a pivotal skill for the Information Age. Most keyword search engines include instructions or short tutorials on their use. For this independent challenge, you'll connect to one of the Web search engines and learn how to use it. To complete this project, you must have access to the Internet, and you must have a Web browser such as Netscape Navigator or Microsoft Internet Explorer.

To complete this independent challenge:

1. Start your browser and connect to one of the following sites:

   www.lycos.com   www.altavista.com

   www.yahoo.com   www.excite.com

   www.hotbot.com

2. Read through the instructions carefully, paying close attention (and maybe taking notes) on the options available for advanced searches, exact matches, and Boolean operators (AND, OR, NOT). Next, try a few searches to make sure you've got the hang of it.

3. Write a mini-manual explaining how to use your search engine and providing examples of different types of searches.

WORD PROCESSING LAB

Word processing software is the most popular computerized productivity tool. In this lab, you will learn how word processing works. When you have completed this lab, you should be able to apply the general concepts you learned to any word processing package you use at home, at work, or in your school lab.

1. Click the Steps button to learn how word processing software works. As you proceed through the Steps, answer all of the QuickCheck questions that appear. After you complete the Steps, you will see a QuickCheck Report. Follow the instructions on the screen to print this report.

2. Click the Explore button to begin. Click File, then click Open to display the Open dialog box. Click the file *Timber.tex*, then press the Enter key to open the letter to Northern Timber Company. Make the following modifications to the letter, check the spelling, then print it out. You do not need to save the letter.

   a. In the first and last lines of the letter, change "Jason Kidder" to your name.

   b. Change the date to today's date.

   c. The second paragraph begins "Your proposal did not include…" Move this paragraph so that it is the last paragraph in the text of the letter.

d. Change the cost of a permanent bridge to $20,000.

3. In Explore, open the file *Stars.tex*. Make the following modifications to the document, then print it out. You do not need to save the document.

   a. Center and boldface the title.

   b. Change the title font to size 16 Arial.

   c. Boldface the words DATE, SHOWER, and LOCATION.

   d. Move the January 2-3 line to the top of the list.

   e. Double-space the entire document.

4. In Explore, compose a one-page, double-spaced letter to your parents or to a friend. Make sure that you date the letter and check your spelling. Print the letter and sign it. You do not need to save your letter.

SPREADSHEETS LAB

Spreadsheet software is used extensively in business, education, science, and humanities to simplify tasks that involve calculations. In this lab, you will learn how spreadsheet software works. You will use spreadsheet software to examine and modify worksheets as well as to create your own worksheets.

1. Click the Steps button to learn how spreadsheet software works. As you proceed through the Steps, answer all of the QuickCheck questions that appear. After you complete the Steps, you will see a QuickCheck Report. Follow the instructions on the screen to print this report.

2. Click the Explore button to begin this assignment. Click OK to display a new worksheet. Click File, then click Open to display the Open dialog box. Click the file *Income.xls*, then press the Enter key to open the Income and Expense Summary worksheet. Notice that the worksheet contains labels and values for income from consulting and training. It also contains labels and values for expenses such as rent and salaries. The worksheet does not, however, contain formulas to calculate Total Income, Total Expenses, or Profit. Do the following:

   a. Calculate the Total Income by entering the formula =sum(C4:C5) in cell C6.

   b. Calculate the Total Expenses by entering the formula =sum(C9:C12) in cell C13.

   c. Calculate the Profit by entering the formula =C6-C13 in cell C15.

   d. Manually check the results to make sure that you entered the formulas correctly.

e. Print your completed worksheet showing your results.

3. You can use a spreadsheet to keep track of your grade in a class. In Explore, click File, then click Open to display the Open dialog box. Click the file *Grades.xls* to open the Grades worksheet. This worksheet contains all of the labels and formulas necessary to calculate your grade based on four test scores.

Suppose you receive a score of 88 out of 100 on the first test. On the second test, you score 42 out of 48. On the third test, you score 92 out of 100. You have not taken the fourth test yet. Enter the appropriate data in the Grades worksheet to determine your grade after taking three tests. Print out your worksheet.

4. Worksheets are handy for answering "what if" questions. Suppose you decide to open a lemonade stand. You're interested in how much profit you can make. What if you sell 20 cups of lemonade? What if you sell 100? What if the cost of lemons increases?

In Explore, open the file *Lemons.xls* and use the worksheet to answer questions (a) through (d), then print the worksheet for question (e):

a. What is your profit if you sell 20 cups per day?

b. What is your profit if you sell 100 cups per day?

c. What is your profit if the price of lemons increases to $0.07 and you sell 100 cups?

d. What is your profit if you raise the price of a cup of lemonade to $0.30? (Lemons still cost $0.07 and assume you sell 100 cups.)

e. Suppose your competitor boasts that she sold 50 cups of lemonade in one day and made exactly $12.00. On your worksheet, adjust the cost of cups, water, lemons, and sugar and the price per cup to show a profit of exactly $12.00 for 50 cups sold. Print this worksheet.

5. It is important to make sure that the formulas in your worksheet are accurate. An easy way to test accuracy is to enter 1's for all values on your worksheet, then check the calculations manually. In Explore, open the *Receipt.xls*, which calculates sales receipts. Enter 1 as the value for Item 1, Item 2, Item 3, and Sales Tax %. Manually calculate what you would pay for three items that cost $1.00 each in a state where sales tax is 1% (.01). Do your manual calculations match those of the worksheet? If not, correct the formulas in the worksheet and print out a formula report of your revised worksheet.

6. In Explore, create your own worksheet showing your household budget for one month. You may use real or fictional data. Make sure that you put a title on the worksheet. Use formulas to calculate your total income and your total expenses for the month. Add another formula to calculate how much money you were able to save. Print a formula report of your worksheet. Also, print your worksheet showing realistic values for one month.

DATABASES LAB

The Databases Lab demonstrates the essential concepts of file and database management systems. You will use the lab to search, sort, and report the data contained in a file of classic books.

1. Click the Steps button to review basic database terminology and to learn how to manipulate the classic books database. As you proceed through the Steps, answer the QuickCheck questions that appear. After you complete the Steps, you will see a QuickCheck Report. Follow the instructions on the screen to print this report.

2. Click the Explore button. Make sure that you can apply basic database terminology to describe the classic books database by answering the following questions:

a. How many records does the file contain?

b. How many fields does each record contain?

c. What are the contents of the Catalog # field for the book written by Margaret Mitchell?

d. What are the contents of the Title field for the record with Thoreau in the Author field?

e. Which field has been used to sort the records?

3. In Explore, manipulate the database as necessary to answer the following questions:

a. When the books are sorted by title, what is the first record in the file?

b. Use the Search button to search for all books in the West location. How many do you find?

c. Use the Search button to search for all books in the Main location that are checked in. What do you find?

4. In Explore, use the Report button to print out a report that groups the books by status and sorts them by title. On your report, circle the four field names. Put a box around the summary statistics showing which books are currently checked in and which books are currently checked out.

LESSON	MEDIA ELEMENT	LESSON	MEDIA ELEMENT
Introducing document production software	LITERACY · TYPING · VIDEO	Presenting numerical data	LIES
Improving the quality of writing	IMPROVE YOUR WRITING · GRAMMAR · SCREENTOUR · SCREENTOUR · WORD PROCESSING	Introducing databases	DATABASES
Formatting documents	FONTS · SCREENTOUR	Understanding database searches	INFORMATION CAREERS · SEARCH ENGINES
Examining electronic publishing	PUBLISHING	Using database information	SCREENTOUR
Automating document production	WHO WROTE IT?	Putting it all together	ONLINE CARD CATALOGS · INTERNET CITATIONS
Introducing spreadsheets	SPREADSHEETS · SPREADSHEET TIPS · SCREENTOUR	Issue: Do Computers Increase Productivity?	PRODUCTIVITY PARADOX
Understanding spreadsheet basics	SPREADSHEET ERRORS · SCREENTOUR		

VISUAL WORKSHOP

Refer to the figure.

1. Identify the different components of each spreadsheet for each of the three screens.

2. Identify and label the graphics, charts, labels, cells, titles, formulas, formatting, and any other components you believe to contribute significantly to the presentation of the data.

3. Explain how each component works as part of the spreadsheet to enhance and deliver the information.

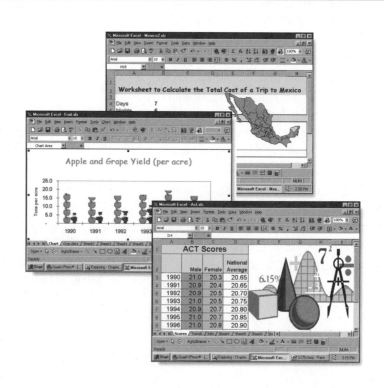

Computer Files and Data Storage

In this unit, you will learn about computer files and data storage. You will learn to distinguish the various types of files. This unit explains how computers store and retrieve data and provides you with a practical foundation for using a computer to manage your own data. You will find out which storage device to use when you save data and how to create a valid filename that the computer will accept. You will also learn what happens in the computer when you save, retrieve, or modify a file.

Introducing computer files

In everyday conversation, people use the terms "data" and "information" interchangeably. Computer professionals have special definitions for the terms "data," "information," and "file." Although we might refer to them as technical definitions, they are not difficult to understand. **Data** is defined as the words, numbers, and graphics that describe people, events, things, and ideas. **Information** is defined as the words, numbers, and graphics used as the basis for human actions and decisions. A **file** is defined as a named collection of program instructions or data that exists on a storage medium such as a hard disk, a floppy disk, or a CD.

DETAILS

- There are several categories of files, such as data files, executable files, configuration files, drivers, and modules. A computer file is classified according to the data it contains, the software that was used to create it, and the way you should use it. Table D-1 provides information on each of these file categories and includes the file extensions for these file types, which you will learn about in the next lesson.

- A **data file** contains words, numbers, sounds, and pictures that you can view, edit, save, send, play, and print. Typically, you create data files when you use application software. For example, you create a data file when you store a document that you have written using word processing software or when you store a picture, graph, sound clip, or video. In addition, word processing software often includes a dictionary data file that contains a list of words that the software uses to check spelling.

  Whether you create or purchase a data file, you typically use it in conjunction with application software that helps you manipulate the data in the file. You usually view, revise, and print a data file with the same software that you used to create it. You can think of data files as being passive: the computer processes the data, but the data generally does not direct the process.

- An **executable file** contains the instructions that tell a computer how to perform a specific task. For example, the word processing program that tells your computer how to display and print text is stored on disk as an executable file. Other executable files on your computer system include the operating system, utilities, and programs for application software. You can think of an executable file as being active: the instructions stored in the file cause the computer to do something.

  To use executable files, you run or start them. Most operating systems help you identify the executable files that you can run. There are several ways to run an executable file: in DOS, you type the filename of the program; in Windows 3.1, you click a program icon; and in Windows 95, Windows 98, and Mac OS, you either select the program from a menu or click the program icon. When using the Windows operating system, you can identify executable files by their unique program icons or by their .exe or .com filename extensions. See Figure D-1.

  The programs that you run are an example of one type of executable file. Your computer also has other kinds of executable files that are not data files but are nevertheless essential for hardware and software operations. For example, a word processing program might request that the computer use an executable file called Grammar.dll to check the grammar in a document. The instructions are stored in a format that the computer can interpret, but this format is not designed to be readable to users.

- In addition to data files and executable files, a computer typically contains other files that are essential for hardware or software operations. These configuration files, help files, temporary files, and program support module files have extensions such as .bat, .sys, .cfg, .dll, .ocx, .vbx, .ini, .mif, .hlp, and .tmp. Because these files—even the temporary files—are crucial to the correct operation of your computer system, it is important not to delete them.

TABLE D-1: *Filename extensions for configuration files and program modules*

TYPE OF FILE	DESCRIPTION	FILENAME EXTENSION
Batch file	A sequence of operating system commands that are executed automatically when the computer boots.	.bat
Configuration file	Information about programs that the computer uses to allocate the resources necessary to run them.	.cfg, .sys, .mif, .ini
Help	The information that is displayed by online Help.	.hlp
Temporary file	A sort of "scratch pad" that contains data while a program is running, but that is discarded when you exit the program.	.tmp
Program support modules	Program instructions that are executed in conjunction with the main .exe file for a program.	.ocx, .vbx, .dll

FIGURE D-1: *Program icons*

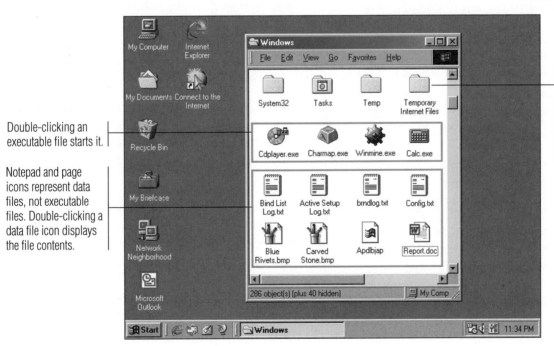

Double-clicking an executable file starts it.

Notepad and page icons represent data files, not executable files. Double-clicking a data file icon displays the file contents.

Folders might contain executable files, but the folder is not executable. Double-clicking a folder opens it and lists its contents.

Learning about file management

Program and data files have unique names and/or locations to ensure that the computer can locate them. When you create a data file, you must provide the file with a name to distinguish it from other files and to help you locate it. It is important to understand filenames—how to create filenames and which conventions to follow when you name a file.

DETAILS

FILENAME EXTENSIONS

☞ A **filename** is a unique set of letters and numbers that identifies a file and should describe its contents.

☞ A valid filename is created by following specific rules. The rules for creating a valid filename are referred to as **filenaming conventions**. Each operating system has a unique set of filenaming conventions. The filenaming conventions used by several operating systems are listed in Table D-2.

☞ It is sometimes difficult to select a DOS or Windows 3.1 filename that is unique and descriptive within the eight-character limit. When you name files under operating systems that permit filenames of more than eight characters, you have greater flexibility. Regardless of which operating system you are using, you must be aware of filenames that are not allowed for that operating system, such as Aux or Com1, and you should create filenames that help you remember the file contents.

☞ A filename usually has two parts: the filename itself and the filename extension. A **filename extension** further describes the file contents. The extension is separated from the filename with a period. If a file were named PamelasResume.doc, you would read it as "Pamela's Resume dot doc." When DOS was originally introduced, computer users had to manually add a three-letter extension to each filename to identify the file contents. Increasingly, however, the software automatically assigns the filename extension.

☞ Filename extensions for data files are classified into one of two categories: generic extensions and application-specific extensions. A **generic filename extension** indicates the general type of data contained in a file and usually means that you can open the file using one of several software packages.

For example, a .txt extension tells you that the file is in the general category of text data files. A .bmp extension tells you that the file contains graphical data and that you can open it using almost any graphics software package. Table D-3 provides a list of generic file extensions.

☞ Many application programs create data files with an **application-specific filename extension**. An application-specific filename extension is associated with a particular application and indicates which application software was used to create a file. See Table D-4.

☞ Knowledge of filename extensions comes in handy when you receive a file on a disk or over the Internet but don't know much about its contents. If you are familiar with filename extensions, you will know which application to use when you want to open the file.

☞ As a computer user, you are not usually responsible for naming executable files. These files are included with the application software you purchase, and the programmers who write them name the files. It is useful to know, however, that the executable files you can run generally have either a .COM (for command) extension or an .EXE (for executable) extension. The computer runs some executable files without your intervention; these files have filename extensions such as .SYS, .DLL, .DRV, and .VBX.

☞ Wildcards are used in most operating systems to make it easier to manipulate a collection of files. See Figure D-2. **Wildcards** include characters such as ? (question mark) and * (asterisk) to help locate patterns of filenames. The question mark is used to represent a single character. The asterisk is used to represent a group of characters.

TABLE D-2: *Filenaming conventions*

	DOS AND WINDOWS 3.1	WINDOWS 95/98/NT/2000	MAC OS	UNIX/LINUX
Maximum length of filename	8-character filename plus an extension of 3 characters or less	255-character filename including an extension of 3 characters or less	31 characters (no extensions)	14–256 (depending on UNIX/Linux version) including an extension of any length
Spaces allowed	No	Yes	Yes	No
Numbers allowed	Yes	Yes	Yes	Yes
Characters not allowed	/ [ ] ; = " \ : , | * ?	\ ? : " < > | * /	None	| @ # $ % ^ & * ( ) { } [ ] " \ ' ; < >
Filenames not allowed	Aux, Com1, Com2, Com3, Com4, Con, Lpt1, Lpt2, Lpt3, Prn, Nul	Aux, Com1, Com2, Com3, Com4, Con, Lpt1, Lpt2, Lpt3, Prn, Nul	None	Depends on the version of UNIX or Linux
Case sensitive	No	No	Yes	Yes (use lowercase)

TABLE D-3: *Generic filename extensions*

TYPE OF FILE	FILENAME EXTENSION	TYPE OF FILE	FILENAME EXTENSION
Text	.txt .dat .rtf	**Animation/video**	.flc .fli .avi .mpg .mov
Sound	.wav .mid	**Web documents**	.html .htm
Graphics	.bmp .pcx .tif .wmf .jpg .gif		

FIGURE D-2: *Wildcards help you locate filenames*   SCREENTOUR

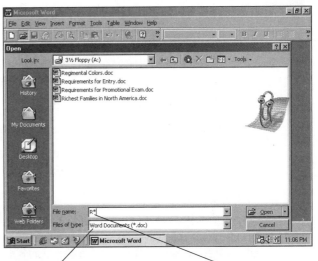

*.doc uses a wildcard to specify all files that have a .doc extension.

If you want to find a document that begins with the letter "R" when using Microsoft Word, you could use the * wildcard to help. Type R* in the File name text box to request a list of all files that begin with the letter "R".

TABLE D-4: *Application-specific filename extensions*

APPLICATION SOFTWARE	FILENAME EXTENSION	APPLICATION SOFTWARE	FILENAME EXTENSION
WordPerfect	.wpd	**Microsoft Excel**	.xls
Microsoft Word and WordPad	.doc	**Microsoft Access**	.mdb
Lotus Word Pro	.sam	**Microsoft PowerPoint**	.ppt
Microsoft Works	.wps	**Adobe Acrobat Reader**	.pdf
Microsoft Works	.wks	**WinZip**	.zip
Lotus 1-2-3	.wk4		

Understanding logical file storage

Your computer system might contain hundreds—or even thousands—of files stored on disks or other storage devices. So, in addition to knowing the filenaming conventions, it is important to understand how files are stored on the disk. **Logical storage** is the conceptual way that data is stored on your disk. Metaphors of directory structures are sometimes called logical models because they represent the way that you logically conceive of these structures. Figure D-3 illustrates two metaphors: the file cabinet metaphor, which depicts files being stored in file folders nested inside one another in a file cabinet, and the tree structure metaphor, which depicts files as leaves on a tree with many branches.

DIRECTORIES,
FOLDERS, FILES

DETAILS

- The **directory** is a list of files for each disk, CD, or DVD that is maintained by the operating system. For every file on the storage device, the directory contains information about each file, such as the filename, the filename extension, the date and time when the file was created, and the file size. The operating system's file manager utility can be used to view the directory of a disk and display information about each file stored in the directory on the computer. The file manager can also indicate the number of files in the directory as well as the amount of storage space used and the amount still available on the computer.

- The **root directory**, which is the main directory of a disk, provides a useful list of files. It could be difficult, however, to find a particular file if your directory contains several hundred files, so the root directory is subdivided.

- **Subdirectories** or **folders** divide your directory into smaller lists, which help you organize a large number of files. For example, you can create one folder to hold all of your word processing documents and another folder to hold all of your files that contain graphical images. Folders can be further divided into subfolders.

- **Device letters** followed by a colon, such as A: and C:, are used to identify storage devices or drives. You will learn more about storage devices in the next lesson.

- A folder name is separated from a drive letter and a filename by a special symbol. In DOS and Microsoft Windows, this symbol is the backslash (\). For example, the root directory of drive C might have a subdirectory called Graphics, written as C:\Graphics. When you type directory names, don't confuse the backslash (\) with the regular slash (/), which slants in the opposite direction.

- A **file specification** (or "path") is the drive letter, subdirectory (folder), and filename that identify a file. Suppose you create a folder on drive A named Word for your word processing documents. Now suppose you create a file of a list of things to do named To-do.doc and put it on drive A in the Word subdirectory. The file specification for that document would be A:\Word\To-do.doc.

- The **file size** is the number of characters that a file contains.

Using file management software

To keep track of the hundreds or even thousands of files stored on disks and other storage devices, computer operating systems provide file manager utility software that helps you locate, rename, copy, move, and delete files. File managers vary from one operating system to another, but all are based on similar concepts. Figure D-4 shows how Microsoft programmers used both the file cabinet and the tree structure metaphors to create the file manager utility called Windows Explorer.

▶ A file cabinet metaphor depicts a storage device as a drawer of a filing cabinet containing folders and documents.

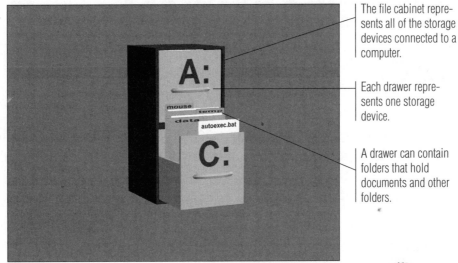

The file cabinet represents all of the storage devices connected to a computer.

Each drawer represents one storage device.

A drawer can contain folders that hold documents and other folders.

▶ Using the tree structure metaphor, you can visualize the directory of a disk as a tree on its side. The trunk and branches are folders and the leaves are files.

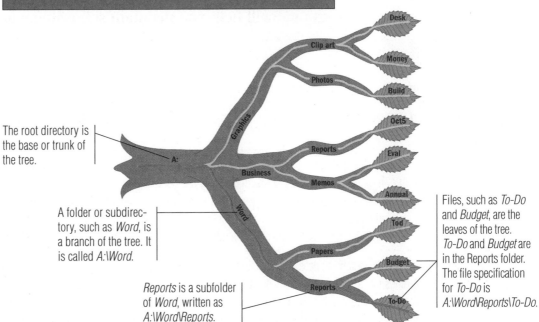

The root directory is the base or trunk of the tree.

A folder or subdirectory, such as *Word*, is a branch of the tree. It is called *A:\Word*.

Reports is a subfolder of *Word*, written as *A:\Word\Reports*.

Files, such as *To-Do* and *Budget*, are the leaves of the tree. *To-Do* and *Budget* are in the Reports folder. The file specification for *To-Do* is *A:\Word\Reports\To-Do*.

FIGURE D-4: *Windows Explorer*

CD
SCREENTOUR

The root directory A: is represented by a disk drive icon.

The red line shows the path for the file *A:\Word\Reports\To-Do.doc*.

A folder icon represents the *Word* subdirectory.

Another folder icon represents *Reports*—a subfolder of *Word*.

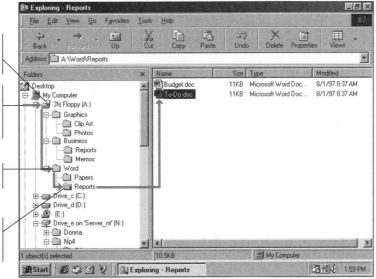

◀ Windows Explorer borrows the folders from the filing cabinet metaphor and places them in a hierarchical structure similar to a tree on its side so that you can easily trace a path to a particular file.

Understanding physical file storage

To keep track of the files on a disk or storage device, the computer has a filing system that is maintained by the operating system. Once you know how the operating system manages your computer's filing system, you can use it effectively to store and retrieve files. The logical view of storage is a convenient mental model that helps you understand the computer's filing system, but the data is not really stored that way. **Physical file storage** refers to the way in which data is actually stored on the disk. Understanding both logical and physical file storage will help you maintain solid file management.

DETAILS

- **Storage technology** refers to a storage device and the media it uses.

- A **storage medium** ("storage media" is the plural) is the disk, CD, DVD, tape, paper, or other substance that contains data. See Figure D-5.

- A **storage device** is the mechanical apparatus, such as a disk drive, that records and retrieves the data from the storage medium. Most computers have more than one storage device that the operating system uses to store files. A letter and a colon identify each storage device. On microcomputers, floppy disk drives are usually identified as A: and B:. The hard disk drive is usually identified as C:. Additional storage devices can be assigned letters from D through Z. A tape drive typically has no device letter. Figure D-6 shows the device letter assignments for a microcomputer that is "fully loaded" with storage devices.

- Data is stored in digital form on storage devices. Your computer must translate the information you enter from documents, graphics, videos, or sound recordings into a digital series of 1s and 0s. Computers use a variety of codes to convert this information into digital data. You will learn more about these codes in the next unit. For now, note that each 1 or 0 that represents data is referred to as a **bit** and is the smallest unit for digitizing data. Eight bits make up one **byte**. In a document, each byte represents one character. For example, the phrase "profit margin" requires 13 bytes of storage space because the phrase contains 13 characters (including the space between the two words).

- The process of **storing data** is often referred to as writing data or saving a file because the storage device writes the data on the storage medium to save it for later use.

- The process of **retrieving data** is often referred to as reading data, loading data, or opening a file. The terms reading data and writing data are often associated with mainframe applications. The terms save and open are standard Windows terminology.

- The **speed** of a storage device is measured in terms of its access time and its data transfer rate. Quick access to data is important, so fast storage devices are preferred over slower devices.
  - **Access time** is the average time that it takes a computer to locate data on the storage medium and read it. Access time for microcomputer storage devices, such as a disk drive, is measured in milliseconds. One **millisecond (ms)** is one-thousandth of a second. Lower numbers indicate faster access times. The best access times are found in random access devices.
  - **Random access** (also called "direct access") is the ability of a disk-based storage device to jump directly to any location on the storage medium that holds the requested data. This ability provides quick access to files anywhere on a disk. **Sequential access** is a slower method of accessing data, in which the data is read from the beginning to the end until the requested data is located.
  - **Data transfer rate** is the amount of data that a storage device can move from the storage medium to the computer per second. Higher numbers indicate faster transfer rates. For example, a CD-ROM drive with a 600 KBps data transfer rate is faster than one with a 300 KBps transfer rate.

5¼" floppy disk

3.5" Double density floppy disk

◄ Floppies and Zip disks are typically used for transporting or shipping data files. They do not have the capacity to store most of today's software, however, so they would not be the main storage device for a computer system.

3.5" High density floppy disk

Zip disk

Tape cartridge

CD-ROM

► On microcomputers, it is conventional for the floppy disk drive to be drive A and the hard disk drive to be drive C. The device letters for other storage devices vary. On one computer the CD-ROM drive might be drive E, whereas on another computer it might be drive R.

A tape drive typically has no device letter.

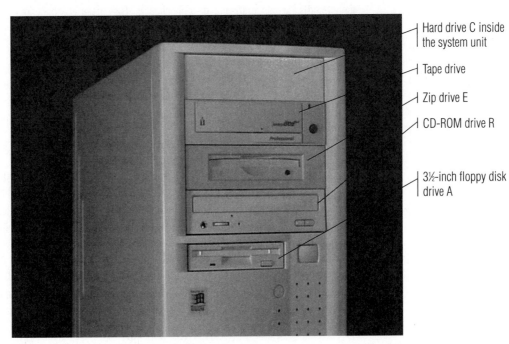

Hard drive C inside the system unit

Tape drive

Zip drive E

CD-ROM drive R

3½-inch floppy disk drive A

Exploring physical file storage

A storage device stores data on a storage medium. This lesson takes a closer look at how files are physically stored on a storage medium.

DEFRAGMENTATION

DETAILS

- Before a computer stores data on a storage medium, it creates the equivalent of electronic storage bins called **tracks**. On magnetic disks, the tracks are arranged in concentric circles that are further divided into wedge-shaped **sectors**, as shown in Figure D-7. Optical technologies store data in tracks that spiral out from the center of the disk. On computer tapes, tracks run parallel to the edge of the tape.
  - Tracks and sectors are numbered to provide addresses for the data storage "bins." The numbering scheme depends on the storage device and the operating system. The floppy disks used by the Windows operating system have 80 tracks and 18 sectors on each side.
  - To speed up the process of reading and writing data, a disk drive handles a group of sectors called a **cluster**. The number of sectors that form a cluster depends on the type of computer and capacity of the disk. Each cluster is numbered, and the operating system maintains a list of which sectors correspond to each cluster.

- When the computer stores a file on a disk, the operating system records the cluster number that contains the beginning of the file in a file allocation table (FAT). The **FAT** is an operating system file that helps the computer store and retrieve files from disk storage by maintaining a list of files and their physical locations on the disk. The FAT is such a crucial file that if it is corrupted by a **head crash**, which occurs when the hard disk drive surface is damaged, you generally lose access to all data stored on your disk because the list of clusters that contain files is no longer readable.
  - When you want to store a file, the operating system looks at the FAT to see which clusters are empty. It then records the data for the file in empty clusters. The cluster numbers are recorded in the FAT. The name of the new file and the number of the first cluster that contains the file data are recorded in the directory.
  - A file that does not fit into a single cluster will spill over into the next adjacent or contiguous cluster, unless that cluster already contains data. If the next cluster is full, the operating system stores the file in a nonadjacent cluster and sets up instructions called pointers. These pointers "point" to each piece of the file, as shown in Figure D-8.
  - When you want to retrieve a file, the operating system looks through the directory for the desired filename and the number of the first cluster that contains the file data. The FAT tells the computer which clusters contain the remaining data for the file. The operating system moves the read-write head to the cluster that contains the beginning of the file and reads it. If the file is stored in more than one cluster, the read-write head must move to the next cluster to read more of the file. It takes longer to access a file stored in nonadjacent clusters than to access one stored in adjacent clusters because the disk or head must move farther to find the next section of the file.

- With random access storage, files tend to become **fragmented**—that is, each file is stored in many nonadjacent clusters. Drive performance generally declines as the drive works harder to locate the clusters that contain the parts of a file. To regain peak performance, you can use a defragmentation utility to rearrange the files on a disk so that they are stored in adjacent clusters. Figure D-9 explains more about fragmentation and defragmentation.

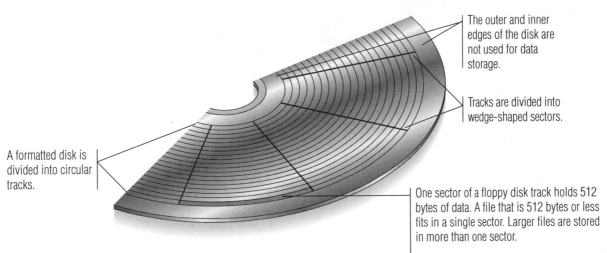

FIGURE D-7: *Data is stored in tracks and sectors*

The outer and inner edges of the disk are not used for data storage.

Tracks are divided into wedge-shaped sectors.

A formatted disk is divided into circular tracks.

One sector of a floppy disk track holds 512 bytes of data. A file that is 512 bytes or less fits in a single sector. Larger files are stored in more than one sector.

FIGURE D-8: *How the FAT works*

InfoWeb

FAT

▶ Each colored cluster on the disk contains part of a file. Clusters 3 and 4 (blue) contain the *Bio.txt* file. Cluster 9 (aqua) contains the *Pick.wps* file. Clusters 7, 8, and 10 contain the *Jordan.wks* file.

A computer locates and displays the *Jordan.wks* file, by looking for its name in the file allocation table. By following the pointers listed in the Status column, the computer can then see that the file is continued in clusters 8 and 10.

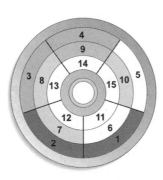

CLUSTER	STATUS	COMMENT
1	1	Reserved for operating system
2	1	Reserved for operating system
3	4	First cluster of *Bio.txt*. Points to cluster 4, which holds more data for *Bio.txt*
4	999	Last cluster of *Bio.txt*
5	0	Empty
6	0	Empty
7	8	First cluster for *Jordan.wks*. Points to cluster 8, which holds more data for the *Jordan.wks* file
8	10	Second cluster for *Jordan.wks*. Points to cluster 10, which holds more data for the *Jordan.wks* file
9	999	First and last cluster containing *Pick.wps*
10	999	Last cluster of *Jordan.wks*

FIGURE D-9: *Defragmenting a disk*

▶ On this fragmented disk, the purple, yellow, and blue files are stored in non-contiguous clusters. Accessing the clusters for these files is not efficient because of the time required to move the read-write head over the data.

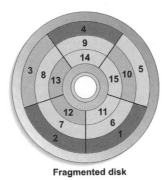

Fragmented disk

Defragmented disk

◀ When the disk is defragmented, the clusters of data for each file are moved to contiguous clusters. Data access becomes more efficient because drive head and disk movement are minimized.

Comparing storage devices

You can envision a document stored in your computer's memory as a long series of 1s and 0s. These bits are sent to a storage device, which writes data to a storage medium. The data is not literally written as 1s and 0s; instead, the 1s and 0s have to be transformed into changes in the surface of the storage medium. Exactly how this transformation happens depends on the storage technology. Magnetic and optical storage technologies are used for the majority of today's microcomputers, minicomputers, and mainframe computers.

DETAILS

- The five major categories of microcomputer storage devices are floppy disk, hard disk, tape, CD, and DVD.

- Storage technology comparisons are often based on storage versatility, durability, capacity and speed. Knowing the characteristics of a storage device or storage medium is one factor in determining which device is best for a particular task.
  - **Versatility**: Some storage devices can access data from only one type of medium. More versatile devices can access data from several different media.
  - **Durability**: Some technologies are less susceptible than others to damage from mishandling or other environmental factors such as heat and moisture that could cause data loss.
  - **Capacity**: **Storage capacity** is the maximum amount of data that can be stored on a storage medium. Data is stored as **bytes**—each byte usually represents one character. Data is usually measured in terms of **kilobytes** (KB), about 1,024 bytes; **megabytes** (MB), about 1 million bytes; **gigabytes** (GB), about 1 billion bytes; or **terabytes** (TB), about 1 trillion bytes. When you read that the storage capacity of a computer is 20.4 GB, it means that the hard disk on that computer can store up to 20.4 billion bytes of information. This capacity is equivalent to that needed to hold approximately 5,400,000 single-spaced pages of text.

- Floppy disk and Zip disk storage is used for three purposes: distribution, storing data, and backup. To use floppy disks or Zip disks, your computer must have the appropriate disk drive. Figure D-10 compares the capacities of floppy and Zip disks.

- The storage device that records and retrieves data on a floppy disk is the floppy disk drive. Figure D-11 shows how to put a disk in both floppy disk and Zip disk drives.

- Even with random access, however, a floppy disk drive is not a particularly speedy device. It takes about 0.5 second for the drive to spin the disk up to maximum speed and then move the read-write head to a particular sector. A Zip drive is about 20 times faster.

- Hard disk storage is the preferred type of main storage for most computer systems because it provides faster access to files than floppy or Zip disk drives. Like floppy disks, hard disks provide random access to files. Unlike floppy disks, which begin to rotate only when you request data, hard disks are continually in motion, so there is no delay as the disk spins up to maximum speed. As a result, hard disk access is faster than floppy disk access.

- Tape storage was the most popular form of mainframe storage in the 1960s. Using tape as a storage device is slow and inconvenient, however, because tape requires sequential—rather than random—access. Microcomputer users quickly abandoned tape storage for the convenience and speed of random access disk drives. While no longer the primary storage device of choice, tape storage is gaining popularity as a means for backing up existing data.

- CD-ROM and DVD-ROM technology are becoming popular storage media for software publishers to distribute large programs and data files. They are read-only storage media, which means that the computer can only retrieve data from a CD-ROM or a DVD-ROM and cannot save any new data to either medium. In this respect, CD-ROM and DVD-ROM technology differs from hard disk storage, on which you can read, write, and erase data.

InfoWeb
FLOPPIES AND
ZIPS

SIZE	5¼ INCH	3½ INCH	3½ INCH	3½ INCH ZIP
Density	High	Double	High	N/A
Capacity	1.2 MB	720 KB	1.44 MB	100 MB
Sectors per side	15	9	18	32
Tracks per side	80	80	80	3,065

FIGURE **D-11**: *Using a floppy or Zip disk*

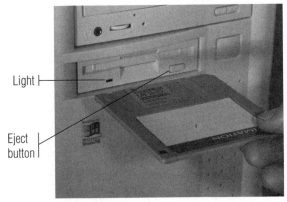

Light ⊢

Eject
button ⊢

▲ A 3½-inch disk drive has an eject button to release the disk and a drive light to indicate when the drive is in use. You insert the disk so that the label goes in last. Virtually every computer has a 3½-inch disk drive.

⊦ Light

▲ A Zip drive uses special Zip disks that are slightly larger than a 3½-inch floppy disk. The green light indicates that the drive is ready. A yellow light indicates that the drive is in use. Insert the Zip disk so that the label enters last. Zip disks are increasing in popularity.

Additional uses for floppy and Zip disks

Although floppy disk and Zip disks are not the preferred storage media for your computer, they still have value. In the university setting, floppy disks are often used to store student data. If you have your own computer, you would tend to store your data on the hard disk. In a student lab, however, you don't have your own computer. Because you never know which computer you will be assigned, you need to store your data on a disk so that you can carry it with you. Another use for floppy disks is to make duplicate copies of your data files. It is important to make backup copies of your work in case something happens to the originals. This process is known as backing up your files. Yet another common use for floppy disks is to share data with other computer users. For example, if you want to give a copy of a report to several colleagues, you can copy the report to floppy disks and give the disks with the files on them to your colleagues. Today, instead of floppy disks, many computer users use computer networks or electronic mail to share data.

Understanding magnetic storage

Today, the most commonly used medium for storage is magnetic storage. Floppy disks, hard disks, and tape are all popular types of magnetic storage media. With **magnetic storage**, the computer stores data on a disk or tape by magnetizing selected particles of an oxide-based surface coating. The particles retain their magnetic orientation until that orientation is changed, thereby making disks and tape fairly permanent, but nevertheless modifiable storage media.

DETAILS

- A read-write head mechanism in the disk drive reads and writes the magnetized particles that represent data. Figure D-12 shows how a computer stores data on a magnetic media.

- A floppy disk is a flexible Mylar plastic disk covered with a thin layer of magnetic oxide. Floppy disks get their name from this thin Mylar disk. They are also called floppies or diskettes. If you cut open the disk casing (something you should never do, unless you want to ruin the disk), you would see that the Mylar disk inside is thin and flexible. Figure D-13 shows the construction of a 3½-inch disk.
  - Physical characteristics: Floppy disks come in several sizes. Today's microcomputers typically use 3½-inch disks. A 3½-inch circular disk made of flexible Mylar is housed inside a protective case of rigid plastic. When the disk is inserted in the disk drive, the spring-loaded access cover slides to the side to expose the disk surface for reading and writing data.
  - Double-sided disks: In the past, floppy disks stored data only on one side; today, most floppy disks store data on both sides. A double-sided disk stores twice as much data as a single-sided disk.

- Disk density: Disk density refers to the size of the magnetic particles on the disk surface. The disk density limits the amount of data you can reliably store on the disk. Double-density disks, abbreviated as DD, are also referred to as low-density disks. A high-density disk, abbreviated as HD, stores more data than a double-density disk. The higher the disk density, the smaller the magnetic particles it stores, and the more data it can store.

- Special high-capacity floppy disks, including Zip and Jaz, are manufactured by Iomega Corporation.

- Formatted disks: The amount of data that a computer can store on each side of a disk depends on the type of disk, its density, and the way that the disk is formatted. The formatting process creates a series of concentric tracks on the disk, with each track being divided into smaller segments called sectors. Most of today's computers use a double-sided disk that is formatted with 80 tracks per side and 18 sectors per track, creating 1,440 sectors. On IBM-compatible computers, each sector of a track holds 512 bytes of data, so a file that is 512 bytes or less fits in a single sector. Larger files are stored in more than one sector.

Protecting your data

You can intentionally change or erase files stored on magnetic media. If you run out of storage space on a disk, you can erase files you no longer need to make more space available. Data stored on magnetic media such as floppy disks can also be unintentionally altered by the environment and by device or media failure. In the environment, magnetic fields, dust, mold, smoke particles, and heat are the primary culprits causing data loss. Placing a magnet on your disk is a sure way of losing data. Even though the metal detectors in an airport use a magnetic field, the field is not strong enough to disrupt the data on your floppy or hard disks. In fact, you are more likely to damage your disks by leaving them on the dashboard of your car in the sun or by carrying them around in your backpack, where they will pick up dust and dirt.

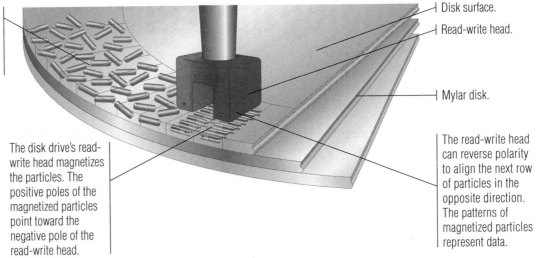

Before data is stored, the particles in the magnetic surface of the disk are scattered in random patterns.

The disk drive's read-write head magnetizes the particles. The positive poles of the magnetized particles point toward the negative pole of the read-write head.

Disk surface.

Read-write head.

Mylar disk.

The read-write head can reverse polarity to align the next row of particles in the opposite direction. The patterns of magnetized particles represent data.

FIGURE **D-13**: *A 3½-inch floppy disk*

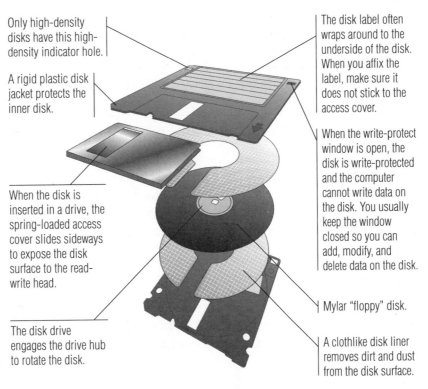

Only high-density disks have this high-density indicator hole.

A rigid plastic disk jacket protects the inner disk.

When the disk is inserted in a drive, the spring-loaded access cover slides sideways to expose the disk surface to the read-write head.

The disk drive engages the drive hub to rotate the disk.

The disk label often wraps around to the underside of the disk. When you affix the label, make sure it does not stick to the access cover.

When the write-protect window is open, the disk is write-protected and the computer cannot write data on the disk. You usually keep the window closed so you can add, modify, and delete data on the disk.

Mylar "floppy" disk.

A clothlike disk liner removes dirt and dust from the disk surface.

What really happens when you erase a file

When you erase a file, the operating system changes the status of the appropriate clusters in the FAT. For example, if a file is stored in clusters 1, 2, 5, and 7 and you erase it, the operating system changes the status for those four clusters to "empty." The data is not physically removed or erased from those clusters. Instead, the old data remains in the clusters until a new file is stored there. This rather interesting situation means that if you inadvertently erase a file, you might be able to get it back by using the operating system's undelete utility. Of course, you can undelete a file only if you haven't recorded something new over it, so it's best to discover and correct mistakes immediately. Not all operating systems provide an undelete utility. To find out if one is available, you can consult the reference manual for your operating system.

Understanding hard disk storage

Hard disk storage is the preferred type of storage for most computer systems. You will frequently see the terms "hard disk" and "hard disk drive" used interchangeably.

HARD DRIVE UPDATE

DETAILS

- A **hard disk platter** is a flat, rigid disk made of aluminum or glass and coated with a magnetic oxide. A **hard disk** is one or more platters and their associated read-write heads.

- Microcomputer hard disk platters are typically 3½ inches in diameter—the same size as the circular Mylar disk in a floppy. The storage capacity of a hard disk, however, far exceeds that of a floppy disk. As noted earlier, floppy disks begin to rotate only when you request data; in contrast, hard disks are continually in motion, so there is no delay as the disk spins up to maximum speed. As a result, hard disk access is faster than floppy disk access. Hard disk storage capacities of 20.4 GB and access speeds of 6–11 ms are not uncommon. See Figure D-14.

- Hard disks store data on the same track and sector locations on both platters before moving the read-write heads to the next sector. A vertical stack of tracks is called a **cylinder**—the basic storage bin for a hard disk.

- Like floppy disks, hard disks provide random access to files by positioning the read-write head over the sector that contains the requested data.

- The read-write heads in a hard disk hover a microscopic distance above the disk surface. If a read-write head runs into a dust particle or some other contaminant on the disk, it might cause a **head crash**, which damages some of the data on the disk. To help eliminate contaminants from contacting the platters, a hard disk is sealed in its case. A head crash can also be triggered by jarring the hard disk while it is in use. It is best to handle and transport hard disks with care.

- It is important to track how much space is available on your computer's hard disk. Your computer operating system shows the capacity of your hard disk and the portion of the capacity that is currently used for data. See Figure D-15.

- **Removable hard disks** or hard disk cartridges contain platters and read-write heads that can be inserted and removed from the drive much like a floppy disk. Removable hard disks increase the potential storage capacity of your computer system. They also provide security for your data by making it possible for you to remove the hard disk cartridge and store it separately from the computer.

How a disk cache helps speed things up

To further increase the speed of data access, your computer might use a disk cache. A disk cache (pronounced "cash") is a special area of computer memory into which the computer transfers the data that you are likely to need from disk storage. Suppose your computer retrieves the data from a particular sector of your disk. There is a high probability that the next data you need will be from an adjacent sector—the remainder of a program file, for example, or the next section of a data file. The computer therefore reads the data from nearby sectors and stores it in the cache. If the data you need next is already in the cache, the computer doesn't need to wait while the mechanical parts of the drive locate and read the data from the disk. A disk cache speeds up the performance of your computer system, because accessing data from the cache is an electrical operation. Figure D-16 explains how disk caching works.

FIGURE D-14: *How a hard drive works*

▶ The hard disk platters are stored inside the drive case or cartridge to prevent dust and other contaminants from interfering with the read-write heads.

The platter surfaces are formatted into cylinders and sectors. A cylinder is a vertical stack of tracks. To find a file, the computer must know the platter, cylinder, and sector in which the file is stored.

The drive spindle supports one or more hard disk platters. Both sides of the platter are used for data storage. More platters mean more data storage capacity. Hard disk platters rotate as a unit on the drive spindle to position a specific sector under the read-write heads. The platters spin continuously, making thousands of revolutions per minute.

Each data storage surface has its own read-write head, which moves in and out from the center of the disk to locate a specific track. The head hovers only a few micro inches above the disk surface, so the magnetic field is much more compact than on a floppy disk. As a result, more data is packed into a smaller area on a hard disk platter.

FIGURE D-15: *Hard disk capacity information*

1. To view disk utilization statistics in Windows, double-click the **My Computer** icon to open the My Computer window.

2. Click the storage device icon for which you want information.

Disk capacity statistics are displayed in the My Computer window.

A graph shows the percentage of disk capacity that is available for files.

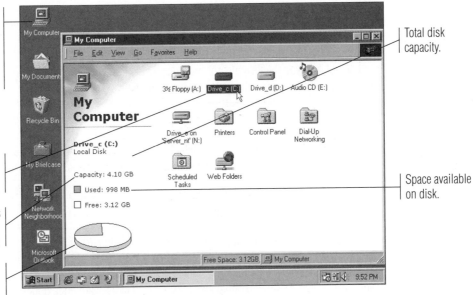

Total disk capacity.

Space available on disk.

FIGURE D-16: *How disk caching works*

1. The computer asks for data that is stored on disk. The disk-cache manager retrieves the requested data (red arrows) and sends it to the main memory so the computer can use it.

2. The disk-cache manager also reads related data (orange arrows) from the disk and keeps it in the cache.

3. When the computer asks for more data, the disk-cache manager first checks the cache to see if the data is there. If the requested data is in the cache, it is immediately sent for processing. If the requested data is not in the cache, the disk-cache manager must take the time to locate the data on the disk, retrieve the data, and then send it to the main memory.

Understanding optical storage

In addition to magnetic storage, optical storage is possible. **Optical storage** stores data as microscopic light and dark spots on the disk surface. With optical storage, data is burned into the storage medium using beams of laser light. CD and DVD technologies are classified as optical storage.

**CD-ROM
UPDATE**

DETAILS

- When data is burned into the storage medium, the burns form patterns of small pits in the disk surface to represent data. The dark spots, as shown in Figure D-17, are called pits. The lighter, nonpitted surface areas of the disk are called lands.

- The transition between the pits and the lands is interpreted as the 1s and the 0s that represent data.

- The pits on optical media are permanent, so the data cannot be changed. Optical media are very durable, but do not give you the flexibility of magnetic media for changing the data once it is stored. Figure D-18 shows how data is stored and read on an optical disk.

- Optical storage gets its name because it is possible to see the data using a high-powered microscope.

- CD-ROM (pronounced "cee dee rom") stands for Compact Disc Read-Only Memory. CD-ROMs are the most popular type of optical storage. Virtually every computer on the market today comes equipped with a CD-ROM.

- CD-ROM technology is derived from the compact disc digital-audio recording system. A computer CD-ROM disk, like its audio counterpart, contains data that has been stamped on the disk surface as a series of pits.

- To read the data on a CD-ROM, an optical read head distinguishes the patterns of pits that represent bytes.

- CD-ROM disks provide tremendous storage capacity. A single CD-ROM disk holds up to 680 MB, equivalent to more than 300,000 pages of text, and the disks are quite durable. The surface of each disk is coated with a clear plastic, making the data permanent and unalterable. Unlike magnetic media, CD-ROMs are not susceptible to humidity, fingerprints, dust, or magnets. You can rinse CD-ROMs off with water. Their useful life is estimated to exceed 500 years.

- CD-ROM disks are limited by the fact that they are read only. Read only means that the computer can retrieve data from a CD-ROM but cannot save any new data on it. In this respect, CD-ROM technology differs markedly from hard disk storage, on which you can write, erase, and read data. A CD-ROM drive therefore supplements a hard disk drive, because the former is a read-only storage device.

- A CD-ROM disk is relatively inexpensive to manufacture, making it an ideal way for software publishers to distribute large programs and data files. CD-ROM is the medium of choice for delivery of multimedia applications because it provides the large storage capacity necessary to hold sound, video, and graphics files.

▶ The pits on an optical storage disk as seen through an electron microscope. Each pit is 1 micron in diameter—1,500 pits lined up side by side would be about as wide as the head of a pin.

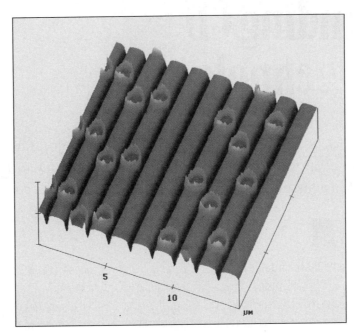

FIGURE **D-18**: *Optical storage devices read data using reflected laser light*

When a CD-ROM disk is manufactured, a laser burns pits into a reflective surface. These pits become dark, non-reflective areas of the disk.

Areas that are not pits have a reflective surface.

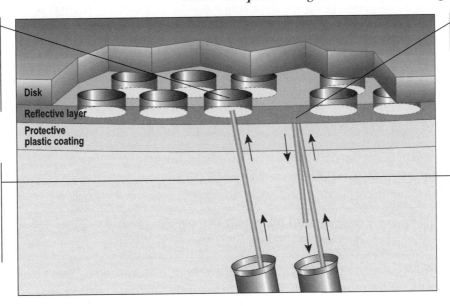

Disk

Reflective layer

Protective plastic coating

The CD-ROM drive uses a low-power laser beam to read the data on the disk. When the beam strikes a pit, no light is reflected.

When the laser strikes a reflective surface, light bounces back into the read head. The patterns of dark spots and reflective spots represent data.

Understanding CD and DVD technology

In addition to CD-ROM, other CD (compact disc) and DVD (digital video disk) technologies are classified as optical storage. This lesson looks at CD and DVD technologies and discusses the disk drives needed to use these technologies.

InfoWeb
DVD
TECHNOLOGY

DETAILS

- **CD-R (compact disc-recordable)** technology allows you to create your own CDs. CD-R technology allows the computer to record data on a CD-R disk using a special CD-R recording device. A CD-R drive uses a laser to change the reflectivity of a dye layer on a blank CD-R disk. With this technology, the data on a CD-R disk is not actually stored as pits on the disk surface. Dark spots in the dye layer appear to be pits. Disks that have been produced with the CD-R device can be used on most optical drives, such as a regular CD-ROM drive (like the one you might have on your computer) or a DVD drive. As with regular CD-ROMs, the data on a CD-R disk cannot be erased or modified once you have recorded it. Most CD-R drives, however, allow you to record your data in multiple sessions. The disks that you create in these sessions can be read only on drives that have **multisession support**. Most drives manufactured after 1998 include multisession support.

- **CD-RW (compact disc-rewritable)** technology allows you to write data on a CD, then change the data. This process requires special CD-RW disks and a CD-RW drive. CD-RW uses **phase-change technology** to alter the crystal structure of the disk surface. The crystal structure's ability to reflect light depends on its state, so altering this structure creates patterns of light and dark similar to the pits and lands on a CD-ROM disk. The crystal structure can be changed from light to dark, and back again, many times. CD-RW technology is useful for archiving and backing up data, but it is not yet a substitute for a hard disk.

- **DVD (digital video disk or digital versatile disk)** is a variation of CD technology that was designed to provide enough storage to hold a full-length movie. DVD movies can be played on a DVD player connected to a television set. DVD-ROM disks require a DVD drive connected to your computer. Although DVD cannot be read by a CD-ROM drive, a DVD drive can read CD-ROM, CD-R, and CD-RW disks. This flexibility makes DVD a versatile and powerful technology.

- A DVD-ROM disk is stamped with data at the time of manufacture and does not allow you to add or change data on the disk. A single-sided DVD-ROM disk can store 4.7 GB of information. Such disks are ideally suited for distributing large multimedia applications, such as games, encyclopedias, maps, and telephone number databases.

- DVD manufacturers introduced **DVD-RW** in 1999. DVD-RW makes it possible to write data on DVD disks by using phase-change technology similar to CD-RWs.

- **DVD-RAM** is another technology that allows you to write to the medium and that uses a blend of technologies to record data. Disks created by DVD-RAM cannot be read in DVD-RW drives, and vice versa.

- As you have just learned, when you are using CD or DVD technologies, you need a disk drive capable of accessing the information on the CD or DVD. Figure D-19 shows how to use a CD-ROM drive. You can use such a drive to listen to your audio CDs while you work on other applications on your computer.

- CD-ROM and DVD-ROM drives are classified according to their speed. Table D-5 compares CD-ROM and DVD-ROM drive speeds. Remember that the data transfer rate is the amount of data that a storage device can move from the storage device to the computer.

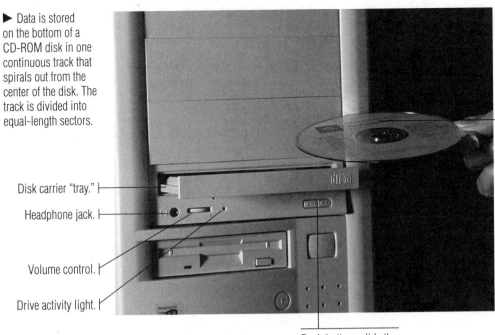

▶ Data is stored on the bottom of a CD-ROM disk in one continuous track that spirals out from the center of the disk. The track is divided into equal-length sectors.

The printed side of the disk does not contain data. It should be face up when you insert the disk because the lasers read the bottom of the disk.

Disk carrier "tray."

Headphone jack.

Volume control.

Drive activity light.

Push buttons slide the disk carrier in or out.

TABLE **D-5**: *Data transfer rates for CD-ROM and DVD-ROM drives*

SPEED	CD-ROM DRIVE	DVD-ROM DRIVE
1X	150 KBps	1,250 KBps
2X	300 KBps	2,500 KBps
4X	600 KBps	5,000 KBps
6X	900 KBps	7,500 KBps
8X	1,200 KBps	10,000 KBps
16X	2,400 KBps	
20X	3,000 KBps	
40X	6,000 KBps	
48X	7,200 KBps	

Archiving data using optical storage

Archiving refers to the process of moving data off a primary storage device and to a supplemental storage device when that data is not frequently accessed. CD-R is a useful technology for archiving data. Archived data does not generally change, but the data you back up might change frequently. Consequently, CD-R technology is not an acceptable replacement for a hard disk. You cannot delete or change data once it is recorded, and the process of creating a CD-R disk is very slow. In fact, it can take from 20 to 60 minutes to record a full CD-R.

Understanding tape storage

In the 1960s, magnetic tape was the most popular form of mainframe computer storage. When IBM introduced its first microcomputer in 1981, the legacy of tape storage continued in the form of a cassette tape drive, similar to those used for audio recording and playback.

TAPE

DETAILS

- Using tape as a primary storage device instead of a hard disk would be slow and inconvenient because tape requires **sequential access** rather than random access. With sequential access, data is stored and read as a sequence of bytes along the length of the tape. To find a file stored on a microcomputer tape storage device, you advance the tape to the approximate location of the file, and then wait for the computer to slowly read each byte until it finds the beginning of the file. Figure D-20 explains how data is stored and retrieved from tape.

- The large reels of computer tapes are called open reel tapes and resemble spools of 16mm film. Access speeds for open reel tapes are measured in seconds, rather than milliseconds.

- Microcomputer users quickly abandoned tape storage for the convenience and speed of random access disk drives. Recently, however, tape storage for microcomputers has experienced a revival—not as a principal storage device, but as a way of making backup copies of the data stored on hard disks. The data on magnetic storage can be easily destroyed, erased, or otherwise lost. Protecting the hard disk is of particular concern to users because it contains so much data—data that would be difficult and time-consuming to reconstruct. Therefore, it is a good idea to have a copy of the data tucked safely away somewhere as a backup.

- A tape backup is a copy of the data from a hard disk that is stored on magnetic tape and used to restore lost data. It is relatively inexpensive and can rescue you from the overwhelming task of trying to reconstruct lost data. If you lose the data on your hard disk, you can copy the data from the tape backup onto the hard disk. Typically, you do not use the data directly from the tape backup because the sequential access is too slow to be practical. For a backup device, access time is less important than the time it takes to copy data from your hard disk to tape. Drive manufacturers do not usually supply such performance specifications, but most users can expect a tape drive to back up 100 MB in 15 to 20 minutes.

- The most popular tape drives for microcomputers use **tape cartridges**, but there are several tape specifications and cartridge sizes. A tape cartridge is a removable magnetic tape module similar to a cassette tape. See Figure D-21. QIC (quarter-inch cartridge) is a tape cartridge that contains one-quarter-inch-wide tape. When you purchase tapes, check the tape drive manual to verify that the tapes are the correct type for your tape drive.

- After the initial time-consuming backup of the hard drive, most tape backup software allows you to selectively back up only those files that have changed since the last backup, making subsequent backups quicker.

- Even though tape storage is sequential, most tape backup software will allow you to back up and restore individual files and directories.

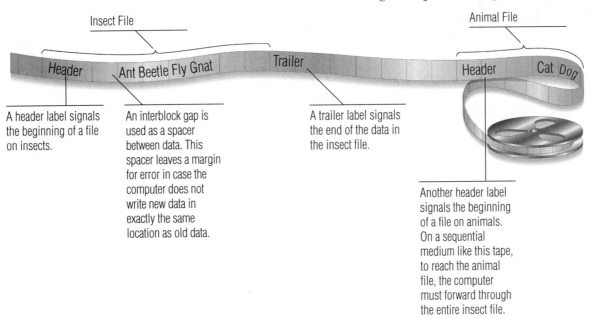

Insect File

Animal File

Header | Ant Beetle Fly Gnat | Trailer | Header | Cat Dog

A header label signals the beginning of a file on insects.

An interblock gap is used as a spacer between data. This spacer leaves a margin for error in case the computer does not write new data in exactly the same location as old data.

A trailer label signals the end of the data in the insect file.

Another header label signals the beginning of a file on animals. On a sequential medium like this tape, to reach the animal file, the computer must forward through the entire insect file.

FIGURE D-21: *Tape drive*

▶ Tape drives are typically incorporated in microcomputer systems to back up the contents of the hard drive. An external tape drive such as this one is a stand-alone unit that can be easily moved from one computer to another. Internal tape drives are installed in the system unit, similar to a floppy or CD-ROM drive.

External tape drive.

A tape cartridge sequentially stores a backup of the data from the computer's hard disk drive.

Using files

As you will recall, most users create, open, or save data files using application software. You are now ready to apply what you've learned about files and file management to see how you would typically use files when you work with application software. Using word processing software to produce a document is a common way to use files on a computer, so we'll take a look at the file operations for a typical word processing session. Examine the details in this lesson to get an overview of the file activities of a typical word processing session.

USING FILES

DETAILS

Word.exe is loaded into memory from the hard disk.

1. Running an Application
Suppose you want to create a document about the summer vacation packages your company offers. You decide to create the document using the word processing software, Microsoft Word. Your first step is to start the Word program. When you run Word, the program file is copied from the hard drive to the memory of the computer.

2. Creating a File
You begin to type the text of the document. As you type, your data is stored in the memory of the computer. Your data will not be stored on disk until you initiate the Save command.

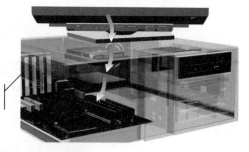

Your data is stored in memory while you type.

3. Saving a Data File
When you create a file and save it on disk for the first time, you must name the file so that you can later retrieve it by name. Earlier in this unit, you learned that the name you give to a file must follow the file naming conventions for the operating system. You name the file *A:Vacation.doc.* By typing *A:* you direct the computer to save the file on the floppy disk in drive A. The computer looks for empty clusters on the disk where it can store the file. It then adds the filename to the directory, along with the number of the cluster that contains the beginning of the file. Once you have saved your file, you can continue to work on the document, exit the Word program, or work on another document.

A:Vacation.doc is copied from memory to the floppy disk.

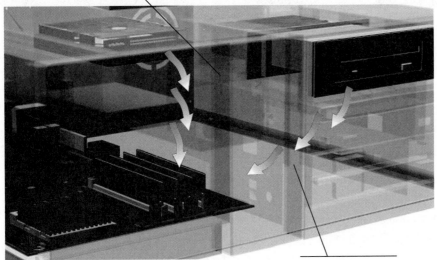

Word.exe is loaded into memory.

A:Vacation.doc is copied from disk into memory.

4. Retrieving a Data File

Suppose that a few days later, you decide that you want to re-read *Vacation.doc*. You need to start Microsoft Word. Once the Word program is running, you can retrieve the *Vacation.doc* file from the disk on which it is stored.

When you want to use a data file that already exists on disk storage, you must tell the application to open the file. In Microsoft Word, you either type the name of the file, *A:Vacation.doc*, or select the filename from a list of files stored on the disk. The application communicates the filename to the operating system.

The operating system looks at the directory and FAT to find which clusters contain the file, then moves the read-write head to the appropriate disk location to read the file. The electronics on the disk drive transfer the file data into the main memory of the computer, where your application software can manipulate it. Once the operating system has retrieved the file, the word processing software displays it on the screen.

The changes you make to the document are stored in memory. When you save your revisions, they overwrite the previous version of *Vacation.doc*.

5. Revising a Data File

When you see the *Vacation.doc* file on the screen, you can modify it. Each character that you type and each change that you make are stored temporarily in the main memory of the computer, but not on the disk.

The *Vacation.doc* file is already on the disk, so when you are done with the modifications you have two options. Option 1 is to store the revised version in place of the old version. Option 2 is to create a new file for your revision and give it a different name, such as *Holiday.doc*.

If you decide to go with option 1—store the revised version in place of the old version—the operating system copies your revised data from the computer memory to the same clusters that contained the old file. You do not have to take a separate step to delete the old file—the operating system automatically records the new file over it.

If you decide to go with option 2—create a new file for the revision—the application prompts you for a filename. Your revisions will be stored under the new filename. The original file, *Vacation.doc*, will remain on the disk in its unrevised form.

Issue Is Data Getting Lost?

PAST AND FUTURE

Before quitting his boring Madison Avenue job and moving to Hollywood, "Mark," a hot-shot advertising designer, copied a collection of his digital graphic and video ideas from his computer at work onto a 12 GB tape. His plan was to purchase a new computer with a 12 GB tape drive, then pull the data off the tape and onto his new hard drive. It was a great plan, except that when he arrived in California, he discovered that the tape drive manufacturer no longer produced the 12 GB model. He was unable to purchase any tape drive that would read the tape that contained his data! Without begging his former boss for access to his old computer, Mark would never be able to retrieve his data.

Mark's data access problem might be indicative of a big problem looming in the future. Today, computers store most of the data generated by banks, credit bureaus, government agencies, and other organizations. In addition, a large amount of historical data is being digitized and stored in computer-readable format. Some experts are concerned that much of this digital data might ultimately be lost as a result of media failures and changes in technology that make some types of media obsolete.

Storage technology has advanced dramatically over the last 40 years. In 1956, IBM researchers introduced the world's first computer disk storage system. It stored 5 MB of data on fifty 24-inch disks. Today, the capacity of a hard disk exceeds 20 GB—that's 4,000 times the capacity of a 1950s storage device. CD and DVD technologies offer optical storage as an alternative to magnetic storage technology, and we can expect new high-capacity storage technologies in the not-too-distant future.

Research is under way on holographic and molecular storage technologies. Holographic storage is essentially a three-dimensional snapshot of data stored in a crystal medium. In the laboratory, researchers have achieved storage densities of 48 MB per cubic centimeter, but expected storage density is 10 GB per cubic centimeter. To put it in perspective, a couple of holographic storage cubes about the size of a pair of dice could hold the contents of a half-mile-high stack of books. Even higher capacity might be possible with molecular storage, which manipulates individual molecules to represent data bits. Researchers have produced a "nano-abacus" with this technology, though a molecular storage device for your PC is still some years away.

Although these new technologies offer the promise of faster, more dependable data storage, the issue of compatibility still exists. In the future, your holographic storage device is not likely to read the CD-R disks that you use today to archive your data. Five years from now, how will you access today's data? To illustrate the problem, consider a related issue: Could you access data that was stored 20 years ago?

Twenty years ago, 8-inch floppy disks were a popular and state-of-the-art storage medium for microcomputers. Suppose that you needed to read the information stored many years ago on a set of 8-inch floppy disks. Obviously, you would need an 8-inch disk drive—hardly standard equipment on today's PCs. The companies that manufacture storage devices tend to drop support for old technologies soon after introducing new models.

You might have difficulty purchasing a new 8-inch floppy disk drive, but perhaps you might locate a used drive. You would still need the correct type of cable and circuit board to connect the drive to the computer. The circuit board would have to be compatible with a modern PC. You would also need driver software that would enable your computer to control that ancient 8-inch disk drive. Drivers are typically designed for a particular operating system. Drivers designed for the operating systems that were popular 20 years ago are not likely to work under Windows. Ultimately, you would wish that the person who saved those 8-inch disks had also saved the entire computer system, including the 8-inch disk drive.

The data storage problem might be getting worse because of competing standards. For example, the current battle between the incompatible DVD-RW and DVD-RAM formats means that data stored using one technology cannot be read using the other technology. Suppose that consumers decide that they prefer CD-RW technology and DVD-RAM technology becomes obsolete. Five years from now, if you have a DVD containing data, it could be difficult to read it. This situation has led some experts to call for more industry cooperation in setting standards for storage devices and media. For now, however, computer users should be aware that today's data disks, CDs, or DVDs might not be usable on tomorrow's storage devices.

EXPAND THE IDEAS

1. Can you currently access all of the data that you have stored on computers in the past? Write a one-page paper explaining your answer. Include any research and facts that support your claims.

2. Do you know anyone who has lost data due to obsolete equipment? How could this situation have been avoided? Compile your ideas into a poster presentation.

3. Think about all of the data that is collected daily in our society, court papers, government documents, school, and university records. If you were in charge of safeguarding this data, how would you plan and prepare to ensure the future access to it? Find several examples of articles, documentaries, or news stories on securing access to data. Write a summary of each article or media piece. Analyze your findings. Was the media voice consistent? Why or why not?

4. Could future data access problems be prevented if the computer industry had a better set of storage standards? Find several examples of articles, documentaries, or news stories that discuss data storage standards. Write a summary of each article or media piece. Analyze your findings. Was the media voice consistent? Why or why not?

5. Storage issues are not limited to computer data; they also include audio and images. There have been many storage technologies that are no longer used or supported. A few of these dinosaurs include vinyl records (78, 45, and 33 rpm), 16mm film, 8mm film, 8-track audiotapes, 8-inch floppy disks, and SONY Betamax tapes. Have you heard of these "old" formats? Can you think of others? Does obsolete technology affect all types of media in the same way? Write a two-page paper supporting your position. Be sure to include your resources.

End of Unit Exercises

STUDY TIPS

Study Tips help you organize and consolidate the information in a unit by making lists, outlines, charts, and sketches. You can use paper and pencil or word processing software to complete most of the Study Tips activities.

1. Indicate which filenames in the following list are not valid under the operating system used in your school's computer lab. Which filenaming convention does each nonvalid filename violate?

Wp.exe	Ppr	Win.exe
Autoexec.bat	Results*.wks	Monthly.wk1
Report#1.txt	Smith&Smith.doc	Sep/94.wri
Asia map.doc	Ocean.tif	Mn43-44.dbf

2. Explain the difference between the terms in the following pairs: data and information, logical storage and physical storage, executable files and data files, generic filename extensions and application-specific filename extensions, reading data and writing data, magnetic storage and optical storage, bit and byte, random access and sequential access, CD-ROM and CD-RW.

3. Make a list of the file operations that you can perform with file manager utility software.

4. Write a short description of how a file allocation table helps the operating system locate files.

5. Explain how a disk becomes fragmented and why it is a good idea to periodically defragment your computer's hard disk.

6. Suppose that a friend is buying a new computer and can't decide whether to get a CD-ROM drive, a CD-RW drive, a DVD-ROM drive, a DVD-RAM drive, or a DVD-RW drive. Explain the advantages and disadvantages of each.

7. You could specify all the files with a .doc extension by *.doc, how would you specify the following files?
   a. All the files with .txt extensions
   b. All the files that contain "minutes"
   c. All the files that begin with "Ship"
   d. All the files on the disk
   e. All the files that begin with the letter "R"

8. Suppose you need to retrieve a file from Sarah's computer. She tells you that the file is stored as D:\Data\Payables.xls.
   a. What is the filename?
   b. What is the filename extension?
   c. On which drive is the file stored?
   d. Will you need a specific software program to retrieve the file?
   e. What type of file is it likely to be?
   f. In which directory is the file stored?

FILL IN THE BEST ANSWER

1. A computer file is classified according to the _____ it contains, the _____ that was used to create it, and the way you should use it.

2. The asterisk is a(n) _____ character that is used to represent a group of characters in a filename or filename extension.

3. Most executable files have a(n) _____ extension.

4. You can delete files with a .bat, .sys, or .cfg file extension because they are temporary. True or False? _____

5. Storage capacity is measured in _____, and access time is measured in _____.

6. A magnet can disrupt data on _____ storage, but _____ storage technology is more durable.

7. The formatting process creates a series of concentric _____ and pie-shaped _____ on the disk.

8. Data files that are entered by the user, changed often, or shared with other users are generally stored on _____ media.

9. The computer can move directly to any file on a(n) _____ access device, but must start at the beginning and read through all the data on a(n) _____ access device.

10. Newer technologies are decreasing the use of _____ for distribution; instead, vendors are using _____ to distribute software.

11. The primary storage device on a microcomputer is the _____.

12. CD-R technology allows you to write data on a disk, then change the data. True or False? _____

13. The _____ keeps track of the physical locations of files on a disk.

14. Folders are also called _____.

15. The main directory of a disk is called the _____ directory.

16. _____ storage devices store data as microscopic light and dark spots on the surface of a CD or DVD disk.

17. When you use Windows application software to create a data file, you don't always have to add a(n) _____.

18. Nested file folders and directory trees are ways of representing _____ storage.

19. _____ technology is a variation of CD technology that was designed to provide enough storage capacity to hold a full-length movie.

20. A data transfer rate of 150 KBps is better than a rate of 100 KBps. True or False? _____

INDEPENDENT CHALLENGE 1

Many software applications use a specific filename extension for data files created with that application. Determine the filename extensions used by five applications on your own computer or a lab computer.

To complete this independent challenge:

1. Run each software application and attempt to retrieve a file. If the software application uses a specific filename extension, you will usually see it indicated in a box on the screen. For example, you might see *.DOC if you are using Microsoft Word.

2. For each of the five programs you select, specify the program name, sketch a picture of the program icon (if you are using Windows), indicate the executable filename (if you are using DOS), and indicate the filename extension used by the program. If the program does not use a specific filename extension, indicate so.

INDEPENDENT CHALLENGE 2

You should be aware of the storage devices on your computer so that you can employ the best device for each task. To identify these devices, you will need to take a hands-on look at either your computer at home or a computer in your school lab.

Answer the following questions to complete this independent challenge:

1. Where is this computer located?

2. What is the hard disk capacity?

3. What is the hard disk drive letter?

4. Is there a floppy disk drive?

5. What is the floppy disk drive letter?

6. Is there a Zip disk drive?

7. Is there a tape storage device?

8. Is there a CD-ROM drive?

9. Which storage device do you typically use for your data files?

10. Which storage device holds most of the applications software that you use?

11. Which device would you use for backups?

INDEPENDENT CHALLENGE 3

How will you organize the information that you store on your hard drive? Your hard disk drive is like a filing cabinet. You can create file folders to hold your files. There is no single right "way" to organize files, but it is important that your filing system work for you. Take some time to think about the filing system you plan to create. Of course, the filing system is flexible, so you can always change folder names and create new ones.

To complete this independent challenge:

1. Read the following possibilities for creating folders and then comment on the advantages and disadvantages of each.

   a. Create a folder for each file that you create.

   b. Store all files in the root directory under a single folder called MyFiles.

   c. Create a folder for each application you plan to use and store only documents you generate with that application in that folder.

   d. Create folders for broad topics such as Memos, Letters, Budget Items, Personal, and store documents that match those headings in the appropriate folder, regardless of the applications used to create the files.

   e. Create folders based on specific topics, such as Applications, Personal, Taxes, and so on. Store all files related to those specific topics in the appropriate folder, regardless of the applications used to create the files.

   f. Create folders based on specific topics, such as Applications, Personal, Taxes, and so on. Create sub-folders for similar types of files, then store all files related to that specific topic and applications used to create the files in the appropriate folders and subfolders.

2. Write a description and then draw a picture to show how you plan to organize the folders on your computer.

INDEPENDENT CHALLENGE 4

Organizations take different approaches to data storage. Depending on the volume of their date, the value of their data, and the need for data security, they may have different plans, procedures, devices, and strategies.

To complete this independent challenge:

1. Interview the person responsible for maintaining data for an organization in your community. Then, create a short paper that summarizes the answers to the following questions:

a. What is the job title of the person responsible for this organization's data storage?

b. What preparation did this individual have to qualify for this position?

c. What are this individual's job responsibilities?

d. How does this person keep up with trends that affect data storage?

e. What type of data does this organization store?

f. How much of this data is stored on a computer? How else is the data stored?

g. What types of storage devices does this organization use?

h. What is the capacity of each storage device?

i. What happens when the storage devices reach their capacity?

j. What problems are associated with maintaining the data for this organization?

INDEPENDENT CHALLENGE 5

Use at least three different Internet sites to research storage devices. You can pay vastly different amounts for the same media and storage devices. Your goal is to use the Internet to obtain the best prices. You have to consider shipping and handling costs as part of the price.

To complete this independent challenge:

1. Create a chart, such as the following:

Shopping list item	Brand name	Merchant	Price

2. Fill in the shopping list item, brand name, merchant, price, and shipping and handling costs for each of the following:

- Package of 10 3½-inch floppy disks and a high-density 3½-inch floppy disk drive
- Hard disk drives (10 GB and 20 GB)
- Tape cartridges and a tape drive
- Zip disks and a Zip disk drive
- CD-ROM drive
- Pack of CD-R disks and a CD-R disk drive
- DVD drive

INDEPENDENT CHALLENGE 6

Many software applications use a specific filename extension for data files created with that application.

To complete this independent challenge:

1. Suppose you have a disk with the following files:

Minutes.doc	Report.doc	Budget.xls
Jacsmemo.doc	Report1.doc	Shipjan.xls
Shipfeb.xls	Shipmar.xlx	Shipapr.xls
Minutes.txt	Roger.txt	Roadmap.bmp

If you could specify all the files with a .doc extension by *.doc, how would you specify the following files?

a. All the files with .txt extensions

b. All the files that contain "minutes"

c. All the files that begin with "Ship"

d. All the files on the disk

e. All the files that begin with the letter "R"

LAB: DIRECTORIES, FOLDERS, FILES

Graphical user interfaces such as MacOS and Windows use a filing system metaphor for file management. In this lab, you will learn the basic concepts of these file system metaphors. With this background, you will find it easy to understand how to manage files with graphical user interfaces.

1. Click the Steps button to learn how to manipulate directories, folders, and files. As you proceed through the Steps, answer all of the QuickCheck questions that appear. After you complete the Steps, you will see a QuickCheck Report. Follow the instructions on the screen to print this report.

2. Make sure you are in Explore. Change to drive C as the default drive. Double-click the c:\ folder to display its contents, then answer the following questions:

   a. How many data files are in the root directory of drive C?

   b. How many program files are in the root directory of drive C?

   c. Does the root directory of drive C contain any subdirectories? How can you tell?

   d. How many files are in the Programs folder?

   e. Complete the diagram to show the arrangement of folders on drive C. Do not include files.

3. Click the Explore button. Make sure drive A is the default drive. Double-click the a:\ folder to display the folder contents, then answer the following questions:

   a. How many files are in the root directory of drive A?

   b. Are the files on drive A data files or program files? How can you tell?

   c. Does the root directory of drive A contain any subdirectories? How can you tell?

4. Open and close folders, and change drives as necessary to locate the following files. After you find the file, write out its file specification:

   a. *config.sys*   d. *meeting.doc*

   b. *explorer.exe*   e. *newlogo3.bmp*

   c. *toolkit.wks*   f. *todo.doc*

LAB: DEFRAGMENTATION

In this lab, you will format a simulated disk, save files, delete files, and undelete files to see how the computer updates the FAT. You will also find out how the files on your disk become fragmented and what a defragmentation utility does to reorganize the clusters on your disk.

1. Click the Steps button to learn how the computer updates the FAT when you format a disk and save, delete, and undelete files. As you proceed through the Steps, answer all of the QuickCheck questions that appear. After you complete the Steps, you will see a QuickCheck Report. Follow the instructions on the screen to print this report.

2. Click the Explore button. Click the Format button to format the simulated disk. Try to save files 1, 2, 3, 4, and 6. Do they all fit on the disk?

3. In Explore, format the simulated disk. Try to save all files on the disk. What happens?

4. In Explore, format the simulated disk. Save FILE-3, FILE-4, and FILE-6. Next, delete FILE-6. Now, save FILE-5. Try to undelete FILE-6. What happens and why?

5. In Explore, format the simulated disk. Save and erase files until the files become fragmented. Draw a picture of the disk to show the fragmented files.

Indicate which files are in each cluster by using color, crosshatching, or labels. List which files in your drawing are fragmented. Finally, defragment the disk and draw a new picture showing the unfragmented files.

LAB: USING FILES

In this lab, you manipulate a simulated computer to view what happens in memory and on disk when you create, save, open, revise, and delete files. Understanding what goes on "inside the box" will help you quickly grasp how to perform basic file operations with most application software.

1. Click the Steps button to learn how to use the simulated computer to view the contents of memory and disk when you perform basic file operations. As you proceed through the Steps, answer all of the QuickCheck questions that appear. After you complete the Steps, you will see a QuickCheck Report. Follow the instructions on the screen to print this report.

2. Click the Explore button and use the simulated computer to perform the following tasks:

   a. Create a document containing your name and the city in which you were born. Save this document as Name.

   b. Create another document containing two of your favorite foods. Save this document as Foods.

   c. Create another file containing your two favorite classes. Call this file Classes.

   d. Open the Food file and add another one of your favorite foods. Save this file without changing its name.

   e. Open the Name file. Change this document so it contains your name and the name of your school. Save this as a new document called School.

   f. Write down how many files are on the simulated disk and the exact contents of each file.

   g. Delete all files.

3. In Explore, use the simulated computer to perform the following tasks:

   a. Create a file called MUSIC that contains the name of your favorite CD.

   b. Create another document that contains eight numbers and call this file Lottery.

   c. You didn't win the lottery this week. Revise the contents of the Lottery file, but save the revision as Lottery2.

   d. Revise the MUSIC file so it also contains the name of your favorite musician or composer, and save this file as Music2.

   e. Delete the Music file.

   f. Write down how many files are on the simulated disk and the exact contents of each file.

LESSON	MEDIA ELEMENT		LESSON	MEDIA ELEMENT
Learning about file management	FILENAME EXTENSIONS	SCREENTOUR	Understanding optical storage	CD ROM UPDATE
Understanding logical file storage	DIRECTORIES, FOLDERS, FILES	SCREENTOUR	Understanding CD and DVD technology	DVD TECHNOLOGY
Exploring physical file storage	FAT	DEFRAGMENTATION	Understanding tape storage	TAPE
Comparing storage devices	FLOPPIES AND ZIP		Using files	USING FILES
Understanding hard disk storage	HARD DRIVE UPDATE	VIDEO	Issue: Is Data Getting Lost?	PAST AND FUTURE

VISUAL WORKSHOP

Examine the figure and answer the following questions.

1. The figure is showing the directory for which drive?
2. Name the two other drives shown in the directory window.
3. Name two data files shown in the directory window.
4. Identify two files that were created with the same program.
5. How much storage space is used by all of the files in the directory?
6. How much storage space remains available on the disk?
7. How many files are in the directory?
8. Which operating system is this directory for?
9. Name two generic files in this directory.
10. What type of style directory is this?
11. Are filename extensions listed?

12. If there are filename extensions, give the filenames and filename extensions.
13. What would happen if you double-click the file Company Logo.bmp?
14. Which is the smallest file in the directory?
15. What would happen if you double-click the file Requirements for Entry.doc?

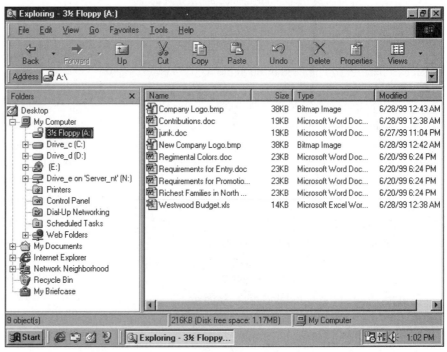

Computer Architecture

OBJECTIVES

Examine the inside of a system unit

Define data representation and transport

Understand data representation

Understand computer memory: RAM

Categorize computer memory

Define the CPU

Understand CPU architecture

Understand the instruction cycle

Understand CPU performance

Learn about input/output (I/O)

Plan for expansion

Learn about the boot process

In this unit, you'll take a more detailed look inside the case of a modern computer system. The basic concepts explored in this unit apply to microcomputer, minicomputer, and mainframe computers. You'll investigate some technical concepts about how computers store and process data. You'll learn how, when, and why you should expand your computer system. Once you understand how a computer works, you will have greater success when troubleshooting problems you encounter at school, at work, or at home. After reading this unit, you'll also be better equipped to understand much of the computer jargon you hear in conversations and read in computer ads.

Examining the inside of a system unit

Computer architecture refers to the design and construction of a computer system. The architecture of any computer can be broadly classified by considering two characteristics: what the computer uses for power, and how the computer physically represents, processes, stores, and moves data. Computers are electronic devices that are powered by electricity. They use electrical signals and circuits to represent, process, and move data.

The arrangement of elements inside the case of a desktop computer differs somewhat from that found inside a notebook computer. The limited space inside a notebook computer means that circuit boards and other components are more tightly packed together.

DETAILS

○── If you have never opened a computer case, you might be surprised to find that the inside of a computer contains circuit boards, a power supply, and storage devices. A few wires and cables connect the storage devices to the power supply and circuit boards. Figure E-1 shows what's inside a typical tower microcomputer.

○── Most of the components inside a computer are integrated circuits, commonly called chips, microchips, or microprocessors. An **integrated circuit** (**IC**) is a thin slice of crystal packed with microscopic circuit elements such as wires, transistors, capacitors, and resistors. A single integrated circuit less than a quarter-inch square could contain more than 1 million microscopic circuit elements. See Figure E-2.

○── The completed circuit is packaged in either a plastic or a ceramic carrier that provides connection pins to other computer components. These carriers exist in several configurations or **chip packages**, including DIP, DIMM, PGA, and SEC. A DIP (dual in-line package) has two rows of connecting pins. Once used for memory, DIPs now contain specialized circuitry. A DIMM (dual in-line memory module) is a small circuit board containing several chips typically used for memory in today's computers. A PGA (pin grid array), which houses most of today's powerful microprocessors, is a square chip with pins arranged in concentric squares. A SEC (single-edge contact) cartridge is a popular chip package for many of today's most powerful processors.

○── Inside the system unit, integrated circuits are housed on a circuit board called the main board, or **motherboard**. The motherboard is connected to peripheral devices that collect input and produce output. Figure E-3 illustrates how a microcomputer motherboard connects the chips that carry out basic computer functions.
- Some chips are soldered to the board, whereas other chips are plugged into the board and can be removed. Removable chips allow you to upgrade your computer components.
- The motherboard contains the processor chip, the memory chips, and the chips that carry out basic input and output. Circuits etched into the motherboard act like wires, providing a path so that the computer can transport data from one chip to another as needed for processing.
- The motherboard contains expansion slots that allow you to connect peripheral devices to the computer.

FIGURE E-1: *Inside a computer's system unit*

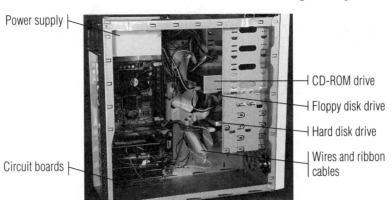

INSIDE THE CASE

VIDEO

Power supply

CD-ROM drive

Floppy disk drive

Hard disk drive

Wires and ribbon cables

Circuit boards

FIGURE E-2: *Integrated circuit*

VIDEO

INTEGRATED CIRCUITS

A single integrated circuit less than a quarter-inch square could contain more than 1 million microscopic circuit elements.

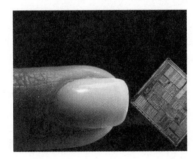

FIGURE E-3: *A computer motherboard*

MOTHERBOARDS

Random access memory chips, which temporarily hold data, are mounted on small circuit boards that plug into the motherboard.

Some chips are mounted on a small circuit board called an "expansion card," which plugs into a long slot on the motherboard.

Support chips and other components, such as a battery for the computer's real-time clock, are typically soldered to the motherboard.

ROM chips contain the programs that start the computer, run system diagnostics, and control low-level input and output activities.

Circuitry, called a "bus," transports data between components on the motherboard.

A microprocessor chip, which contains circuitry that performs arithmetic and logical operations, plugs directly into the motherboard.

Many expansion cards include a port, which provides a connection point for peripheral devices, such as a scanner or monitor.

Defining data representation and transport

Data representation refers to the form in which information is conceived, manipulated, and recorded. Because a computer is an electronic device, it uses electrical signals to represent data. Data transport is the way that data travels from one location to another. In a computer, data travels on electronic pathways.

DETAILS

- The type of signal that a computer uses to represent data depends on whether the computer is a digital or analog device.
  - A **digital device** works with discrete numbers or digits, such as 0 and 1. In this context, "discrete" means that the numbers are distinct and separate. For example, the number 0 is discrete, or distinct, from the number 1.
  - An **analog device** operates on continuously varying data. A dimmer switch that has a rotating dial that increases or decreases brightness smoothly over a range from bright to dark is an analog device.

- Today, most computers are digital computers. Figure E-4 can help you visualize how computers might use electrical pulses to move data along a circuit.

- Digital computers represent numbers, letters, and symbols with codes that use a series of 1s and 0s. They represent numeric data using the binary number system, or base 2. Computers also use several other codes designed for computer data; you will learn about these codes in the next lesson.

- The binary number system contains only two digits: 0 and 1. These digits can be converted to electrical "ons" or "offs" inside a computer. The numeral 2 cannot be used in the binary number system; thus, instead of writing 2, you would write 10. Figure E-5 shows the first 10 numbers represented in the binary number system.

- Typically, data travels from one location to another within the computer on an electronic pathway, or circuit, called a **data bus**. The term *bus* figuratively describes this circuit's function. Picture a school bus that goes to a neighborhood and picks up a load of children, drops them off at school, and then goes to the next neighborhood on its route to pick up a second bus load of children. A computer data bus works in similar fashion. A computer data bus "picks up" a load of data from one of the components on the motherboard, then transfers the data to another motherboard component. After dropping off this load, the bus collects another load, as shown in Figure E-6.

- In terms of computer architecture, the data bus is a series of electronic circuits that connect the various electrical elements on the motherboard. The circuits in a digital computer have only two possible states. For convenience, you can think of one of those states as "on" and the other state as "off." If you equate the "on" state with 1 and the "off" state with 0, you can grasp the basic principle of how a digital computer works. When data is being transported along computer circuitry or processed within an integrated circuit, the 1s and 0s have to be converted into an electrical signal.

- The bus contains data lines and address lines. **Data lines** carry the signals that represent data. **Address lines** carry the locations of data to help the computer find the data it needs to process.

Why 1s and 0s?

In a digital computer, each number or letter is represented by a series of electrical signals. Think about the way Morse code uses dashes and dots to represent letters. In a similar way, digital computers represent numbers, letters, and symbols with a code that uses a series of 1s and 0s. Data that is represented digitally can be easily moved or stored electronically as a series of "ons" and "offs."

A pulse of electricity moving down a circuit could represent 1 bit.

FIGURE E-5: *Binary numbers*

Decimal		Binary			
Place	Place	Place	Place	Place	Place
10	1	8	4	2	1
	0				0
	1				1
	2			1	0
	3			1	1
	4		1	0	0
	5		1	0	1
	6		1	1	0
	7		1	1	1
	8	1	0	0	0
	9	1	0	0	1
1	0	1	0	1	0

FIGURE E-6: *How the data bus works*

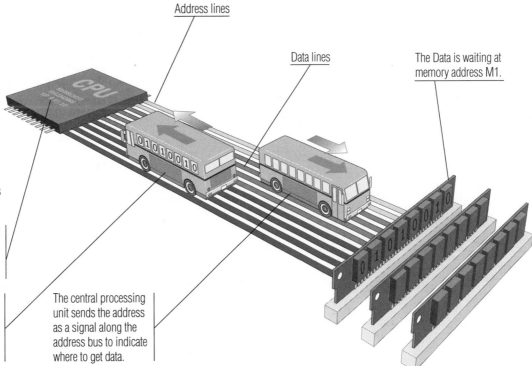

A computer data bus "picks up" a load of bits from one of the components on the motherboard, then transfers these bits to another motherboard component. After dropping off one load of bits, the bus collects another load.

The central processing unit needs the data stored at memory address M1

The bus picks up the data and transports it along the address lines to the central processing unit.

The central processing unit sends the address as a signal along the address bus to indicate where to get data.

Address lines

Data lines

The Data is waiting at memory address M1.

Understanding data representation

You now know that data exists in the computer as a series of electronic signals represented as 1s and 0s. Each 1 or 0 that represents data is referred to as a **bit**. Most computer coding schemes use eight bits to represent each number, letter, or symbol. A series of eight bits is referred to as a **byte**. Study Figure E-7 to make sure you understand how the term *byte* is related to the terms *bits* and *characters*.

DETAILS

- Digital computers use many different coding schemes to represent data. The coding scheme used by a computer depends on whether the data is numeric- or character-based.

- Numeric data consists of numbers that represent quantities and that might be used in arithmetic operations. For example, your annual income is numeric data. You use it in arithmetic operations every April when you calculate your income taxes. Your age is also a number. Computers use the binary number system to represent numbers.

- Character data is composed of letters, symbols, and numerals that will not be used in arithmetic operations. Examples of character data include your name, hair color, phone number, and Social Security number. Because you will not use your Social Security number or your phone number in arithmetic operations, they are considered character data made up of *numerals*, not numbers.

- Digital computers typically represent character data using either the **ASCII** (pronounced "ASK ee") **code** or **EBCDIC** (pronounced "EB seh dick") **code**. ASCII stands for American Standard Code for Information Interchange. It is used to represent symbols and numerals as well as uppercase and lowercase letters. ASCII is a data representation code used on most microcomputers, on many minicomputers, and on some mainframe computers. EBCDIC stands for Extended Binary Coded Decimal Interchange Code. IBM-brand mainframe computers often use the eight-bit EBCDIC code. Figure E-8 shows the ASCII and the EBCDIC codes.

The smallest unit of information in a computer is a bit. A bit can be a 0 or a 1. The electronic circuits in a computer carry one bit as a pulse of electricity through an open switching circuit.

A collection of eight bits is called a **byte**. This byte is composed of the eight bits 01111001.

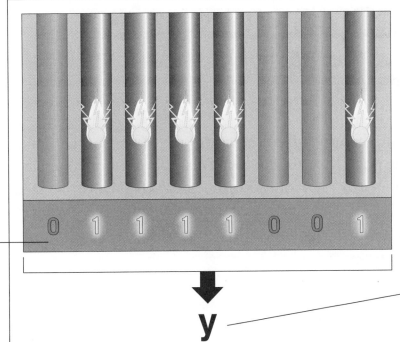

A byte represents one **character**—a letter, numeral, or punctuation symbol. This byte, 01111001, represents a lowercase *y*.

Each letter, number, and most symbols have an ASCII and EBCDIC code.

SYMBOL	ASCII	EBCDIC	SYMBOL	ASCII	EBCDIC	SYMBOL	ASCII	EBCDIC
(space)	0100000	01000000	?	0111111	01101111	^	1011110	
!	0100001	01011010	@	1000000	01111100	_	1011111	
"	0100010	01111111	A	1000001	11000001	a	1100001	10000001
#	0100011	01111011	B	1000010	11000010	b	1100010	10000010
$	0100100	01011011	C	1000011	11000011	c	1100011	10000011
%	0100101	01101100	D	1000100	11000100	d	01100100	10000100
&	0100110	01010000	E	1000101	11000101	e	1100101	10000101
'	0100111	01111101	F	1000110	11000110	f	1100110	10000110
(	0101000	01001101	G	1000111	11000111	g	1100111	10000111
)	0101001	01011101	H	1001000	11001000	h	01101000	10001000
*	0101010	01011100	I	1001001	11001001	i	1101001	10001001
+	0101011	01001110	J	1001010	11010001	j	1101010	10010001
,	0101100	01101011	K	1001011	11010010	k	1101011	10010010
–	0101101	01100000	L	1001100	11010011	l	1101000	10010011
.	0101110	01001011	M	1001101	11010100	m	1101101	10010100
/	0101111	01100001	N	1001110	11010101	n	1101110	10010101
0	0110000	11110000	O	1001111	11010110	o	1111111	10010110
1	0110001	11110001	P	1010000	11010111	p	1110100	10010111
2	0110010	11110010	Q	1010001	11011000	q	1110001	10011000
3	0110011	11110011	R	1010010	11011001	r	1110010	10011001
4	0110100	11110100	S	1010011	11100010	s	1110100	10100010
5	0110101	11110101	T	1010100	11100011	t	1110100	10100011
6	0110110	11110110	U	1010101	11100100	u	1110101	10100100
7	0110111	11110111	V	1010110	11100101	v	1110110	10100101
8	0111000	11111000	W	1010111	11100110	w	1110111	10100110
9	0111001	11111001	X	1011000	11100111	x	1111000	10100111
:	0111010	01111010	Y	1011001	11101000	y	1111001	10101000
;	0111011	01011110	Z	1011010	11101001	z	1111010	10101001
<	0111100	01001100	[	1011011	01001010	{	1111011	
=	0111101	01111110	\	1011100		}	1111101	
>	0111110	01101110	]	1011101	01011010			

Understanding computer memory: RAM

Memory is electronic circuitry linked directly to the processor that holds data and program instructions when they are not being transported from one place to another. Four major types of memory exist: random access memory (RAM), virtual memory, read-only memory (ROM), and CMOS memory. Each type of memory is characterized by the kind of data it contains and the technology it uses to hold the data.

MEMORY TECHNOLOGY

GRACE HOPPER

DETAILS

○━ Memory is sometimes called primary storage, but this term is easily confused with disk storage. It is preferable to use the term *memory* to refer to the circuitry that has a direct link to the processor and to use the term *storage* to refer to media, such as disks, that are not directly linked to the processor.

○━ **Random access memory** (**RAM**) is an area in the computer system unit that temporarily holds user data, operating system instructions, and program instructions. Every time you turn on your computer, a set of operating system instructions is copied from disk into RAM. These instructions, which help control basic computer functions, remain in RAM until you turn the computer off.

You can think of RAM as analogous to a chalkboard. You can use a chalkboard to write formulas, erase the formulas, and then write notes for a report. In a similar way, RAM can hold numbers for a spreadsheet, then the text of an essay for a word processor. Each time you enter data, you change the contents of RAM. Because its contents can be changed, RAM is a reusable resource.

○━ RAM is volatile. That is, the memory holds data only as long as the computer power is on. It is therefore important to save your work frequently. If the computer is turned off or the power goes out, all data stored in RAM instantly and permanently disappears.

○━ The contents of RAM are necessary for the computer to process data. The results of processing are kept temporarily in RAM until they are needed again or until they are stored on disk.

○━ In RAM, microscopic electronic parts called **capacitors** hold the electronic signals for the ASCII, EBCDIC, or binary code that represents data. A charged capacitor represents an "on" bit. A discharged capacitor represents an

"off" bit. Just changing the charge of a capacitor can change the contents of RAM. You can visualize the capacitors as being arranged in banks of eight. Each bank holds eight bits, or one byte of data.

○━ A **RAM address** on each bank helps the computer locate the data contained in the bank. Figure E-9 shows how RAM works.

○━ Today, the storage capacity of RAM is measured in megabytes (MB). Microcomputers typically have between 64 MB and 256 MB of RAM, which means that they can hold between 64 million and 256 million characters of data or instructions. The amount of RAM your computer needs depends on the software you are using. You can purchase additional RAM to the limit set by the computer manufacturer.

○━ The processor works at a certain speed, but would be forced to slow down if it had to wait for data from RAM. Most RAM today can have access speeds as fast as 8 nanoseconds. Older, slower memory has access speeds of 60 to 80 nanoseconds. A **nanosecond** is one-billionth of a second. Computer pioneer Grace Hopper showed that a nanosecond is the time it takes electricity to travel a 12-inch piece of wire.

○━ RAM is typically configured as a series of DIPs soldered onto the small circuit board called a DIMM. See Figure E-10. Metallic teeth on the edge of the DIMM plug into special RAM slots on the motherboard, which makes it easy to replace defective RAM or add RAM capacity.

○━ SDRAM (synchronous dynamic RAM) is a type of volatile memory circuitry that runs in synchronization with the bus that transports data to and from the processor. SDRAM is faster than other types, so it works well even with fast processors.

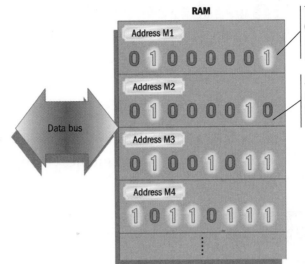

Each RAM location has an address and holds one byte of data by using eight capacitors to represent the eight bits in a byte.

RAM is connected to the data bus so that the computer can transport data to and from the central processing unit.

The two charged capacitors in this RAM location represent the letter A.

A different sequence of charged capacitors represents the letter B.

Today, most RAM is configured as small circuit boards called DIMMs, which plug into special slots in the motherboard.

How much RAM?

The amount of RAM a computer needs depends on the operating system and the applications software you plan to use. RAM requirements are usually specified on the outside of the software box. When you purchase additional RAM, you must make sure that it is the correct type, size, and configuration for your computer system. RAM costs have dropped from about $10 per megabyte to as low as $2.50 per megabyte. To run many of today's software programs effectively, your computer should have at least 32 MB of RAM; most computers today come equipped with at least 128 MB.

Categorizing computer memory

In addition to RAM, your computer uses three other types of memory to hold data: virtual memory, ROM, and CMOS. These types of memory supplement the functions provided by RAM.

DETAILS

- **Virtual memory** is the ability of a computer to use disk storage to simulate RAM. It allows computers without enough RAM to nevertheless run large programs, manipulate large data files, and run more than one program at a time. In the context of computing, "virtual" usually means "simulated." Figure E-11 explains how virtual memory works.

  One disadvantage of virtual memory is reduced performance. With most of today's operating systems, the computer uses space on its hard drive as an extension of RAM. It takes longer to retrieve data from virtual memory than from RAM because the disk is a mechanical device and access time is therefore slower. A disk access time of 10 milliseconds is quite a bit slower than a RAM access speed of 80 nanoseconds. Like data held in RAM, data held in virtual memory becomes inaccessible if the power goes off.

- **ROM** (read-only memory) is a set of chips containing instructions that help a computer prepare for processing tasks. The instructions in ROM are permanent. You have no way to change them, unless you remove the ROM chips from the motherboard and replace them with another set.

  ROM contains a small set of instructions called the **ROM BIOS** (Basic Input Output System). See Figure E-12. The BIOS is a small but critical part of the operating system that tells the computer how to access the disk drives and look for the operating system. When you turn on your computer, RAM is empty. The CPU performs a series of steps by following the instructions stored in ROM. This series of steps is called the boot process; it is discussed in more detail later in this unit. Some steps in the boot process are permanently stored in ROM.

- **CMOS memory** (pronounced "SEE moss") makes it possible for some boot instructions to be not permanent. CMOS is an acronym for Complementary Metal Oxide Semiconductor. It is powered by a battery that is integrated in the motherboard to retain vital data about your computer system configuration, such as hard disk drive specifications and the date and time—even when your computer is turned off. If information about the hard disk was permanently stored in ROM, you would never be able to replace your hard disk drive with a larger one, because the computer could not access the new hard disk using information about the old disk. In many of today's computers, the CMOS chip is housed within the same chip carrier as the ROM BIOS.

  CMOS provides your computer with a type of memory that is more permanent than RAM, but less permanent than ROM. When your system configuration changes, the data in the CMOS memory must be updated. See Figure E-13. To change the CMOS data, you usually run a CMOS setup program. Some operating systems have special utilities that help you update the CMOS settings so that hardware can be changed on any computer system. For example, the **Plug and Play** feature of most of today's computers helps you update CMOS if you install a new peripheral device.

The difference between memory types: RAM is temporary; virtual memory is disk-based; ROM is permanent; CMOS is battery-powered and more permanent than RAM but less permanent than ROM.

3. The spreadsheet program can now be loaded into the RAM vacated by the least-used segment of the word processing program.

1. Your computer is running a word processing program that takes up most of the program area in RAM, but you want to run a spreadsheet program at the same time.

2. The operating system moves the least-used segment of the word processing program into virtual memory on disk.

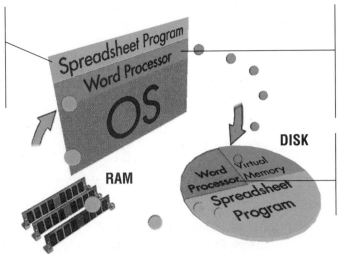

FIGURE E-12: *ROM BIOS is housed in one or more ROM chips on the motherboard*

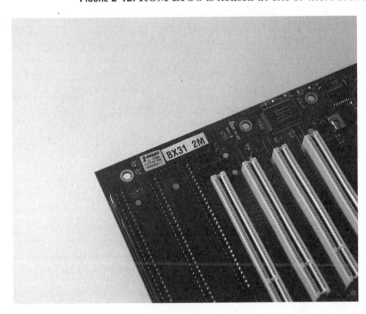

FIGURE E-13: *CMOS holds computer configuration settings*

SCREENTOUR

CMOS holds computer configuration settings, such as the date and time, hard disk capacity, number of floppy disks, and RAM capacity.

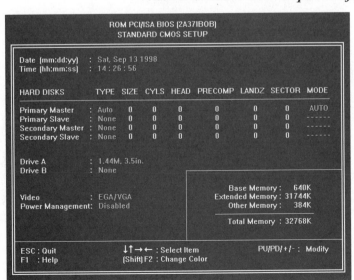

Defining the CPU

Digital computers represent data by using a series of electrical signals; data can be held in memory or transported over the data bus. But a computer does more than store and transport data. It processes data, performs arithmetic, sorts lists, formats documents, and so on. The computer processes data in the CPU.

InfoWeb
CPUs

Lab
CPU SIMULATOR

DETAILS

- The **CPU** (**central processing unit**) is the circuitry in a computer that performs arithmetic and logic operations and executes instructions. The CPU receives instructions and data from RAM, processes it, and then places the data in RAM to be displayed or stored. See Figure E-14.

- At one time, CPUs were large, unreliable, expensive devices that used a lot of electrical power. The ENIAC pictured in Figure E-15 was built in 1944, had 20 processing units, each of which was about 2 feet wide and 8 feet high. Today, this circuitry fits on an integrated circuit less than 560 mils (0.56 inch) square.

- The CPU on a mainframe usually consists of one or more integrated circuits and circuit boards. In a microcomputer, the CPU is a single integrated circuit called a **microprocessor**. The microprocessors in today's microcomputers might be housed in a large SEC, as shown in Figure E-16, or in a smaller square PGA.

- Most of today's PCs are designed around microprocessors manufactured by Intel or AMD. Intel created the first processor for the first IBM PC. Computers that contain Intel processors are more expensive than computers that contain "work-alike" processors from other manufacturers. Intel also produces a budget processor called a Celeron, which has slightly less sophisticated architecture than the Pentium models.

- Companies such as Cyrix and AMD produce "work-alike" processors. Computers with such processors are generally less expensive than an equivalent computer with an Intel processor.

- Macintosh computers use a 68000-series or PowerPC microprocessor. Until 1994, Macintosh computers contained a 68000-series microprocessor manufactured by Motorola. More recent models, called Power Macs, contain a PowerPC microprocessor that implements RISC architecture to provide relatively fast performance at a low cost. You'll learn more about RISC in a later lesson.

Evolution of the microprocessor

The original IBM PC used the Intel 8088 microprocessor, one of the first models in the x86 family of microprocessors. Most of the microprocessors manufactured by Intel are still members of the x86 family, but have evolved into the Pentium lines. The x86 chip family (286, 386, 486) descended from Intel's 8086 microprocessor. For the next-generation chip (80586),

however, Intel broke with the tradition of naming the chip based on its last three numbers. Initially, the 80586 chip was dubbed the P5, until it was officially renamed the Pentium in 1993. From 1993 forward, the Intel chips use Pentium as part of their name. In 1995, Intel produced the P6 generation of processors, called the Pentium Pro. In 1997, the company

launched two new processors: the Pentium with MMX technology, which was a jazzed-up version of the original Pentium chip and contained circuitry to speed the execution of multimedia applications; and the Pentium II, which added MMX technology to the Pentium Pro chip. Current Intel chips include Pentium II Xeon, Pentium III, and Pentium III Xeon.

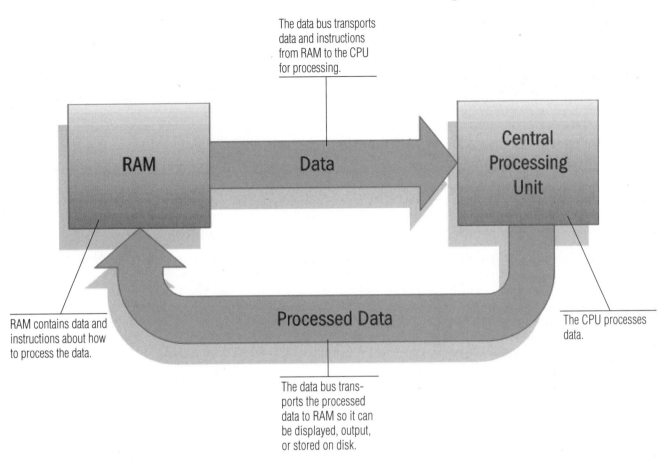

The data bus transports data and instructions from RAM to the CPU for processing.

RAM

Data

Central Processing Unit

Processed Data

RAM contains data and instructions about how to process the data.

The CPU processes data.

The data bus transports the processed data to RAM so it can be displayed, output, or stored on disk.

FIGURE E-15: *The ENIAC CPU*

FIGURE E-16: *A typical CPU in today's computers*

Understanding CPU architecture

The CPU has two main parts: the arithmetic logic unit and the control unit. Each of these units performs specific tasks to process data. A computer accomplishes a complex task by performing a series of very simple steps, referred to as instructions. Each instruction tells the computer to carry out one specific arithmetic, logical, or control operation. Many instructions are required to accomplish a task such as adding a column of numbers. This lesson looks at how the ALU and the control unit work together in a computer instruction.

RISC

DETAILS

○— The **arithmetic logic unit (ALU)** is the circuitry that performs arithmetic operations such as addition and subtraction. It also carries out logical operations such as comparing two numbers to see if they are the same. The ALU uses registers to hold the data that is being processed. In the ALU, the result of an arithmetic or logical operation is held temporarily in the accumulator. See Figure E-17.

○— The **control unit** is the circuitry that directs and coordinates processing. It makes a significant contribution to processing data efficiently, directing the movement of data, and scheduling processing. It retrieves each instruction in sequence from RAM, placing the instruction in a special instruction register. The control unit then interprets the instruction to find out what needs to be done. It helps get data into the ALU and tells the ALU what operation to perform. Based on its interpretation, the control unit sends signals to the data bus to fetch data from RAM and to the arithmetic logic unit to perform a process, as shown in Figure E-18.

○— The control unit uses an **instruction pointer** to keep track of the sequence of instructions to be processed. Using this pointer as a guide, it retrieves each instruction in sequence from RAM and places it in a special **instruction register**. The control unit then interprets the instruction to find out what needs to be done.

○— An **instruction set** is the list of instructions that a CPU can perform. Every task that a computer performs must be described in terms of the limited list of instructions in the instruction set. Like other data in the computer, instructions are stored as 1s and 0s. Using 1s and 0s for instructions allows the computer to store and transport the instructions as a series of electrical signals.

○— A computer instruction has two parts: the op code and the operands. An **op code** (short for "operation code") is a command word for an operation, such as add, compare, or jump. The **operands** for an instruction specify the data or the address of the data for the operation.

For example, a computer instruction might read JMP M1. Here, the op code is JMP and the operand is M1. The op code JMP means jump, or go, to a different instruction. The operand M1 is the RAM address of the instruction.

Figure E-19 shows part of a simple instruction set for a microprocessor. You will look at the instruction cycle in the next lesson.

○— As programmers developed various instruction sets for computers, they tended to add increasingly more complex instructions that took up many bytes in memory and required several clock cycles for execution. A computer based on a CPU with a complex instruction set came to be known as a **complex instruction set computer** (**CISC**).

○— The microprocessor of a **reduced instruction set computer** (**RISC**) has a limited set of instructions that it can perform very quickly. In theory, RISC computers should be faster than CISC computers for most processing tasks. In reality, a balance or hybrid of CISC and RISC technologies produces the most efficient and flexible computers.

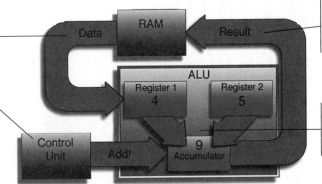

1. The data to be processed arrives from RAM and is held in registers.

2. A signal from the control unit indicates which arithmetic or logical operation to perform.

4. The results are usually sent to RAM so they can be output or stored on disk.

3. The ALU performs the operation and places the result in the accumulator.

FIGURE E-18: *How the control unit works*

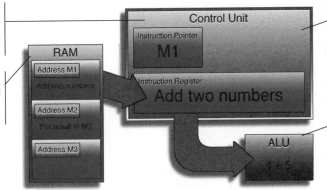

1. The control unit retrieves an instruction from RAM and puts it in the instruction register.

2. The RAM address of the instruction is kept in the instruction pointer. When the instruction has been executed, the address in the instruction pointer changes to indicate the RAM address of the next instruction to be executed.

3. The control unit interprets the instruction in its instruction register.

4. Depending on the instruction, the control unit will get data from RAM, tell the ALU to perform an operation, or change the memory address in the instruction pointer.

FIGURE E-19: *Part of a simple microprocessor instruction set*

INSTRUCTION SETS

OP CODE	OPERATION	EXAMPLE
INP	Input the given value into the specified memory address	INP 7 M1
CLA	Clear the accumulator to 0	CLA
MAM	Move the value from the accumulator to the specified memory location	MAM M1
MMR	Move the value from the specified memory location to the specified register	MMR M1 REG1
MRA	Move the value from the specified register to the accumulator	MRA REG1
MAR	Move the value from the accumulator to the specified register	MAR REG1
ADD	Add the values in two registers, place the results in the accumulator	ADD REG1 REG2
SUB	Subtract the value in the second register from the value in the first register, place the result in the accumulator	SUB REG1 REG2
JMP	Jump to the instruction at the specified memory address	JMP P2

Understanding the instruction cycle

The term **instruction cycle** refers to the process in which a computer executes a single instruction. The instruction cycle is repeated each time the computer executes an instruction. Figure E-20 summarizes the steps in this cycle. As you'll recall, the ALU performs arithmetic and logical operations and the control unit retrieves data from RAM and tells the ALU which operation to perform. Figure E-21 explains how the ALU, control unit, and RAM work together to process instructions.

FIGURE E-20: *The instruction cycle*

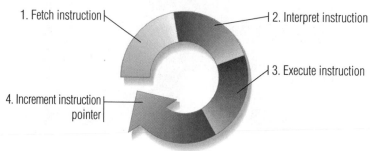

1. Fetch instruction
2. Interpret instruction
3. Execute instruction
4. Increment instruction pointer

FIGURE E-21: *Processing instructions*

1. The instruction pointer indicates the memory location that holds the first instruction (M1).

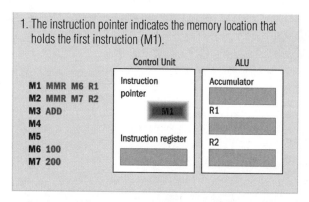

2. The computer fetches the instruction and puts it into the instruction register.

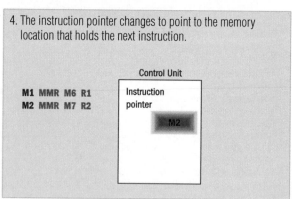

3. The computer executes the instruction that is in the instruction register; it moves the contents of M6 into register 1 of the ALU.

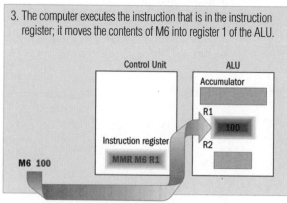

4. The instruction pointer changes to point to the memory location that holds the next instruction.

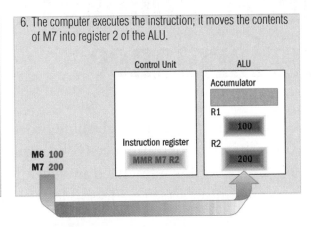

5. The computer fetches the instruction and puts it in the instruction register.

M1 MMR M6 R1
M2 MMR M7 R2

Control Unit

Instruction pointer

M2

Instruction register

MMR M7 R2

6. The computer executes the instruction; it moves the contents of M7 into register 2 of the ALU.

Control Unit

ALU

Accumulator

R1

100

Instruction register

R2

MMR M7 R2

200

M6 100
M7 200

7. The instruction pointer changes to point to the next instruction.

Control Unit

Instruction pointer

M3

8. The computer fetches the instruction and puts it in the instruction register.

M1 MMR M6 R1
M2 MMR M7 R2
M3 ADD

Control Unit

Instruction pointer

M3

Instruction register

ADD

9. The computer executes the instruction. The result is put in the accumulator.

Control Unit

ALU

Accumulator

300

R1

100

Instruction register

R2

ADD

200

Moore's Law

Advances in integrated circuits have been unprecedented. As the capacity of integrated circuits has increased, so has their ability to process instructions. In 1965, Gordon Moore, cofounder of chip-production giant, Intel Corporation, predicted that the number of transistors on a chip would double every 18 to 24 months. Much to the surprise of engineers and Moore himself, Moore's law accurately predicted 30 years of chip development. In 1958, the first integrated circuit contained two transistors. The Pentium III Xeon processor, introduced in 1999, has 9.5 million transistors.

Understanding CPU performance

All CPUs are not created equal; some process data more quickly than others. A computer system with a high-performance CPU might not necessarily provide great overall performance. CPU speed is influenced by several factors, including clock rate, word size, cache, and instruction set size. This lesson looks at the factors that affect CPU performance.

DETAILS

⊶ A computer contains a **system clock** that emits pulses to establish the timing for all system operations. The system clock operates at a speed quite different from that of a clock that keeps track of the time of day. It determines the speed at which the computer can execute an instruction and, therefore, limits the number of instructions that the computer can complete within a specific amount of time. The time to complete an instruction execution cycle is measured in **megahertz (MHz)**, or millions of cycles per second.

Although some instructions require multiple cycles to complete, you can think of processor speed as the number of instructions that the processor can execute in one second. Today, microprocessor speeds exceed 600 MHz. If all other specifications are identical, higher megahertz ratings mean faster processing.

⊶ **Word size** refers to the number of bits that the CPU can manipulate at one time. It is based on the size of the registers in the CPU and the number of data lines in the data bus. For example, a CPU with an 8-bit word size is referred to as an 8-bit processor; it has 8-bit registers and manipulates 8 bits at a time. Processing more data in each cycle contributes to increased performance. Today's faster computers use 32-bit or 64-bit microprocessors. All other factors being equal, a larger word size means faster processing.

⊶ **Cache** is special high-speed memory that gives the microprocessor more rapid access to data, because a high-speed microprocessor can execute an instruction so quickly that it often waits for data to be delivered from RAM. Cache is sometimes called RAM cache or cache memory. The cache ensures that data is immediately available whenever the CPU requests it. All other factors being equal, more cache means faster processing.

⊶ Computers with a single processor execute one instruction at a time—that is, "serially." Usually, the processor must complete all four steps in the instruction cycle before it begins to execute the next instruction. Using a technology called **pipelining**, however, the processor begins executing an instruction before it completes the previous instruction. See Figure E-22. Pipelining speeds up processing in a computer with a single processor, and it can also be implemented on computers with multiple processors.

⊶ A computer that has more than one processor can execute multiple instructions at the same time. This method of executing instructions is called parallel processing. **Parallel processing** increases the amount of processing that a computer can accomplish in a specific amount of time. Special software is required to take advantage of parallel processing. Figure E-23 explains this concept in more detail.

⊶ As the saying goes, a chain is only as strong as its weakest link. A computer system might also have weak links. Even if it has a high-performance processor, a computer system with a slow hard disk, no disk cache, and a small amount of RAM is likely to perform slowly at tasks such as starting programs, loading data files, printing, and scrolling through long documents.

Disk cache and RAM cache are not identical. Disk cache works with data between the disk and memory. RAM cache works with data between RAM and the CPU.

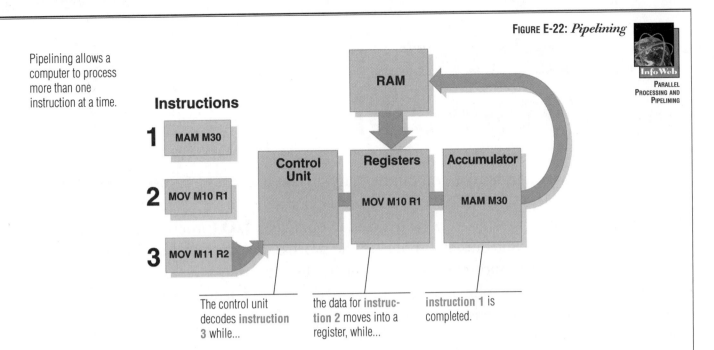

FIGURE E-22: *Pipelining*

PARALLEL PROCESSING AND PIPELINING

Pipelining allows a computer to process more than one instruction at a time.

The control unit decodes **instruction 3** while...

the data for **instruction 2** moves into a register, while...

instruction 1 is completed.

FIGURE E-23: *Parallel processing*

Parallel processing uses more than one processor to increase the number of instructions that can be executed in a specific amount of time.

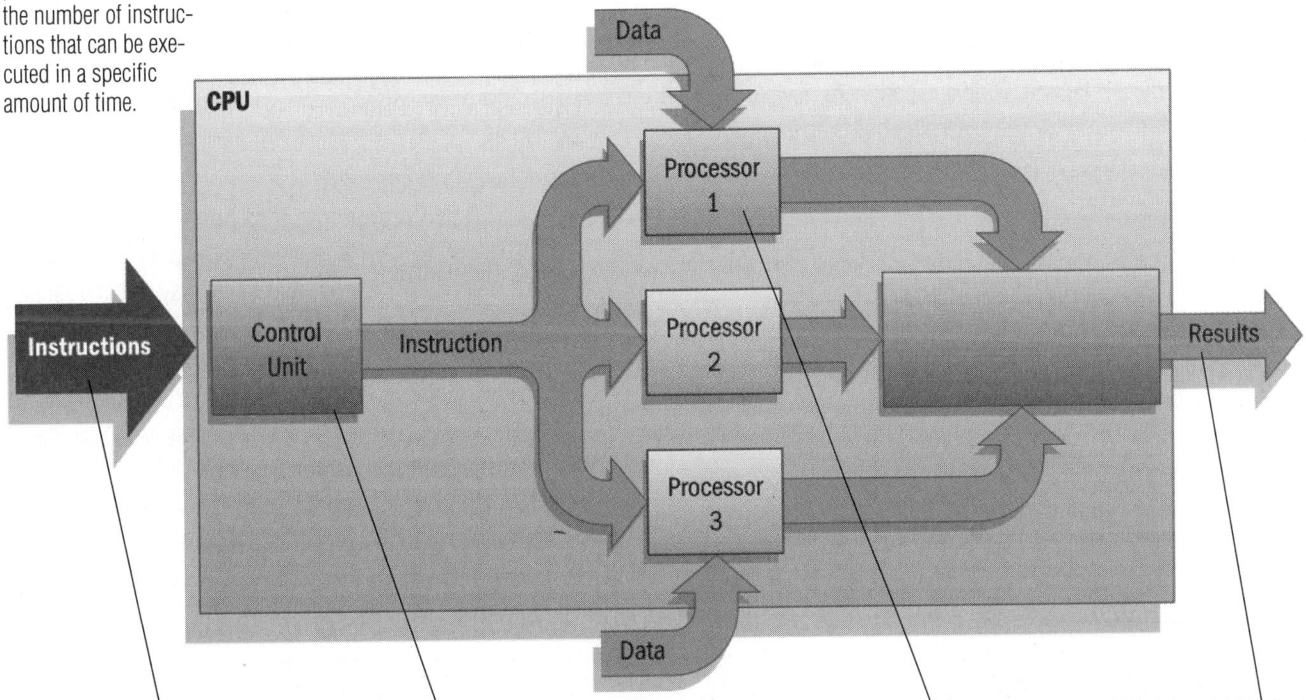

1. Instructions are queued and waiting to enter the CPU.

2. The control unit sends an instruction to the next available processor.

3. Each processor completes its assigned instruction using data that has been transported from RAM into the CPU registers. Because the processors finish at different times, the results might not be in sequence.

4. The results are placed in the correct sequence and sent out of the CPU.

Learning about input/output (I/O)

When you purchase a computer, you can be fairly certain that before its useful life ends, you will want to add equipment to expand its capabilities. If you understand computer I/O, you will see how it is possible to expand a computer system. **I/O** (pronounced "eye-oh") is computer jargon for input/output. It refers to the process of collecting data for the microprocessor to manipulate and transporting results to display, print, and storage devices. I/O between the CPU and peripheral devices often involves a long path that moves data over the expansion bus, slots, cards, ports, and cables. Figure E-24 provides an overview of I/O architecture.

DETAILS

☞ You have already learned that a data bus transports data between RAM and the CPU. The data bus also extends to other parts of the computer. The segment of the data bus that transports data between RAM and peripheral devices is called the **expansion bus**. The expansion bus is an extension of the data bus that terminates at an expansion slot.

☞ An **expansion card** is a small circuit board that can connect a device to your computer and add capabilities to your computer, such as controlling a storage, input, or output device.

An expansion card, which is also referred to as an expansion board or controller card, plugs into an expansion slot. It provides the I/O circuitry for peripheral devices. Today's microcomputers typically contain a **graphics card** for connecting the monitor, a **modem** for transmitting data over phone or cable lines, and a **sound card** for connecting speakers, headphones, and a microphone. You usually have to add expansion cards if you want to connect a scanner, digitize videos, or link your computer to a network. Figure E-25 shows how expansion cards simply slide into an expansion slot and then can be secured to the system unit with a small screw.

☞ A microcomputer motherboard typically has three types of expansion slots: AGP, PCI, and ISA. These slots have different lengths, so you can readily identify them on the motherboard. Refer to Figure E-26.

- **AGP (accelerated graphics port)** slots are primarily used for graphics cards and are faster than a PCI slot. They provide a high-speed data pathway that is useful for 3-D graphics.
- **PCI (peripheral component connect)** slots offer faster transfer speeds and a 64-bit data bus. They typically house graphics cards, sound cards, video capture cards, modems, or network interface cards.
- **ISA (industry standard architecture)** slots are an older technology, used today for some modems and other relatively slow devices. Many new computers have few or no ISA slots.

Modems

Many computer systems include a modem. Modems are used to transmit and receive data over phone lines to other computers and to connect to the Internet. The speed of transmission is usually described in terms of baud rate, which is determined by the number of signal changes that occur in one second during transmission. Faster baud rates mean faster data transmission.

A fax-modem is a modem that can send a document that is in the memory of your computer to any standard fax machine, where it prints in hard copy format. Modems with fax capability can also receive fax transmissions from standard fax machines or other fax-modems.

If your computer system includes a modem, it probably has communications software as well. Some communications software packages allow you to set up your computer as an answering machine or voice-mail system.

FIGURE E-24: *I/O architecture transports data to motherboard components and to peripheral devices*

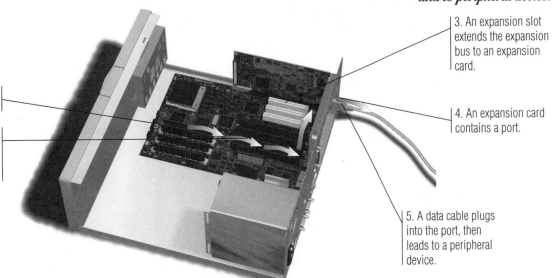

1. Data originates in RAM.

2. The expansion bus transports data along circuits on the motherboard.

3. An expansion slot extends the expansion bus to an expansion card.

4. An expansion card contains a port.

5. A data cable plugs into the port, then leads to a peripheral device.

FIGURE E-25: *Expansion card in expansion slot*

▶ Expansion cards simply slide into an expansion slot, then can be secured to the system unit case with a small screw.

An expansion card has a "card edge" connector with metal contacts that connect the circuitry on the card to the circuitry on the motherboard. ▼

FIGURE E-26: *Expansion slots*

AGP, PCI, and ISA slots are different lengths, so you can easily identify them by opening your computer's system unit and looking at the motherboard.

ISA slots ⊢

⊣ AGP slot

⊣ PCI slots

COMPUTER ARCHITECTURE ◀ **E-21**

Planning for expansion

Most microcomputers have four to eight expansion slots. The number of empty slots in your computer determines its expandability. Expanding your system involves purchasing and installing additional hardware. Expansion hardware is required when adding printers, modems, and many other peripheral devices. Each peripheral device has specific requirements.

DETAILS

- To find out if you have adequate expansion capability, turn your computer off, unplug it, and then open the system unit case.

- An **expansion port** is a connector that passes data in and out of a computer or peripheral device. To connect a peripheral device to an expansion card, you plug a cable from the peripheral device into the expansion port on the expansion card. An expansion port is often housed on an expansion card so that it is accessible through a hole in the back of the computer system unit; alternatively, it might be connected directly to the motherboard. Figure E-27 shows the shapes of frequently used expansion ports.

- If a cable is supplied along with a peripheral device, you can usually match the shape of the cable connector to the port. If you must purchase a cable, you need to know the correct type and designation (such as DB-9 or C-50). The first part of the designation indicates the shape of the connector. DB and C connectors are trapezoidal; DIN connectors are round. The second part of the designation indicates the number of pins. Figure E-28 shows examples of common connectors and cables.

- A **parallel port** provides a connection for transmitting data eight bits at a time over a cable with eight separate data lines. Because all eight bits travel at the same time, parallel transmission is relatively fast. This type of transmission is typically used to send data to a printer. In a microcomputer, the parallel port is either built into the motherboard or mounted on an expansion card. The cable that connects two parallel ports contains 25 wires. Eight of the wires carry data, and the rest carry control signals that maintain orderly transmission and reception. Because the wires that carry data run parallel to each other, the signals in the cables tend to interfere with one another over long distances.

- A **serial port** provides a connection for transmitting data one bit at a time. A serial port connects your computer to a device that requires two-way data transmission (such as a modem) or to a device that requires only one-way data transmission (such as a mouse). A serial cable contains one data line and an assortment of control lines. Because a serial cable requires fewer data lines, it is less susceptible to interference than a parallel cable.

- The system unit provides openings called **bays** for mounting disk, CD-ROM, and tape drives. An external bay provides an opening for installing a device that you need to access from the outside of the case, such as a floppy disk drive. An internal bay provides a mounting bracket for devices that don't need outside accessibility, such as a hard disk drive.

- A **docking station** is essentially an additional expansion bus into which you plug your notebook computer. It provides expansion slots for cards that would not fit into a notebook case.

- A **PCMCIA slot** (Personal Computer Memory Card International Association) is a special type of expansion slot developed for notebook computers, which do not have space in the case for full-size expansion slots and cards. A PCMCIA slot is a small, external slot into which you can insert a PCMCIA card. PCMCIA cards are credit-card-sized circuit boards that incorporate an expansion card and a device. They can contain modems, memory expansion, or even hard disk drives. Unlike traditional expansion cards, PCMCIA devices can be plugged in or removed without turning the computer off.

To many computer users, the back of a computer is a confusing array of unlabeled ports, connectors, and cables. This figure will help you become familiar with the shapes of the most frequently used expansion ports.

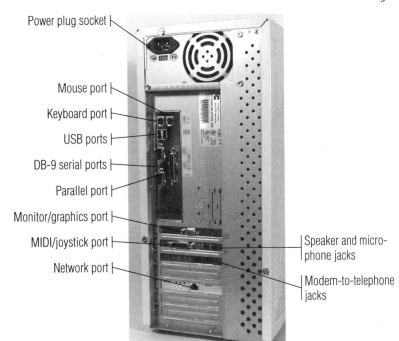

Power plug socket

Mouse port

Keyboard port

USB ports

DB-9 serial ports

Parallel port

Monitor/graphics port

MIDI/joystick port

Network port

Speaker and micro-phone jacks

Modem-to-telephone jacks

InfoWeb
CONNECTORS

FIGURE E-28: *Microcomputer cables and connectors*

	CONNECTOR	DESCRIPTION	DEVICES
	Serial DB-9	Connects to serial port, which sends data over a single data line one bit at a time at speeds of 56 Kbps.	Mouse or modem
	Parallel DB-25M	Connects to parallel port, which sends data simultaneously over eight data lines at speeds of 12,000 Kbps.	Printer, external CD-ROM drive, Zip drive, external hard disk drive, tape backup device
	USB	Connects to universal serial bus (USB), which sends data over a single data line at speeds of 12,000 Kbps; supports up to 127 devices.	Modem, keyboards, joystick, scanner, mouse
	SCSI C-50F	Connects to SCSI ("scuzzy") port, which sends data simultaneously over 8 or 16 data lines at speeds between 5 MBps and 80 MBps; supports up to 16 devices.	Hard disk drive, scanner, CD-ROM drive, tape backup device
	IEEE 1394	Connects to the "FireWire" port, which sends data at 400,000 Kbps.	Video camera, DVD drive
	VGA DB-15	Connects to the video port.	Monitor

Learning about the boot process

The sequence of events that occurs between the time you turn on a computer and the time it is ready for you to issue commands is referred to as the **boot process.** Microcomputers, minicomputers, and mainframe computers all require a boot process. In this lesson, you'll learn about the microcomputer boot process. The main objective of the boot process is to get operating system files into RAM. Table E-1 summarizes the six steps in the boot process.

TROUBLE-
SHOOTING

TROUBLE-
SHOOTING

DETAILS

○━ *Power up:* The first things that happen when you turn the power on are that the fan in the power supply begins to spin and the power light on the case of the computer comes on. See Figure E-29.

○━ *Start boot program:* When you turn on the computer, the microprocessor begins to execute the boot program stored in ROM.

○━ *Power-on self-test:* The power-on self-test (POST) diagnoses problems in the computer. The computer checks whether the RAM, expansion cards, keyboard, and drives are functioning correctly.

○━ *Load operating system:* After successfully completing the POST, the computer continues to follow the instructions in ROM to load the operating system into RAM. See Figure E-30.

If your computer has a hard disk, you generally want drive C to be the default drive, so it is best not to put disks in any of the floppy disk drives until the boot process is complete. The computer first checks drive A to see whether it contains a disk. If a disk is present in this drive, then drive A becomes the default drive. If there is no disk in drive A but the computer has a drive C, the computer uses drive C as the default drive. The computer continues to use the default drive for the rest of the computing session unless you specify a different one.

Next, the computer tries to locate and load operating system files from the default drive. If these files do not exist on the disk, the boot process stops, and the screen displays an error

message such as "Non-system disk or disk error," "Cannot load a file," or "Bad or missing command interpreter." If you encounter one of these messages, turn off the computer and make sure that drive A is empty; then turn the computer on again. If the error message reappears, you should seek the assistance of a technical support person.

○━ *Check configuration and customization:* Early in the boot process, the computer checks CMOS to determine the amount of installed RAM and the types of available disk drives. Often, however, more configuration data is needed for the computer to properly access all available devices. In the next stage of the boot process, the computer searches the boot disk for configuration files.

It also searches the default drive for customized startup instructions. On some computers, these instructions are stored in a file called Autoexec.bat or a Windows startup group, which you can modify to customize your computing environment.

○━ *Ready for commands and data:* The boot process is complete when the computer is ready to accept your commands. Usually, the computer displays the operating system main screen or prompt at the end of the boot process. If you are using Windows, you will see the Windows desktop. If you are using DOS, you will see the operating system prompt.

○━ Problems may show up during the boot process. If Windows cannot complete the boot process, you can select Safe Mode and shut down your computer, then restart it.

Step Number	Step	What Happens
1	Power up	When you turn on the power switch, the power light is illuminated, and power is distributed to the internal fan and motherboard
2	Start boot program	The microprocessor begins to execute the instructions stored in ROM
3	Power-on self-test	The computer performs diagnostic tests of RAM, extension cards, keyboard, and disk drives
4	Load operating system	The operating system is copied from a disk to RAM
5	Check configuration and customization	The microprocessor reads configuration data and executes any customized startup routines specified by the user
6	Ready for commands and data	The computer is ready for you to enter commands and data

FIGURE E-29: *The light and fan*

When you turn on a computer, you should see the power light and hear the fan.

Power light

Fan

FIGURE E-30: *Loading the operating system*

1. If the computer finds a disk in drive A, that drive becomes the default drive.

2. If the computer cannot find a disk in drive A, it uses drive C as the default drive.

3. The computer loads the operating system from the default drive into RAM.

Just think how wealthy you would be if you had invented the computer, held a patent for its technology, and could collect even $1 in royalties for every computer ever sold. In 1973, a company called Sperry-Rand claimed to hold a patent on the technology for electronic digital computers. If the courts had upheld this claim, then no company would have been able to manufacture computers without obtaining a license from and paying royalties to Sperry-Rand. As you might expect, other computer companies, such as IBM, took issue with Sperry-Rand's claim. During the ensuing court battle, opposition lawyers suggested a surprising number of candidates as the "inventor" of the computer. You can read the brief sketches of these candidates and their machines, and then do some supplementary research on the Web, before deciding who you think invented the computer.

During the period 1821-1832, Charles Babbage drew up plans for a machine that he called the Analytical Engine. Like modern computers, this device was designed to be programmable. It would accept input from a set of punched cards that contained the instructions for performing calculations. The plans for the Analytical Engine called for it to store the results of intermediary calculations in a sort of memory. Results would be printed on paper. Babbage intended to power his device using a steam engine, which was the cutting-edge technology of his day. Unfortunately, Babbage worked on this machine for 11 years but never completed it.

In 1939, John Atanasoff began to construct a machine that came to be known as the Atanasoff-Berry Computer (ABC). Like today's computers, the ABC was powered by electricity, but it used vacuum tubes instead of integrated circuits. This machine was designed to accept input, store the intermediary results of calculations, and produce output. Unlike today's computers, the ABC was not a multipurpose machine. Instead, it was designed for a single purpose—finding solutions to systems of linear equations.

Atanasoff never completed the ABC, but he shared his ideas and technology with John Mauchly and J. Presper Eckert, who were working on plans for the ENIAC (Electronic Numerical Integrator and Computer). Like the ABC, the ENIAC was powered by electricity and used vacuum tubes for its computational circuitry. The machine could be "programmed" by rewiring its circuitry and it produced printed output. ENIAC went online in 1946. Eckert and Mauchly filed for a patent on their technology and formed a company that became Sperry-Rand.

The ENIAC was not originally designed to store a program in memory, along with data. The stored program concept—a key feature of today's computers—was proposed by John von Neumann, who visited the ENIAC project and then collaborated with Eckert and Mauchly on the EDVAC computer, which was completed in 1949. The EDVAC was an electronic, digital computer that could accept input, process data, store data and programs, and produce output. Like the ENIAC, the EDVAC used vacuum tubes for its computational circuitry. Whereas the ENIAC worked with decimal numbers, however, the EDVAC worked with binary numbers much like today's computers.

In 1938, German scientist Conrad Zuse developed a binary, digital computer called the Z-1. Zuse had designed his machine as a programmable, general-purpose device with input, storage, processing, and output capabilities. Unlike the ABC and ENIAC, the Z-1 was not a fully electronic device. Instead of using electrical signals to represent data, it used mechanical relays.

Zuse's work was cloaked in secrecy during World War II, and scientists in Allied countries had little or no knowledge of his technology. It is somewhat surprising, therefore, that a similar machine was constructed in the United States by Howard Aiken, who was working with funding from IBM. The Harvard Mark I, completed in 1944, was powered by electricity, but used mechanical relays for its computational circuitry.

No list of computer inventors would be complete without Alan Turing, who worked with a group of British scientists, mathematicians, and engineers to create a completely electronic computing device in 1943. Called the Colossus, Turing's machine was essentially a huge version of Atanasoff's ABC—a special-purpose device (designed to break Nazi codes) powered by electricity, with vacuum tubes for its computing circuitry.

The roster of possible computer "inventors" includes Babbage, Atanasoff, Eckert and Mauchly, von Neumann, Zuse, Aiken, and Turing. Patents were filed only by IBM for Aiken's Mark I and by Eckert and Mauchly for the ENIAC. Should any of these inventors be collecting royalties on computer technology?

EXPAND THE IDEAS

1. The Sperry-Rand lawsuit ended with a ruling that the Eckert and Mauchly patent was not valid because the ENIAC inventors derived their ideas from Atanasoff. Do you think that this decision was correct? Write a one-page paper supporting your answer.

2. To be credited with the invention of the computer, do you think that the inventor would be required to have completed a working model? Why or why not? Research patent information to provide background information on what is required.

3. What key components do you believe define a computer? Detail the specific characteristics that made the "computer" different from any other machine.

4. Research the development and invention of the automobile. What are the similarities between the invention of the automobile and the invention of the computer? Find several examples of articles, documentaries, or news stories. Write a summary of each article or media piece. Analyze your findings. Was the media voice consistent? Why or why not?

5. Do you know anyone who holds a patent and gets a royalty for an invention? If you don't know anyone personally, research a recent invention. What made it a unique invention and eligible for patent and royalty rights? Compile your findings into a poster presentation.

End of Unit Exercises

STUDY TIPS

Study Tips help you organize and consolidate the information in a unit by making lists, outlines, charts, and sketches. You can use paper and pencil or word processing software to complete most of the Study Tips activities.

1. Use Figure E-8 to write out the ASCII code for the following phrase: *Way Cool!*

2. Imagine you are a teacher. Write a one- or two-page script explaining the instruction cycle to your class. Design at least three visual aids you would use as illustrations.

3. Think about the concepts in this unit: digital electronics, memory, central processing unit, and I/O. Using these concepts, put together your own description of how a computer processes data. You can use a narrative description and/or sketches.

4. For each type of memory (RAM, ROM, CMOS, and virtual), answer the following questions:
   a. What role does it play in the overall process of computing?
   b. What types of data does it hold?
   c. Does it store data permanently or temporarily?

5. Write the name of the memory category best suited for each task: **RAM**, **virtual memory**, **ROM**, or **CMOS**.
   Holds user data such as documents
   Holds program instructions such as a word processor
   Holds boot program
   Holds configuration data for the hard disk type
   Temporary
   Permanent
   Battery-powered
   Disk-based

6. Write a brief description of each type of memory:
   RAM _____
   _____

   Virtual memory _____
   _____

   ROM _____
   _____

   CMOS _____
   _____

FILL IN THE BEST ANSWER

1. A(n) _____ is a collection of microscopic circuit elements such as wires, transistors, capacitors, and resistors packed onto a very small square of silicon.

2. The _____ number system represents numeric data as a series of 1s and 0s.

3. Each _____ in a digital computer is either on or off.

4. Data travels from one location to another within a computer on a circuit called a(n) _____.

5. The smallest unit of information in a computer is a(n) _____.

6. A series of eight bits is referred to as a(n) _____

7. A computer uses the _____ or _____ codes to represent character data.

8. Having a steady power source is important for a computer because RAM is _____.

9. RAM is measured in_____.

10. In RAM, microscopic electronic parts called _____ hold the electrical signals that represent data.

11. If your computer does not have enough RAM to run several programs at once, your computer operating system might use _____ to simulate RAM with disk-based memory.

12. The series of instructions that a computer performs when it is first turned on are permanently stored in _____.

13. System configuration information, such as the format of the hard disk drive, is stored in battery-backed memory called _____.

14. A microcomputer uses a(n) _____ as its CPU.

15. The _____ in the CPU performs arithmetic and logical operations such as adding or comparing two numbers.

16. The _____ in the CPU directs and coordinates the operation of the entire computer system.

17. A computer instruction has two parts: the _____ and the _____.

18. The four steps in the instruction cycle are _____, _____, _____, and _____.

19. Factors that affect the speed of a microprocessor are _____, _____, _____, and _____.

20. A(n) _____ is an electronic path that transports data between RAM and expansion slots.

21. A(n) _____ is a small circuit board that plugs into an expansion slot.

22. A(n) _____ _____ is a connector that passes data in and out of a computer or peripheral device and is often housed on an expansion card so that it is accessible through a hole in the back of the computer system unit.

23. Two types of expansion ports are _____ and _____.

24. A DB-9 connector has _____ pins.

25. When you boot your computer, the _____ is copied from a disk to RAM.

INDEPENDENT CHALLENGE 1

It is important that you familiarize yourself with the type of computer with which you are working. You may need to consult the computer resource person at your school or the manual that came with your computer to answer these questions.

To complete this independent challenge:

1. With the computer running, identify all of the components of your computer.

  a. What type of computer are you using?
  b. How much RAM does the computer have?
  c. Which microprocessor is inside your computer?
  d. What is the clock speed of your computer?
  e. Do you have a high-speed bus? If so, what kind?
  f. Is your system set up for cache memory? What kind and how much?

2. Turn the computer off.

  a. Draw a sketch of and label each of the components you see.
  b. What kind of system unit case do you have?
  c. Which devices are connected to external slots?
  d. Do you have any expansion slots?
  e. If you are using a notebook computer, do you have a PCMCIA slot?
  f. Do you have a docking station?
  g. How many bays does your computer have? Internal? External?

INDEPENDENT CHALLENGE 2

Computers would not be available for individual use today if not for the invention of the integrated circuit. Just four months apart in 1959, Jack Kilby and Robert Noyce independently created working models of the circuit that was to transform the computer industry. Jack Kilby worked at Texas Instruments, and you can find reproductions of his original research notes on the Web. Robert Noyce developed the integrated circuit while CEO of Fairchild Semiconductor. He left Fairchild to form Intel.

To complete this independent challenge:

1. Use your library and Internet resources to research the impact of the integrated circuit on the computer industry. You can take a tour of the history of innovation on Texas Instruments' Web site by going to *www.ti.com/corp/docs/company/history/tihistory.htm*.

2. Complete one of the following written assignments:

  a. Write a two- to three-page paper summarizing how the integrated circuit was used in the first five years after it was invented.
  b. Write two one-page biographical sketches: one of Jack Kilby and one of Robert Noyce.
  c. Create a diagram of the "family tree" of computer technologies that resulted from the development of the integrated circuit.

INDEPENDENT CHALLENGE 3

Pretend you are a computer industry analyst preparing an article on computer memory for a popular computer magazine.

To complete this independent challenge:

Gather as much information as you can about RAM, including current pricing, the amount of RAM that comes installed in a typical computer, tips for adding RAM to computers, and so forth. If you have Internet access, you might find useful information at various Web sites. Use a word processor to write a one- to two-page article that would help your magazine's readers understand RAM.

INDEPENDENT CHALLENGE 4

In this unit, you learned about the microprocessor of a reduced instruction set computer (RISC).

To complete this independent challenge:

Research RISC, then write a one- to two-page paper about RISC technology. You might look at the use of RISC processors for the type of powerful workstation typically employed for engineering and CAD applications.

In 1994, Intel released the Pentium microprocessor. Within a matter of weeks, rumors began to circulate that the Pentium chip had a bug that caused errors in some calculations. As the rumors spread, corporate computer users became nervous about the numbers that appeared on spreadsheets calculated on computers with the Pentium processor.

To complete this independent challenge, write a short essay to answer these questions:

1. How can a computer make such mistakes? Are computers with Pentium processors destined for the dumpster? Is there any way users can save the money they have invested in their Pentium computers?

2. Suppose you own a computer store that sold many computers with the flawed Pentium microprocessor. Your customers are calling you to get the facts. Use your library and Internet resources to gather as much reliable information as you can about the Pentium flaw. Use this information to write a one-page information sheet for your customers. You might use the following resources:

- Your favorite search engine to look for information about the Pentium bug
- Intel's Internet site: *www.intel.com*
- The article "The Truth Behind the Pentium Bug," *Byte*, March 1995.

LAB: CPU SIMULATOR

In a computer's CPU, the ALU performs instructions orchestrated by the control unit. Processing proceeds at a lightning pace, but each instruction accomplishes only a small step in the entire process. In this lab, you work with an animated CPU simulation to learn how computers execute assembly language programs. In the Explore section of the lab, you have an opportunity to interpret programs, find program errors, and write your own short assembly language programs.

1. Click the Steps button to learn how to work the simulated CPU. As you proceed through the Steps, answer all of the QuickCheck questions that appear. After you complete the Steps, you will see a QuickCheck Report. Follow the instructions on the screen if you want to print this report.

2. Click the Explore button. Use the File menu to open the program called Add.cpu. Use the Fetch Instruction and Execute Instruction buttons to step through the program. Then answer the following questions:

a. How many instructions does this program contain?

b. Where is the instruction pointer after the program is loaded, but before it executes?

c. What does the INP 3 M1 instruction accomplish?

d. What does the MMR M1 REG1 instruction accomplish?

e. Which memory location holds the instruction that adds the two numbers in REG1 and REG2?

f. What is in the accumulator when the program execution is complete?

g. Which memory address holds the sum of the two numbers when program execution is completed?

3. In Explore, use the File menu to open the program called count5.cpu. Use the Fetch Instruction and Execute Instruction buttons to step through the program. Then answer the following questions:

a. What are the two input values for this program?

b. What happens to the value in REG1 as the program executes?

c. What happens when the program executes the JPZ P5 instruction?

d. What are the final values in the accumulator and registers when program execution is complete?

4. In Explore, click File, then click New to make sure the CPU is empty. Write a program that follows these steps to add 8 and 6:

a. Input 8 into memory address M3.

b. Input 6 into memory address M5.

c. Move the number in M3 to Register 1.

d. Move the number in M5 to Register 2.

e. Add the numbers in the registers.

f. Move the value in the accumulator to memory address M1.

g. Tell the program to halt.

Test your program to make sure it produces the answer 14 in address M1. When you are sure that your program works, use the File menu to print your program.

5. In Explore, use the File menu to open the program called *Bad1.cpu*. This program is supposed to multiply two numbers together and put the result in memory location M3. The program contains an error, however.

a. Which memory location holds the incorrect instruction?

b. What instruction will make this program produce the correct result?

6. In Explore, use the CPU simulator to write a program to calculate the volume, in cubic feet, of the inside of a refrigerator. The answer should appear in the accumulator at the end of the program. The inside dimensions of the refrigerator are 5 feet by 3 feet by 2 feet. Test your program, then print it.

LAB: TROUBLESHOOTING

Computers sometimes malfunction, so it is useful to have some skill at diagnosing, if not fixing, some of the hardware problems you might encounter. In this lab, you use a simulated computer that has trouble booting. You learn to make and test hypotheses that help you diagnose the cause of boot problems.

1. Click the Steps button to learn how to make and test hypotheses about hardware malfunctions during the boot process. As you proceed through the Steps, answer all of the QuickCheck questions that appear. After you complete the Steps, you will see a QuickCheck Report. Follow the instructions on the screen if you want to print this report.

2. Click the Explore button. Use the File menu to load *System11.trb*. Click the Boot Computer button and watch what happens on the simulated computer (in this case, what does not happen!). State a hypothesis about why this computer does not boot. Use the Check menu to check the state of various cables and switches. When you think you know the cause of the problem, select it from the Diagnosis list. If you correctly diagnosed the problem, write it down. If your diagnosis was not correct, form another hypothesis and check it, until you correctly diagnose the problem.

3. Sometimes problems that appear very similar result from different causes. In Explore, use the File menu to load *System03.trb*, then diagnose the problem. Do the same for *System06.trb*. Describe the problems with these two systems. Then describe the similarities and differences in their symptoms.

4. In Explore, use the File menu to load *System02* and *System08*. Both systems produce keyboard errors, but these errors have different causes. Describe what caused the problem in *System02*, and what caused the problem in *System08*. Once you have diagnosed these problems, what can you do about them?

5. In Explore, use the File menu to load Systems 04, 05, 07, 09, and 14. These systems produce similar symptoms when booting, but they have different problems. Diagnose the problem with each system and indicate the key factor (the symptom or what you checked) that led to your diagnosis.

LESSON	MEDIA ELEMENT	LESSON	MEDIA ELEMENT
Examining the inside of a system unit	INSIDE THE CASE / INTEGRATED CIRCUITS / MOTHERBOARDS / VIDEO / VIDEO	Understanding CPU architecture	RISC / INSTRUCTION SETS
Defining data representation and transport	VIDEO	Understanding CPU performance	PARALLEL PROCESSING AND PIPELINING
Understanding computer memory: RAM	MEMORY TECHNOLOGY / GRACE HOPPER	Learning about input/output (I/O)	VIDEO
Categorizing computer memory	SCREENTOUR	Planning for expansion	CONNECTORS
Defining the CPU	CPUs / VIDEO / CPU SIMULATOR	Learning about the boot process	TROUBLESHOOTING / TROUBLESHOOTING

VISUAL WORKSHOP

Identify the six components labeled on the figure and write a short description of each.

1._____
2._____
3._____
4._____
5._____
6._____

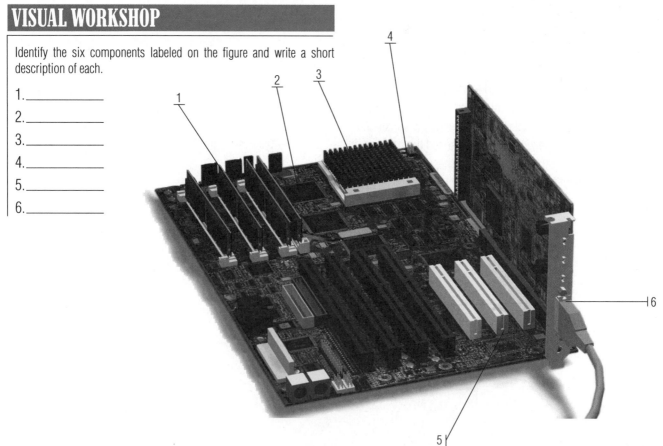

Computer Networks and E-mail

The idea that microcomputer users could benefit by connecting their computers into a network became feasible in the mid-1980s with the introduction of reliable, reasonably priced software and hardware designed for microcomputer networks. The availability of this hardware and software ushered in a new era of computing, which has provided an increasing number of ways for people to collaborate, communicate, and interact. The purpose of this unit is to help you understand the type of local area network you would typically find in a college, university, or business. The unit begins with an overview of computer networks, and then presents practical information on network hardware and software, including network applications such as groupware and electronic mail.

Defining computer networks

A computer network is a collection of computers and other devices that communicate to share data, hardware, and software. A network that is located within a relatively limited area, such as a building or campus, is referred to as a **local area network (LAN)**. LANs are found in most businesses, government offices, and educational institutions. Most users and technical support people refer to LANs simply as "networks." A network that covers a large geographical area is referred to as a **wide area network (WAN)**. Not all networks are the same. The various types of networks provide different services, use different technology, have different resources, and require users to follow different procedures.

LANs

DETAILS

- A computer that is not connected to a network is referred to as **a stand-alone computer**. When you physically connect your computer to a local area network, using a cable or other communications channel, your computer becomes a **workstation** on the network, and you become a "network user." A network workstation is not the same as a "high-end workstation," which consists of a high-performance microcomputer.

- Each device on a network, including workstations, servers, and printers, is referred to as a **node**. See Figure F-1.

- Your workstation has all of its usual resources, referred to as **local resources**, such as your hard drive, software, data, and printer. You also have access to **network resources**, which typically include application software, storage space for data files, and printers other than those available on your local workstation.

- A **network server** is a computer that is connected to the network and that "serves," or distributes, resources to network users.

- A **network printer** provides output capabilities to all network users.

- The main advantage of a computer network is that all users can share the same resources, instead of each user maintaining his or her own resources. See Figure F-2. For example, a LAN permits many users to share a single printer. Most organizations with LANs are able to reduce the overall number of printers needed, trim printer maintenance costs, and use the money saved to buy higher-quality printers.

Software licenses for networks

It would be very inexpensive for an organization to purchase a single copy of a software package and then place it on the network for everyone to use. In an organization with 100 users, for example, word processing software might cost $295 for a single copy, instead of $29,500 for 100 copies. Using a single-user license for multiple users, however, violates copyright law. Most single-user software licenses allow only one person to use the software at a time. Many software publishers offer a network license that permits use by multiple people on a network. Typically, such a network license will cost more than a single-user license, but less than purchasing single-user licenses for all of the users. For example, a word processing software package that costs $295 for a single-user license might have a $5,000 network license that allows as many as 100 people to use the software.

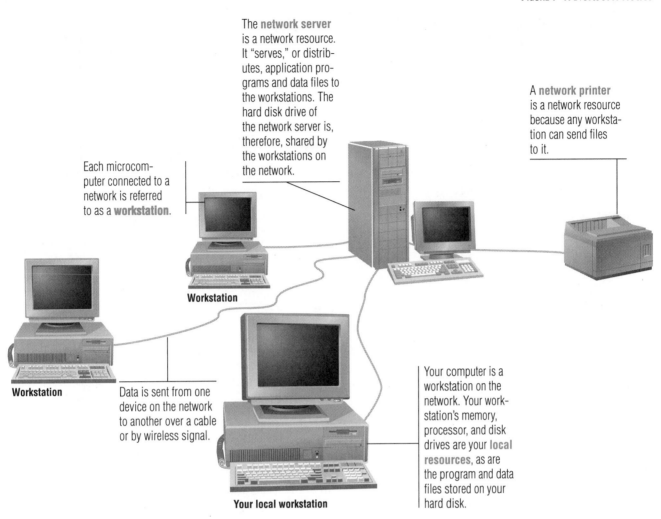

The **network server** is a network resource. It "serves," or distributes, application programs and data files to the workstations. The hard disk drive of the network server is, therefore, shared by the workstations on the network.

A **network printer** is a network resource because any workstation can send files to it.

Each microcomputer connected to a network is referred to as a **workstation**.

Workstation

Workstation

Data is sent from one device on the network to another over a cable or by wireless signal.

Your computer is a workstation on the network. Your workstation's memory, processor, and disk drives are your **local resources**, as are the program and data files stored on your hard disk.

Your local workstation

FIGURE F-2: *Sharing resources*

Administering computer networks

Most organizations restrict access to the software and data on a network by requiring users to log in. When you log in, you identify yourself to the network as a user by entering a valid user ID and password. Your user ID and password are the basis for your user account. As the login process continues, your workstation becomes connected to network drives, allowing you to use programs and data files stored on a server and to access network resources such as a network printer.

DETAILS

- A **user account** provides access to network resources and accumulates information about your network use by tracking when you log in and log out. To access your user account, you follow a login process.

- Your **user ID**, sometimes referred to as your user name, is a unique set of letters and numbers that serves as your "call sign" or "identification." On many networks, your user ID is derived from your real name. It might be case sensitive, but typically does not include spaces. For example, Pamela Bunin's user ID might be Pbunin, Pam.Bunin, or Pamela_Bunin.

- Your **password** is a special set of symbols known only to you and the network administrator. You can let people know your user ID so that they can send you messages over the network, but you don't want to reveal your password because it would violate your responsibility to help maintain network security. On most networks, users can select their own passwords. Table F-1 offers some password do's and don'ts.

- A **network administrator**, also called a network supervisor, is the person responsible for maintaining a network. He or she creates your account and provides you with a user ID and starter password that give you security clearance to use network resources initially. For security reasons, the network administrator might limit your access to open, change, or store files on network drives, folders, or files.

- **Drive mapping** is network terminology for assigning a drive letter to a network server disk drive. Your workstation gains access to the file server and its hard drive when the server hard drive is mapped to a drive letter. Once a drive letter has been mapped, you can access data files and application software from that drive just as you would from your local hard disk drive. Drive mappings vary from one network to another. As a network user, it is useful to know the type of network drive mapping employed so that you can find programs and files on the network more easily. The Windows operating system provides a utility called Network Neighborhood, as shown in Figure F-3, that helps you discover the network drive mapping and the other resources that are available to your workstation.

- Most application software sends files you want to print to a printer that is connected to your computer's parallel port. Network workstations, however, often do not have printers connected to the parallel port. Instead, they access network printers. You can specify whether a printer is connected to the network or to your local computer. The printer that you most typically use is referred to as the **default printer**. As shown in Figure F-4, if you have a local printer in addition to a network printer, you can often change the default printer by selecting another printer to use.

- Files sent to a network printer are placed in a print queue. A **print queue** is a special holding area on a network server where files are stored until they are printed. A **print job** is a file that has been sent to the printer. When more than one user sends a file to the print queue, the files are added to the print queue and printed in the order in which they are received. Most networks would not allow two files to travel simultaneously over the network. Before the printer has completed one printout, however, other files may arrive to be printed.

FIGURE F-3: *Network Neighborhood*

Clicking the Network Neighborhood icon opens a dialog box that lists the devices connected to your network.

To check a network drive mapping, first double-click a server icon to open it. Then, right-click a folder and select the Map Network Drive option.

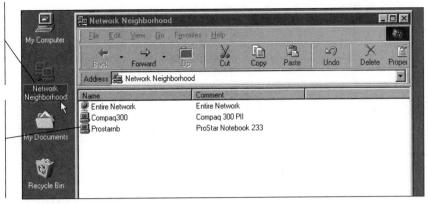

FIGURE F-4: *Change the default printer on a network*

You can select a printer by using the Start button to access the Printers dialog box.

You can use the Print dialog box provided by your application software.

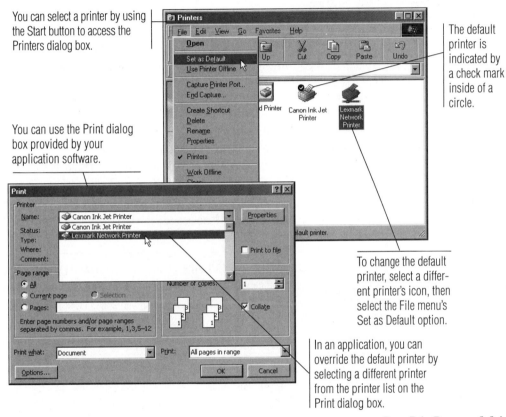

The default printer is indicated by a check mark inside of a circle.

To change the default printer, select a different printer's icon, then select the File menu's Set as Default option.

In an application, you can override the default printer by selecting a different printer from the printer list on the Print dialog box.

TABLE F-1: *Password do's and don'ts*

DO	DON'T
Select a password that is at least six characters long and that you can remember.	Select a password that can be found in the dictionary.
Use numbers as well as letters in your password.	Use your name, nickname, Social Security number, birth date, or name of a close relative.
Combine two or more words or use the first letters of the words in a poem or phrase.	Write your password where it is easy to find— under the keyboard is the first place a password thief will look.
Change your password periodically.	

Using computer networks

One advantage of a network is that, with proper licensing more, than one user on a network can simultaneously use the same program. This process is called **sharing** a program. When you use a computer network, you'll discover that finding, retrieving, and storing files on a network is not very different from the process you use on a stand-alone computer. When you use a network, however, you must remember to use additional resources, and you must be more conscious of security.

DETAILS

☞ Starting a program: When you start a program on a stand-alone computer, the program is copied from your hard disk into RAM. When you start a program that is stored on the hard disk of a network server, the program is copied from the hard drive of the server to the RAM of your workstation. Once the program is in memory, it runs just as if you had started it from your workstation hard disk drive. Figure F-5 shows how this process works.

☞ Sharing a program: Sharing a program over a network has many benefits. First, less disk storage space is required because the program is stored only once on the server, instead of being stored on the hard disks of multiple stand-alone computers. Second, when a new version of the software is released, it is easier to update one copy of the program on the server than to update many copies stored on stand-alone computers. Third, purchasing a software license for a network can be less expensive than purchasing single-user licenses for all workstations on the network.

☞ Using data files on a network: Suppose that while connected to a network, you create a document using a word processing program. You can store the document either on your local hard disk or on the server hard disk. If you store the file on your local hard disk, you can access it only from your workstation. If you store the file on the hard disk of the server, however, you or any other user can access it from any workstation on the network, as shown in Figure F-6.

☞ Locking files: Although a program file on the file server can be accessed by more than one user simultaneously, most of the data files on a network server can be opened by only one user at a time. When one user has a file open, it is locked to other users. File locking is a sensible precaution against losing valuable data. Groupware addresses the need for more than one person to work on the same file at one time. You'll learn about groupware in a later lesson.

| **Why networks lock files** | Suppose two users were allowed to change the same file at the same time. Each user would open a copy of the original file and make changes to it. The first user to finish making changes would save the file on the server. So far, so good—the first user has replaced the | original version of the file with an edited version. Remember, however, that the second user has been making revisions to the original file, but has no idea of the first user's revisions. When the second user saves his or her revised version of the file, the changes made by the first | user are overwritten by the second user's version. This action would be counterproductive, because one user's changes might contradict the other user's changes. Therefore, when one user has a data file open on a network, it is locked to other users. |

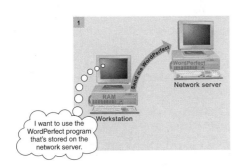
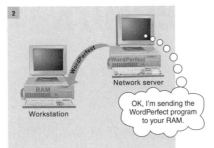
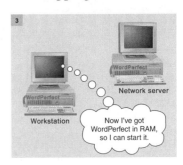

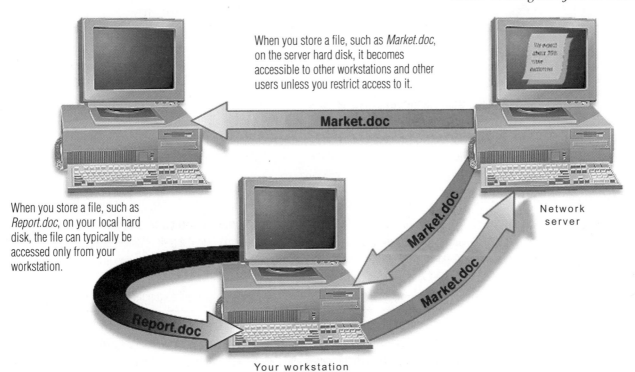

When you store a file, such as *Market.doc*, on the server hard disk, it becomes accessible to other workstations and other users unless you restrict access to it.

When you store a file, such as *Report.doc*, on your local hard disk, the file can typically be accessed only from your workstation.

What is an intranet?

INTRANETS

An **intranet** is a mini-Internet designed primarily for use by employees within a particular organization, rather than by the general public. It uses TCP/IP and Internet software to handle data communications within an organization. Intranets provide Web pages and e-mail. The distinction between a LAN and an intranet isn't always clear. LANs and intranets are both networks that service users in a limited local area. The Internet, intranets, and LANs were all specifically invented and designed for efficient digital data transmission.

Identifying network server types

When you use a stand-alone computer, all of your data is processed by your computer's microprocessor. When your computer is connected to a network, the device that processes your data depends on the types of servers present on the network. A **file server** is a computer that "serves," or distributes, application programs and data files to the workstations. The hard disk drive of the file server is shared by the workstations on the network. A typical local area network uses a microcomputer as a file server, although a minicomputer or a mainframe computer can also be a file server. Server types include dedicated servers, nondedicated servers, print servers, application servers, and host computers.

CLIENT/SERVER

DETAILS

- A **dedicated file server** is devoted solely to the task of delivering programs and data files to workstations. As you can see in Figure F-7, a dedicated file server does not process data or run programs for the workstations. Instead, programs take advantage of the memory and processor of the workstation. Saying that a dedicated file server is "dedicated" does not mean that a network has only one server. In fact, many networks have more than one dedicated file server.

- In some cases, a network computer performs a dual role as both file server and workstation. This setup is referred to as a **nondedicated file server** or **peer-to-peer architecture** capability. Unlike a dedicated file server, a nondedicated file server is not devoted *solely* to the task of delivering programs and data to workstations. When you use a nondedicated server, your computer functions like a normal workstation, but other workstations can access programs and data files from the hard disk of your computer, as shown in Figure F-8. More than one computer on a network can act as a nondedicated server.

- An **application server**, as shown in Figure F-9, is a computer that runs application software and forwards the results of processing to workstations as requested. An application server makes it possible to use the processing power of both the server and the workstation. Use of an application server splits processing between the workstation client and the network server. This type of network is also referred to as **client/server architecture**.

- Some networks include a **host computer**, usually a minicomputer or mainframe with attached terminals. A **terminal** has a keyboard and a screen, but does not have a local storage device and does little or no processing on its own. When you use a terminal connected to a host computer, all processing takes place on the host. Although this system fits the definition of a network, it is more commonly called a **time-sharing system**. The terminals essentially share the host's processor by each being allocated a fraction of each second of processing time. **Terminal emulation software** makes a microcomputer function like a terminal. If you want to process data received from a host, you must use communications software to transfer the data to your computer instead of using terminal emulation software.

- A **print server** receives files from workstations, then forwards them to a specific network printer. It can be the same computer as the file server, or it can be another microcomputer, minicomputer, or mainframe computer connected to the network. A print server manages the print queue.

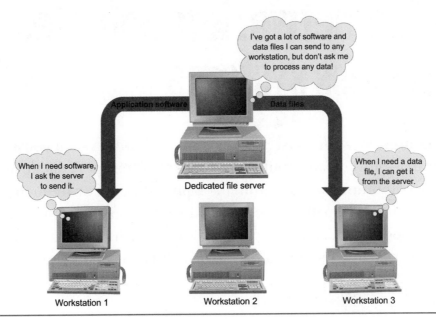

FIGURE F-7: *A dedicated file server*

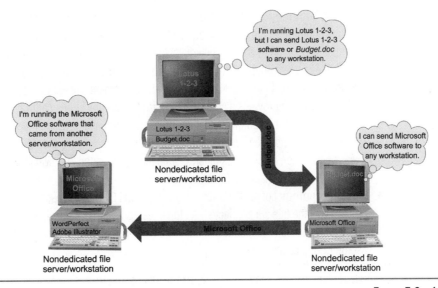

FIGURE F-8: *A nondedicated file server*

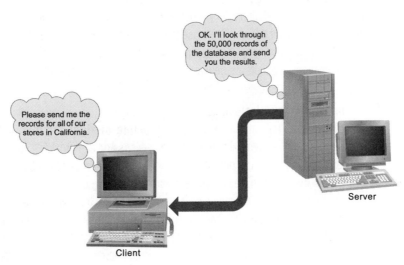

FIGURE F-9: *An application server*

Exploring network topologies and wireless systems

A network is a **communications system**. A communications system consists of a combination of hardware, software, and connecting links that transport data over communications channels. A **communications channel** is a physical path or frequency for a signal transmission. The pattern or path of the interconnections in a communications system is referred to as its **topology**. A communications system, such as a network, can use a single topology, or it can contain a mixture of topologies. It can even be wireless.

WIRELESS NETWORKS

SATELLITES

DETAILS

○── Commonly used communications system topologies, shown in Figure F-10, include star, bus, and ring.

- In a **star topology**, like the one used to connect telephone lines to the phone company's switching station, communication lines fan out from a central location and each line provides essentially a private link to a centralized hub. The advantage of the star topology is that every connection is dedicated to one user and the particular user gets use of the full bandwidth of the channel. Its disadvantage is the high cost of the media and equipment needed to supply individual connections.

- A **bus topology** provides a common or shared communications pathway. This topology is typically used by cable TV companies, which string cables from one house to the next in a long chain. A bus topology can supply the same signal to multiple users, as is the case with cable TV signals. If each user or device on a bus wants different signals, however, the bandwidth must be divided and no one will get to use the channel's full bandwidth.

- A **ring topology** connects devices in a continuous loop—it is essentially a bus topology in which the ends of the bus are connected. A signal leaves the sending device, travels in sequence to each device connected to the loop, and then returns to the sending device. Ring topologies are used in some local area networks.

○── Instead of using cables, some **wireless networks** use radio, microwave, or infrared signals to transmit data from one network device to another. Wireless networks are handy in environments where wiring is difficult to install. In addition, they provide mobility, making it possible to carry a notebook or handheld computer throughout a large warehouse to take inventory, for example. Wireless networks are also useful for temporary installations, when drilling holes to install wiring is not practical or economical. Wireless communications channels are generally slower than cables, susceptible to signal interference, eavesdropping, and jamming.

- **Infrared transmissions** use a frequency range just below the visible light spectrum to transport data. Infrared transmission is an example of **line-of-sight communication.** Infrared devices include handheld remote controls for televisions and can provide a communications link for transferring data between a computer and peripheral devices. See Figure F-11.

- A **microwave** is an electromagnetic wave with a frequency of at least 1 gigahertz (GHz). Data converted into microwaves can be sent over a microwave link. **Microwave transmissions** send a high-frequency signal from a transmitting station to a receiving station that cannot be more than 25 or 30 miles away. At farther distances, the curve of the earth blocks the line-of-sight transmission path. Many communications systems transmit microwave signals between a **land-based ground station** and a telecommunications satellite.

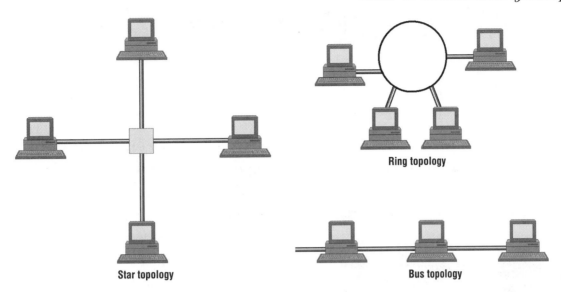

Star topology

Ring topology

Bus topology

FIGURE F-11: *Using infrared sensors to send a file to a printer*

VIDEO

By pointing the infrared port of the computer at the printer's infrared sensor, you can send data to the printer without using a cable.

Satellite systems

ANIMATION

A telecommunications satellite contains a **transponder** that receives a signal on one frequency, amplifies the signal, and then retransmits the signal on another frequency. A **satellite** in **geosynchronous orbit** (GEO) stays above the same part of the earth by orbiting at the same speed as the earth and provides continuous coverage of a particular area. Many recent telecommunications satellites are launched into **low-earth orbit** (LEO) about 1,000 miles above the earth. These satellites do not stay in the same location above the earth. A LEO communications system requires a web of satellites to maintain communications. See Figure F-12.

FIGURE F-12: *Low-earth orbit communications system*

Understanding network hardware

The three main components of a network are network cables, network hardware, and network software. Knowing about the network components will help you recognize whether a computer is on a network, help you troubleshoot loose connections, and move and reconnect a computer on a network computer system.

BANDWIDTH   ETHERNET

DETAILS

▣ A **communications medium** carries one or more communications channels and provides a link between transmitting and receiving devices.

▣ **Bandwidth** is the transmission capacity of a communications channel.

▣ **Network cables** provide the physical connections or communications channels for the computers in a network.

- The media most frequently used in today's communications systems include twisted-pair cable, coaxial cable, and fiber-optic cable. You will learn more about network cables in the next lesson.
- The network cables are connected to each workstation using cable connectors and expansion cards. You can think of network cables, connectors, and expansion cards as components that fit together to form links.

▣ **Network hardware** directs the flow of data over the network cables.

- A desktop computer **network interface card** (**NIC**—pronounced "nick") is a small circuit board designed to plug into an expansion slot on a computer motherboard. A notebook computer NIC usually resides on a PCMCIA card. Each workstation on a network must have a NIC. A NIC is the key component for connecting a computer to a local area network. It sends data from your workstation, server, printer, or other device out over the network and collects incoming data. The NIC on a wireless network contains the transmitting devices necessary to send data to other devices on the LAN. Figure F-13 shows NICs for desktop and notebook computers.
    Different types of networks use different types of NICs. If you want to add a computer to a network, you need to know the network type so that you can purchase the appropriate NIC. Popular network types include **Ethernet** and **Token Ring**. You can purchase NICs for these networks in either 10-megabit or 100-megabit speeds. The 100-megabit cards provide faster data transfer rates.
- On most of today's networks, the cable from a workstation NIC connects to a **network hub**, which is a device that joins communication lines together. See Figure F-14. In a typical network configuration, cables from one or more workstations connect to the hub, and a single cable then connects the hub to a server.

▣ **Radio waves** provide wireless transmission for mobile communications. A radio communications link uses a **transmitter** to send a signal at a particular frequency, and a **receiver** at the other end of the transmission picks up the signal.

▣ **Network software** controls the flow of data, maintains security, and keeps track of user accounts. You will learn more about network software in a later lesson.

Desktop (left) and notebook (below) NICs are expansion cards that can be used to connect a computer to a network.

FIGURE F-14: *A hub*

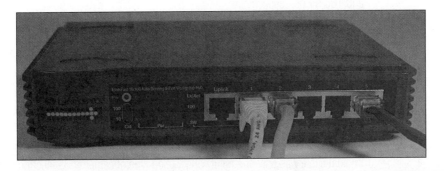

Satellite dishes

Transmissions from a satellite transponder are sent to satellite dishes. A **satellite dish** "catches" satellite transmissions on its parabolic surface, then reflects these signals to a feedhorn. A **feedhorn** contains a small metal probe that acts as a microwave antenna. It funnels signals to a device called a low noise block (LNB) downconverter, which converts the microwave signal into an electrical current, amplifies it, and lowers its frequency. The downconverted signal is conveyed by cable to the indoor receiver. Figure F-15 illustrates the major parts of a satellite dish.

FIGURE F-15: *A satellite dish can be used to receive data as well as cable TV signals*

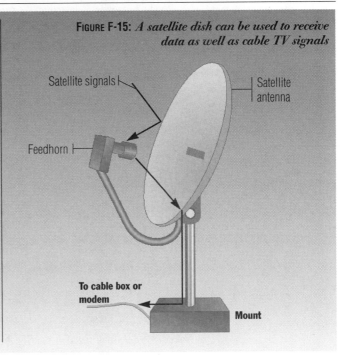

Satellite signals

Satellite antenna

Feedhorn

To cable box or modem

Mount

Exploring network cables

Most networks use cables to connect servers, workstations, and printers. This lesson looks at the three most commonly used network cables: twisted-pair cables, coaxial cables, and fiber-optic cables.

FIBER OPTICS

DETAILS

○━ Today's networks typically use **twisted-pair cable**, as described in Figure F-16. Sometimes called UTP (unshielded twisted-pair) or STP (shielded twisted-pair), this type of cabling resembles a telephone cable, consists of copper wires twisted together, and terminates in a square plastic RJ-11 or RJ-45 plug or connector. Twisted-pair cables are classified into five categories based on their transmission capacity.

- Category 1 is considered **voice-grade cable**, which means it is recommended for transmitting voice but not data signals.
- Category 2 is a better grade suitable for voice and data.
- Categories 3, 4, and 5 are **data-grade cable** suitable for communications at 16 MBps, 20 MBps, and 100 MBps, respectively.

○━ **Coaxial cable**, which is shown in Figure F-17 and which resembles cable-TV cable with a round, silver **BNC connector** at either end, is a high-capacity communications cable consisting of a copper wire conductor, nonconducting insulator, foil shield, woven metal outer shielding, and plastic outer coating. Coaxial cable is typically used to carry cable television signals, because it has a high capacity that can accommodate signals for more than 100 television stations. It also provides good capacity for data communications and is used where twisted-pair cable is inadequate.

- Coaxial cable is sometimes called "category 6 cable" and has a bandwidth that exceeds 100 MBps.
- Coaxial cable was once the most widely used type of cable for connecting computers in LANs. Today, because it is less durable, more expensive, and more difficult to work with, it is being replaced by twisted-pair cable. For situations requiring high bandwidth, both twisted-pair and coaxial cable are being replaced by fiber-optic cable.

○━ **Fiber-optic cable**, shown in Figure F-18, consists of a bundle of extremely thin tubes of glass. Each tube, called an optical fiber, is much thinner than a human hair. Fiber-optic cable usually consists of a strong inner support wire; multiple strands of optical fiber, each covered by a plastic insulator; and a tough outer covering.

How fiber-optic cable works

The use of optical fibers for communications is a relatively new development. Unlike twisted-pair or coaxial cables, fiber-optic cables do not conduct or transmit electric signals. Instead, miniature lasers send pulses of light that represent data through the fibers. Electronics at the receiving end of the fiber convert the light pulses back into electrical signals. Each fiber is a one-way communications channel, which means that at least two fibers are required to provide a two-way communications link.

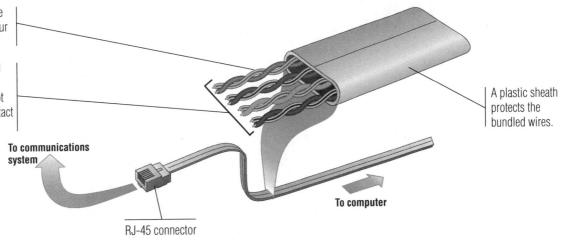

A twisted-pair cable usually contains four pairs of wires.

Each wire is coated with plastic, so the copper wires do not come in direct contact with each other.

A plastic sheath protects the bundled wires.

To communications system

To computer

RJ-45 connector

FIGURE F-17: *Coaxial cable*

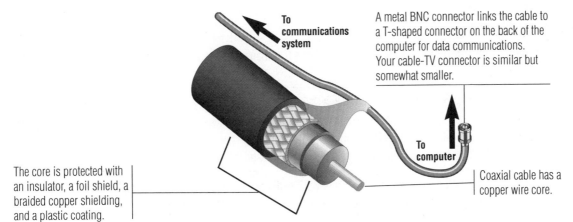

To communications system

A metal BNC connector links the cable to a T-shaped connector on the back of the computer for data communications. Your cable-TV connector is similar but somewhat smaller.

To computer

The core is protected with an insulator, a foil shield, a braided copper shielding, and a plastic coating.

Coaxial cable has a copper wire core.

FIGURE F-18: *Fiber-optic cable*

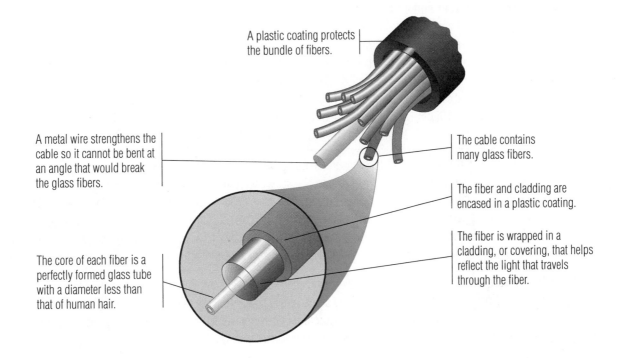

A plastic coating protects the bundle of fibers.

A metal wire strengthens the cable so it cannot be bent at an angle that would break the glass fibers.

The cable contains many glass fibers.

The fiber and cladding are encased in a plastic coating.

The fiber is wrapped in a cladding, or covering, that helps reflect the light that travels through the fiber.

The core of each fiber is a perfectly formed glass tube with a diameter less than that of human hair.

Understanding network software

The software on a local area network typically includes many of the same applications you might use on a stand-alone computer. A network requires network software or a network operating system to control the flow of data, maintain security, and keep track of user accounts. Today, networks often run specialized applications designed for multiple users, such as groupware and workflow software, that facilitate the flow and sharing of documents.

NOS

GROUPWARE

WORKFLOW
SOFTWARE

DETAILS

- A **network operating system (NOS)** is the software that manages network resources, controls the flow of data, maintains security, and tracks user accounts.

- Today's popular desktop operating systems, such as Windows 95/98/NT Workstation and 2000 Professional, include the software necessary to establish communications with a network server. When you install a NIC and start your computer, the operating system will detect the NIC and guide you through the process of installing its driver software. This network software handles the communications between your workstation and the network server.

- Earlier desktop operating systems, such as Windows 3.1, did not include network software. A network that uses Windows 3.1 must therefore use a network operating system, such as **Novell NetWare**. Network operating systems such as Novell NetWare are optimized for installations that need an efficient file server.

- A network operating system usually contains two components: network server software and network client software.
  - **Network server software** is installed on a file server. It controls file access from the server hard drive, manages the print queue, and tracks user data such as IDs and passwords.
  - **Network client software** is installed on the local hard drive of each workstation. It gathers your login information, handles drive mapping, and directs printouts to the network printer. This type of software is essentially a device driver for the NIC. It establishes the connection between your workstation and other devices on the network.
  - The server and client components do not have to match. For example, the network client software that is provided as part of Windows 95/98, NT Workstation, and 2000 Professional allows you to access servers running a variety of software, including Linux, UNIX, and Novell NetWare as well as Windows NT Server and Windows 2000 Server.

- **Groupware** is application software that supports collaborative work by managing schedules, shared documents, and intragroup communications. In most organizations, people exchange information using memos, phone conversations, and face-to-face meetings. Employees collect, organize, and share information that must be stored in a centralized repository. Essentially, groupware manages a pool of documents and allows users to access those documents simultaneously. A key feature of groupware is document version management, which maintains all revisions within a document when more than one group member revises a document. The workgroup can accept or reject each revision, as shown in Figure F-19.

- **Workflow software**, also referred to as document routing software, automates the process of electronically routing documents from one person to another in a specified sequence and time. It facilitates a process or a series of steps. As illustrated in Figure F-20, workflow software is based on a "process-centered model" as opposed to groupware's "information-centered model." With workflow software, the focus is on a series of steps. With groupware, the focus is on the documents.

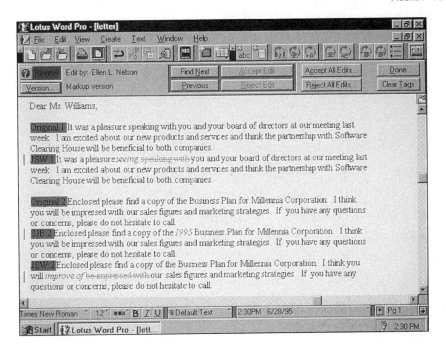

Groupware provides simultaneous access to a pool of documents

Workflow software facilitates a process

Running applications on a network

Most of your favorite word processing, spreadsheet, graphics, and presentation software programs will work on a network just as if they were running from your local hard drive. In addition, some applications that you use on a stand-alone computer have built-in features for networking that appear only when the software is installed on a network.

After a new Windows-based program has been installed on a network server, the network manager needs to complete a **workstation installation** of the software. A workstation installation usually copies some—but not all—of the program files to your local hard disk. It then updates your Windows menu to include a listing for the new program.

Transporting data over networks

To ensure that the data you transmit over a network is not altered, both the sending and the receiving computers must strictly follow communications protocols. A **communications protocol** is a set of rules that ensures the orderly and accurate transmission and reception of data. When two devices communicate, they must agree on protocols for starting and ending a transmission, recognizing errors, sending data at the appropriate speed, and formatting or packaging the data.

PACKET SWITCHING

DETAILS

☞ Phone conversations and television broadcasts are continuous and sequential events that require a continuous circuit and use circuit-switching technology. In contrast, data communications are not necessarily continuous and require **packet-switching** technology that divides a message into smaller units called **packets**. Most LANs use packet-switching technology. Each packet in one message is addressed to the same destination, but any packet can travel a different route over the network than other packets. At the receiving end of the transmission, all of the packets are gathered together and reassembled. Packet switching uses bandwidth efficiently. Packets are shipped over the circuit on a "first come, first served" basis. Figure F-21 illustrates how this procedure works.

☞ A **network access method** is a set of specifications that defines how data will be physically transmitted from one network node to another. A NIC supports a particular network access method, which, from a user's perspective, is determined by the type of NIC and cables that connect the network to nodes. Devices on a network must use the same network access method to communicate and share network resources. Today's popular network access methods include Ethernet and Token Ring.

- **Ethernet**, the most popular network access method, transmits data at 10 or 100 MBps. Ethernet nodes are arranged in a bus or star topology. Several variations of Ethernet exist, each of which is characterized by the type of cable that connects the workstations.
- A **Token Ring** network is based on a ring topology. It uses a special message called a **token** to prevent collisions. The token travels around the network carrying a signal to indicate whether the network is busy or available to carry a data packet. Figure F-22 illustrates how Token Ring technology works.

☞ **TCP/IP** is a standard set of communications rules used by every computer that connects to the Internet. This communications protocol is used by both the Internet and intranets. TCP/IP is also a popular protocol for Ethernet and Token Ring LANs.

☞ Other popular LAN protocols include IPX/SPX and NetBIOS/NetBEUI.

- **IPX/SPX (Internetwork Packet Exchange/Sequenced Packet Exchange)** is the protocol used by Novell NetWare, the most popular stand-alone microcomputer network software.
- **NetBIOS/NetBEUI (NetBIOS Extended User Interface)** is a Microsoft network protocol, that is shipped with the Windows operating system.

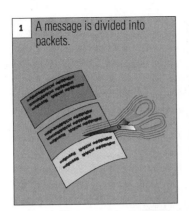

1 A message is divided into packets.

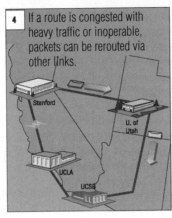

2 Each packet is addressed to the destination.

TO UCLA
TO UCLA
TO UCLA

3 A packet might travel the shortest path to its destination.

Stanford
U. of Utah
UCLA
UCSB

ANIMATION

4 If a route is congested with heavy traffic or inoperable, packets can be rerouted via other links.

Stanford
U. of Utah
UCLA
UCSB

5 When the packets arrive at their destination, they are reassembled.

FIGURE F-22: *How Token Ring works*

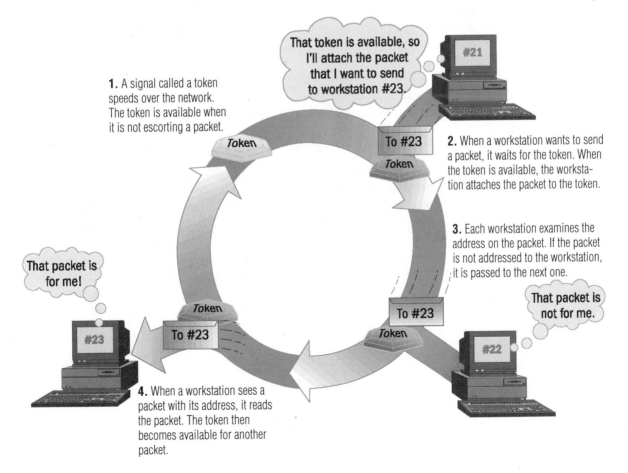

1. A signal called a token speeds over the network. The token is available when it is not escorting a packet.

That token is available, so I'll attach the packet that I want to send to workstation #23.

#21

To #23

Token

2. When a workstation wants to send a packet, it waits for the token. When the token is available, the workstation attaches the packet to the token.

3. Each workstation examines the address on the packet. If the packet is not addressed to the workstation, it is passed to the next one.

That packet is for me!

That packet is not for me.

#23

#22

To #23

To #23

Token

4. When a workstation sees a packet with its address, it reads the packet. The token then becomes available for another packet.

Building a low-cost LAN

Data communications are not the exclusive property of large corporations, huge government agencies, and giant telecommunications companies. You can set up your own network in your own home and use it to share data, collaborate on computer projects, and try out some multiplayer games.

BUILDING A NETWORK

DETAILS

- In addition to a Phillips-head screwdriver and patience, … you will need:
  - At least two computers. To make it easier for you, these computers should run Windows 95, Windows NT, Windows 98, or Windows 2000, all of which include the built-in networking software that will handle the network protocols.
  - One NIC for each computer. The simplest and least expensive networks use 10BaseT Ethernet cards.
  - One hub. A 10BaseT hub, like the one shown in Figure F-23, includes five ports so you can connect as many as five devices to your network. If you don't have five computers, the extra ports provide room for expansion.
  - Cables. 10BaseT cables, sometimes referred to as **network patch cables**, are sold in various lengths with RJ-45 plugs at each end and are suitable for distances up to 100 feet. For each computer, you will need a cable long enough to reach the hub. Look for Category 5 UTP cables.

- The first step in setting up your network is to install the NIC in each computer. Be sure to "ground" yourself to release static electricity that might damage components on the computer's motherboard. Place the NIC in an unused expansion slot on the motherboard. See Figure F-24.

- The cables connect each computer to the hub. One end of the cable plugs into the NIC, and the other end plugs into one of the ports on the hub for each computer. This set of connections creates a "star" as the cables branch out from the hub like points on a star.

- The hub has to be powered by plugging it into a wall outlet. It is advisable to use a UPS (uninterruptible power supply).

- When you turn on each computer, Windows should detect the NICs. A Windows Wizard will display a series of dialog boxes to guide you through the installation process. For your first network, you should select the Client for Microsoft Networks protocol and indicate that you want to share files and printers, as shown in Figure F-25.

- Network Neighborhood on your Windows desktop can be used to map the drive letters and printers.

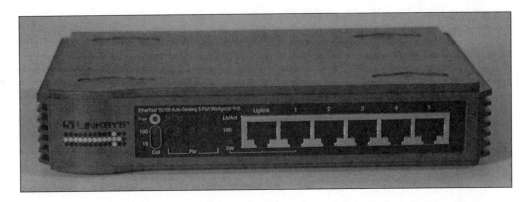

FIGURE F-24: *Installing a network card*

FIGURE F-25: *Using the Windows Network dialog box*

Select Client for Microsoft Networks

Click to open File and Print Sharing dialog box

Select File and Print Sharing options

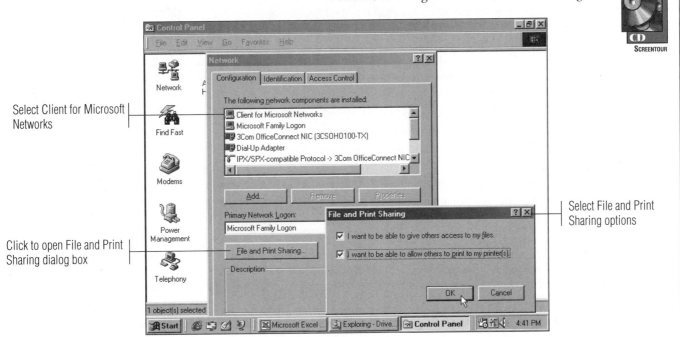

Introducing e-mail

Electronic mail, or e-mail, is correspondence conducted between two or more users on a network. Rather than waiting for a piece of paper to be physically transported, you can send an electronic version of a message directly to someone's electronic "mailbox."

InfoWeb
E-MAIL

Lab
E-MAIL

DETAILS

☞ How e-mail works: An **e-mail message** is essentially a document sent electronically from one user to another. An **e-mail system** is the hardware and software that collects and delivers e-mail messages. Typically, a local area network provides electronic mail services to its users. The software on the network server that controls the flow of e-mail is called **e-mail server software**. The software on a workstation that helps each user read, compose, send, and delete messages is called **e-mail client software**.

☞ Store and forward technology: E-mail messages are stored on a server. When you want to read this mail, the server forwards the messages to your workstation. For this reason, e-mail is called a **store-and-forward technology**. Because the server stores the messages, your workstation does not need to be on when someone sends you e-mail. See Figure F-26.

☞ **E-mail servers** are the computers that store and forward e-mail. They can be part of a local area network or the Internet. Many businesses and education institutions operate e-mail servers as part of their LANs. LAN users can send and receive e-mail whenever they are logged onto the network. Many e-mail servers also exist on the Internet. These servers provide e-mail services to the general public for a small fee or for free. For example, an e-mail account is included in the monthly subscription fee for America Online (AOL), AT&T WorldNet, and CompuServe. Advertiser-supported Internet sites such as Hotmail and MailCity provide free e-mail accounts. See Figure F-27. If you have an account on an Internet mail server, you would collect your mail by establishing an Internet connection using a phone line and your computer's modem.

☞ Sending e-mail out of network: Many e-mail systems connect to other e-mail systems through electronic links called **gateways**. When you send an e-mail message to a user on another computer network, the message is transferred through the gateway to a larger e-mail system, which delivers the message to the recipient's network or host computer system. In today's connected world, the e-mail address is sufficient to route a message to its destination anywhere in the world.

☞ Receiving e-mail: When someone sends you e-mail, the message is stored on a host or network server in an area you can think of as your mailbox. When you log into the e-mail system and check your mail, the message is listed as new mail. Figure F-28 shows how a user's mailbox might look when accessed with the Microsoft Outlook Express e-mail client software.

☞ E-mail addresses: E-mail must be addressed correctly so that it will arrive at its destination. Typically, an **e-mail address** is a person's network user ID, an @ symbol, and the name of the user's e-mail server. For example, if a student whose user ID is dee_greene has an e-mail account on the e-mail system at Rutgers University, her e-mail address might be dee_greene@rutgers.edu. Your e-mail address will most likely change if you "move" to a different network or Internet e-mail server. When your address changes, you should remember to notify your friends, colleagues, family, and clients of your new contact information. You can also subscribe to an e-mail forwarding service such as www.bigfoot.com; such a service provides you with a permanent e-mail address that remains the same on the forwarding service regardless of where you move your actual e-mailbox. The e-mail forwarding service forwards your mail to the LAN-based or Internet-based e-mail server that is currently handling your mail.

☞ Features: Some electronic mail systems offer extra features, such as the following: priority mail, which immediately alerts the recipient that an e-mail message has arrived; return receipt, which sends a message back to you when a recipient receives your message; carbon copy, which sends a copy of the message to another user; blind carbon copy, which sends a copy of the message to other users but does not include the addresses or names of those other people who also got the message; and group addressing, which allows you to send a copy of an e-mail message to all members of a group at the same time.

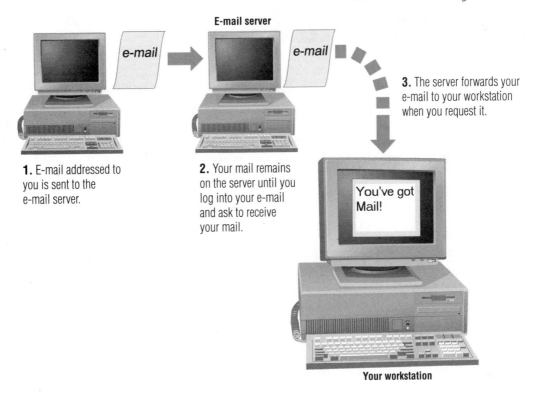

E-mail server

1. E-mail addressed to you is sent to the e-mail server.

2. Your mail remains on the server until you log into your e-mail and ask to receive your mail.

3. The server forwards your e-mail to your workstation when you request it.

You've got Mail!

Your workstation

FIGURE F-27: *Free e-mail accounts are available on advertiser-supported Internet sites*

msn Hotmail™
Microsoft®

Français
Deutsch
日本語

Hotmail wins!
CNET Editor's Choice Award

New user? **Sign up now!**

Login Name

Password

Enter

FIGURE F-28: *An e-mailbox lists new messages*

Buttons at the top of the mail window help you reply to, forward, send, print, and delete messages.

Your Inbox lists all the messages in your e-mailbox. An icon that looks like an unopened envelope indicates unread mail.

The text of the new message is displayed in the lower section of the window.

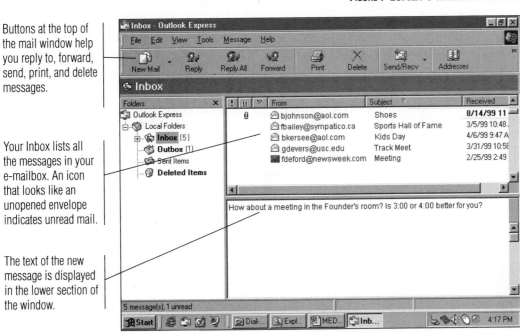

SCREENTOUR

Managing e-mail

Using e-mail is not exactly the same as using the post office. With e-mail, you can send messages immediately. You can send the same message to multiple people just as easily as you can send a message to a single person. In addition, it is a simple process to reply automatically to messages you receive.

DETAILS

- Creating new messages and replying to e-mail: E-mail software has a button or menu option for creating new mail messages. When you get an e-mail message to which you want to reply, you can click the Reply button on your e-mail software's toolbar. The composition window or message form is where you write and reply to messages. See Figure F-29. Depending on how your system is set up, it may automatically "quote" the original message in the composition window. You should type the text of your reply with the original text in the message to remind the recipient of the context of the discussion.

- Sending e-mail: In the To text box, type the recipient's mail address or select it from an address book that contains a list of e-mail addresses for the people with whom you correspond frequently. In the Subject area, specify the topic of the e-mail. You can specify other recipients in the cc: option (carbon copy) or use the bcc: (blind carbon copy) option to "hide" the names of recipients from each other.

- Sending attachments: Most e-mail systems allow you to send an **e-mail attachment**, which is a file such as a document, worksheet, or graphic that travels through the e-mail system along with the e-mail message. See Figure F-30.

- The advantages of e-mail can also create potential problems. Table F-2 offers tips to help you avoid e-mail problems.

TABLE F-2: *Tips to avoid e-mail problems*

TIP	DESCRIPTION
Read your mail regularly.	When you use e-mail, your correspondents expect a quick response. You lose much of the advantage of e-mail if you check your mailbox only once every two weeks!
Delete messages after you read them.	Your e-mail is stored, along with everyone else's, on a file server where storage space is valuable. Leaving old messages in your mailbox takes up space that could be used more productively.
You don't have to reply to every e-mail message.	Don't reply unless you have a reason to respond, such as to answer a question. Sending a message to say "I got your message" just creates unnecessary mail traffic.
If you receive mail addressed to a group, it might be better to reply to only one person in the group.	You might receive mail as a member of a mailing list; the same message will be sent to everyone on the list. If you use the automatic reply feature of your e-mail system, the message is likely to be sent to everyone on the list. Use this option only if your reply is important for everyone to see.
Think before you send.	It is easy to write a message in haste or in anger and send it off before you have time to think it through. If you're upset, write your message, but wait a day before you send it.
Don't write anything you want to remain confidential.	E-mail is easily forwarded to other people. Don't write unflattering e-mail messages.
Don't get sloppy.	Your e-mail is a reflection of you, your school, and your employer. Use a spelling checker if one is available; if not, proofread your message before you send it. Use standard grammar, punctuation, and capitalization.
Use proper netiquette. InfoWeb SMILEYS	Netiquette is online jargon for "Internet etiquette." It is a series of customs or guidelines for maintaining civilized communication in online discussions and e-mail messages. For example, netiquette guidelines point out that a message in all uppercase means you're shouting. You should avoid this style of message unless you want other people to regard your message as an emotional outburst. You can, however, use "smileys," such as :-) to express emotions and feelings in your e-mail.

When you reply to an e-mail message, your e-mail client automatically fills in the To, From, and Subject lines.

Typically, you will type the text of your reply above the text of the original message.

The ">" symbol indicates the text of the message to which you are replying.

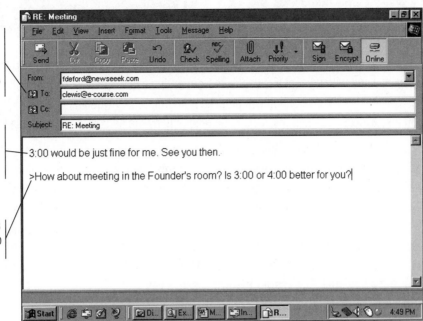

FIGURE F-30: *Sending an attachment*

1. Create a new message and address it to the person to whom you are sending the attachment.

2. Use the menus or the toolbar buttons provided by your e-mail software to attach the file containing the attachment.

3. An icon indicates the name of the file you attached. Send the mail following your usual procedures. The recipient of the message can click the icon to see the attachment.

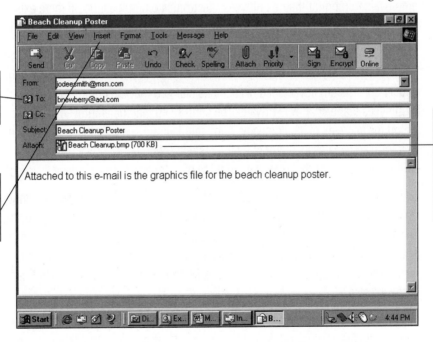

E-MAIL PRIVACY

When you drop an envelope in the corner mailbox, you probably expect it to arrive at its destination unopened and with its contents kept safe from prying eyes. When you make a phone call, you might assume that your conversation will proceed unmonitored by wiretaps or other listening devices. Can you also expect an e-mail message to be read only by the person to whom it is addressed?

In a recent poll conducted by *MacWorld* magazine, managers from 25 percent of the companies surveyed said that they read employee e-mail. But this intentional eavesdropping is only one way in which the contents of your e-mail messages might become public. The recipient of your e-mail can forward it to one or more people—people who you never intended for it to reach. Your e-mail messages could pop up on a technician's screen in the course of system maintenance or repairs. Also, keep in mind that e-mail messages—including those that you have deleted from your own PC—might be stored on backups of the e-mail server. You might wonder if such open access to your e-mail is legal. The answer in most cases is yes.

In the United States, the federal Omnibus Crime Control and Safe Streets Act of 1968 and the Electronic Communications Privacy Act of 1986 prohibit public and private employers from engaging in surreptitious surveillance of employee activity through the use of electronic devices. However, two exceptions to these privacy statutes exist. The first exception permits an employer to monitor electronic communications if one party to the communication has consented to the monitoring. An employer must inform employees of this policy before undertaking any monitoring. The second exception permits employers to monitor their employees' electronic communications if there exists a legitimate business need and if the monitoring takes place within the business-owned communications system.

Employees have not been successful in defending their rights to e-mail privacy. For example, in 1996, a Pillsbury employee was fired from his job for making unprofessional comments in an e-mail to his supervisor. The employee sued because he claimed that the company had repeatedly assured its employees that e-mail was private. The court ruled that the employee's right to privacy did not outweigh the interests of the company. Although it would seem that the company violated the requirement to inform employees as required by the first exception to the privacy statutes, the fact that the company owned the e-mail system gave it the right to monitor any correspondence carried out over that system.

Like employees of a business, students who use a school's e-mail system cannot be assured of e-mail privacy. When a CalTech student was accused of sexually harassing a female student by sending lewd e-mail to her and to her boyfriend, investigators retrieved all of the student's e-mail from the archives of the e-mail server. The student was expelled from the university even though he claimed that the e-mail had been "spoofed" to make it look as though he had sent it, when it had actually been sent by someone else.

Why would an employer want to know the contents of employee e-mail? Why would a school be concerned with the correspondence of its students? It is probably true that some organizations simply snoop on the off chance that some important information might be discovered. Other organizations have more legitimate reasons for monitoring e-mail. An organization that owns an e-mail system could be held responsible for the consequences of actions related to the contents of e-mail messages on that system. For example, a school has a responsibility to protect students from harassment. If it fails to do so, it could be sued along with the author of the offending e-mail message. Organizations also recognize a need to protect themselves from false rumors and industrial espionage. For example, a business would want to know if an employee was supplying its competitor with information on product research and development.

Many schools and businesses have established e-mail privacy policies, which explain the conditions under which you can and cannot expect your e-mail to remain private. Court decisions, however, seem to support the notion that because an organization owns and operates its e-mail system, the organization owns the e-mail messages that are generated on its system. The individual who authors an e-mail message does not own it and therefore has no rights related to it. A company can, therefore, legally monitor your e-mail. You should use your e-mail account with the expectation that some of your mail *will* be read from time to time. Think of your e-mail as a postcard, rather than a letter, and save your controversial comments for face-to-face conversations.

EXPAND THE IDEAS

1. Do you think that most people believe that their e-mail is private? Do you think most people believe that mail sent through the U.S. Postal Service is private? Detail the specific characteristics that make the e-mail system different from other mail systems.

2. Do you agree with CalTech's decision to expel the student who was accused of sending harassing e-mail to another student? Why or why not? Find several examples of articles, documentaries, or news stories for similar cases. Write a summary of each article or media piece. Analyze your findings. Was the media voice consistent?

3. Should the laws be changed to make it illegal to monitor e-mail without court approval? Why or why not? Write a two-page essay with supporting facts to support your opinion.

4. Would you have different privacy expectations regarding an e-mail account at your place of work and an account that you purchase from an e-mail service provider? Find several examples of articles, documentaries, or news stories that discuss privacy. Write a summary of each article or media piece. Analyze your findings. Was the media voice consistent? Why or why not?

5. How has e-mail changed over the past 10 years? Research the history of e-mail and then compile your findings into a poster presentation.

End of Unit Exercises

STUDY TIPS

Study Tips help you organize and consolidate the information in a unit by making lists, outlines, charts, and sketches. You can use paper and pencil or word processing software to complete most of the Study Tips activities.

1. List three reasons why sharing programs is effective for an organization.

2. List three password do's and three password don'ts when creating a password for a network. Explain the reason for each.

3. Draw a diagram and explain the processing roles for servers and workstations for each of the following types of networks: (1) a network with a dedicated file server, (2) a peer-to-peer network, (3) a client/server network, (4) a time-sharing system.

4. Explain the difference between sharing files on a network and using a groupware product on a network.

5. Draw a conceptual diagram of a network showing the following components: (1) three workstations, (2) one file server, (3) one network printer, (4) a hub, (5) NICs for workstations, a printer, and a server, (6) cables connecting all of the network nodes.

6. Make a list of important points pertaining to network operating systems.

7. Summarize the software licensing issues that affect local area networks.

8. Explain how store-and-forward technology applies to e-mail systems.

9. Describe three ways to avoid problems with your e-mail.

10. Explain what an e-mail attachment is and describe when you might send one.

FILL IN THE BEST ANSWER

1. A network server is a(n) _____ connected to the network that "serves," or distributes, resources to network users.

2. Your _____ is a special set of symbols known only to you and the network administrator.

3. An application server splits _____ between the workstation client and the network server.

4. A network that is located within a relatively limited area is referred to as a(n) _____.

5. Each device on a network, including workstations, servers, and printers is called a(n) _____.

6. Assuming proper licensing, while Jenny uses a spreadsheet program from the file server, Atkin, who is working on the same network, can use the same spreadsheet program concurrently at his workstation. True or False? _____

7. If you do not reply to every e-mail message that you receive, it is considered rude and improper e-mail netiquette. True or False? _____

8. _____ cable is typically used for LANs and cable television.

9. Wireless communications channels are generally slower than cables. True or False? _____

10. Twisted-pair and coaxial cables transmit _____ signals, whereas fiber-optic cables transmit pulses of _____.

11. The pattern or path of interconnections in a communications system is referred to as its _____.

12. A ring topology connects devices in a continuous loop. True or False? _____

13. In a(n) _____ topology, like the one used to connect telephone lines to the phone company's switching station, communication lines fan out from a central location and each line provides essentially a private link to a centralized hub.

14. A network server _____ is a computer connected to a network that distributes files to network users.

15. _____ is network terminology for assigning a drive letter to a file server disk drive.

16. Three reasons why sharing programs is effective for an organization are _____, _____, and _____.

17. The circuit board that connects a computer to a local area network is called a(n) _____.

18. If a network computer functions both as a file server and as a workstation, it is referred to as a(n) _____.

19. A(n) _____ is devoted to the task of delivering program and data files to workstations.

20. Novell NetWare would be classified as _____ software.

21. If an organization is planning to use software on a network, it should purchase a(n) _____ so that multiple users can legally use the software.

22. If you are a team leader and you want your team members to collaborate on a project using the network to complete their contributions as a series of steps, you might purchase a(n) _____ product.

23. Data communications are not necessarily continuous and require _____-switching technology that divides a message into smaller units called _____.

24. A(n) _____ is a mini-Internet designed primarily for use by employees within a particular organization, rather than by the general public, that provides Web pages and e-mail.

25. Ethernet and Token Ring are popular network _____ methods.

INDEPENDENT CHALLENGE 1

Creating passwords requires some thought and creativity. As a new employee at the Dumont Board of Education, Michael Christopher Williams has to create a password to be able to access the LAN. Based on the guidelines presented in this unit, help to select a password for him.

To complete this independent challenge:

1. Rank the following, listing the most secure password first:
   - XX32nsa (a totally random selection of letters and numbers)
   - MichChrisWill (for Michael Christopher Williams)
   - RRRYBGDTS (the first letters of "row, row, row your boat gently down the stream")
   - SMAILLIW (Michael's last name spelled backward)
   - Maureen (Michael's wife's name)
   - Elmhurst (Michael's hometown)

2. List five possible passwords for yourself if you were to go on a secure network.

3. List five bad examples of passwords for yourself.

INDEPENDENT CHALLENGE 2

Research your school network. Determine who is the network administrator at your school and prepare to interview him or her or to gain access to the system to find out about the network.

To complete this independent challenge, answer the following questions:

1. What is the network operating system?

2. Which drives are mapped to a student workstation?

3. Is the file server a microcomputer, minicomputer, or mainframe computer?

4. Is the print server a different device than the file server?

5. What licenses are provided for software use on the network?

6. Is there a hub?

7. What are the communications links? Communications channels?

INDEPENDENT CHALLENGE 3

Client/server architecture is becoming more and more popular in corporations.

To complete this independent challenge:

Find out more about client/server computing. Use library and Internet resources to look for case studies and articles about corporations that are using client/server applications. Write a one- or two-page description of an effective use of client/server computing. Be sure to include a list of references.

INDEPENDENT CHALLENGE 4

Assume that you are the network administrator at a small manufacturing company. While doing some maintenance work on the e-mail system, you happen to view the contents of a message transmitted between two employees. The employees seem to be discussing a plan to steal equipment from the company.

To complete this independent challenge:

Find out more about e-mail privacy. Use library and Internet resources to look for case studies and articles about corporations finding out about employee activities though e-mail. Write a one- or two-page essay that explains what you would do, including the factors that would affect your decision. Include any references from your research that support your decision. Be sure to cite any articles or documents that you use in your essay.

LAB: E-MAIL

E-mail that originates on a local area network with a mail gateway can travel all over the world. That's why it is so important to learn how to use e-mail. In this lab, you use an e-mail simulator, so even if your school computers don't provide you with e-mail service, you will know the basics of reading, sending, and replying to e-mail messages.

1. Click the Steps button to learn how to work with e-mail. As you proceed through the Steps, answer all of the QuickCheck questions that appear. After you complete the Steps, you will see a QuickCheck Report. Follow the instructions on the screen to print this report.

2. Click the Explore button. Write a message to re@films.org. The subject of the message is "Picks and Pans." In the body of your message, describe a movie you have seen recently. Include the name of the movie, briefly summarize the plot, and give it a thumbs up or a thumbs down. Print the message before you send it.

3. In Explore, look in your Inbox for a message from jb@music.org. Read the message, then compose a reply indicating that you will attend. Send a carbon copy to mciccone@music.org. Print your reply, including the text of JB's original message, before you send it.

4. In Explore, look in your Inbox for a message from leo@sports.org. Reply to the message by adding your rating to the text of the original message as follows:

Equipment:	Your Rating:
Rollerblades	2
Skis	3
Bicycle	1
Scuba gear	4
Snowmobile	5

Print your reply before you send it.

LAB: BUILDING A NETWORK

Here's your chance to become a computer lab manager and see if you can please all of the students who use your labs. In the Building a Network Lab, you control a simulated computer network that provides services to student computer labs and to students dialing in from home. By monitoring usage and installing new equipment, see if you can make all of your students happy!

1. Click the Steps button to learn how to use the simulation to monitor and configure the network. As you work through the Steps, answer all of the QuickCheck questions that appear. After you complete the Steps, you will see a report that summarizes your performance on the QuickChecks. Follow the directions on the screen if you would like to print this report.

2. Use a photocopier to make several copies of the Network Statistics table shown at the end of the lab. In Explore, use File/Open to set up the network configuration stored as msu.net. Record the statistics for one day on a copy of the Network Statistics table, then answer questions (a) through (e).

   a. How many hours during the day are more than 25 percent of the lab users without computer access?

   b. Are remote users satisfied with the level of dial-in service?

   c. Would you characterize the printer load as high or low?

   d. Does the current demand exceed the capacity of the file server?

   e. What should you do to improve the network to meet demand?

3. In Explore, install a network hub and a file server in the Tech Room. Install a print server with an attached printer in Lab 1. Install another print server and attach a printer in Lab 2. Install three workstations in Lab 1 and five workstations in Lab 2. Record the statistics for one day on a copy of the Network Statistics table, then answer questions (a) through (e).

   a. How many hours during the day are more than 25 percent of the lab users without computer access?

   b. Are remote users satisfied with the level of dial-in service?

   c. Would you characterize the printer load as high or low?

   d. Does the current demand exceed the capacity of the file server?

   e. What should you do to improve the network to meet demand?

4. In Explore, use File/Open to set up the network configuration stored as wfcc.net. Use no more than 30 devices to construct what you think is an optimal network for the students in the simulation. (*Hint:* Don't forget to save your network frequently on your floppy disk as you are working on it.) Make sure that you test your network for at least five days. The percentage of students unable to access workstations and modems should rarely exceed 25 percent. Server and printer loads should never reach 100 percent. After you are satisfied with your network, print out your network configuration report.

Network Statistics

Time	Lab Users Without Workstations	Remote Users Without Workstations	File Server Load	Printer Load
8:00				
9:00				
10:00				
11:00				
Noon				
1:00				
2:00				
3:00				
4:00				
5:00				
6:00				
7:00				
8:00				
9:00				
10:00				
11:00				

LESSON	MEDIA ELEMENT	LESSON	MEDIA ELEMENT
Defining computer networks	LANs · VIDEO	Understanding network software	NOS · GROUPWARE · WORKFLOW SOFTWARE
Administering computer networks	SCREENTOUR	Exploring data transport on networks	PACKET SWITCHING · ANIMATION
Using computer networks	INTRANETS	Building a low-cost LAN	BUILDING A NETWORK · SCREENTOUR
Identifying network server types	CLIENT/SERVER	Introducing e-mail	E-MAIL · E-MAIL · SCREENTOUR
Exploring network topologies and wireless systems	WIRELESS NETWORKS · SATELLITES · VIDEO	Managing e-mail	SMILEYS · SCREENTOUR
Understanding network hardware	BANDWIDTH · ETHERNET	Issue: How Private Is E-mail?	E-MAIL PRIVACY
Exploring network cables	FIBER OPTICS		

VISUAL WORKSHOP

Explain the network topology shown in the figure. How would you access programs and data files if you were working on Workstation 2? Write a one-page essay on a typical session, describing how the files and programs would transfer between computers and the role each computer would play in the session.

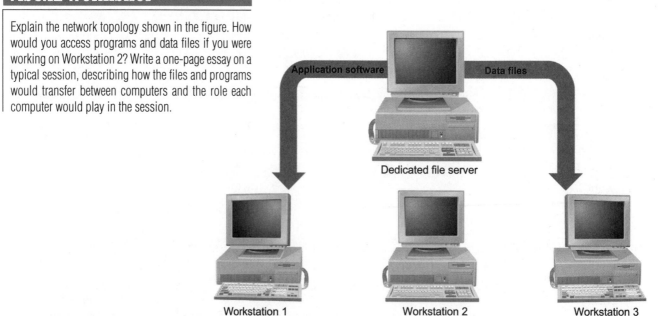

Application software   Data files

Dedicated file server

Workstation 1   Workstation 2   Workstation 3

The Internet

Unit G

Your computer can provide you with access to a digital "information highway"–the Internet. Journalists writing about the Internet have popularized the term **"cyberspace,"** which means a computer-generated world that exists in a realm between imagination and reality. The unit explores the Internet phenomenon, examines how the Internet works, and introduces you to the Internet's powerful potential. You will learn Internet terminology, how to the use of Web browsers, and ways to create, publish, and manage Web sites. The unit concludes with a discussion of how to connect your computer to the Internet.

Introducing the Internet

Connecting two or more networks creates an **internetwork**, also referred to as an internet. This lesson takes a look at the most well-known internetwork, the **Internet**, which is a collection of local, regional, national, and international computer networks that are linked together to exchange data and distribute processing tasks. Over the past 30 years, the Internet has evolved from a fledgling experiment with four computers into a vast international information network. The Internet connects millions of microcomputers, minicomputers, mainframes, and supercomputers and that provides information to people of all ages and interests.

INTERNET HISTORY

INTERNET STATISTICS

DETAILS

- ☞ The history of the Internet begins in 1957, when the Soviet Union launched Sputnik, the first artificial satellite. In response to this display of Soviet technical expertise, the U.S. government resolved to improve its science and technical infrastructure. One of its initiatives was the Advanced Research Projects Agency (ARPA), created by the Department of Defense. The plan was to construct a network of geographically dispersed computers that would continue to function even if one of the computers on the network was destroyed. In 1969, four computer networks were connected to each other, creating ARPANET. Connecting two or more networks creates an internetwork, so ARPANET was one of the first examples of an internet (with a lowercase "i").

- ☞ In 1985, the National Science Foundation (NSF) used ARPANET technology to create a similar, but larger network, linking not just a few large computers, but entire local area networks at each site. The NSF network was an internet, but as this network grew through the world, it became known as the "The Internet" (with an uppercase "I"). See Figure G-1.

- ☞ Early Internet pioneers used primitive command-line interfaces to send e-mail, transfer files, and run scientific calculations on Internet supercomputers. It wasn't until the early 1990s that software developers created user-friendly Internet access tools such as search engines to find files.

- ☞ A computer on the Internet that provides services such as Web pages, e-mailboxes, or data-routing services is referred to as an **Internet host,** a "host computer," or simply a "host." Internet host computers include **Web servers**, which maintain the World Wide Web; **FTP servers**, which maintain a collection of files that you can transfer to your own computer; and **Usenet servers** and **IRC servers** (Internet relay chat servers), which handle the exchange of comments among members of Internet discussion groups and chat groups.

- ☞ By 1986, the Internet had grown to 2,000 host computers. By 1999, the Internet had mushroomed to include more than 50 million computers worldwide, see Figure G-2, and more than 200,000 new users were signing up for Internet accounts each day. Today, the Internet is the largest and most widely used network in the world, serving an estimated 200 million people worldwide.

- ☞ **Internet traffic** is the number of bytes transmitted from one Internet host computer to another.

    - By 1997, Internet traffic exceeded 100 terabytes a week. A **terabyte** is 1,000,000,000,000 bytes. An **exabyte** is quintillion (10^{18}) bytes. Although we have no way to know for sure, the Internet probably has a long way to go before it contains an exabyte of data.
    - E-mail generates much of the traffic on the Internet. It is the most popular Internet activity—used by 63 percent of all Internet users—and accounts for more than 34 trillion messages per year in the United States alone.

▶ The simple NSF network shown here and described in the 1985 video, expanded to become today's Internet, providing access to information on every continent.

FIGURE **G-2:** *Distribution of Internet host computers throughout the world*

▶ The distribution of Internet host computers throughout the world varies from areas with a single host (represented by a red circle) to areas with 1 million hosts (represented by purple circles).

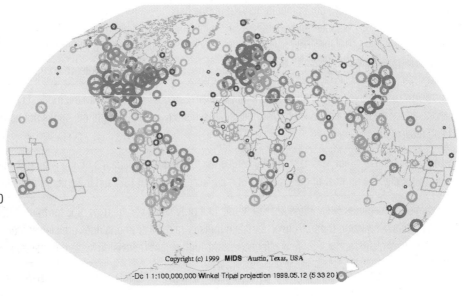

Number of Hosts

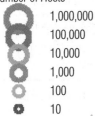

1,000,000
100,000
10,000
1,000
100
10
1

Copyright (c) 1999 **MIDS** Austin, Texas, USA

-Dc 1 1:100,000,000 Winkel Tripel projection 1999.05.12 (5 33 20)

Introducing Internet technology

To understand how you can use the Internet to access information from a computer that is located thousands of miles away, it is helpful to have a little background on the Internet communications network.

- A **network service provider** (NSP), such as MCI or Sprint, maintains a series of communications links for Internet data. These links interconnect at several **network accesses points** (NAPs) so data can travel between NSPs.

- The cables, wires, and satellites that carry Internet data form an interlinked communications network. Data traveling from one Internet computer to another is transmitted from one link in the network to another, along the best possible route. If some links are overloaded or temporarily out of service, the data can be routed through different links. The major Internet communications links make up the **Internet backbone**. Figure G-3 illustrates a layer of the Internet backbone maintained by MCI in the continental United States.

- When you connect your computer to the Internet, you connect to a company that in turn connects to the backbone. An **Internet service provider (ISP)** is a company that maintains a host computer and charges a monthly fee for providing Internet access to businesses, organizations, and individuals.
  - An ISP provides you with communications software and a user account.
  - You supply a modem that connects your computer to your phone line.
  - Your computer dials the ISP's computer and establishes a connection over the phone line.
  - Once you are connected, the ISP routes data between your computer and the Internet backbone.

  Figure G-4 illustrates the communications channels that make it possible for your computer to access the Internet.

- The **connection speed** is the maximum speed at which your modem can communicate with the modems maintained by your ISP. Most of today's modems have a maximum speed of 56 kilobits per second (KBps) although this rate is not necessarily the speed at which you send and receive data.

- The **transfer rate** is the speed at which you can actually send and receive data. It depends on many factors, including the quality of the phone lines in your city, the number of other people who are accessing your ISP, and the amount of traffic on the Internet.

- Although most ISPs offer connections over phone lines, a phone line provides a very narrow pipe for transmitting data. Its typical capacity is only 56,600 bits per second (bps). Connections and transfer rates over phone lines are slower than connections over cables or satellite links. As a result, some ISPs now offer access through a cable television system or personal satellite dish.

- A connection that uses a phone line to establish a temporary Internet connection is referred to as a **dial-up connection**. When your computer hangs up, the connection is broken.

- The efficient flow of data over the communications links on the Internet requires a standard mechanism for routing data to its destination. **Internet communications software** allows your computer to transmit and receive data using the Internet's TCP/IP communication protocols. **TCP/IP** is an acronym for Transport Control Protocol/Internet Protocol, a set of communication rules used by every computer that connects to the Internet. Standard TCP/IP software handles Internet communication between computers that are directly cabled to a network. **SLIP** (Serial Line Internet Protocol) and **PPP** (Point-to-Point Protocol) are versions of TCP/IP that are designed to handle Internet communications over dial-up connections.

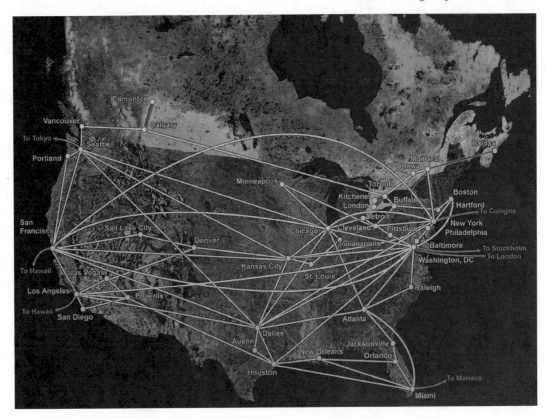

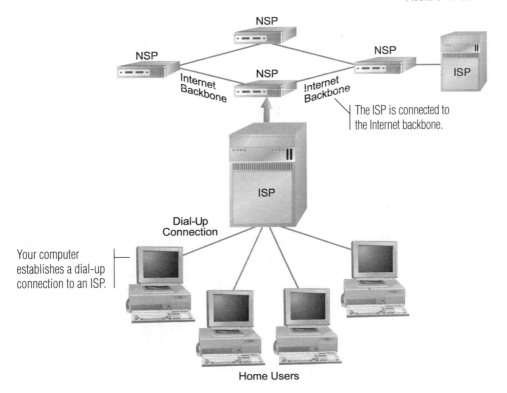

Understanding hosts, domains, and URLs

The Internet includes computers that perform different functions. Some of these computers handle communications and route e-mail, but most publicity about the Internet focuses on computers that provide information such as stock quotes, movie reviews, and sports scores. Regardless of its function, every computer connected to the Internet has a unique identifying number called an IP address.

InfoWeb
DOMAIN NAMES

DETAILS

- An **IP address** is a set of four numbers between 0 and 255 that are separated by periods. For example, 204.146.144.253 is the IP address of the Coca-Cola Company. When data travels over the Internet, it carries the IP address of its destination. At each intersection on the backbone, the data's IP address is examined by a computer called a **router** that forwards the data toward its destination.

- Internet host computers have permanent IP addresses. When your computer establishes a dial-up connection, it is assigned a temporary IP address from a pool maintained by your ISP. When you disconnect from the ISP, your computer's temporary IP address goes back into the pool of IP addresses.

- Although an IP address works for intercomputer communications, it is difficult to remember long strings of numbers. Therefore, many host computers also have an easy-to-remember name, such as cocacola.com. The official term for such a name is **Fully Qualified Domain Name (FQDN)**, or **domain name**. A domain name ends with a three-letter extension that indicates its **top-level domain**. A top-level domain groups the computers on the Internet into the categories shown in Table G-1. In the domain name cocacola.com, *com* indicates that the computer is maintained by a commercial business.

- Outside the United States, country codes serve as top-level domains. For example, Australia's top-level domain is au, Israel's is il, and the United Kingdom's is uk.

- An organization called InterNIC maintains the registry for IP addresses and domain names. By 1997, InterNIC had assigned more than 16 million IP addresses. Both organizations and individuals can register a domain name for an annual fee. Many ISPs will help you process your registration.

- Computers with domain names are popularly referred to as sites. A **site** is a metaphor for a virtual place that exists in cyberspace. For example, a Web site provides a virtual location that you can visit to view information in the form of Web pages. You might envision www.amazon.com as a physical bookstore, but you actually connect to its **Web site**—a location on a computer somewhere on the Internet.

- A Web site is composed of one or more **Web pages**. Each Web page is stored as a separate file and referred to by a unique URL (Uniform Resource Locator). A **URL**, like a domain name, is an Internet address. Whereas the domain name is the IP address of a computer, a URL is the address of a document on a computer. See Figure G-5.

- E-mail that travels over the Internet requires an Internet e-mail address that consists of a user ID and the user's mail server domain name. When Internet e-mail reaches an intersection on the Internet backbone, a router sends it on toward the mail server specified by the domain name. Figure G-6 illustrates the parts of an Internet mail address.

FYI

Although the domain name is always lowercase, the other parts of a URL might be uppercase. When you type URLs, you should be sure to use the correct case

DOMAIN	DESCRIPTION	DOMAIN	DESCRIPTION
org	Professional and nonprofit organizations	**gov**	U.S. government agencies
com	Commercial businesses	**mil**	U.S. military organizations
edu	Colleges and universities	**int**	Organizations established by international treaties
net	Internet administrative organizations		

FIGURE G-5: *Components of a URL*   FIGURE G-6: *Components of an e-mail address*

http://www.course.com/products/titles.html

Protocol   Web server name   Folder name   Document name and filename extension

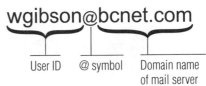

wgibson@bcnet.com

User ID   @ symbol   Domain name of mail server

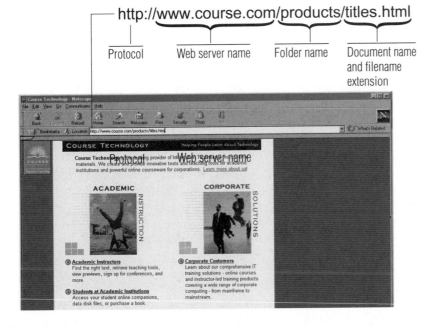

Protocol   Web server name

Explaining the URL

Protocol: The first part of the URL is the protocol. **HTTP** (Hypertext Transfer Protocol) is the protocol or communications system that allows Web browsers to communicate with Web servers. Many of today's Web browsers assume that any address you type begins with http://. If you are using such a browser, you can omit http:// when you type the URL.

Server name: The next part of the URL identifies the Web server. A Web **server** is a computer that uses **Web server software** to transmit Web pages over the Internet. Most Web server names consist of domain names prefixed with www. By entering the Web server name, you access the site's home page. A **home page** is similar to the title page in a book. It identifies the site and contains links to other pages at the site.

Folder name: A Web site is usually stored in a folder. The URL of a Web page reflects the name of any folder or folders in which it is stored.

Web page: A Web site usually contains more than one page. Each page is stored as a separate file. The filename is followed by a special filename extension that identifies the file as an HTML document. Filename extensions for Web pages are typically **.htm** or **.html**.

Introducing the World Wide Web

Unlike the Internet, which is simply a mass of cables and connection points that form a communications network, the World Wide Web (more commonly referred to as the Web) is an Internet service that stores and provides information. The Web is partially responsible for the explosion of interest in the Internet. As an easy-to-use, graphical source of information, the Web opened up the Internet to millions of people who were interested in finding and exchanging information.

THE WEB

WEB PORTALS

THE WORLD WIDE WEB

DETAILS

- In the mid-1960s, Ted Nelson was trying to devise a computer system that could store literary documents, link them according to logical relationships, and allow readers to comment and annotate what they read. He envisioned a set of documents, which he called a "hypertext," connected by a set of "hypertext links" that could be navigated to view additional material related to a topic. He called this project "Xanadu."

- The World Wide Web was created with little fanfare in 1990 at the European Laboratory for Particle Physics (CERN). Within a few years, however, the Web had captured the interest of the news media and the public. Today, Web surfers (as Web users are sometimes called) can visit an estimated 800 million Web pages on more than 2.8 million Web sites containing more than 15 terabytes of data.

- The official description of the World Wide Web is a "wide-area hypermedia information retrieval initiative aiming to give universal access to a large universe of documents."

- The World Wide Web consists of documents, called Web pages, that contain information on a particular topic. A Web page might also include one or more **hyperlinks** (or **links**, as they are commonly called) that point to other Web pages. Links make it easy to follow a thread of related information, even if the pages are stored on computers located in different countries. Figure G-7 shows a conceptual model of linked Web pages.

Using Web portals

A **Web portal** is a Web site that provides a group of particular Web services, such as a search engine, e-mail access, chat rooms, and links to shopping, weather, news, and sports. Popular Web portal sites include America Online (AOL), AT&T WorldNet, CompuServe, Excite, Go Network, Lycos, Microsoft Network (MSN), and Yahoo!. Access to these portal sites is typically free to anyone who has access to the Internet. Some Web portals are maintained by ISPs. They typically charge a membership fee of $10 to $30, which includes dial-up connections, an e-mail account, and a personal Web page. You can access the portal sites for free, however, even if you are not a member.

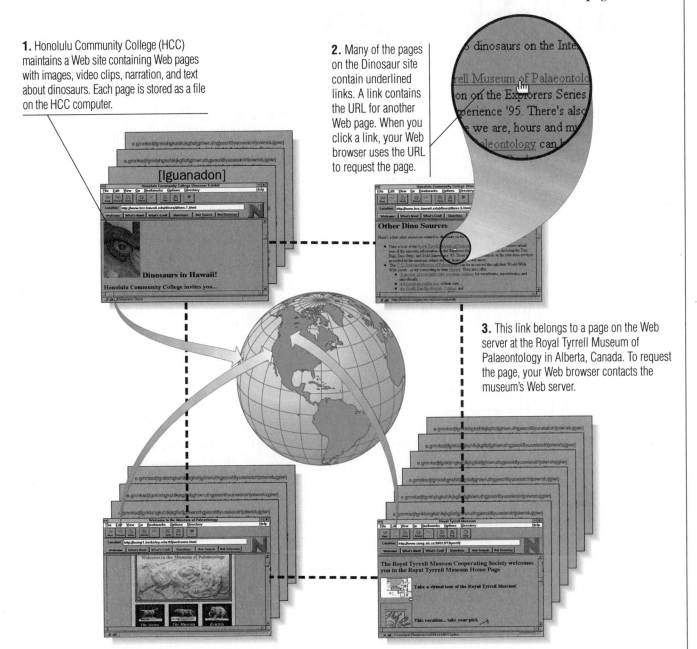

1. Honolulu Community College (HCC) maintains a Web site containing Web pages with images, video clips, narration, and text about dinosaurs. Each page is stored as a file on the HCC computer.

2. Many of the pages on the Dinosaur site contain underlined links. A link contains the URL for another Web page. When you click a link, your Web browser uses the URL to request the page.

3. This link belongs to a page on the Web server at the Royal Tyrrell Museum of Palaeontology in Alberta, Canada. To request the page, your Web browser contacts the museum's Web server.

5. Another link might take you to the University of California Museum of Paleontology. You can use your Web browser to take a virtual tour of the world's dinosaur museums. Your "travel time" from place to place is just the few seconds that it takes to click a link and have a page arrive at your computer.

4. The museum's Web server sends the page to your computer over your Internet connection, then your browser displays it for you.

Using Web browsers

In the past, you needed a separate client software program to access each type of server. For e-mail, you needed an e-mail client software such as Eudora. For FTP, you needed FTP client software. Originally, programs such as Archie, WAIS, TelNet, Gopher, and Newsreader client software were all part of the Internet user's software toolbox. Today, however, a **Web browser** has replaced this awkward collection of client software providing Internet users with a single, all-purpose tool for accessing many types of servers.

DETAILS

- The two most popular Web browsers are Netscape Navigator and Microsoft Internet Explorer.

- Web browsers are used to view Web pages, transfer files between computers, access information, send e-mail, and interact with other Internet users.

- To access a Web page, you either type a URL in the Address text box or click a Web page link. The server then sends the data for the Web page over the Internet to your computer. This data has two components: the information you want to view and a set of instructions that tells your browser how to display it. The instructions include specifications for the color of the background, the size of the text, and the placement of graphics. Additional instructions tell your browser what to do when you click a link.

- Your browser's menu and toolbars help you navigate the Web as you follow links. The Back and Forward buttons trace and retrace your path through the links you've followed from one Web page to another during one session. Your browser:
  - Stores a list of the pages you visit during each session.
  - Displays the list of pages you visit as links. You can click one of these links to revisit a page.
  - Stores a list of your favorite sites, often called **bookmarks** or **favorites**, so that you can link directly to them instead of entering a URL.

- Your browser's home page is usually the first page displayed when your browser starts. You can always return to this page by clicking the Home button. Most browsers let you pick any Web page as the home page, so select one that you use often, such as your favorite search engine or Web portal. In Figure G-8, the Internet Explorer browser is displaying the Go Network portal.

- The Web is constantly changing as new Web sites come online and old sites close. Consequently, links are not always valid. Sometimes when you click a link, nothing happens, or you get an error message like the one shown in Figure G-9. If a Web server is offline for maintenance or busy from heavy traffic, you won't be able to get the Web pages you requested, or you might get them only slowly.

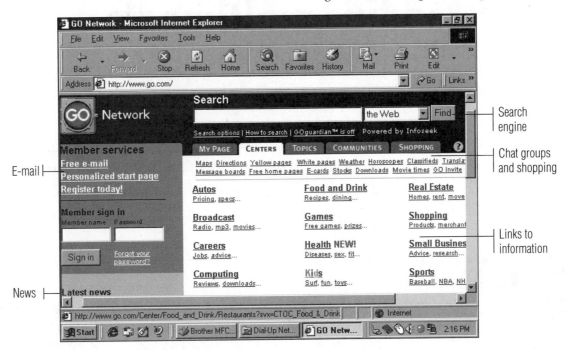

Search engine

Chat groups and shopping

E-mail

Links to information

News

CD
SCREENTOUR

The page cannot be found error is sometimes called a "404 error."

A "page cannot be found" message indicates that a page has moved or no longer exists.

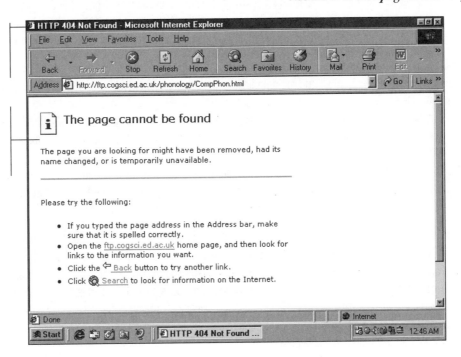

Understanding multimedia on the Web

As you know from your reading, the Internet contains a wealth of information. When people envision multimedia on the Internet, they tend to think of the Web and its wide variety of multimedia elements, including sound, animation, and video. It may seem difficult to imagine Web pages that do not include these multimedia elements, but prior to 1995 most Web pages were simply text.

PLUGINS

DETAILS

- A media element is stored on the Web server in a file. A link for the media element would typically be displayed on a Web page that contains additional information about the topic. When you click a Web page to play a media element, the Web server sends a copy of the media file to your computer. Files can be sent to your computer in one of two ways, depending on how the Web server has been set up.
  - In one case, the Web server sends you a copy of the entire media file before starting to play it. For large video files, you might wait several minutes before the video begins to play.
  - A newer technology, referred to as **streaming media**, sends a small segment of the media file to your computer and begins to play it. While this first segment plays, the Web server sends the next part of the file to your computer, and so on until the media segment ends. Thus, with streaming media technology, your computer plays a media file while receiving it.

- As you browse the Web, you'll find multimedia that are displayed "in place" and multimedia that "run in a separate window." Of the two, in-place technology is more sophisticated.
  - **In-place multimedia technology** plays a media element as a seamless part of a Web page. For example, an **animated GIF**, like the one shown in Figure G-10, uses in-place technology so that the animation appears to play right on the Web page.
  - **Multimedia overlay technology** adds a separate window to your screen in which multimedia elements appear. With some overlay technologies, you must manually close the window when the multimedia segment finishes. Figure G-11 illustrates a media window that overlays a Web page.

- A software module that provides your computer with the capability to view or play a specific type of file is called a **player**, **plug-in**, or **viewer**. In the context of the Web, a plug-in adds a feature to your browser, such as the capability to play media. Popular plug-ins include Acrobat Reader, MacroMedia Shockwave, RealNetworks RealPlayer, and Apple QuickTime.

  Media player software that is provided with Windows includes controls to start, stop, and rewind media file types such as sound files with .wav extensions and videos with .avi extensions. Many media players play only one type of media file; for example, RealAudio player works with only .ra sound files. Before you can use a media element on the Web, your computer must have the corresponding media player.

  Your browser maintains a list of the media players that have been installed on your computer. When you click a link that requires a player that is not present, the browser will display an error message and provide a link to the media player's Web server. Web servers usually give you an opportunity to download and install required media players on your system.

- The way in which most people use the Web is shaped by pull technology. With **pull technology**, you use your browser to request Web pages and "pull" them into view on your computer screen. You get only those pages that you request, and a Web server will not send you information unless you request it.

FIGURE G-10: *An animated GIF*

SCREENTOUR

An animated GIF runs in place as part of a Web page. In this example, the spacecraft rotates to illustrate its operation in space.

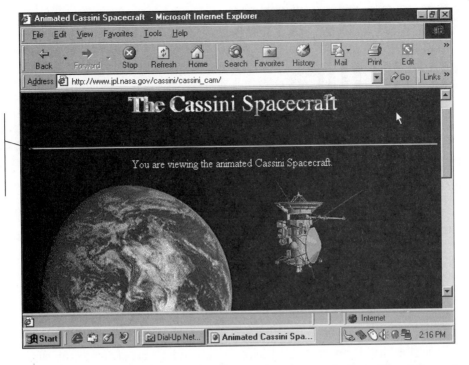

FIGURE G-11: *Multimedia overlay technology*

SCREENTOUR

Some multimedia elements play in a window that overlays the Web page.

Push Technology

Push technology sends you information that you didn't directly request. To receive pushed information from a Web site, you first register and then download the push plug-in software. Each push technology requires its own plug-in. At most sites, the registration and the plug-in are free. Once you've registered, you receive pushed information whenever your computer is connected to the Internet. For example, if you register at a site that pushes stock information, then every time you connect to the Internet, your computer will receive and display current stock prices. Another example of push technology is a webcast, which broadcasts a stream of continually changing information over the Web. A webcast can be used for special event coverage.

Downloading and uploading files

As you become more familiar with the Web, you may find yourself wanting to transfer files either from the Web to your computer or from your computer to the Web. The process of transferring a file from a remote computer to your computer's disk drive is called **downloading**. The process of transferring a file from your computer to a remote computer is called **uploading**. This lesson takes a closer look at transferring files via the Web.

FTP SOFTWARE

DOWNLOAD SITES

DETAILS

○━┳ When you are viewing a Web page, the Web page is held temporarily in the RAM of your computer but is not stored as a file on disk. If a Web page contains a graphic, sound, or video, you can store that file on disk for later use. Most Web browsers allow you to easily download Web page elements such as pictures, sounds, animations, and videos. See Figure G-12.

○━┳ In addition to downloading Web elements, you may want to download other files, such as program files or data files. You may also want to upload files to a colleague. Uploading and downloading files via the Internet offer many advantages of time and resources. For example, imagine a writer living in British Columbia who needs to send a very large manuscript file that includes images to an editor in New York. Because she is very close to a deadline, she cannot take the time to print out the documents, save the file to a Zip disk, and send it all via the mail (several days) or even overnight delivery service (one day.) She can quickly upload the file to an Internet server, however, so the editor in New York can download it as soon as the file transfer is complete.

○━┳ Although most Web browsers allow you to download files, not all allow you to upload. Nevertheless, you can both upload and download files, using **FTP** (File Transfer Protocol), which is a set of rules for transferring files between computers.

○━┳ **FTP client software**, such as WinFTP (published by Ipswitch, Inc.), includes the ability to both upload and download from FTP servers.

○━┳ Many FTP servers allow people to log in using "anonymous" as the user ID and their e-mail address as the password. For security reasons, however, most FTP servers provide upload capabilities only to people who have valid user accounts. To upload a file using your browser or FTP client software, you need to know the domain name for the FTP server on which you have an account. You must log in using your user ID and password.

○━┳ The Internet is a terrific source of free software. Its sites list thousands of downloadable shareware programs. For example, many publishers offer free trial versions of commercially available software that you can download and use for a specified trial period, as shown in Figure G-13.

  • Downloading and installing software from the Web typically involve four simple steps: (1) download the file, (2) find the file on your computer, (3) open the file, and (4) complete the installation.

  • A download site will usually provide the detailed instructions on how to download and install the software. Most downloadable software is stored as **self-extracting files**. A self-extracting file is a single file that holds all of the modules for the software and that is compressed to reduce its size and minimize download time. When the download is complete, the compressed file must be "extracted" to return it to its original size and its original modules. The software can then be installed on your computer.

CD
SCREENTOUR

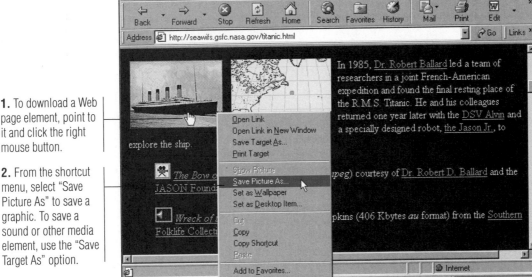

1. To download a Web page element, point to it and click the right mouse button.

2. From the shortcut menu, select "Save Picture As" to save a graphic. To save a sound or other media element, use the "Save Target As" option.

FIGURE G-13: *Downloading and installing software*

CD
SCREENTOUR

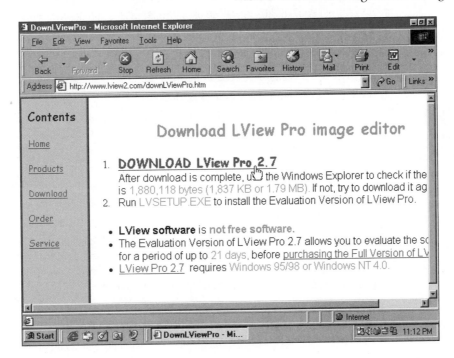

Compressing files

To compress or "zip up" a file or group of text or graphic files, you need to use compression software. Compression software effectively reduces the size of text and BMP files. WinZip and PKZip are popular file compression utilities that you can obtain by mail from a shareware distributor, download from the Internet, or purchase from a local computer store. Compressed files include the .zip filename extension. They must be uncompressed before you can use them. You can use WinZip or PKZip to uncompress compressed files. You should make it a rule to compress any e-mail attachments that exceed 100 KB.

Interacting online

The most popular way to interact with other people on the Internet is via e-mail. As you have learned, your e-mail interactions can include sending mail, receiving mail, replying to mail you receive, forwarding mail you receive, and even sending attachments. There are other ways to interact online as well, such as discussion groups, chat groups, and multiplayer games. This lesson looks at some ways of interacting online.

CHAT AND DISCUSSION GROUPS

CYBERSPACE

GAMES

DETAILS

☞ Discussion Groups: In a **discussion group**, participants share their views on a specific issue or topic. The Internet has thousands of discussion groups on such diverse topics as snowboarding, urban policy, rave music, and William Gibson's cyberspace novels. Discussion groups take place **asynchronously**, meaning that the discussion participants are not interacting online at the same time. You can leave a message asking a question about a particular topic. Over the next few days, other participants can post comments and responses, post new questions, or simply read the posted comments and responses.

☞ Chat Groups: In a chat group, participants share their thoughts on a variety of topics; unlike discussion groups, however, chat groups are not limited to one topic. Although chat groups are sometimes called discussion groups, there is a distinct difference between the two. Discussion groups take place asynchronously, but chat groups take place **synchronously**, meaning that people are interacting online at the same time.

   To participate in a chat group, you generally choose a nickname and then enter a chat room. As chat participants type, their messages appear on your screen. You'll see the messages from everyone in the chat room. Chat groups can be an effective forum for professional interaction—for example, when physicians in different locations use the Internet to collaborate on a diagnosis. Generally speaking, however, chat groups are often less focused than discussion groups and can branch off into a variety of topics.

☞ Recently, chat groups have come under fire because of their potential dangers in terms of personal safety and privacy. Use common sense in your chat room interactions.

- Don't represent yourself as something you're not.
- Don't provide personal information, such as your name or address.
  Internet society, like society as a whole, has its share of deviants and rip-off experts. Most chat groups, however, are civilized, as shown in Figure G-14. Many Internet users today enjoy interacting on the Internet via chat groups.

☞ Multiplayer Games: Online **multiplayer gaming** is another aspect of Internet interaction. From simple competitive word games to massive adventure games, the world of Internet gaming has it all. See Figure G-15.

   Some multiplayer games are synchronous, whereas others are asynchronous. As with chat groups, to participate in a synchronous game, you and the other players must be online at the same time. To participate in asynchronous games, you post each move to the game's referee, and then you can pick up the results and submit new moves the next time you are online. Many multiplayer games require a small fee to participate.

FIGURE G-14: *A chat session*

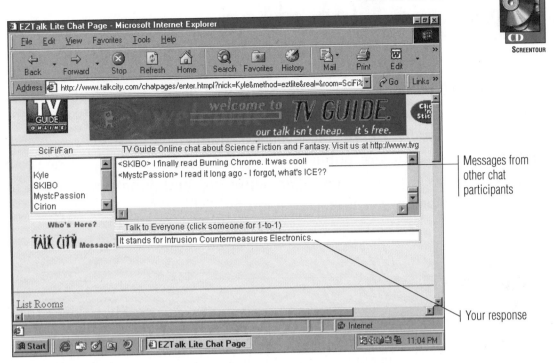

Messages from other chat participants

Your response

FIGURE G-15: *Multiplayer games*

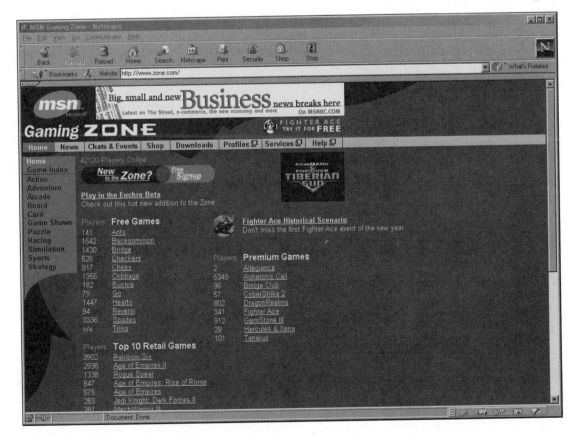

Creating Web sites

Using the Web as a source of information and interaction is great, but eventually you might want to become a Web author and publish your own pages. You might become even more ambitious and decide to create and manage your own Web site. The Web provides opportunities for publishing tasks ranging from a single page to an entire Web site. Using today's software tools, Web authoring and publishing are not much more difficult than word processing or desktop publishing.

InfoWeb
E-COMMERCE
CONSTRUCTION

DETAILS

☞ Why would you want to publish on the Web? You might have information that you want to make available to the public, such as your résumé or a calendar of events for your club. You might have services or products that you would like to offer to people in any geographic location. You might want to collect information from people by using surveys or questionnaires. You might publish a series of Web pages as part of a corporate site to describe the products and services available from your department. Freelance artists or programmers could use a series of Web pages to publish examples of their work. A university instructor might publish a series of Web pages containing the syllabus, study guide, and assignments for a course. Web publishing can help you get your message out as well as collect data.

☞ A single Web page is simple to create and can be used to electronically publish useful information such as your résumé or a small-business fact sheet. Another use for a single Web page is to provide a list of links to sites with information on a particular topic. See Figure G-16.

☞ A series of interlinked Web pages acts like a mini-site, but does not have its own domain name.

☞ A full Web site, with its own domain name, provides a solid point of presence on the Internet. See Figure G-17. Businesses and organizations of all types and sizes establish Web sites to provide information to their customers and to sell products. Many online businesses try to use a recognizable domain name, such as www.landsend.com, which helps customers arrive at the site without a lengthy search.

☞ Basic Web pages contain text, graphics, and links. You need only a few tools to create and publish them. More-sophisticated Web pages might include animation, sound, video, and even interactive elements, such as questionnaires or surveys. To incorporate these more complex features in your Web pages, you might need to use more sophisticated publishing tools and your Web server might require special server software.

Building an e-commerce site

With the availability of security software to protect customers' credit card numbers, online shopping has become very popular. **E-commerce** refers to the process of buying products and services by means of the Internet. It encompasses online shopping, applies to innovative auction sites, and includes stock trading. E-commerce is not the exclusive domain of big business; in fact, individuals can easily set up their own e-commerce sites by creating simple Web pages that display product information and include telephone numbers to call when placing an order. Many Web hosting services and portal sites offer an **e-commerce enabled Web site**, which simplifies the process of constructing an online storefront. The software that runs an e-commerce site, displays your merchandise, collects orders, and processes credit cards typically resides in the computers of the Web hosting service.

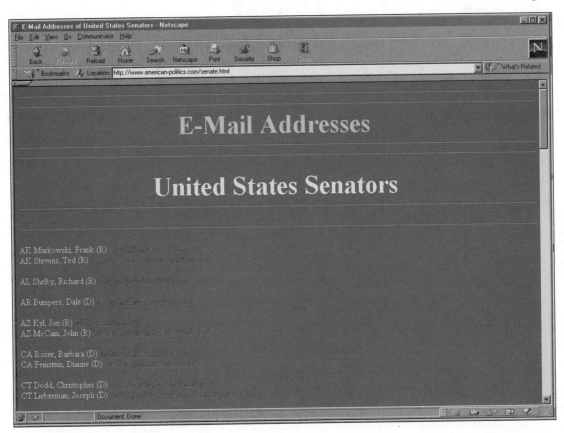

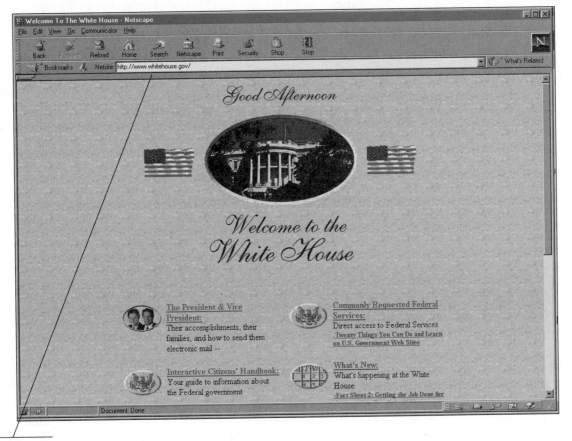

Domain name

Understanding HTML

Every Web page is stored on a computer as an **HTML (Hypertext Markup Language)** document. Although you don't need to be concerned about HTML tags when you are simply viewing Web pages, you do need to be familiar with HTML when you develop Web pages. A little background will help you understand HTML and the way in which your Web browser interprets HTML.

InfoWeb
HTML

InfoWeb
AUTHORING TOOLS

Lab
WEB PAGES & HTML

DETAILS

- An HTML document contains special instructions called HTML tags that tell a Web browser how to display the text, graphics, and background of a Web page. If you look at the text of a Web page before a browser displays it, you'll see the HTML tags set off in angle brackets. See Figure G-18.

- A basic HTML document has two parts: the title and the body. The head of the document specifies a title that appears on the title bar of the Web browser when the Web page is displayed. The body of the document contains informational text, graphics, and links.

- HTML uses tags to identify directions. Some HTML tags work in pairs. A tag without a slash is the opening tag; and a tag with a slash is the ending tag. For example, the <B> tag means to begin boldface text and a companion </B> tag means to end the boldface text. Every HTML document should begin with the tag <HTML> and end with the tag </HTML>. Some tags do not have a corresponding ending tag; for example, you only need a single <BR> tag to create a line break. Table G-2 contains a basic set of HTML tags that you can use to create HTML documents for Web pages.

- HTML tags are basic Web page development tools that can be used to create interesting Web pages. They have limitations, however. Consequently, additional Web page development tools have been developed to overcome HTML's limitations.
  - **DHTML** (Dynamic HTML) allows elements of a Web page to be changed while the page is being viewed.
  - **XML** (Extensible Markup Language) is a document format similar to HTML but allows the Web page developer to define customized tags and produce special effects not available with HTML.
  - **Java** is a programming language developed for Web applications.
  - **ActiveX controls** allow Web pages to perform software-like tasks rather than simply display data.

- The traditional way to create an HTML document is with a basic text editor. You simply type the HTML tags and the text for your Web page, then save the file with an .htm filename extension. Using familiar software tools, such as your word processing program, can help you create Web pages, but the tools don't provide a high level of control over the final appearance of your Web page. Your word processing program will do its best to translate a word processing document into an HTML document. Word processing programs were designed to create printed documents, however, and they often include features not available in HTML. In the final analysis, exact formats and arrangements displayed in your word processing program may not translate as you might expect or want on the Web page.

- Remembering the purpose of each HTML tag, typing the tags into a document, and revising them are fairly tedious tasks. **Web authoring software** makes it much easier to create HTML documents using word processor-style interfaces, pre-designed templates, and wizards. Top Web authoring software titles include Microsoft FrontPage and Claris Home Page. Most of these packages provide a word processor-style interface, but allow you to implement only those features that are available in HTML. As you use the Web authoring software to enter text, select type styles, and insert graphics, the software automatically inserts appropriate HTML tags.

- Many Web authoring software packages also provide tools to manage an entire Web site. In addition to helping you create individual Web pages, they maintain a page of links and automatically test links to pages at other sites to ensure that the links remain valid. If the software package includes Web server software, you can test your Web site on your own computer.

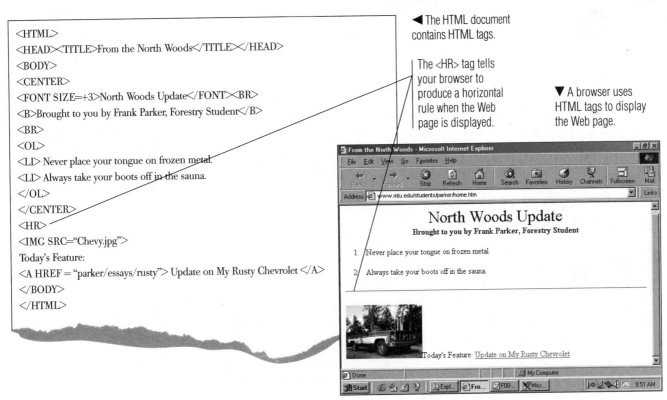

```
<HTML>
<HEAD><TITLE>From the North Woods</TITLE></HEAD>
<BODY>
<CENTER>
<FONT SIZE=+3>North Woods Update</FONT><BR>
<B>Brought to you by Frank Parker, Forestry Student</B>
<BR>
<OL>
<LI> Never place your tongue on frozen metal.
<LI> Always take your boots off in the sauna.
</OL>
</CENTER>
<HR>
<IMG SRC="Chevy.jpg">
Today's Feature:
<A HREF = "parker/essays/rusty"> Update on My Rusty Chevrolet </A>
</BODY>
</HTML>
```

◄ The HTML document contains HTML tags.

The <HR> tag tells your browser to produce a horizontal rule when the Web page is displayed.

▼ A browser uses HTML tags to display the Web page.

TABLE G-2: *Basic HTML tags*

HTML TAG	DESCRIPTION AND USE
<HTML> </HTML>	Place the HTML tag at the beginning of a document and place the /HTML tag at the end of the document.
<HEAD> <TITLE>... </TITLE> </HEAD>	Place immediately after the HTML tag. The text between the TITLE tags will appear on the title bar.
<BODY> </BODY>	Place all text and tags for the body of your Web page between the BODY tags.
<FONT SIZE=+3> </FONT>	To specify a font size use a positive or negative number in place of +3.
 	The BR tag creates a line break. Use two to create a blank line.
<UL> </UL> or <OL> </OL>	UL creates a bulleted list; OL creates a numbered list. Start each list item with the LI tag.
<CENTER> ... </CENTER>	Text between the CENTER tags will be centered.
<B> ... </B>	Text between the B tags will appear in boldface.
<I> ... </I>	Text between the I tags will appear in italics.
<A HREF =" "> ... </A>	To create an underlined link, place the URL for the link between the quotation marks then type the link name between the tags.
<IMG SCR=" ">	To display a graphic, place its filename between the quotation marks.
<HR>	The HR tag inserts a horizontal line.

Publishing Web sites

Today, the Internet connects computers all over the globe and supplies information to people of all ages and interests. It provides an opportunity for people with diverse backgrounds to interact and engage in life-long education. When communicating on the Web via e-mail or through Web pages, it is important to be sure that your message is understood. Sometimes, it is not easy to find the right balance between art and functionality to produce a really great Web page. This lesson provides tips for planning, designing, creating, and publishing Web pages on the Internet.

AUTHORING TIPS

DETAILS

- ⊶ If you decide to publish on the Web, it is important to follow basic rules for good Web page design. See Table G-3. Viewers will lose patience and move on to other Web sites if it takes too long for your pages to appear or if the text is illegible.

- ⊶ A really great Web page is one that clearly communicates its purpose. In addition to following the basic rules for Web page design, here are some other protocols you should follow when designing Web pages:
  - Plan your Web page so that it fulfills its purpose. It is easier to communicate your message if you have a clear idea of what you want your Web page to say.
  - Design a template to unify your pages. A design template is a set of specifications for the location and format of all elements that should appear on your Web pages. It visually ties together a series of Web pages and provides a consistent interface. You template design might include any of the following elements: background, title, text, lists, headings, subheadings, video clips, graphics, music, animations, and navigation buttons. Get design ideas and develop a sense of style by looking at Web pages similar to those you plan to create.
  - Include navigation elements. A carefully selected set of navigational buttons or links makes it easier for users to jump from page to page in a logical order. Navigation elements should be clearly visible and easy to understand. See Figure G-19.
  - Respect the copyrights and intellectual property rights of other Web sites. Make sure you obtain permission before you use material from other Web sites and always give credit appropriately.
  - Identify your pages. Always include a title, a way for people to contact you, copyright information, and the latest updated information.
  - Include dates. Incorporate a "last updated" date into the main page of your site. Date any articles, essays, and other documents to help the reader place information in context.

- ⊶ The end of the publishing process involves some very important steps.
  - Test each page locally. Verify that every element displays correctly in a browser. It is important to remember that your hard drive is much faster than a dial-up connection, so the text and graphics for your Web page will appear more quickly when you test locally than they will appear for someone viewing your page over the Internet.
  - Transfer pages to a Web server. Whether you're publishing a single page, a series of pages, or an entire Web site, you must put your pages on a Web server. Although Web server software is available for your home computer, you probably don't want to leave your computer on all the time with a live phone line link to the Internet. Instead, you should look for a site that will host your pages. Many universities allocate space for student home pages and resumes. ISPs, such as America Online and AT&T WorldNet, also offer space for individual home pages. If you are setting up a site for your business, consider **a Web hosting service** that provides space on its Internet servers for a monthly fee.
  - Test your links. Test the links on your pages, transfer your pages to your Web server, and then test all of your links again.
  - Update your site to keep it current. Review the information on your pages and verify that the links are still valid. Change, test, and revise pages offline, then post them when they are complete.

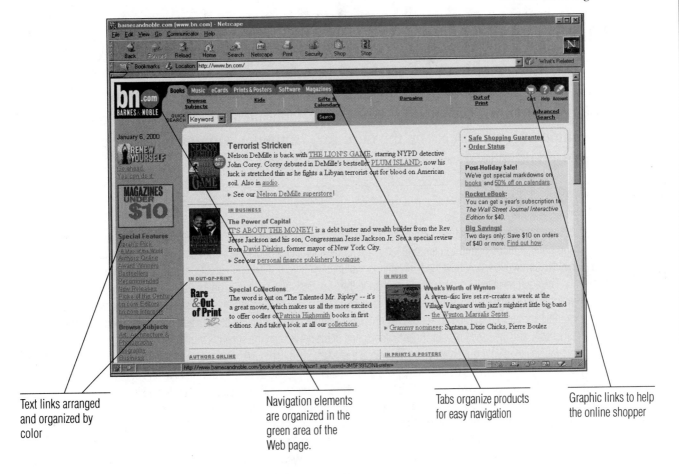

Text links arranged and organized by color

Navigation elements are organized in the green area of the Web page.

Tabs organize products for easy navigation

Graphic links to help the online shopper

TABLE **G-3**: *Basic Web design rules*

Text	For readability, use black type for large sections of text. Maintain narrow line widths. Text that stretches across the entire width of the screen is more difficult to read than text in columns. Make sure you proofread your document for spelling errors.
Background	White or a very pale color makes a good background. Avoid drab gray and don't let your background color or graphic make it difficult to read the text.
Graphics	Try not to use graphics files that exceed 30 KB because larger files take too long to transfer, load, and appear on a Web page. Use graphics with .gif or .jpg extensions. To include a large graphic, present it as a small "thumbnail" with a link to the larger version of the graphic.

Connecting to the Internet

Although you can access the Internet using the cable television system, a personal satellite dish, or a cellular phone system, most people use a telephone line. To access the Internet from your home computer, you must set up the necessary computer equipment, locate an ISP, install the appropriate software on your computer, and then dial in.

ISPs

MODEMS

DETAILS

▸ Set up the necessary computer equipment. The basic equipment for setting up online communications consists of a computer, a modem, and a telephone line. The modem converts data from your computer into signals that can travel over telephone lines. Follow the instructions included with your modem to set it up, as shown in Figure G-20.

The equipment that you use does not change the activities you can pursue online, but it can affect the speed at which you can accomplish these tasks. A fast computer, such as a 600 MHz Pentium, speeds up some activities such as viewing graphics online. A fast modem speeds the process of sending and receiving data. In addition to the speed of your processor and the speed of your modem, the speed of the server and the speed of your communications link will affect the overall speed of your online activities. Both PCs and Macintosh computers can connect to online services.

- As you'll recall, the connection speed is the maximum speed at which your modem can communicate with the modems maintained by your ISP. You can check your connection speed by double-clicking the connection icon in the Windows taskbar to open the connection dialog box, as shown in Figure G-21.
- The telephone line that you use for voice communication is suitable for most online activities. Corporations sometimes use faster communications links, such as ISDN or T1 lines. Your telephone line—though not the speediest communications link—is certainly the least expensive. When you are using your telephone line for online activities, you can't simultaneously use it for voice calls; while you are online, people who call you will get a busy signal. If you pick up the telephone receiver to make an outgoing call while you are online, your online connection might terminate.

▸ Locate an ISP. An ISP supplies you with a user account on a host computer that has access to the Internet. When you connect your personal computer to the host computer using a modem and the appropriate software, you gain access to the Internet. Your school might provide Internet access for students and faculty who want to use the Internet from off campus. An Internet connection provided by an educational institution is typically free. Commercial ISPs, such as CompuServe, AT&T WorldNet, and America Online, also provide Internet access. In addition, some telephone companies, cable TV companies, and independent telecommunications firms offer Internet connections.

▸ Install the appropriate software. Many ISPs provide their subscribers with a complete software package that includes browser and Internet communications software. **Internet communications software** allows your computer to transmit and receive data using the Internet TCP/IP communications protocol. The Windows operating system also provides Internet communications software, as shown in Figure G-22.

▸ Establish computer communications. Today, the software supplied by most Internet service providers is self-configuring. In other words, the first time you run the software, it examines your computer system and automatically selects the appropriate software settings. You must deal with technical specifications only if your computer equipment, modem, and telephone line are not standard.

▸ Dial in. Most Internet communications software presents an icon on your computer's desktop or appears on the Start menu. You start the software by clicking the icon, which automatically tells the computer to load your Internet communications client software, which will use SLIP, PPP, or a similar protocol to handle TCP/IP protocols as your computer transmits and receives data through the modem. The Internet communications client software dials the ISP using a stored phone number.

If your user ID and password have been stored as well, the communications client software will automatically log you in. If any of these elements has not been stored, you will have to enter it manually when prompted to do so to establish a connection to the Internet. Some people prefer not to store their user ID and password in the client software for security reasons.

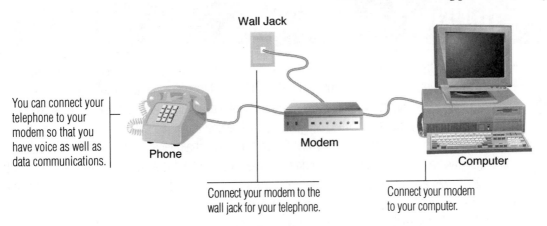

Wall Jack

You can connect your telephone to your modem so that you have voice as well as data communications.

Phone

Modem

Computer

Connect your modem to the wall jack for your telephone.

Connect your modem to your computer.

FIGURE G-21: *Checking your connection*

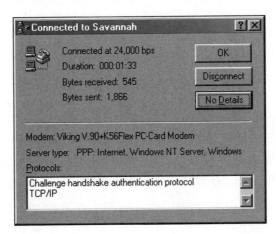

FIGURE G-22: *Dial-up Networking*

CD

SCREENTOUR

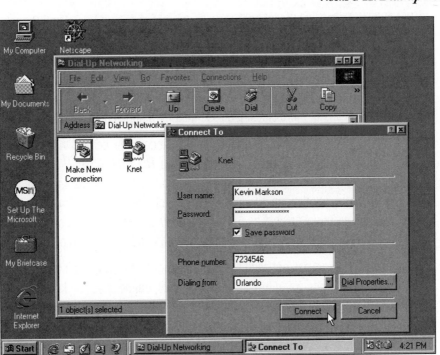

InfoWeb

INFORMATION QUALITY

In an episode of the *X-Files*, Agent Scully warns Mulder about his search into the unexplored realm of extraterrestrial and paranormal phenomena: "The truth is out there, but so are lies." And so it is on the Internet, where truth mingles with lies, rumors, myths, and urban legends. The Internet is uncensored and unregulated. Anyone with a Web page or an e-mail account can rapidly and widely distribute information, which is often redistributed and forwarded like a chain letter on steroids. As an example, one e-mail message, circulated in the summer of 1999, contained this alarming first-person account: "When Zack was 2 years old, I put on the waterproof sunscreen. I don't know how, but he got some in his eyes. I called the poison control center and they told me to rush Zack to the ER now. I found out for the first time that many kids each year lose their sight to waterproof sunscreen. Zack did go blind for two days. It was horrible."

Worried parents forwarded this e-mail message to their friends, and many of them threw their sunscreen in the trash. In August of that year, members of an NBC television news team reported that they had researched the story, but failed to find evidence of any child becoming blind from sunscreen. They concluded their report by saying, "This is one of those stories that has spun out of control—touted as fact, when in reality, it's nothing more than a modern Internet myth."

The Internet has also been blamed for circulating reports that the U.S. Navy shot down TWA Flight 800. Pierre Salinger, an ex-TV reporter and a former advisor to President John F. Kennedy, made front-page headlines in November 1996 when he displayed documents that described how the Navy was testing missiles off Long Island and accidentally hit Flight 800. Although Salinger would not reveal the source of the documents, it turned out that they had been circulated on the Internet months earlier.

The *Chicago Tribune* described Salinger's error as "merely the latest outbreak of the disturbing new information-age phenomenon of bogus news," and went on to say that "America is awash in a growing and often disruptive avalanche of false information that takes on a life of its own in the electronic ether of the Internet, talk radio, and voice mail until it becomes impervious to denial and debunking."

But is it fair to say that the Internet has a monopoly on false information? Probably not. Even well-established newspapers, magazines, and television news shows report stories that are later found to be misleading or untrue. In an article published online in *Salon*, Scott Rosenberg asks, "Who's more responsible for the spread of misinformation, the Internet or the news media? Well, ask yourself how you first heard of Salinger's memo: was it from the Net, or from a TV broadcast? The sad truth is that the old media are far more efficient disseminators of bogus news than the new."

Before the Internet became a ubiquitous part of modern life, certain "rules of thumb" helped to distinguish truth from lies and fact from fiction. In *The Truth About URLs*, Robin Raskin writes, "When printed junk mail floods our overcrowded mailboxes we have some antennae for the bogus causes and the fly-by-night foundations. We've come to expect *The New York Times* to be a credible source of information; we're not as sure about *The National Enquirer*... It takes years to establish these sorts of cultural cues for knowing whether we're getting good information or a bum steer."

Perhaps the Internet has not been around long enough for us to establish the cultural cues we need to distinguish fact from fiction in Web pages, e-mails, online chats, and discussion groups. You can get some help from the Web itself. A number of sites keep track of the myths and legends that circulate on the Internet. Before you spread dire warnings about sunscreen or call a press conference to report a government coverup, you can check one of these sites for the real scoop. See Figure G-23.

▶ It is easy to spread conspiracy theories on the Internet, but several "watchdog" sites try to present the "facts" that dispute or confirm the theories.

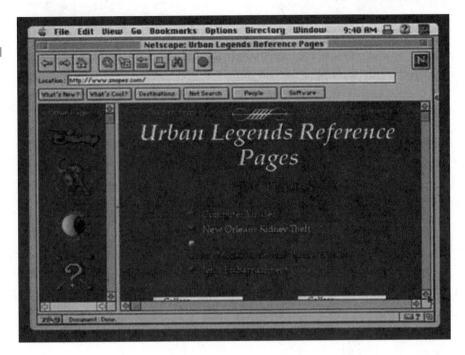

EXPAND THE IDEAS

1. Do older people with less Internet experience tend to be more naïve about Internet information than younger people who have been "raised" on the Internet? Find several examples of articles, documentaries, or news stories on verifying facts and data on the Internet. Write a summary of each article or media piece. Analyze your findings. Was the media voice consistent? Why or why not?

2. Have you ever received e-mail chain letters or alarming messages about fake viruses? What was your reaction? Write a paper detailing the steps you should follow to verify or negate the validity of such messages.

3. Have you heard of or received e-mail detailing some incredible story or consumer event? Did you believe it? Did you spread the story to your friends before fully examining the source and research the facts? How could this situation have been avoided? Compile your ideas into a poster presentation.

4. Can you think of another way in which information spreads so quickly? How does society monitor and check the facts for other forms of media like newspapers and television? Find several examples of articles, documentaries, or news stories on journalism and integrity in journalism. Form a discussion group and share your articles. Then compile a group presentation on your articles; summarizing them for the class. How are the situations in the articles similar and how are they different? What steps were taken to verify the facts? Were these steps appropriate? Sufficient? What else would you have done to monitor the facts?

5. Do you have your own set of rules to help you evaluate information on the Internet? Write a two-page paper detailing how you evaluate information. Do you follow an existing model? Be sure to include your resources.

End of Unit Exercises

STUDY TIPS

1. Make a list of the Internet services you can access using a Web browser. Explain how each one works and how it would benefit you in your daily life.

2. Indicate the type of software you can use to do each of the following. Write a brief description of how you would do each task.

   a. Download a file.

   b. Upload a file.

   c. View a Web page.

   d. Play a video.

3. Describe what happens when you view a Web page and how it differs from downloading a file.

4. Describe the differences between a Web server, an e-mail server, a Web page on your computer, an FTP site, and a Web site.

5. Explain tools you can use to create HTML documents.

FILL IN THE BEST ANSWER

1. The _____ is a collection of local, regional, national, and international computer networks that are linked together to exchange data and distribute processing tasks.

2. Internet traffic is measured in _____.

3. The _____, created in 1969, connected computers at four universities and is the predecessor of the Internet.

4. A(n) _____ is 1 quintillion (10^{18}) bytes.

5. All the computers on the Internet use a standard set of communication rules called _____.

6. A(n) _____ such as MCI or Sprint maintains a series of communication links for Internet data.

7. The address http://www.cyberspace.com is a(n) _____.

8. The top-level domain com is for _____, and the top-level domain edu is for _____.

9. A computer domain name is popularly referred to as a(n) _____.

10. Your browser's _____ page is the first one you see when your browser starts.

11. A technology called _____ essentially plays a media file while your computer receives it.

12. A(n) _____ is a software module that adds a specific feature to your browser, such as the capability to play videos.

13. A Web _____ is a Web site that provides a group of popular Web services such as a search engine, e-mail access, chat rooms, and links to shopping.

14. The process of transferring a file from a remote location to your computer's disk drive is called _____.

15. Most downloadable software is stored as a(n) _____ file, a single file that holds all of the modules for the software.

16. Basic Web pages contain only _____, _____, and _____.

17. A basic HTML document has two parts: the title and the _____.

18. _____ software is specifically designed to create HTML documents that will be displayed as Web pages.

19. When you include _____ in your Web pages, you should use those with .gif or .jpg filename extensions.

20. _____ refers to the process of buying products and services by means of the Internet.

INDEPENDENT CHALLENGE 1

Understanding and knowing how to use the Internet will help you in many areas of your life.

To complete this independent challenge:

1. Draw a conceptual diagram that shows how the Internet connects computers. Include and label the following elements: backbone, dial-up connection, host computers, router, NSP computer, ISP computer, and home computer.

2. List the steps you would take to connect your computer at home to the Internet.

3. Provide an example of an IP address, a domain name, a URL, and an e-mail address. In your own words, describe the elements each contains.

4. On the Internet, you can interact with people in discussion groups, chat groups, and interactive games. Describe the difference between synchronous and asynchronous interactions, and explain how each relates to chats, discussion groups, and games.

INDEPENDENT CHALLENGE 2

Although the Internet is only 30 years old, it has a rich and fascinating history. Use Internet or library resources to write a research paper about the Internet. In your paper, be sure to answer—but do not limit yourself to—the following questions.

To complete this independent challenge, answer these questions:

1. What are the key events in the development of the Internet?

2. What is the timeline for these key events?

   a. What is the Internet's current status?

   b. What changes are likely to take place in the future?

   c. What ethical issues do you think are raised by the existence of the Internet?

3. The Internet, like most societies, has certain standards for behavior. What's generally acceptable online behavior in cyberspace culture?

4. Design a poster of Internet rules. Decide which audience your poster targets: children, high school students, college students, business people, and so on. Try to use words and images that will appeal to your target audience.

INDEPENDENT CHALLENGE 3

Surfing the Web will take you to many interesting sites. As you visit each site, you will notice differences among the Web pages. To some extent, good design is a matter of taste, and, when it comes to Web page design, there are usually many possible solutions that will provide a pleasing look and efficient navigational tools. On the other hand, some designs just don't seem to work because they make the text difficult to read or navigate.

To complete this independent challenge:

1. Select a Web page that you think could use improvement. You may find the page by browsing on the Web or by looking in magazines for screen shots of Web pages.

2. Save and print the page or photocopy the magazine picture.

3. Use colored pencils or markers to sketch your plan for improving the page. Annotate your sketch by pointing out the features you have changed and explaining why you think your makeover will be more effective than the original Web page.

INDEPENDENT CHALLENGE 4

Many people have their own home pages. A home page is a statement of who you are and what your interests may be. You can design your own home page. Depending on the tools you have available, you might be able to create a real page and publish it on the Web. If these tools are not available, you will still be able to complete the initial design work.

To complete this independent challenge:

1. Write a brief description of the purpose of your home page and your expected audience. For example, you might plan to use your home page to showcase your résumé to prospective employers.

2. List the elements you plan to include on your home page. Briefly describe any graphics or media elements you want to include.

3. Create a document that contains the information you want to include on your home page.

4. Make a sketch of your home page showing the colors you plan to use and the navigation elements you plan to include. Annotate this sketch to describe how these elements follow effective Web page design guidelines.

5. If you have the tools available to create the entire HTML document for your home page, do so. Make sure that you test the page locally using your browser. Use the Print option on the File menu of your browser to print your page.

6. If you have permission to publish your Web page on a Web server, do so. Provide your instructor with the URL for your page.

The URL for each Web page uniquely identifies each site. When selecting a URL, businesses try to include their names or products in the URL in an effort to better promote themselves on the Internet. As being on the Web becomes more common in our society, many companies are including URLs in their print advertisements. As you encounter URLs, you need to be aware that sometimes they are not what they appear to be.

To complete this independent challenge:

1. Look through a local paper and list five local businesses in your area that incorporate Web site information into their advertisements. Cut out the advertisements and circle the URL.

2. Find the URLs for five of the following businesses or organizations:

   Nike, Trek Bicycles, Burger King, McDonalds, The New York Times, The Washington Post, GM, IBM, Microsoft, the U.S. Congress, the U.S. Department of Agriculture, your college or university, the New York Yankees, the Chicago Bulls, your favorite baseball team, your favorite football team, your local town government, a hospital in your area

3. Search the Web and find three URLs whose names don't clearly identify the business or product. Search the names that you think would have been better choices.

   - Did you find that those names were used by another company?
   - Why do you think these businesses could not use the name you might have selected?

4. The top-level domain makes a difference in a Web site. List the differences between the following sites, identifying each:

   - FCC.gov and FCC.com
   - FBI.com and FBI.gov
   - MIT.com and MIT.edu

One of the most popular services on the Internet is the World Wide Web. This lab is a Web simulator that teaches you how to use Web browser software to find information. You can use this lab regardless of whether your school provides you with Internet access.

1. Click the Steps button to learn how to use Web browser software. As you proceed through the Steps, answer all of the QuickCheck questions that appear. After you complete the Steps, you will see a QuickCheck Summary Report. Follow the instructions on the screen to print this report.

2. Click the Explore button on the Welcome screen. Use the Web browser to locate a weather map of the Caribbean Virgin Islands. What is its URL?

3. A scuba diver named Wadson Lachouffe has been searching for the fabled treasure of the pirate Greybeard. A link from the Adventure Travel Web site, *www.atour.com*, leads to Wadson's Web page called "Hidden Treasure." In Explore, locate the Hidden Treasure page and answer the following questions:

   a. What was the name of Greybeard's ship?
   b. What was Greybeard's favorite food?
   c. What does Wadson think happened to Greybeard's ship?

4. In the Steps, you found a graphic of Jupiter from the photo archives of the Jet Propulsion Laboratory. In the Explore section of the lab, you can also find a graphic of Saturn. Suppose one of your friends wanted a picture of Saturn for an astronomy report. Make a list of the blue, underlined links your friend must click in the correct order to find the Saturn graphic. Assume that your friend will begin at the Web Trainer home page.

5. Enter the URL *http://www.atour.com* to jump to the Adventure Travel Web site. Write a one-page description of this site. In your paper, include a description of the information at the site, the number of pages the site contains, and a diagram of the links it provides.

6. Chris Thomson is a student at UVI and has his own Web pages. In Explore, look at the information Chris has included on his pages. Suppose you could create your own Web page. What would you include? Use word processing software to design your own Web pages. Make sure you indicate the graphics and links you would use.

WEB PAGES & HTML LAB

It's easy to create your own Web pages. As you learned in this chapter, many software tools are available to help you become a Web author. In this lab you'll experiment with a Web authoring wizard that automates the process of creating a Web page. You'll also try your hand at working directly with HTML code.

1. Click the Steps button to activate the Web authoring wizard and learn how to create a basic Web page. As you proceed through the Steps, answer all of the QuickCheck questions. After you complete the Steps, you will see a QuickCheck Summary Report. Follow the instructions on the screen to print this report.

2. In Explore, click the File menu, then click New to start working on a new Web page. Use the wizard to create a home page for a veterinarian who offers dog day-care and boarding services. After you create the page, save it on drive A or C, and print the HTML code. Your site must have the following characteristics:

   a. Title: Dr. Dave's Dog Domain

   b. Background color: Gold

   c. Graphic: Dog.jpg

   d. Body text: Your dog will have the best care day and night at Dr. Dave's Dog Domain. Fine accommodations, good food, play time, and snacks are all provided. You can board your pet by the day or week. Grooming services also available.

   e. Text link: "Reasonable rates" links to *www.cciw.com/np3/rates.htm*

   f. E-mail link: "For more information:" links to *daveassist@drdave.com*

3. In Explore, use the File menu to open the HTML document called *Politics.htm*. After you use the HTML window (not the wizard) to make the following changes, save the revised page on drive A or C, and print the HTML code. Refer to Table G-2 for a list of HTML tags you can use.

   a. Change the title to Politics 2000.

   b. Center the page heading.

   c. Change the background color to FFE7C6 and the text color to 000000.

   d. Add a line break before the sentence "What's next?"

   e. Add a bold tag to "Additional links on this topic:".

   f. Add one more link to the "Additional links" list. The link should go to the site *http://www.elections.ca* and the clickable link should read "Elections Canada."

   g. Change the last graphic to display the image "next.gif."

4. In Explore, use the Web authoring wizard and the HTML window to create a home page about yourself. You should include at least a screenful of text, a graphic, an external link, and an e-mail link. Save the page on drive A, then print the HTML code. Turn in your disk and printout.

LESSON	MEDIA ELEMENT			LESSON	MEDIA ELEMENT			
Introducing the Internet	INTERNET HISTORY	INTERNET STATISTICS	VIDEO	Interacting online	CHAT AND DISCUSSION GROUPS	CYBERSPACE	GAMES	SCREENTOUR
Understanding hosts, domains, and URLs	DOMAIN NAMES			Creating Web sites	E-COMMERCE CONSTRUCTION			
Introducing the World Wide Web	THE WEB	WEB PORTALS	THE WORLD WIDE WEB	Understanding HTML	HTML	AUTHORING TOOLS	WEB PAGES & HTML	
Using Web browsers	SCREENTOUR			Publishing Web sites	AUTHORING TIPS			
Understanding multimedia on the Web	PLUGINS	SCREENTOUR	SCREENTOUR	Connecting to the Internet	MODEMS	ISPs	SCREENTOUR	
Downloading and uploading files	FTP SOFTWARE	DOWNLOAD SITES	SCREENTOUR, SCREENTOUR	Issue: Is the Truth Out There?	INFORMATION QUALITY	VIDEO		

VISUAL WORKSHOP

Enter the letter from the diagram that correctly matches each element in the list below and write a brief description of each.

1. The Internet backbone _____

2. A NAP or NSP _____

3. A dial-up connection _____

4. An ISP _____

5. A PC with a modem _____

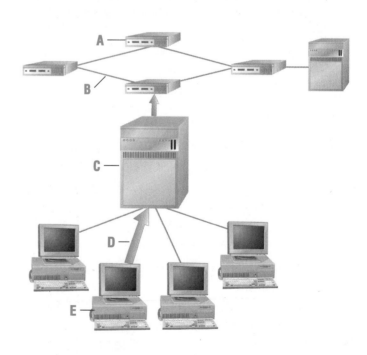

Data Security and Control

Unit H

In this unit, you will learn about human errors and equipment failures that can lead to lost or inaccurate data. You will learn about threats to the data stored on computer systems, such as intentional acts of vandalism and computer crime in which data is tampered with or stolen. The lesson on risk management explains the steps you can take to protect your data. You can begin to assess your risk of losing important data, becoming the target of computer vandalism, or being affected by inaccurate data. This unit also explores security on the Internet and the technology available to protect you as you download files and perform commercial transactions. On a practical level, you will learn how to disinfect disks that contain viruses, make backups, and design an effective backup plan for your data. You will find out why data backup is one of the most effective security measures for protecting your data.

Knowing what can go wrong

Data stored on computers is vulnerable to human error and power problems. Today's computer users battle to avoid lost, stolen, and inaccurate data. **Lost data**, also referred to as **missing data**, comprises data that is inaccessible, usually because it was accidentally removed. **Stolen data** is not necessarily missing, but has been accessed or copied without authorization. **Inaccurate data** is not accurate because it was entered incorrectly, was deliberately or accidentally altered, or was not edited to reflect current facts.

DETAILS

☛ Operator error: Despite the sometimes sensational press coverage of computer criminals and viruses, the most common cause of lost data is a mistake made by a computer user; this problem is known as **operator error**. Operator error refers to mistakes such as entering the wrong data or deleting a file that is still needed. The number of operator errors can be reduced if users pay attention to what they're doing and establish habits that can help them avoid mistakes. Many organizations have reduced the incidence of operator errors by using direct source input devices. A **direct source input device**, such as a bar code reader, collects data directly from a document or object. Computer software designers can also help prevent operator error by designing products that anticipate mistakes users are likely to make and that provide features to help users avoid those mistakes. See Figure H-1.

☛ Computer software problems: Commercial software is complex and, therefore, is sometimes released with program errors that can affect the integrity of your data. Although catastrophic loss of data due to programming errors is rare, it is important to be aware of your data and to look for inaccuracies that may be caused by the program itself.

☛ Power problems: Because computers are powered by electricity, they are susceptible to power failures, spikes, and surges. A **power failure** is a complete loss of power to the computer system. A power failure is usually caused by something over which you have no control. Even a brief interruption in power can force your computer to reboot and lose all of the data in RAM. Although a power failure results in lost data from RAM, it is unlikely to cause data loss from disks.

Two other common power-related problems are spikes and surges. Both of these can damage sensitive computer components. A **power spike** is an increase in power that lasts only a short time—less than one millionth of a second. A **power**

surge lasts a little longer, a few millionths of a second. Spikes and surges are caused by malfunctions in the local generating plant and the power distribution network, and they are potentially more damaging than a power failure. Both can destroy the circuitry that operates your hard disk drive or damage your computer's motherboard.

• A UPS (uninterruptible power supply) represents the best protection against power problems. A **UPS** is a device containing a battery that provides a continuous supply of power and other circuitry to prevent spikes and surges from reaching your computer. It is designed to provide enough power to keep your computer working through momentary power interruptions. A UPS gives you enough time to save your files and exit your programs in the event of a longer power outage. Figure H-2 shows a typical UPS. A UPS is essential equipment for Internet and LAN servers but is also recommended for individual computer users. Because lightning can cause a power surge, many experts recommend that you unplug your computer equipment, including your modem, during electrical storms.

• As a low-cost alternative, you can plug your computer into a **surge strip** (also called a surge protector or surge suppressor) to protect it and your modem from power spikes and surges. Just remember that a surge strip does not contain a battery to keep the computer running and protect the data in RAM if the power fails. Figure H-3 shows a surge strip.

• When you shop for a surge strip, do not purchase a **power strip** such as the one shown in Figure H-4. Although a power strip contains multiple outlets for power plugs as does a surge strip, it does not contain the electronics necessary to filter out power spikes and surges.

1. The user selects the file Sales Summary. Pressing the Delete key initiates an operation that will, in effect, destroy the data in the selected file.

2. The Microsoft Windows operating system displays a prompt asking the user to confirm the deletion. The file is deleted only if the user clicks the Yes button.

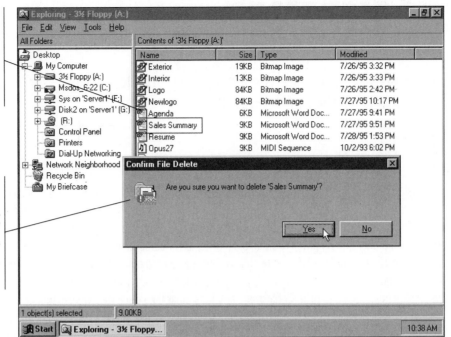

A light on the case lets you know that the UPS is charged and ready

To connect a UPS, plug it into a wall outlet, then plug your computer and monitor cables into the outlets on the UPS.

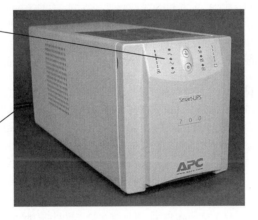

▶ The cost of such a device can range from $100 to $600, depending on the power requirements of the computers and the features of the UPS.

VIDEO

UPS

FIGURE H-3: *A surge strip*

A surge strip typically contains the electronics necessary to prevent spikes and surges from damaging your computer. Many, but not all, surge strips also contain a place to plug the phone cable that leads to your modem.

FIGURE H-4: *A power strip*

A power strip simply provides multiple outlets, but cannot protect your computer and modem from power spikes and surges.

Avoiding disasters

In addition to falling prey to human error and power problems, data is also vulnerable to hardware failure, natural disasters, and vandalism.

COMPUTER INSURANCE

DETAILS

○━ Hardware failure: The reliability of computer components is expressed as mean time between failures, or **MTBF**. The MTBF is calculated by observing test equipment in a laboratory, then dividing the number of failures by the total number of hours of observation. This statistic is an estimate based on laboratory tests of a few sample components. The measurement is somewhat misleading to most consumers, however, because the tests are conducted in a regulated laboratory environment where power problems, failure of other components, and regular wear and tear do not exist. For example, a 125,000-hour MTBF means that, on average, a hard disk drive is likely to function for 125,000 hours or 14 years without failing. In the real world, your hard disk drive might work for only 10 hours before it fails. With this fact in mind, it is important to plan for hardware failures, rather than hope they won't happen.

Much of the equipment that fails does so within the first hours or days of operation, but after that it can be expected to work fairly reliably until it nears the end of its useful life. The effect of a hardware failure depends on which component fails. Most hardware failures are simply an inconvenience. For example, if your monitor fails, you can obtain a replacement monitor, plug it in, and get back to work. On the other hand, a hard disk drive failure can be a disaster because you might lose all data stored on the hard disk drive. Although an experienced computer technician might be able to recover some of the files on the hard disk drive and transfer them to another hard disk, it is more often the case that all programs and data files stored on the hard disk are permanently lost. The effects of a hard disk drive failure are considerably reduced if you have complete, up-to-date backups of the programs and data files on your hard disk. Data backup is discussed later in this unit.

○━ Natural disasters: Computers are not immune to unexpected damage from smoke, fire, water, and breakage; therefore, it is a good practice to carry insurance to cover your equipment. Under the terms of many standard household and business insurance policies, a computer is treated like any other appliance. You should make sure, however, that your insurance policy covers the full cost of purchasing a new computer at current market prices.

Replacing your damaged computer equipment will not replace your data. Some insurance companies provide extra coverage for the data on your computer. With this type of coverage, you would receive a sum of money to compensate you for the time it takes to reload your data on a replacement computer. This procedure assumes that you have a backup of your data. Without a backup, much of your data cannot be reconstructed. A good insurance policy provides funds to replace computer equipment, but the only insurance for your data is an up-to-date backup tape or disk.

○━ Vandalism: Your data can also be destroyed by vandalism. Computer vandals are people who, acting for thrills or illegal gain, attack the data of other computer users. Computer viruses can destroy data. Read the message in Figure H-5. What would you do if this message appeared on your computer screen? This virus alert is obviously a hoax that is designed to frighten and embarrass computer users when they find out that they have spread this fake virus alert to all of their friends and colleagues. Understanding how programs such as viruses work is the first line of defense against attacks and pranks. You will learn more about computer viruses and vandalism in the next lesson.

What are disaster recovery centers?

Disaster recovery centers provide emergency computing facilities to businesses. A business can build its own disaster recovery center or contract with a third party for this service. When disaster strikes, businesses cannot afford to disrupt their operations. Disaster recovery facilities stand ready to take over operations when disaster strikes and until the main systems can be restored. This type of facility is a remote location that can have a complete backup of the hardware, software, and data for a company or simply provide a building where computers can be brought in quickly.

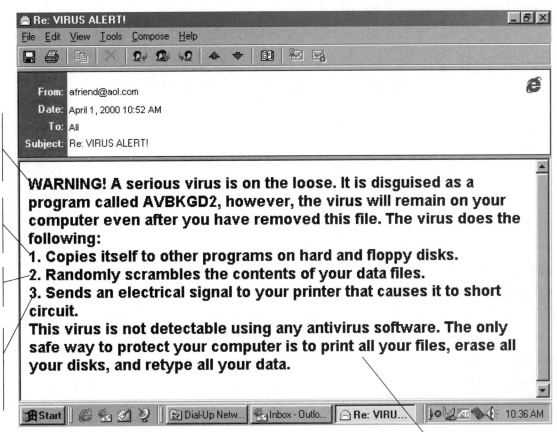

It is possible for a virus to migrate to a file other than the one to which it was originally attached.

Viruses can replicate themselves and spread to other programs on hard or floppy disks.

Viruses can destroy the contents of your hard disk.

The first hint that the message is a fake: Experts have not been able to confirm the existence of any viruses that damage printers.

The prank becomes obvious: Printing out all of your files, then erasing them from computer storage is definitely not the way to deal with a virus attack! If you see a message like this one, ignore it.

Computer crime and the law

"Old-fashioned" crimes that take a high-tech twist because they involve a computer are often prosecuted under traditional laws. Most states have enacted computer crime laws that specifically define computer data and software as personal property. These laws also define as a crime the unauthorized access, use, modification, or disabling of a computer system or data. Under most state laws, intentionally circulating a destructive virus is a crime. Laws are made to deter criminals, bring them to trial if they are caught, and punish them if they are convicted. But laws don't actually protect your data. You therefore need to make frequent backups and take steps to prevent unauthorized access to your data.

Introducing computer viruses and vandalism

Computer data can be damaged, destroyed, or altered by vandalism. Computer vandals are called **hackers**, **crackers**, or **cyberpunks**. The programs that these hackers create are colorfully referred to as malware, pest programs, vandalware, or punkware. More typically, though, these programs are called viruses. The term "virus" technically refers to only one type of program created by hackers.

VIRUSES

MACRO VIRUSES

DETAILS

- A **computer virus** is a program that attaches itself to a file and reproduces itself so as to spread from one file to another. A virus can destroy data, display irritating messages, or disrupt other computer operations. Computer viruses lurk on disks, in RAM, and on the Internet, ready to wreak havoc in your computer.

- The jargon that describes a computer virus sounds similar to medical jargon. Your computer is a "host," and it can become "infected" with a virus. A virus can reproduce itself and spread from one computer to another. You can "inoculate" your computer against many viruses. If your computer has not been inoculated and becomes infected, you can use antivirus software to "disinfect" it.

- A computer virus generally infects the files that your computer executes on your computer system. These files include program files with .exe filename extensions, the system files that your computer uses to boot up, and the macro files that automate tasks in word processing and spreadsheet applications. Most viruses attach themselves to executable files, because these files are the ones that your computer runs. Each time your computer runs an infected program, it also runs the attached virus instructions to replicate or deliver its payload. Because a virus needs to be executed to spread, a data file can only be a carrier; it cannot deliver the payload.

- The term **payload** refers to the ultimate mission of a virus, which may be as harmless as a simple annoying message or as devastating as corrupting the data on your hard disk. Figure H-6 illustrates how a computer virus spreads and delivers its payload.

- A **file virus** attaches itself to an application program, such as a game.

- **Boot sector viruses** are viruses that infect the system files your computer uses every time you turn it on. They can cause widespread damage and persistent problems.

- A **macro virus** infects documents such as those created with a word processor or a spreadsheet. Infected documents are stored with a set of instructions called a macro. A **macro** is essentially a miniature program that usually contains legitimate instructions to automate document and worksheet production. A hacker can create a destructive macro, attach it to a document, and then distribute it over the Internet or on disk—often as an e-mail attachment. When anyone views the document, the macro virus duplicates itself into the general macro pool, where it is picked up by other documents.

- Of the top viruses, macro viruses account for about 75 percent of the virus attacks, as shown in Figure H-7.

- The symptoms of a virus infection depend on the virus. Symptoms indicating that your computer might have contracted a virus could include the following: Your computer displays annoying messages. Your computer develops unusual visual or sound effects. You have difficulty saving files, files mysteriously disappear, or executable files unaccountably increase in size. Your computer suddenly seems to work very slowly or reboots unexpectedly. Some of these problems, however, can be caused by other, non-virus-related factors.

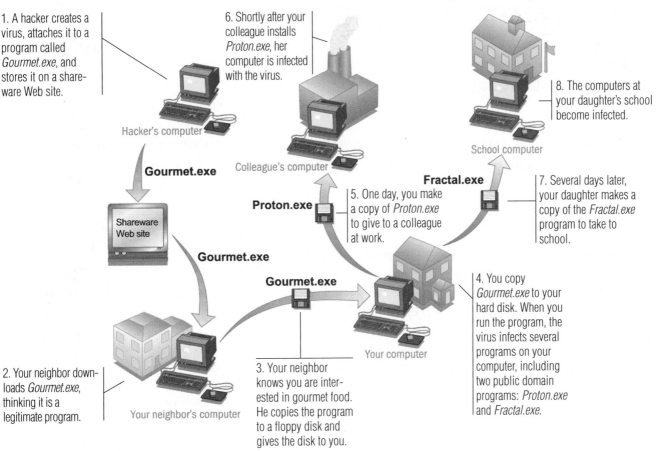

1. A hacker creates a virus, attaches it to a program called *Gourmet.exe*, and stores it on a share-ware Web site.

6. Shortly after your colleague installs *Proton.exe*, her computer is infected with the virus.

8. The computers at your daughter's school become infected.

Gourmet.exe

Hacker's computer

Shareware Web site

Colleague's computer

School computer

Proton.exe

5. One day, you make a copy of *Proton.exe* to give to a colleague at work.

Fractal.exe

7. Several days later, your daughter makes a copy of the *Fractal.exe* program to take to school.

Gourmet.exe

Gourmet.exe

Your computer

4. You copy *Gourmet.exe* to your hard disk. When you run the program, the virus infects several programs on your computer, including two public domain programs: *Proton.exe* and *Fractal.exe*.

2. Your neighbor down-loads *Gourmet.exe*, thinking it is a legitimate program.

Your neighbor's computer

3. Your neighbor knows you are inter-ested in gourmet food. He copies the program to a floppy disk and gives the disk to you.

FIGURE H-7: *Top 10 viruses*

▶ In today's comput-ing environment, macro viruses are the most prolific.
▶ The two most com-mon macro viruses are the Melissa virus, which attaches itself to Microsoft Word docu-ments, and the Laroux virus, which attaches itself to Microsoft Excel spreadsheets.

▶ Experts say that more than 2,000 viruses exist; fewer than 10 viruses cause 90 percent of virus damage.

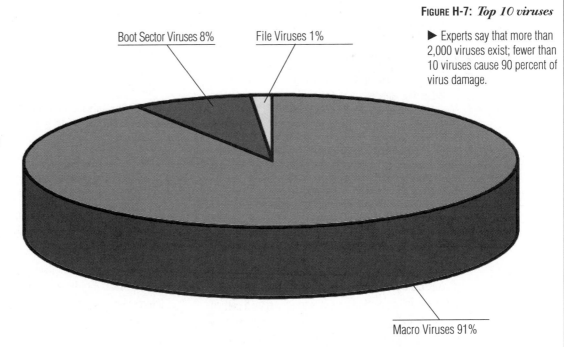

Boot Sector Viruses 8%

File Viruses 1%

Macro Viruses 91%

Exploring viruses and vandalism

Viruses are just one type of software vandalism. Hackers also cause problems by creating programs such as Trojan horses, time bombs, logic bombs, and worms.

InfoWeb
Y2K Bug

DETAILS

A modern **Trojan horse** is a computer program that appears to perform one function while actually doing something else. A Trojan horse sometimes—but not always—harbors a virus. You can think of a Trojan horse as a container that hides a secret program. That program might be a virus, a time bomb, or simply a program that, when run, carries out a nasty task such as formatting your hard disk. The namesake of the computer Trojan horse is a Greek legend. According to the story, Greek soldiers hid inside a wooden statue of a horse. The Trojans thought that the horse was a gift, so they pulled it into their walled city. This act gave the Greek army the access they needed into the city, enabling them to defeat the Trojans.

Figure H-8 shows how one type of Trojan horse program works. This Trojan horse does not harbor a virus because it does not replicate itself.

It is easy to be fooled by Trojan horse programs because they are designed to be difficult to detect. For example, one popular Trojan horse looks just like the login screen on a network. Be suspicious of anything out of the ordinary on your computer system; if your login screen looks a little different one day, check with your technical support person. Be informed about the latest computer pranks circulating in your local area.

Although a virus usually begins to replicate itself immediately, it or another unwelcome surprise can lurk in your computer system for days or months without discovery.

A **time bomb** is a computer program that stays in your system undetected until it is triggered by a certain event in time, such as when the computer system clock reaches a certain date. For example, the Michelangelo virus contains a time bomb designed to damage files on your hard disk on March 6, the birthday of artist Michelangelo. Many hackers seem to favor dates of well-known events, such as Halloween, Friday the 13th, and April Fool's Day for time bomb attacks. A time bomb is usually carried by a virus or Trojan horse.

A **logic bomb** is a computer program that is triggered by the appearance or disappearance of specific data. A logic bomb can be carried by a virus or Trojan horse. Alternatively, a logic bomb can be a stand-alone program.

Time bombs and logic bombs might do mischief in your computer long before the timer goes off. If the bomb is part of a virus, it could replicate itself, spread to other files, and attach itself to files you sent from your computer to other computers.

A software **worm** is a program designed to enter a computer system—usually a network server—through security "holes." Like a virus, a worm reproduces itself. Unlike a virus, a worm does not need to be attached to a document or executable program to reproduce. Worms typically do not affect personal computer users; instead, they affect LAN and Internet users by disrupting their access to files, programs, Web pages, and other services provided by the network.

A lead story in *The Wall Street Journal* reported on the now-famous Internet worm that spread to more than 6,000 Internet host computers. This software worm entered computers through security holes in e-mail systems and then used data stored on the computer to, in effect, mail itself to other computers. The worm spread rapidly, as shown in Figure H-9. The Internet worm was not designed to destroy data. Instead, it filled up storage space and dramatically slowed computer performance. The only way to eradicate the Internet worm was to shut down the e-mail system on the Internet hosts, then comb through hundreds of programs to find and destroy the worm—a process that took as long as eight hours for each host.

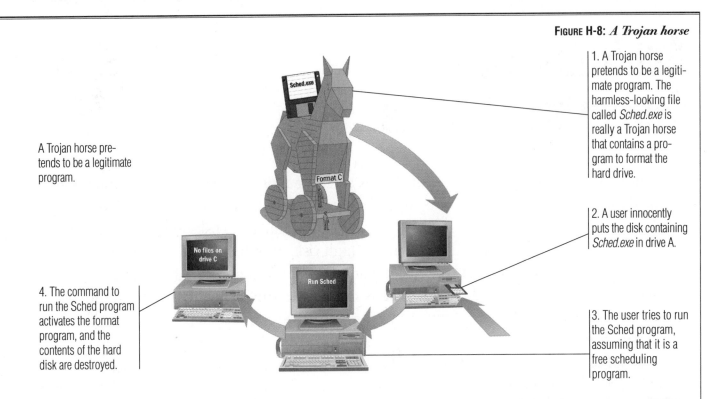

A Trojan horse pretends to be a legitimate program.

1. A Trojan horse pretends to be a legitimate program. The harmless-looking file called *Sched.exe* is really a Trojan horse that contains a program to format the hard drive.

2. A user innocently puts the disk containing *Sched.exe* in drive A.

4. The command to run the Sched program activates the format program, and the contents of the hard disk are destroyed.

3. The user tries to run the Sched program, assuming that it is a free scheduling program.

FIGURE H-9: *A worm attacks the Internet*

The Internet Worm

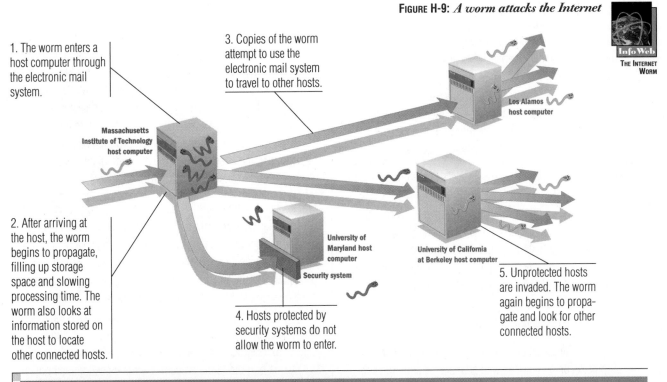

1. The worm enters a host computer through the electronic mail system.

3. Copies of the worm attempt to use the electronic mail system to travel to other hosts.

2. After arriving at the host, the worm begins to propagate, filling up storage space and slowing processing time. The worm also looks at information stored on the host to locate other connected hosts.

4. Hosts protected by security systems do not allow the worm to enter.

5. Unprotected hosts are invaded. The worm again begins to propagate and look for other connected hosts.

Y2K Bug

The year 2000 (Y2K) time bomb refers to the problem with software that does not require a four-digit date field (for example, 89 entered instead of 1989). This "time bomb" was created unintentionally by programmers who were trying to save precious memory space back when memory was a costly commodity in computer systems and code was written to save disk space and processing time. As it turns out, this decision had the potential to cause havoc when the year 2000 arrived. Corporations, businesses, and governments invested a considerable amount of time, money and energy in the last years of the twentieth century into upgrading and correcting their systems to nullify this potential time bomb. As it turned out, whether because of planning or overestimating the problem, the Y2K bug didn't cause any major problems worldwide.

Avoiding and detecting viruses

Computer viruses and other types of malicious software typically lurk on disks containing public domain software or shareware, on disks containing illegal copies of computer programs downloaded from the Internet, and in e-mail attachments. Disks and programs from these sources should be regarded as having a "high risk" of infection. Figure H-10 lists tips for avoiding viruses. If you must use a disk that you suspect might be infected, you can use a virus detection program to check for viruses before you run any programs from the disk.

DETAILS

▢━☞ **Antivirus software** (also called **virus detection software** or an **antivirus program**), examines the files stored on a disk to determine whether they are infected with a virus and then disinfects the disk, if necessary.

▢━☞ Virus detection programs use several techniques to detect viruses, which attach themselves to an existing program, thereby increasing the length of the original program. The earliest virus detection software simply examined the programs on your computer and recorded their lengths. A change in the length of a program from one computing session to the next indicated the possible presence of a virus.

▢━☞ Installing and using antivirus software will help protect your system. If viruses are a recurring problem in your computing environment, you might want to configure your virus detection software to continually monitor the behavior of your computer files and alert you if it spots signs of virus-like activity. The disadvantage to this strategy is that continually monitoring files slows down your computer operation. Alternatively, you can set antivirus software to load and scan every time you boot your system.

▢━☞ Many virus detection programs are available. Many new computers come equipped with preinstalled antivirus software. Shareware virus detection programs are available from Web sites, computer bulletin boards, and shareware dealers. Popular antivirus software includes Norton Antivirus, Dr. Solomon's Anti-Virus, and McAfee VirusScan. Figure H-11 shows what happened when VirusScan detected a virus on a disk in drive A.

▢━☞ In response to early virus detection programs, hackers became more cunning. They created viruses that insert themselves into unused portions of a program file, but do not change its length. Of course, the people who designed virus detection programs fought back. They designed programs that examine the bytes in an uninfected application program and calculate a checksum. A **checksum** is a value that is calculated by combining all of the bytes in a file. Each time you run the application program, the virus detection program recalculates the checksum and compares it with the original value. If any byte in the application program has been changed, the checksum will be different, and the virus detection program assumes that a virus is present.

▢━☞ Another technique used by virus detection programs is to search for a signature. A **virus signature** is a unique series of bytes that can be used to identify a known virus, much as a fingerprint is used to identify an individual. Most of today's virus detection software scans for virus signatures. The signature search technique can identify only those viruses with a known signature. To detect new viruses, you must obtain regular updates for your virus detection program that include new virus signatures.

Some viruses are specifically designed to avoid detection by one or more of the preceding virus detection methods. For this reason, the most sophisticated virus protection schemes combine elements from each of these methods.

▢━☞ Virus detection software finds and eradicates many viruses, but it is not 100 percent reliable. However, it is generally successful in detecting and eradicating most widespread viruses. It should be included in your software collection.

1. Install and use virus detection software.

2. Keep your virus detection software up to date.

3. Make frequent backups after you use virus detection software to scan your files for viruses.

4. Download software only from sources that take steps to make sure files do not contain any viruses. Use a virus detection program to scan downloaded software before you use it.

5. Be careful with disks that contain shareware. Scan them before you run or copy any files from these disks.

FIGURE H-11: *Using antivirus software*

SCREENTOUR

ANTIVIRUS SOFTWARE

When your antivirus software detects a virus, it provides information about the virus and asks whether you want to remove it immediately. In most cases, you will want to use this option. Some viruses cannot be removed without destroying the host file. Unfortunately, if you don't have a pre-virus backup, it is probably too late to make one.

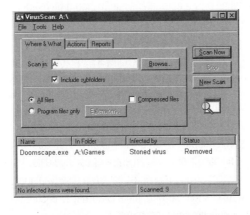

What to do if your computer has a virus

If you detect the symptoms of a virus on your computer system, you should take immediate steps to stop the virus from spreading. If you are connected to a network, alert the network administrator. You should also warn your colleagues and anyone with whom you shared disks or e-mailed files. Although antivirus software will find and remove the virus from your personal computer, the problem might have spread to your backups and removable storage media such as floppy disks, Zip disks, and removable hard disks. You should use your antivirus software to check all of your removable media so you don't reinfect your system the next time you use the media. If your computer is attacked by a macro virus, you might have to manually extract the macros from each infected document. Because new viruses appear every week, you should update your antivirus software regularly by either purchasing updates from the antivirus software publisher or by downloading the updates from the Internet.

Understanding data security and risk management

It is not practical to completely protect computer data from theft, viruses, and natural disasters. In most situations, providing total data security is too time-consuming, too expensive, or too complex. **Data security** is the collection of techniques that provide protection for data. To determine the extent to which you should practice data security, you must do risk management analysis.

RISK
MANAGEMENT

ACCEPTABLE USE
POLICIES

DETAILS

○— **Risk management** is the process of weighing threats to computer data against the amount of data that is expendable and the cost of protecting crucial data. Table H-1 shows steps for formulating a risk management strategy. Once you have completed your risk management analysis, you can establish policies and procedures to help you maintain data security.

○— In a computing environment, a computer policy is referred to as an **acceptable use policy**, which is a set of rules and regulations that specify how a computer system should be used. Policies are most often determined by management and used by large organizations to stipulate who can access computer data. They also help an organization define appropriate uses for its computers and data. The advantages of policies are that they define how a computer system should be used, make users aware of limits and penalties, and provide a framework for legal or job action against individuals who do not follow those policies. Policies are an inexpensive building block in the overall structure of data security. Implementing one does not require any special hardware or software. The cost of policies is the time it takes to compose, update, and publicize them. The disadvantages of policies for data security are that some users disregard them and they do not typically prevent operator errors that can lead to lost or corrupted data.

○— Successful computer users develop habits that significantly reduce their chances of making mistakes. These habits, when formalized and adopted by an organization, are referred to as **end-user procedures**. Procedures help reduce human errors that can erase or damage data. The major advantage of procedures is their ability to reduce operator error. Procedures have two disadvantages. First, they must be kept up to date as equipment and software change. Second, there is no way to ensure that people follow them. Figure H-12 describes some possible policies and procedures.

Policies are rules and regulations that apply to computer use in a general way. Procedures describe steps or activities that are performed in conjunction with a specific task. Because procedures are more specific, they generally take longer to write than policies, making them somewhat more costly for an organization to create and document.

Why practice risk management?

The most popular data security techniques used to reduce the risk of data loss apply to microcomputer, minicomputer, and mainframe computer data. Risk management is important for you as an individual for these reasons. You will likely work with computers within an organization when you graduate, so you will share the responsibility with your coworkers for that organization's data. Second, many organizations maintain sensitive data, such as your credit rating, educational record, and health records. You have a vested interest in maintaining the accuracy and the confidentiality of this data. Finally, you currently have data stored on disks that might be time-consuming to reconstruct. Consider using backup and virus detection to secure your own data.

STEP	FOR THIS STEP
1. Determine the likely threats to your computer data.	You must evaluate the possibility of hardware failure, human error, and vandalism.
2. Assess the amount of data that is expendable.	You must ask yourself, "How much data will I have to reenter if my hard drive is erased?" and " How much of my data would be lost forever because it could not be reconstructed?"
3. Determine the cost of protecting all of your data versus protecting some of your data.	You must define cost to include time as well as money.
4. Select the protective measures that meet your needs.	You must take into account which protective measures are affordable to you, effective against the threats you identified, and easy for you to implement.

FIGURE H-12: *Computer policies and procedures*

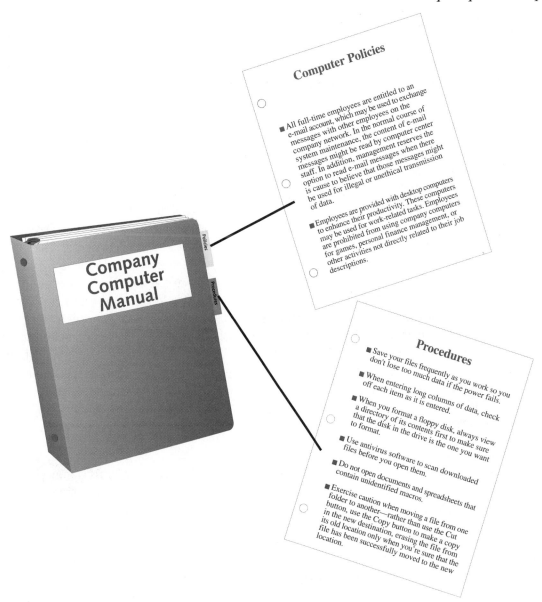

Restricting access to data

One of the best ways to prevent people from damaging equipment is to restrict physical access to a computer system. If potential criminals cannot get to a computer or a terminal, stealing or damaging data becomes more difficult. In today's web of interlaced computer technologies, however, it has also become critical to restrict data access to authorized users and to properly identify authorized users, especially those who are logging in from remote sites located thousands of miles away.

InfoWeb
BIOMETRICS

DETAILS

☞ Ways to restrict physical access: Restrict access to the area surrounding the computer to prevent physical damage to the equipment. Keep floppy disks and data backups in a locked vault to prevent theft and to protect against fire or water damage. Keep offices containing computers locked to prevent theft and to deter unauthorized users. Lock the computer case to prevent theft of components such as RAM and processors. Keep in mind, however, that restricting physical access will not prevent a determined criminal from stealing data.

☞ There are three methods of personal identification used to restrict access: something a person carries, something a person knows, or some unique physical characteristic. Any one of these methods has the potential to positively identify a person, and each has a unique set of advantages and disadvantages.

- Something a person carries: An identity badge featuring a photo, or perhaps a fingerprint or bar code, remains a popular form of personal identification. Designers have created high-tech identity card readers, like the one in Figure H-13, that can be used from any off-site PC. Because an identity badge can be easily lost, stolen, or duplicated, however, it works best on site where a security guard checks the face on the badge with the face of the person wearing the badge. Without visual verification, the use of identity badges from a remote site is not secure, unless combined with a password or **PIN** (personal identification number).

- Something a person knows: User IDs and passwords fall into this category of personal identification. When you work on a multiuser system or network, you generally must have a user ID and password. Data security on a computer system that is guarded by user IDs and passwords depends on password secrecy. If users give out their passwords, choose obvious passwords, or write them down in obvious places, hackers can break in. The brute force method of trying every word in an electronic dictionary to steal a password decreases in effectiveness if a password is based on two words, a word and number, or a nonsense word that does not appear in a dictionary. Table H-2 shows how the composition of passwords affects the opportunity for unauthorized access.

- Some unique physical characteristic: This third method of personal identification, called **biometrics**, bases identification on some physical trait, such as a fingerprint or the pattern of blood vessels in the retina of the eye. Unlike passwords, biometric data can't be forgotten, lost, or borrowed. Once the technological fiction of spy thrillers, biometric devices are today becoming affordable technologies that can be built into personal computer systems. Such technologies include hand-geometry scanners, voice recognition, face recognition, and fingerprint scanners, as shown in Figure H-14.

☞ Passwords are a first line of defense against unauthorized access. What if a hacker breaks in anyway? One way to limit the amount of damage from a break-in is to assign user rights. **User rights** are rules that limit the directories and files that each user can access. They can restrict your ability to erase, create, write, read, and find files. When you receive a user ID and password for a password-protected system, the system administrator gives you rights that allow you to access and perform specified tasks only on particular directories and files on the host computer or file server. Assigning user rights helps prevent both accidental and deliberate damage to data. If users are granted limited rights, a hacker who steals someone's password has only the same access as the person from whom the password was stolen.

A disk-shaped carrier allows a floppy disk drive to read an identity card.

FIGURE H-14: *A fingerprint scanner*

VIDEO

Fingerprint scanners cost less than $200 and can confirm your identity in less than two seconds, even from a pool of thousands of employees.

TABLE H-2: *How password length and composition affect the chances of unauthorized access*

PASSWORD STRATEGY	EXAMPLE	NUMBER OF POSSIBILITIES	TIME TO BREAK PASSWORD
Any name	Ed, Christine	2,000	< 1 second using a name dictionary
Any dictionary word	tie, electrocardiogram	60,000	< 1 second using a standard dictionary
Two words joined together	batfont, funnelgum	3,600,000,000	10 hours
5 characters (a–z only)	scftw, bklpw	11,881,376	2 minutes
5 characters (a–z and 0–9)	u4got, 4ti8s	60,466,176	10 minutes
8 characters (a–z and 0–9)	ouamdaip, hitfptwp	282,110,990,7456	326 days

Trapdoor

Hackers occasionally gain unauthorized access to computer systems through a trap door. A **trap door** is a special set of instructions that allows a user to bypass the normal security precautions and enter the system. Trap doors are often created during development and testing but should be removed before the system becomes operational.

Understanding encryption

When an unauthorized person reads data, the data is no longer confidential. Important data such as credit card accounts, bank records, and medical information must be encrypted to foil hackers who break into computers.

DETAILS

- **Cryptography** is the science of keeping messages secret by encoding them so that only the intended recipient can decode and understand them. It was traditionally a secret science practiced by government-employed mathematicians to safeguard the exchange of private messages between the government and its intelligence officers, military personnel, and ambassadors overseas.

- **Encryption** is the process of scrambling or hiding information so that it cannot be understood until it is decrypted, or deciphered, to change it back to its original form. The process of decoding is called **decryption**. Encryption provides a last line of defense against the unauthorized use of data. Figure H-15 depicts simple encryption and decryption techniques.

  - When a computer encrypts data for storage, the same program that encrypts the data also decrypts it. The encryption method or key needs to be known only by the encrypting computer. Encrypting transmitted data, however, presents a problem because the sender's computer that encrypts the data is not the same one that decrypts the data on the recipient's end of the transmission. Transmitted data must use an encryption **key** that is shared by everyone but that cannot be decrypted by everyone.

  - Data that has not been encrypted is referred to as **plaintext**. When plaintext is encrypted, it is called **ciphertext**. Cryptography generally produces ciphertext by combining plaintext with a secret key (a sequence of numbers or characters) by means of an algorithm. An **algorithm** is a step-by-step procedure for solving a problem or accomplishing a specific task. One problem that has historically plagued cryptography is the difficulty in communicating the secret key to the intended recipient of a ciphertext who is located far away. If the key were to fall into the wrong hands, ciphertext created with that key would no longer be secret.

- **Public key encryption** (PKE) is an encryption method that uses a pair of digital keys: a **public key** known to everyone, and a **private key** known only to the message recipient. The public key encrypts a message; the private key decrypts a message. Figure H-16 explains the basic concept of PKE. Encryption software is virtually a necessity for some businesses, such as financial institutions that transmit and store funds electronically. Several public key encryption systems are currently available, including the popular and easy-to-use **Pretty Good Privacy (PGP)**. Public key encryption is discussed in more detail in the next lesson.

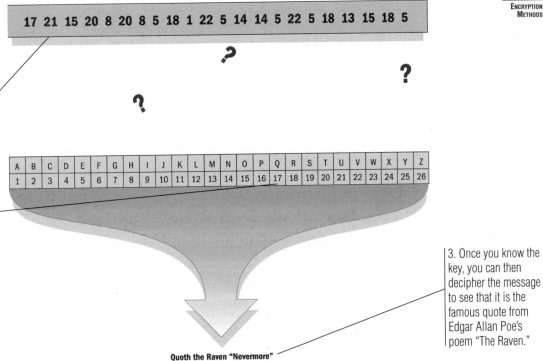

One of the simplest encryption methods substitutes a number for each letter of the alphabet.

1. This message is encrypted using a very simple substitution technique in which the number of each letter's position in the alphabet represents the letter.

2. The key to this encryption looks like this. The 17 in the encrypted message is the letter "Q," the 21 is the letter "U," and so on.

3. Once you know the key, you can then decipher the message to see that it is the famous quote from Edgar Allan Poe's poem "The Raven."

FIGURE H-16: *Public key encryption secures messages*

Public key encryption uses two different digital keys—one to encrypt a message and one to decipher it.

Understanding public key encryption

The explosion in the use of computers as personal communications devices is primarily due to the Internet's increasing popularity as a global medium for the exchange of information, including confidential information. The Internet poses special problems when the information being transmitted might include a credit card number. Savvy programmers can write routines that detect just such information making its way to a known commercial site. Such concerns, along with the desire to ensure privacy in personal communications, generally have encouraged common use of public key encryption on the Internet.

DETAILS

- ☞ In 1976, Whitfield Diffie and Martin Hellman developed a new form of cryptography that did not require the exchange of secret keys between parties. Their invention, called public key encryption, involves a scheme in which each party gets two keys: a public key and a private key. The public and private keys have a special mathematical relationship. Plaintext that is encrypted with the one key can be decrypted only by using the other key. At the same time, knowing the contents of one of the keys provides almost no clues about the contents of the other key. Several public key encryption programs are available for use on the Internet.

  Using this method, George, your correspondent in Figure H-17, is assured of the secrecy of his message to you—which is the first level of protection afforded by public key encryption. One problem for you is verifying that the message you received from George is actually from George. This problem arises because you have released your public key to the world; therefore, someone pretending to be George could have sent you the ciphertext.

- ☞ **Authentication** refers to the process of verifying that a message has been sent by the person who claims to have sent it. This process is particularly important in commercial transactions, because the seller needs assurance that the buyer is who he says he is or that his written promise to pay is not a forgery.

- ☞ Public key encryption addresses the issue of authentication by providing George with a way to sign the message using his private key before encrypting it with your public key. This approach is called creating a **digital signature**.

- ☞ The creation of a digital signature begins with a software algorithm referred to as a **hash function**. The hash function generates a fingerprint that is based on the exact contents of the plaintext, but much smaller than the original plaintext. A hash function produces a fingerprint that is mathematically impossible to reproduce using any other message.

The steps of public key encryption

1. A typical public key encryption program is first used to generate a key pair for the user—the public key and its mathematically related private key. Once you have generated the key pair, you will never need to repeat this step again.

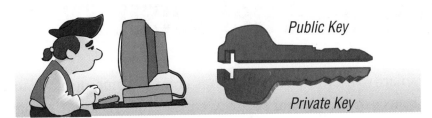

Public Key

Private Key

2. You then distribute your public key to the world (or to those individuals from whom you want to receive encrypted e-mail). Your private key remains private, kept in a safe place where others will not have access to it. In addition, because of the strength of the algorithm used, no one will be able to deduce your private key by examining your public key.

Private Key

```
Hello, World!
My name is Paul.
Here is my public key.


fGta365Lfhjqw54&c01pXs
4tRqb7ShpmKlJUsr7cwiBeGDo
bVivM74&rf#g39kjhVI...
```

3. The other user (George), who sends you an encrypted message, will then use your public key to encrypt the message. Once George has encrypted the message using your public key, the only key capable of decrypting the ciphertext is your private key.

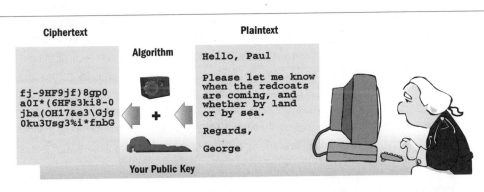

Ciphertext

Algorithm

Plaintext

```
fj-9HF9jf)8gp0
a0I*(6HFs3ki8-0
jba(OH17&e3\Gjg
0ku3Usg3%i*fnbG
```

```
Hello, Paul

Please let me know
when the redcoats
are coming, and
whether by land
or by sea.

Regards,

George
```

Your Public Key

4. George then sends the cyphertext to you, assured that his message to you will be absolutely private because you are the only person capable of decrypting his message—using your private key.

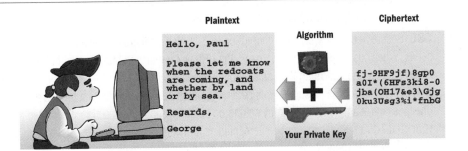

Plaintext

Algorithm

Ciphertext

```
Hello, Paul

Please let me know
when the redcoats
are coming, and
whether by land
or by sea.

Regards,

George
```

```
fj-9HF9jf)8gp0
a0I*(6HFs3ki8-0
jba(OH17&e3\Gjg
0ku3Usg3%i*fnbG
```

Your Private Key

Exploring Internet security

The increasing popularity of online shopping has created some nervousness about the security of online transactions. Special security considerations apply to data and transactions on the Internet. When you download a file from the Internet, you can use virus detection software to make sure that the file is virus-free before you run it, but some Web sites automatically send a program to your computer and run it before you even know it's there. Many security problems on the Internet are the result of two technologies: Java applets and ActiveX controls.

INTERNET SECURITY

DETAILS

⊶ A **Java applet** is a small program that is intended to add processing and interactive capabilities to Web pages. Such an applet may, for example, total the cost of the merchandise you are purchasing online. When you access a Web page containing a Java applet, the program is downloaded automatically to your computer and executed in a supposedly secure area of your computer known as the **sandbox**. Some hackers, however, have been able to breach security and create hostile Java applets that damage or steal data.

⊶ **ActiveX controls** are also downloaded automatically to your computer. They provide another way to add processing capabilities and interaction to Web pages. Unlike Java applets, ActiveX controls are not limited to the sandbox and have full access to your entire computer system. It is possible for hackers to use ActiveX controls to create havoc in your system.

⊶ A **digital certificate** identifies the author of an ActiveX control. A programmer, in effect, signs a program by attaching his or her digital certificate. Theoretically, a programmer would not sign a hostile program, so all programs with a digital certificate should be safe. Your browser will warn you about programs that do not have a digital certificate, so you can decide whether to accept them, as shown in Figure H-18. The only way to entirely avoid dangerous Java applets and ActiveX controls is to tell your browser not to accept them. In reality, many Web pages include legitimate applets and controls. If your browser doesn't accept them, you might miss some valuable features and interactions. Companies with hosts and LANs connected to the Internet often implement a **firewall** to screen out potentially damaging programs. You might consider installing **personal firewall software** to protect your computer from hostile Java applets and ActiveX controls.

⊶ The security of an Internet transaction is about the same as that when you purchase merchandise by mail or by phone. Current Internet security technology does not guarantee that your transaction will remain secure. Legitimate e-commerce sites provide their customers with a secure channel for transmitting credit card data. This secure channel is established by encrypting the transaction with a security protocol such as SSL or S-HTTP.

- **SSL** (Secure Sockets Layer) uses encryption to establish a secure connection between your computer and a Web server. When customers use an SSL page, the URL will begin with https: instead of http:, and you will generally receive a message indicating that transactions are secure.

- **S-HTTP** (Secure HTTP) also encrypts data transmitted between your computer and a Web server, but does so one message at a time rather than by setting up an entire secure connection. Encrypted transactions ensure that your credit card number cannot be intercepted as it travels from your computer, through Internet routers, to a Web server. See Figure H-19.

Your browser will warn you before it accepts an unsigned Java applet or ActiveX control.

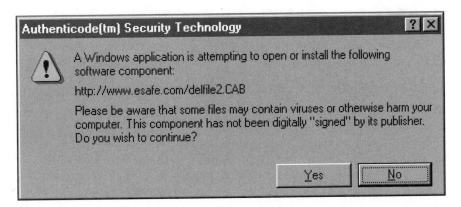

Authenticode(tm) Security Technology

A Windows application is attempting to open or install the following software component:

http://www.esafe.com/delfile2.CAB

Please be aware that some files may contain viruses or otherwise harm your computer. This component has not been digitally "signed" by its publisher. Do you wish to continue?

Yes   No

▶ Lock Icon on Internet Explorer indicates secure transmission.

▶ Key icon on Netscape Navigator indicates secure transmission.

Cookies

A *cookie* is a message sent from a Web server to your browser and stored on your hard disk. Web sites use cookies to remember information about you such as the following: your name, the date of your last visit, your e-mail address, your last purchase, and the links you followed at the site. When you use a Web site that distributes cookies, this information is incorporated into the cookie that the Web server sends to your computer. The next time you connect to that Web site, your browser sends the cookie to the Web server.

Although cookies are usually harmless, some Web sites might ask for information that you would not want to make public. Try to use good sense when responding to requests for personal information.

Providing redundancy

Accidents can destroy data and equipment. The result is **downtime**—computer jargon for the time a computer system is not functioning.

DATA BACKUP

DETAILS

☞ The most dependable way to minimize downtime is by duplicating data and equipment. Duplicating equipment simply means maintaining equipment that duplicates the functions critical to computing activities. This approach is sometimes referred to as **hardware redundancy**. Duplicate servers, routers, and communications lines are key to Internet hosting services that must maintain continuous service for the hundreds of Web pages and e-commerce sites that they host. Hardware redundancy reduces an organization's dependency on outside repair technicians. If it maintains a stock of duplicate parts, an organization can swap parts and be up and running before the manufacturer's repair technician arrives. Duplicate parts are expensive, however, and their costs must be weighed against lost revenue or productivity while repairs are under way.

☞ A **backup** is a duplicate copy of a file or the contents of a disk drive. If the original file becomes lost or damaged, you can use the backup copy to restore the data to its original working condition. Backup is probably the best all-around protection for your data. It provides good data protection from hardware failures, vandalism, operator error, and natural disasters. Although most people recognize that backups are important, they often forget to make backups or they tend to procrastinate. For effective backups, follow the recommendations in Table H-3.

☞ **Tape backups** are the most popular microcomputer backup solution for small businesses, but they are not the only solution. Tape backup requires tape and a tape drive. Refer to Figure H-20. An internal tape drive fits into your computer's system unit. An external tape drive is ideal for notebook computers.

☞ Many microcomputer users back up their data onto floppy disks, Zip disks, removable hard disks, CD-RWs, DVD-RAMs, and even paper. Floppy and Zip disks are unrealistic for backing up the entire contents of today's high-capacity disk drives. It is not necessary to back up every file, however. Many users back up only those directories that contain data files. In the event of a hard disk failure, these users would need to reinstall all of their software from the original disks, and then copy their data files from the backups.If you use the computers in a college computer lab, your situation is somewhat unique because you store your data on a floppy disk instead of the hard disk. In this situation, an effective backup technique is to use a copy disk operating system utility, which makes a copy of a floppy disk.

☞ Software for backups: You must use software to tell the computer what to copy. You might use any of three types of software: a copy utility, a copy disk program, or backup software.

- A **copy utility** is a program that copies one or more files. You can use such a utility to copy files from a hard disk to a floppy disk (or vice versa), between two floppy disks of any size, from a CD-ROM to a hard disk, or from a CD-ROM to a floppy disk. A copy utility is usually included with a computer operating system.
- **Copy Disk** is a program that duplicates the contents of an entire floppy disk. You use such a utility to copy all files from one floppy disk to another floppy disk of the same size. You cannot use Copy Disk for files on a hard disk drive. Refer to Figure H-21 to see how to duplicate a floppy disk.
- **Backup software** is designed to manage hard disk backup to tapes or disks. When you use these software programs, you can select the files you want to back up. Many backup programs offer automated features, which allow you to schedule automatic backups and to back up only those files that have changed since the last backup. Windows presents some unique backup challenges. When you perform a backup, many critical operating system and Registry files are open and therefore are not included in the backup. To ensure that your backup includes every file that you will need to restore your system, make sure that you follow the directions provided by your backup software to make a copy of the Registry.

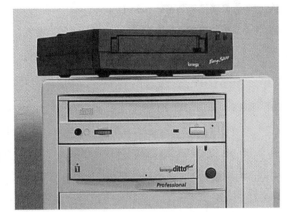

Notebook computers might not have an empty storage bay, so an external tape drive is an ideal solution.

An internal tape drive fits into one of the storage bays of your computer's system unit.

FIGURE H-21: *How to use Copy Disk*

If you are working in a school computer lab and saving your data on a floppy disk, you can use the copy disk utility to back up a floppy.

1. Put your original disk in the floppy drive.

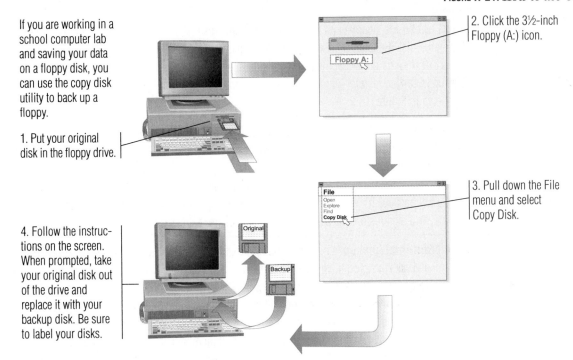

2. Click the 3½-inch Floppy (A:) icon.

3. Pull down the File menu and select Copy Disk.

4. Follow the instructions on the screen. When prompted, take your original disk out of the drive and replace it with your backup disk. Be sure to label your disks.

TABLE H-3: *Good backup habits*

WHAT YOU SHOULD DO	REASONS
Make frequent backups.	You can't restore data that you haven't backed up—if you wait a month between backups, you could lose a month's worth of data.
Scan for viruses before you back up.	Your backup will also be infected if your computer is infected with a virus when you back up.
Store your backup away from your computer.	Your backup could be damaged if it is next to your computer and your computer is damaged by flood, fire, or some other natural disaster.
Test your backup.	You depend on your backup to be able to restore data from your backup to your hard drive. You must be sure that your backup works properly—you would not want to discover when you go to use your backups that your backup files are blank because you have not followed the correct backup procedure.

Creating backups

One of the most distressing computing experiences is to lose all of your data. This problem might be the result of a hardware failure or a virus. Whatever its cause, most users experience only a moment of surprise and disbelief before the depressing realization sinks in that they might have to recreate all of their data and reinstall all of their programs. A backup can pull you through such trying times, making the data loss a minor inconvenience, rather than a major disaster.

DETAILS

- A **full backup** is a copy of all files on a disk. It ensures that you have a copy of every program and data file on the disk. Because a full backup includes a copy of every file on a disk, it can take a long time to make one for a hard disk. Some users consider it worth the extra time, however, because this type of backup is easy to restore. You simply have the computer copy the files from your backup to the hard disk, as shown in Figure H-22.

- A **differential backup** is a copy of all files that have changed since the last full backup. You maintain two sets of backups—a full backup that you make infrequently—say, once a week—and a differential backup that you make more frequently—say, once a day. It takes less time to make a differential backup than to make a full backup, but it is a little more complex to restore data from a differential backup than from a full backup. To restore data using a differential backup, you first restore the data from the last full backup, and then restore the data from the latest differential backup, as shown in Figure H-23.

- An **incremental backup** is a copy of the files that have changed since the last backup. When you use incremental backups, you must have a full backup, and you must maintain a series of incremental backups. The incremental backup procedure sounds like the differential backup procedure, but there is a difference. With a differential backup, you maintain one full backup and one differential backup. The differential backup contains any files that changed since the last full backup. With an incremental backup procedure, you maintain a full backup and a series of incremental backups. Each incremental backup contains only those files that have changed since the last incremental backup. To restore the data from a series of incremental backups, you restore the last full backup, and then sequentially restore each incremental backup, as shown in Figure H-24. Incremental backups take the least time to make, and they provide a little better protection from viruses than other backup methods because your backup contains a series of copies of your files. They are, however, the most complex type of backup to restore.

- Any data backup plan represents a compromise between the level of protection and the amount of time devoted to backup. To be safe, you would need to back up your data every time you change the contents of a file, which would reduce the amount of work you could complete in a day. Realistically, you should make backups at regular intervals (including copies of the Registry). The interval between backups will depend on the value of your data—what that data is worth to you.

A full backup is simply a copy of all files on your hard disk.

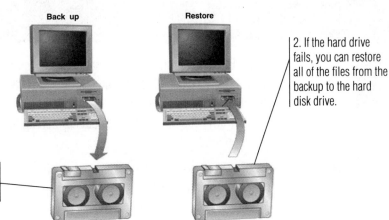

Back up

Restore

2. If the hard drive fails, you can restore all of the files from the backup to the hard disk drive.

1. Back up all files from the hard disk drive to a backup tape.

A differential backup copies any files that have changed since your last full backup.

1. Make a full backup on Monday evening.

2. On Tuesday evening, use a different tape to back up only the files that have been changed since the full backup.

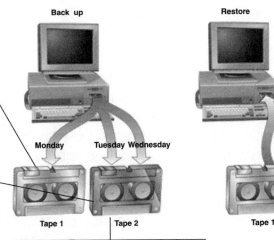

Back up

Restore

Monday   Tuesday Wednesday

Tape 1   Tape 2

Tape 1   Tape 2

4. Now, suppose the hard disk fails. To restore your data, first load the full backup onto the hard disk. This step restores the files as they existed on Monday evening.

5. Next, load the data from the differential backup tape. This step restores the files you changed on Tuesday and Wednesday.

3. On Wednesday evening, back up only the files that have been changed since the full backup. These files are the ones you changed or created on Tuesday and Wednesday. Put these files on the same tape you used for Tuesday's backup.

Of the three backup techniques, an incremental backup takes the least time, but is the most complex to restore.

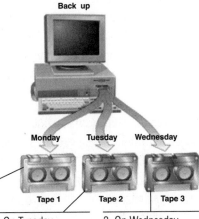

Back up

Monday   Tuesday   Wednesday

Tape 1   Tape 2   Tape 3

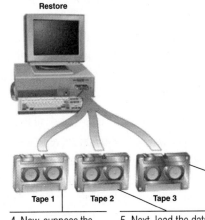

Restore

Tape 1   Tape 2   Tape 3

1. Make a full backup on Monday evening.

2. On Tuesday evening, back up only the files that have been changed or created on Tuesday.

3. On Wednesday evening, back up only the files that have been changed or created on Wednesday.

4. Now, suppose the hard disk fails. To begin the restoration process, first load the data from the full backup.

5. Next, load the data from Tuesday's incremental backup. This step restores the work you did on Tuesday.

6. Finally, load the data from Wednesday's incremental backup. This step restores the work you did on Wednesday.

The accounting firm Ernst & Young estimates that computer crime costs individuals and organizations in the United States between $3 billion and $5 billion each year. Some "old-fashioned" crimes that take a high-tech twist because they involve a computer can be prosecuted using traditional laws. For example, a person who attempts to destroy data by setting fire to a computer might be prosecuted under traditional arson laws.

Traditional laws do not, however, cover the range of possibilities for computer crimes. Suppose a person unlawfully enters a computer facility and steals backup tapes. That person might be prosecuted for breaking and entering. But would breaking and entering laws apply to a person who uses an off-site terminal to "enter" a computer system without authorization? And what if a person copies a data file without authorization? Has that file really been "stolen" if the original remains on the computer?

Many countries have computer crime laws that specifically define computer data and software as personal property. These laws also define as a crime the unauthorized access, use, modification, or disabling of a computer system or data.

In early 1995, cybersleuth Tsutomu Shimomura tracked down a hacker named Kevin Mitnick who had broken into dozens of corporate, university, government, and personal computers. Before being arrested, Mitnick stole thousands of data files and more than 20,000 credit card numbers. U.S. attorney Kent Walker commented, "He was clearly the most wanted computer hacker in the world." Mitnick's unauthorized access and use of computer data are explicitly defined as criminal acts by computer crime laws.

Denying many, but not all, of the accusations against him, Mitnick claimed, "No way, no how, did I break into NORAD. That's a complete myth. And I never attempted to access anything considered to be classified government systems." Although vilified in the media, Mitnick had the support of many hackers, who believed that the prosecution had grossly exaggerated the extent of his crimes. Nonetheless, Mitnick was sentenced to 46 months in prison and ordered to pay restitution in the amount of $4,125 during his three-year period of supervised release. The prosecution was horrified by such a paltry sum—an amount that was much less than its request for $1.5 million in restitution.

Forbes reporter Adam L. Penenberg took issue with the 46-month sentence imposed by Judge Marianne Pfaelzer, and wrote, "This in a country where the average prison term for manslaughter is three years. Mitnick's crimes were curiously innocuous. He broke into corporate computers, but no evidence indicates that he destroyed data. Or sold anything he copied. Yes, he pilfered software—but in doing so left it behind. This world of bits is a strange one, in which you can take something and still leave it for its rightful owner. The theft laws designed for payroll sacks and motor vehicles just don't apply to a hacker."

Unfortunately for Mitnick, the jail term and $4,125 fine were, perhaps, the most lenient part of his sentence. Mitnick, who had served most of his jail term while awaiting trial, was scheduled for a supervised release soon after sentencing. The additional conditions of Mitnick's supervised release include a ban on access to computer hardware, software, and any form of wireless communication. He is prohibited from possessing any kind of passwords, cellular phone codes, or data encryption devices. And just to make sure that he doesn't get into any trouble with technologies that are not specifically mentioned in the terms of his supervised release, Mitnick is prohibited from using any new or future technology that performs as a computer or provides access to one. Perhaps worst of all, he cannot obtain employment with a company that has computers or computer access on its premises.

The Mitnick case illustrates our culture's ambivalent attitude toward hackers. On the one hand, they are viewed as evil cyberterrorists who are set on destroying the glue that binds together the Information Age. From this perspective, hackers are criminals who need to be hunted down, forced to make restitution for damages, and prevented from creating further havoc.

From another perspective, hackers are viewed more as Casper, the friendly ghost in our complex cybermachines—as moderately bothersome entities whose pranks are tolerated by the computer community, along with software bugs and hardware glitches. Seen from this perspective, a hacker's pranks are part of the normal course of study that leads to the highest echelons of computer expertise. "Everyone has done it," claim devotees, "even Bill Gates (founder of Microsoft) and Steve Jobs (founder of Apple computer)."

Which perspective is right? Before you make up your mind about computer hacking and cracking, you might want to further investigate the Mitnick case and similar cases by following the Computer Crime InfoWeb links.

EXPAND THE IDEAS:

1. Should it be a crime to steal a copy of computer data while leaving the original data in place and unaltered? Write a two-page paper supporting your position. Be sure to include your resources.

2. Was Mitnick's sentence fair? Research other famous cases of computer hackers who were caught and prosecuted by the law. Find several examples of articles, documentaries, or news stories on computer crime on the Internet. Write a summary of each article or media piece. Analyze your findings. Was the media voice consistent? Why or why not?

3. Should hackers be sent to jail if they cannot pay restitution to companies and individuals who have lost money as a result of a prank? Write a two-page paper supporting your position. Be sure to include your resources.

4. Have you or anyone you know been a victim of a computer crime? What was the outcome? Could the crime have been avoided? Compile your ideas into a poster presentation.

5. How do you view hackers? Is our culture ambivalent? Do you view them as heinous criminals or more like Casper the friendly ghost? Form a discussion group with several colleagues in the class. Write a two-page summary paper analyzing the opinions of the group.

End of Unit Exercises

STUDY TIPS

Study Tips help you organize and consolidate the information in a unit by making lists, outlines, charts, and sketches. You can use paper and pencil or word processing software to complete most of the Study Tips activities.

1. Create a chart to review the factors that cause data loss or misuse. List the factors you learned about in this chapter in the first column. Then place an X in the appropriate column to indicate whether that factor leads to data loss, inaccurate data, stolen data, or intentionally damaged data. Some factors might have more than one X.

2. Summarize what you have learned about viruses, Trojan horses, time bombs, logic bombs, and software worms.

3. Make a checklist of steps to follow if you suspect that your computer is infected with a virus.

4. List the four steps in the risk management process.

5. List the data security techniques discussed in the Risk Management section. Then indicate the advantages and disadvantages of each technique.

6. Use your own words to write descriptions of full, incremental, and differential backup procedures. Make sure that your descriptions clearly explain the difference between incremental and differential backups.

7. On a sheet of paper, list all of the reasons you can think of for making a backup of computer data.

FILL IN THE BEST ANSWER

1. As a result of a power failure, your computer will lose all data stored in RAM and the hard drive. True or False? _____

2. The circuitry on your computer circuit boards can be damaged by accidentally turning off your computer. True or False? _____

3. MTBF tells you how often an electronic device needs to be serviced. True or False? _____

4. You can eliminate a virus from your computer system by deleting the virus file. True or False? _____

5. Payload is the name of a very common virus. True or False? _____

6. A macro virus duplicates itself into the general macro pool, where it is picked up by other documents. True or False? _____

7. Procedures help reduce human errors that can erase or damage data. True or False? _____

8. Public key encryption uses a pair of keys. True or False? _____

9. The most common cause of lost data is _____.

10. A(n) _____ contains a battery that provides a continuous supply of power to your computer during a brief power failure.

11. A(n) _____ protects your computer from power spikes and surges but does not keep your computer operating if the power fails.

12. The failure of which computer component is potentially the most disastrous? _____

13. The best insurance for your data is _____.

14. A(n) _____ is a program that reproduces itself when the computer executes the file to which it is attached.

15. Suppose that your computer displays a weird message every time you type the word "digital." You might suspect that your computer has contracted a(n) _____.

16. Three symptoms of a computer virus infection are _____, _____, and _____.

17. A(n) _____ is a software program that might contain a virus or a time bomb.

18. A(n) _____ is a program that reproduces itself without being attached to an executable file.

19. Computer crime laws define _____ and _____ as personal property.

20. Two sources of disks that should be considered a "high risk" of virus infection are _____ and _____.

21. Many virus detection programs identify viruses by looking for a unique series of bytes called a(n) _____.

22. _____ is the process of weighing threats to computer data against the amount of data that is expendable and the cost of protecting crucial data.

23. A(n) ———————is a rule designed to prohibit employees from installing software that has not been preapproved by the information systems department.

24. If a network administrator assigns _____, users can access only certain programs and files.

25. Hackers sometimes gain unauthorized entry to computer systems through _____ that are not removed when development and testing are complete.

26. _____ is computer jargon that refers to the time during which a computer system is not functioning.

INDEPENDENT CHALLENGE 1

Describe a situation in which you or someone you know lost data stored on a computer.

To complete this independent challenge:

Write a brief essay that answers the following questions:

1. What caused the data loss?

2. What steps could have been taken to prevent the loss?

3. What steps could you or this other person have taken to recover the lost data?

INDEPENDENT CHALLENGE 2

Assess the risk to the programs and data files stored on the hard disk drive of your computer.

To complete this independent challenge:

Answer the following questions:

1. What threats are likely to cause your data to be lost, stolen, or damaged?

2. How many files of data do you have?

3. If you add up the size of all your files, how many megabytes of data do you have?

4. How many of these files are critical and would need to be replaced if you lost all of your data?

5. What would you need to do to reconstruct the critical files if the hard disk drive failed and you did not have any backups?

6. What measures could you use to protect your data from the threats you identified in Question 1? What is the cost of each of these measures?

7. Taking into account the threats to your data, the importance of your data, and the cost of possible protective measures, what do you think is the best plan for the security of your own data?

INDEPENDENT CHALLENGE 3

Assume that your hard disk drive fails on a Friday afternoon.

To complete this independent challenge:

Explain how you would restore your data over the weekend if you had been using each of the following backup systems:

1. A full backup every Friday evening

2. A full backup every Friday evening, with a differential backup on Wednesday night

3. A full backup every Friday evening, with an incremental backup Monday through Thursday evenings

INDEPENDENT CHALLENGE 4

If you suspect your computer has become infected with a virus, it is prudent to immediately activate virus detection software to scan your files. With the continued spread of viruses, virus detection software has become an essential utility in today's computing environment. Many virus detection software packages are available in computer stores, on computer bulletin boards, and on the Internet.

To complete this independent challenge:

1. Find information about three virus detection software packages. Write a brief report on each one, and compare and contrast the features and benefits of each.

2. Microsoft Word documents can harbor macro viruses. This type of virus is documented in many sources. Using library or Internet resources, find a list of symptoms for the Word macro virus that is currently circulating. Write a one-page report describing what you learned about the Word macro virus and its presence on, or absence from, the documents you have on your disks.

3. Use the latest version of your virus protection software to check your disks to see whether you have the virus and to check the list of signatures in your virus software to see whether the virus is listed there.

INDEPENDENT CHALLENGE 5

The Internet worm created concern about the security of data on military and research computer systems, and it raised ethical questions about the rights and responsibilities of computer users.

To complete this independent challenge:

Select one of the following statements and write a two-page paper that argues for or against it. Use the Internet or library resources to learn more about each viewpoint. Be sure to include the resources you used in a bibliography.

1. People have the right to hone their computing skills by breaking into computers. As a computer scientist once said, "The right to hack is held higher than the right of someone to tell you not to. It's an inalienable right."

2. If problems exist, it is acceptable to use any means to point them out. The computer science student who created the Internet virus was perfectly justified in claiming that he should not be prosecuted because he was just trying to point out that security holes exist in large computer networks.

3. Computer crimes are no different from other crimes, and computer criminals should be held responsible for the damage they cause by paying for the time and cost of replacing or restoring data.

INDEPENDENT CHALLENGE 6

Obtain a copy of your school's student code or computer use policy.

To complete this independent challenge:

Write a brief paper that answers the following questions:

1. To whom does the policy apply: students, faculty, staff, community members, others?

2. What types of activities does the policy specifically prohibit?

3. If a computer crime is committed, would the crime be dealt with by campus authorities or by state law enforcement agents?

4. Does the policy state the penalties for computer crimes? If so, what are they?

INDEPENDENT CHALLENGE 7

Most Internet users have received panicked e-mail about various types of viruses. It turns out that many of these viruses do not exist.

To complete this independent challenge:

1. How can you tell the difference between a real virus alert and a hoax? The best policy is to check a reliable site. You can easily locate sites that list hoaxes by entering "hoax" in any Internet search engine, such as Yahoo! Sites with

reliable reports include www.urbanlegends.com and ciac.llnl.gov/ciac/CIACHoaxes.html.

2. Visit at least one of these sites and find the descriptions of five hoaxes. Write a one-page summary that includes the name and description of each hoax, the way in which the hoax spreads, and reasons why people might believe the hoax.

INDEPENDENT CHALLENGE 8

Many computer experts predicted all sorts of effects ranging from minor glitches to Armageddon as the millennium turned. The Y2K bug caused many companies worldwide to invest large sums of money, time, and manpower in updating their computer systems. Ultimately, the clock turned from 12/31/99 to 1/1/00 throughout the world with very few disruptions due to computer failures.

To complete this independent challenge

Go to the library or Internet, and research the efforts that were instituted to prepare for the date 1/1/00. Write a three-page paper on the Y2K phenomenon. Be sure to address the following topics in your paper:

1. Which dates in particular were the companies concerned about? What major systems were of most concern to people around the world?

2. What types of efforts did major U.S. corporations invest in to prepare for the "event?"

3. Did any systems fail?

DATA BACKUP LAB

The Data Backup Lab gives you an opportunity to make tape backups on a simulated computer system. Periodically, the hard disk on the simulated computer will fail, which gives you a chance to restore the data from your simulated backups and assess the convenience and efficiency of different backup procedures.

1. Click the Steps button to learn how to use the simulation. As you work through the Steps, answer all of the QuickCheck questions that appear. After you complete the Steps, you will see a QuickCheck Summary Report. Follow the directions on the screen to print this report.

2. Click the Explore button. Create a full backup every Friday using only Tape 1. At some point in the simulation, an event will cause data loss on the simulated computer system. Use the simulation to restore as much data as you can. After you restore the data, print the Backup Audit Report.

3. In Explore, create a full backup every Friday on Tape 1 and a differential backup every Wednesday on Tape 2. At some point in the simulation, an event will cause data loss on the simulated computer system. Use the simulation to restore as much data as you can. Print the Backup Audit Report.

4. In Explore, create a full backup on Tape 1 every Monday. Make incremental backups on Tapes 2, 3, 4, and 5 each day for the rest of the week. Continue this cycle, reusing the same tapes each week. At some point in the simulation, an event will cause data loss on the simulated computer system. Use the simulation to restore as much data as you can. Print the Backup Audit Report.

5. Photocopy a calendar for next month. On the calendar, indicate your best plan for backing up data. In Explore, implement your plan. Print out the Backup Audit Report. Write a paragraph or two discussing the effectiveness of your plan.

LESSON	MEDIA ELEMENT	LESSON	MEDIA ELEMENT
Knowing what can go wrong	UPS VIDEO	Restricting access to data	BIOMETRICS VIDEO
Avoiding disasters	COMPUTER INSURANCE	Understanding encryption	ENCRYPTION METHODS
Introducing computer viruses and vandalism	VIRUSES MACRO VIRUSES	Exploring Internet security	INTERNET SECURITY
Exploring viruses and vandalism	Y2K BUG THE INTERNET WORM	Providing redundancy	DATA BACKUP
Avoiding and detect viruses	ANTIVIRUS SOFTWARE SCREENTOUR	Issue: Is It a Crime?	COMPUTER CRIME
Understanding data security and risk management	RISK MANAGEMENT ACCEPTABLE USE POLICIES		

VISUAL WORKSHOP

Fill in the blanks based on the illustration.

1. The illustration depicts the process of making a(n) _____ backup.

2. Tape 1 should contain a(n) _____ backup.

3. Tape 2 and Tape 3 contain data that has changed since the last backup of any sort. True or False? _____

4. To restore this backup, you would first restore tape number _____.

5. With this type of backup, you must make sure to accurately _____ each tape.

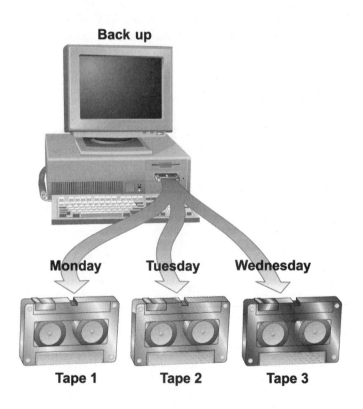

Back up

Monday   Tuesday   Wednesday

Tape 1   Tape 2   Tape 3

Trends in Technology

Unit

1

OBJECTIVES

Exploring evolving trends in ...

Personal computers	
Processors	
Storage devices	
Networking	
Remote and wireless connectivity	
Web design and development	
Productivity software	
Leisure technology	

Technologies, once the domain of science fiction writers and film-makers, are now the items on many people's shopping lists. Today, you can pick up a device small enough to fit comfortably in your pocket, press a few keys or speak into the device and reach anyone anywhere in the world. Now, you have the wealth of the worlds' knowledge through the World Wide Web available at anytime or any-place. Learning about and understanding the technology that makes this all possible is both fascinating and overwhelming—fascinating because of the way technology impacts our daily lives; overwhelming because the science behind the technologies seems to be rapidly changing and evolving. This unit highlights a sampling of technology trends that impact the world around us.

Exploring evolving trends in . . .
Personal computers

New technology for desktops, notebooks, and handheld computers, as well as PC accessories and components, is changing rapidly. Because of this change, these technologies are becoming even smaller, faster, cheaper, and lighter. Today, hard disk drives that range from 10GB-100GB hard disk capacities that a few short years ago were not even thought possible in any market—are readily available for the consumer market. Today, handheld devices have the capacity and processing power that were once only the domain of large mainframe computers. This lesson explores the recent developments and trends in personal computers.

DETAILS

☞ **Multipurpose PCs**: Because desktop computers are too big to take along and notebook computers often have displays and keyboards too small for long-term usage, computer manufacturers are looking for ways to combine the best of both worlds. For example, Compaq Computer is developing a computer that will offer the best of both types of personal computers for the price of one. The new line of business notebooks transform into desktop PCs.

☞ **Internet Appliances**: Internet appliances are PCs that are designed for the sole purpose of accessing the Internet. Dell Computer tried and failed to market a WebPC that cost roughly the same as a desktop. New ventures include the New Internet Computer Company's NIC (www.thinknic.com). The NIC, priced initially at $199 (without the monitor), cost much less than the cheapest PC. It includes just what you need to connect to the Internet: keyboard, mouse, speakers, modem, Ethernet, a lower-end processor, and CD-ROM. It does not have a hard disk and all applications boot from the CD.

☞ **Display Technology: Organic light emitting diode** (OLED) is a new display technology that allows brighter displays at lower costs. Displays using this technology use less energy. Many companies are developing OLEDs for the commercial market. OLEDs are thinner, have higher resolutions, and are more power-efficient than Cathode Ray Tubes or Active Matrix Liquid Crystal displays, which are the dominant technologies used in monitor displays today. OLEDs likely will first appear in smaller devices such as cell phones and watches. Some fast-developing fabrication processes may help to bring OLED technology to flat-panel TVs and computer screens sooner than expected.

☞ **CRT technology**: Advances in Cathode Ray Tube (CRT) technology, still the technology behind most computer monitors, continues to advance with higher refresh rates (about 70Hz) and smaller dot-pitches (ranging now from .22mm horizontal to

.13mm -.16mm vertical). **Flat-faced monitors** have less glare and images have a more realistic flatter appearance, however, they are more expensive. Some believe flat-faced monitors are more environmentally friendly both when in use (because they emit less radiation and are more energy efficient) and when they are disposed (because they are not made with mercury, lead, and glass, which is how CKT monitors are made).

☞ **Input Devices:** From Douglas Englebart's original design in 1964, see Figure I-2, the mouse has come a long way. Recent developments include the force feedback iFeel Mousman, which was launched by Logitech in 2000. The mouse, when used with appropriate software, provides customized sensations. The Cordless Mousman Optical also has no roller ball and no cables. It promises precision tracking and highly sensitive resolution. The optical sensor in the mouse detects 800dpi for accuracy on any surface. Microsoft's Intellimouse replaced the roller ball, which was always in need of cleaning, with an LED that tracks movements and transfers it to the computer.

Harmonic Research of Virginia has developed a prototype of the Lightglove. Users click and move by waving their fingers. Optical sensors respond to the movements, which are picked up by the wristband. The Lightglove also detects typing movements.

☞ **Keyboards:** Keyboard technology has continued to evolve. Advances have been made in wireless keyboards that work with IR (infrared) devices to transmit input to the computer, and can be used up to three feet (one meter) away from a computer or printer. There are new keyboard designs that offer viable alternatives to the typical layout. For example, some new keyboards work as both a conventional desktop keyboard and portable word processor.

Smaller, more efficiently designed keyboards offer full keyboard features in less than one-third the space; and other keyboards save time and space by integrating a trackball and using color-coded keys.

Handheld Devices: Personal Digital Assistant (PDA)

devices from leading vendors, such as Palm Computing and Handspring, typically are small enough to fit in a pocket and have a touch screen that works with a stylus. IBM, Casio, Hewlett Packard, and Compaq also offer a full line of PDAs. The operating systems used on handhelds typically are Palm OS, Windows CE, Windows for Pocket PC, EPOC, and Linux. Some of these devices even come with multimedia features to play video and audio files. Data entry can be through a **hotsync**, which is a cable connection to a computer, or through **graffiti**, which is digital shorthand that converts movement on the screen into text. Collapsible keyboards that can attach to the PDA can be purchased as an accessory for your handheld. You might prefer to use the keyboard when you don't want to use the stylus to enter data.

Clamshell handheld devices are similar in functionality to the Palm-sized devices. These have larger screens than PDAs and tiny keyboards.

Tablet handheld devices are still designed to be portable. These are lighter and smaller than laptop computers but have larger displays and keyboards than the clamshell devices.

FIGURE I-1: *Flat monitors*

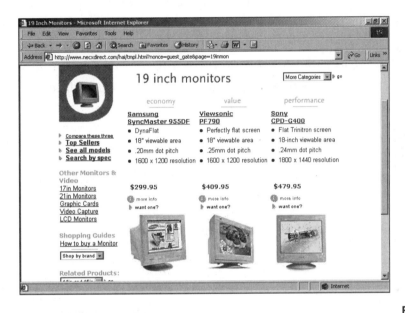

FIGURE I-2: *The first mouse*

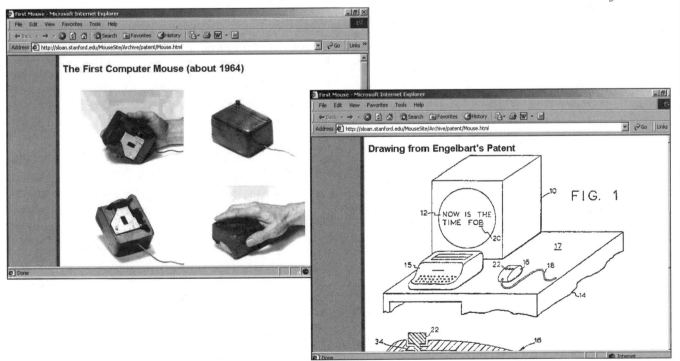

Exploring evolving trends in . . . Processors

The microprocessor is the heart of the personal computer. Advances in microprocessor technology are announced on a daily basis. These advances drive the personal computing market. In addition to the processors in desktop and laptop computers, other devices such a handhelds and cell phones use processors. Advances in processors for these other devices are driving their markets as well. Currently, processors for cell phones and other wireless devices are somewhat limited because different chips generally are needed to handle the devices' memory, processing, and communications tasks. Before purchasing a computer with a new processor, it is a good idea to research the processor. Benchmark tests on processors provide current information about a chip – the manufacturer's claims and the reality.

DETAILS

☞ **Processors**: The three leading manufacturers of processors are Intel, Advanced Micro Deviced (AMD), and Transmeta. These companies manufacture processors for personal computers as well as other devices. Generally a company manufactures several lines of processors; each one in a series builds on the features and the functionality of the processor that came before it. The future trends in processors will be designing ones that require less energy and therefore produce less heat. These changes to processors will allow the devices that use them to become smaller, thinner, and lighter – and so more mobile.

☞ **Intel chips**: Intel manufactures a wide variety of chips. Intel's processors are targeted for specific uses such as servers, workstations, desktops, and mobile. New chips are announced often.

- **Intel Itanium processor:** Designed as a high-end server processor, this chip arrived with a lot of fanfare. It is an 800MHz processor that uses large memory addressibility to address 16M terabytes of memory. The line of Itanium processors is designed for servers and workstations targeted for e-businesses.
- **Intel XEON:** The Intel XEON processors are designed for Dual-Processor (DP) workstations for multitasking environments. It is designed for advanced graphics and visualizations.
- **Intel's Pentium 4:** This 400MHz chip includes features such as Intel NetBurst micro architecture, Rapid Execution Engine, Hyper Pipeline technology, and Execution Trace Cache. It comes at available speeds of 1.7GHz, 1.5 GHz, 1.4GHz, and 1.3GHz.

☞ **Intel's "Wireless Internet on a Chip":** This chip is designed for cell phones and handheld computers. It combines the core components of cell phones with handheld computers, and features energy efficiency. It combines flash memory and analog communication circuits. Intended for use in advanced wireless devices, the chip is based on Intel's XScale processor and will run at speeds of up to 1GHz.

☞ **Transmeta chips:** Transmeta's premier product is the Crusoe processor, see Figure I-3. With Crusoe, Transmeta has pioneered a revolutionary new approach to microprocessor design. For example, it is x86-compatible and it provides a family of solutions specially designed for mobile Internet computing. The Crusoe chip is a low-power chip. This makes it ideal for Internet devices and the ultra-light mobile PC category because it has low power consumption and it has an extended battery life.

The information at the www.transmeta.com site describes the technology associated with the Crusoe chip as follows: "Rather than implementing the entire x86 processor in hardware, the Crusoe processor solution consists of a compact hardware engine surrounded by a software layer. The hardware component is a very simple, high-performance, low-power VLIW (Very Long Instruction Word) engine with an instruction set that bears no resemblance to that of x86 processors. Instead, it is the surrounding software layer that gives programs the impression that they are running on x86 hardware.

This innovative software layer is called the Code Morphing software because it dynamically "morphs" (that is, translates) x86 instructions into the hardware engine's native instruction set."

This is a revolutionary advance in microprocessors. It could become the model around which future microprocessors are built.

Advanced Micro Devices Inc. chips: AMD processors include the Athlon, Duron, and KB family of processors. See

Figure I-4. The Athlon 4 microprocessor chip is optimized for notebooks, the fastest growing segment of the PC market. The Athlon 4 is the first 1 gigahertz mobile processor from AMD, and should extend battery life by as much as 30 percent. AMD offers x86-compatible processors that are suitable for Linux-based designs.

FIGURE I-3: *Crusoe specifications*

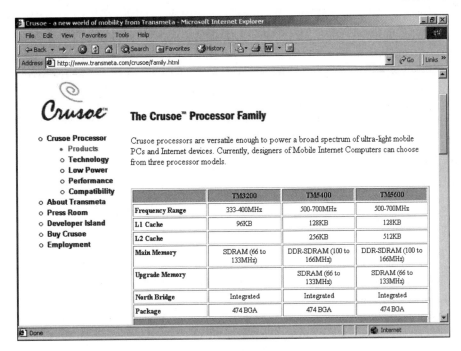

FIGURE I-4: *AMD Chips*

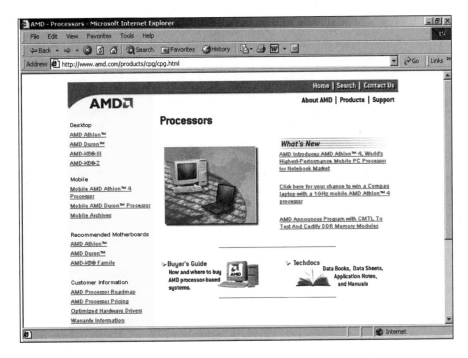

Exploring evolving trends in . . .
Storage devices

There was a time when a one gigabyte hard drive was the stuff dreams are made of. But now, when personal computers come with one gigabyte of storage, standard, you have to wonder where the limits will take us. You might even wonder if it is even necessary to have the storage device attached to the computer. After all, for security reasons, doesn't it make more sense to have the data stored remotely? With recent technological advances, it can seem as though the device is attached, but in fact, your data and applications may be miles away on a server that you never even need to know where it is. This lesson explores the recent trends in storage devices and technologies.

DETAILS

Trends in hard disks

- Speed, Speed, and Speed. Newer hard drives are now running at 7200RPM, rather than 5400RPM.
- Size: Hard disk drives have gotten smaller in physical size. One example is the IBM Microdrive. See Figure I-5. It holds one gigabyte of data storage capacity on a disk that is the size of an American quarter! This has tremendous implications for the digital camera world. The microdrive can hold up to 1,000 high-resolution photographs, a thousand 200-page novels, or almost 18 hours of high-quality digital music. Microdrive is compatible with many devices from many manufacturers, including laptops, digital cameras, handhelds, and card readers. Microdrive has moving parts, which is the only down side. But, because it has moving parts, Microdrive can be categorized with drives.
- **Flash memory** is a solid-state storage device, everything is electronic. Flash memory devices such as CompactFlash, SmartMedia cards, PCMCIA Type I and Type II memory cards are also types of removable storage for small devices such as digital cameras, notebook computers, or home video games but have no moving parts. The BIOS chip in your computer is Flash Memory, but is ROM (Read-Only Memory). Flash memory devices are easy and fast storage devices. Because many of these removable devices were developed to adhere to the PCMCIA standards, they can be used in many devices such as digital cameras, digital music players, and digital voice recorders. Sandisk developed CompactFlash Cards in 1994. It comes in store capacities from 8MB up to 192MB. Toshiba originally developed SmartMedia Card.

Trends in Network drives

- **Network drives** are drives that are directly connected to your LAN and are accessible from all computers on the LAN. One advantage to a network drive is shared space without having the overhead of sharing a folder on a PC. There are some security risks in having access to shared folders on a network that are avoided with the network drives. The disadvantages are transfer rates and expense. These drives are limited to the transfer rates available on the network. Another issue is that these drives are not cheap.
- **Online drives** allow you to store files on a "virtual hard drive" that is available from around the world, as long as you have an Internet connection. At present there are some problems with online drives. For example the storage space available in the online drives is determined outside your control by the vendor and you may find that it is a limited space. More importantly, online drives have slower access than real hard drives.
- **XDRIVE technology** is one online service that provides secure online storage. There are several options including licensed service, which is when the Xdrive software is installed directly onto the client's network. Xdrive claims that their technology makes the interface look and act like your own computer. Hosted Xdrive keeps the main system at Xdrive, and they provide support and technology for the offsite storage. It is not free. Other online services include FreeDrive (www.freedrive.com) and idrive (www.idrive.com). Online service is very popular now. Figure I-6 shows the FreeDrive home page and the idrive home page.

- **Trends in RAID - Redundant Array of Independent disks (RAID):** RAID provides fault tolerance and increased performance. While RAID has been around for a while for the business user, it has recently become available for the personal user. Originally RAID was used for servers only, but now it can be used as disk storage. RAID comes in nine levels; here is a description of the most common levels: Level 0 provides data striping, which means it writes data across multiple disks, increasing performance. Level 1 provides disk mirroring, which means it writes data on two disks at the same time, and when one disk dies, the RAID controller automatically starts reading from the other disk. There is no performance increase. Level 3 reserves one dedicated disk for error correction data, and provides some level of fault tolerance and some increased performance. Level 4 uses large stripes, which means you can read records from any single drive. Level 5 provides data striping at the byte level,

and it also provides striping error correction. This is the highest level: it has the greatest fault tolerance (one disk can die, and all data is still available), and awesome performance. However, you lose some disk space (because of the striping).

- **Pixie dust**: A new technology that IBM is using, informally called "pixie dust," is pushing up the limits of current drive technologies by increasing capacity levels. Pixie dust is a new type of magnetic coating that increases data density. Current high-capacity disk drives can store about 48 billion bytes of data; IBM believes their new disk drive design could quadruple disk drive capacity. IBM is forecasting that their new technique will enable them to increase disk capacity to 100 billion bits per square inch. Staggering to think about. What do these numbers translate to? It means IBM could be manufacturing a new version of its Microdrive that would be capable of storing six billion bytes of data.

FIGURE I-5: *IBM Microdrive*

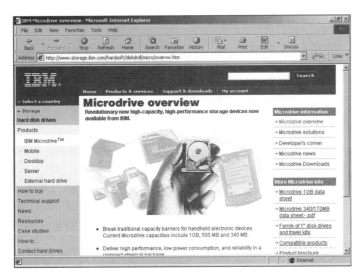

FIGURE I-6: *Popular online services*

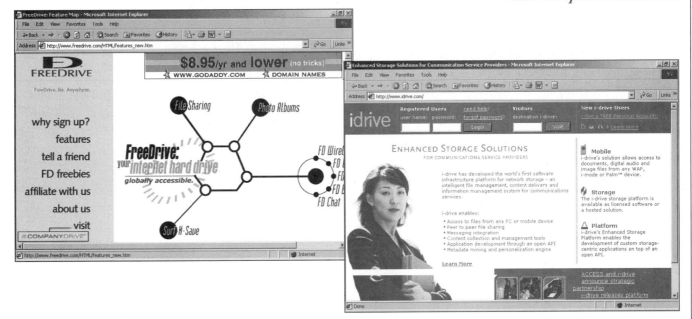

Exploring evolving trends in . . .
Networking

No longer are computers working in isolation. More likely than not, your computer is connected in some way to others through a network. There is the Internet, intranets, LANs, and WANS. Even handheld devices are now more likely than not to be working interactively with other computers, which allow you to be linked to a wider community. New technologies are constantly being developed that allow for greater amounts of data to move at faster rates and in a secure environment. Networks drive connectivity. Whether by cable, satellite, radio, or telephone, networks define our interconnected world. This lesson explores advances in networking technologies and trends including VPNs and VLANs.

DETAILS

Virtual Local Area Network (VLAN): A VLAN is a group of personal computers, servers and other network resources that are on physically different segments of a network, but communicate as though they were on the same wire. A VLAN is a logical grouping. It is a network created by software that combines stations and network devices into a single unit, regardless of the physical LAN segment they are actually attached to. **Segmentation** is the division of a network into separate shared-media sub networks.

Because these networks are software based, there are many advantages. For example, changes do not have to be hard wired. Users and resources that are likely to work together can be grouped in common VLANs to optimize the network. VLANs free up bandwidth to boost traffic through the network and allow more control in securing the network. Figure I-7 shows a schematic of a VLAN solution from the Intel Web site. Other vendors, including Cisco Systems, are working on VLAN technology.

VLAN industry standards are being developed by IEEE (Institute of Electrical and Electronics Engineers—pronounced I triple-E) to make VLANs more accessible to IT managers, who have switches, routers, and network cards from different vendors. Among other things, IEEE VLAN standards provide for VLAN construction so that VLANs established with components developed by different vendors work properly in the VLAN.

Virtual Private Network (VPN): A VPN is a private network that is configured within a public network to regulate the users who can access it. VPNs have been built on common carriers so, in affect, they appear as private networks, but, in fact, they are in a shared network with many other users. VPNs have the security of a private network but take advantage of the built-in facilities of large public networks. Typically, businesses have used VPNs for outsourcing remote access, connecting sites over the Internet, and connecting outside users over an extranet.

Clustering computers: Clustering technologies allow computers to work together to maximize performance. A **cluster** is a group of workstations that share a server or group of servers. They can share work and provide backups in case of failures of any of the connected servers. There are clustering technologies for Windows, Linux, and other operating systems. Shared disk technologies centralize the I/O (input/output) devices.

Dense Wave Division Multiplexing (DWDM): DWDM is a fiber optic transmission technique that employs light wavelengths to transmit data either using parallel transmission by bit or serial transmission by character. DWDM provides multiple channels over fiber optics using different wavelengths of light.

- **Optical networks** developers are facing new challenges that they didn't have with copper or even fiber-based networks. Lucent Technologies offers the WaveStar OptiGate subsystem, which is one example of an optical network. See Figure I-8.

- **Asynchronous Transfer Mode (ATM):** ATM is based on transferring data in packets of a fixed size. The packet is small compared with older technologies. The small, constant packets allow ATM equipment to transmit different types of data over the same line, without interfering with one another. **Constant Bit Rate (CBR)** is a fixed bit rate so that data is sent in a steady stream. **Variable Bit Rate (VBR)** is a specified maximum throughput capacity, but data is sent at even bit rates. **Unspecified Bit Rate (UBR)** doesn't guarantee any throughput levels. **Available Bit Rate (ABR)** provides a guaranteed minimum capacity but allows data to be bursted when the network allows. ATM packets take a fixed route, rather than TCP/IP, where each packet can take different routes to the destination.

- **Standards:** Several wireless standards exist including Bluetooth and HomeRF. The IEEE Standard 802.11b estab-lishes wireless network speed, which can reach up to 11Mbps (depending on distance from base unit) and lets your laptop hook up to your Ethernet wirelessly. The 802.11b was designed for wireless network and Internet access in the 2.4GHz radio band. Many vendors including Cisco Systems have wireless LAN products that include IEEE802.11b Compliant access points to provide point-to-point or point-to-multipoint connections of up to 25 miles away.

FIGURE I-7: *VLAN solution*

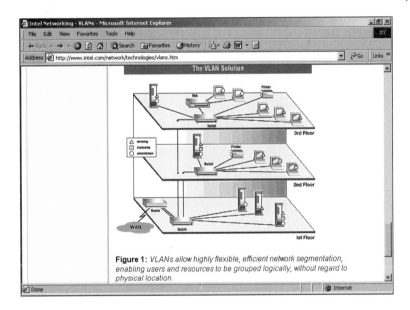

Figure 1: *VLANs allow highly flexible, efficient network segmentation, enabling users and resources to be grouped logically, without regard to physical location.*

FIGURE I-8: *WAVESTAR OptiGate*

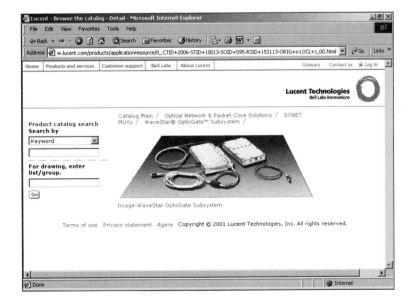

Exploring evolving trends in . . .
Remote and Wireless Connectivity

As our community is becoming more sophisticated, users of technology are becoming less and less willing to accept limits. No longer is the ability to have the world at your fingertips while you sit at your desk enough. Freedom, the ability to get what you want when you want it, is a driving force behind wireless computing. Advances in chip technology and battery life made portable computing a reality. No longer must a device be tethered to a cable to access the Internet or an intranet. Remote and wireless connectivity has freed the user from physical limits. Essential productivity tools include cell phones, portable computers, and personal data assistants. As the costs drop and the technology improves, devices are being developed that combine the features of each of these into a single device. This lesson focuses on the technology that enables you to connect to your company, your friends, and the world from handheld devices anywhere in the world without cables and adapters.

DETAILS

- **3G "Third Generation":** The standard for the next generation of wireless devices that will combine voice and Internet into portable wireless appliances operating with greater bandwidth. Several major companies, such as Lucent, have signed testing agreements to deliver mobile IP (Internet Protocol) standards based on 3G high-speed wireless networks. 3G combines wideband radio communications and IP-based services. 3G depends on technology developments such as WAP and Bluetooth.

- **Wireless WAN and Wireless LAN:** A **WAN (wide area network)** is defined as a telecommunications network that is not limited by geographic boundaries. It is a broad telecommunications structure that includes public (shared user) networks. WANs may be privately owned or rented. A **LAN (local area network)** is defined as a group of computers and associated devices that share a common communications line, such as a cable, and share the resources within a small geographic area, such as an office building or school.

  The advantage to creating a wireless LAN is overcoming the limitations of the cable or wire. The goal of wireless LANs is to have a greater range of access as well as being able to accommodate the transfer of larger amounts of data at greater speeds. Currently, the IEEE 802.11 standards have wireless LANS operating at 11Mbps, which is considerably slower than the 100Mbps found on wired LANs. Projected speeds are

- up to 20Mbps. The technology is catching up, however. The critical factors in establishing working wireless LANS relies on the ability to generate a good site survey in order to determine where to place the access points. Other issues include securing wireless LANs and creating a common standards for product development. Wireless LAN solutions are based on Bluetooth technology and are being created by companies such as CISCO, Linksys, Lucent, Ericsson, Intel, and 3Com.

- **High-Speed Wireless LANS:** The first high-speed wireless LANs promise that they will deliver data rates up to 54Mbps. Because wireless technology still lags behind faster Ethernet-switched technology, this will be the wave of the future. At the moment, though, high-speed wireless LANs are not a stable alternative. Wireless vendors include 3Com, Cisco, and Agere (part of Lucent).

  The high-speed standard is based on the IEEE 802.11 standard, which works in the 5 GHz band and uses a modulation technique called **Orthogonal Frequency Division Multiplexing (OFDM)**. OFDM is a method of digital modulation in which a signal is split into several narrowband channels at different frequencies. Currently, OFDM is used in European digital audio broadcast services and is being considered for digital television transmission.

Wireless Application Protocol (WAP): The Wireless Application Protocol is a global open standard that gives mobile users access to the Internet through handheld devices. More and more technologies are converging in such a way that your cell phone can also act as a PDA and as a browser. WAP plays an important role in these technologies. A device powered with WAP includes a WAP microbrowser that displays hyperlinks to services and information portals. Depending on the device purchased, these links will vary. WAP standards are being incorporated into devices developed by companies such as Erricsson, AT&T Wireless, and Motorola. Figure I-9, shows the homepage of the WAP Forum—the industry association for the WAP standard.

Bluetooth technology: The Bluetooth wireless technology, see Figure I-10, was developed by the Bluetooth Special Interest Group. This group was founded in 1998 to define an industry-wide specification for connecting personal and busi-ness mobile devices. The Bluetooth wireless technology is an open specification for low-cost, personal area network connection among mobile computers, mobile phones, and other devices. The Bluetooth wireless technology specification provides secure, radio-based transmission of data and voice. It eliminates the need for cables.

The Bluetooth wireless technology uses a globally available frequency range. Bluetooth technology includes five usage models. The three-in-one phone model works as a portable phone with a fixed line charge in your home, a mobile phone with cellular charges, and a walkie-talkie. The Internet bridge model is used with a mobile computer to access the Internet. The Interactive conference model is used for transferring selected documents among participants. The headset model is used for connecting a wireless headset to a mobile phone or computer. The automatic synchronizer model is used to synchronize data, such as calendars and addresses, among your desktop, mobile computers, and your phone.

FIGURE I-9: *WAP Forum*

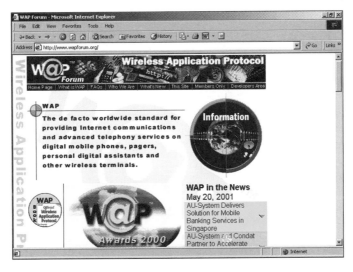

FIGURE I-10: *Bluetooth technology*

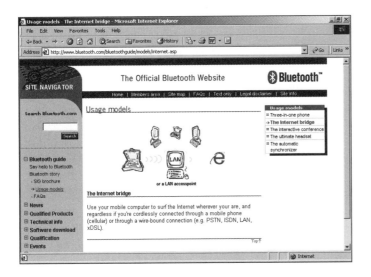

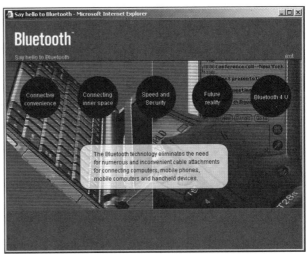

Exploring evolving trends in . . .
Web design and development

Dot-com, e-commerce, the Web; all ubiquitous terms that didn't exist a few short years ago. The technology that is developing for the Web is moving fast. Browsers are the window to the Web, and there have been many advances in browser technology. Browsers are now being built into devices that are designed as Internet appliances. Which browser you use will most likely be the one supplied by the manufacturer of the device. As devices become more specific in delivering services, browsers will be tailored to meet the functions of the appliance and the needs of the consumer. This lesson explores recent trends in Web technologies.

DETAILS

- **Browsers:** Browser technology is not new, but advances in components integrated into browsers is new. As the Web continues to change, so too must the browsers that users use to navigate the Web. The three leading browsers are Internet Explorer, Netscape Navigator, and Opera. Subscribers to AOL often use the proprietary AOL browser. These browsers share similarities and promote differences. New versions of browsers include enhanced and integrated Search and Explorer bars, media bars, instant messaging, Themes and additional shareware.

- **Opera's** software is an alternative browser not supported by either Netscape or Internet Explorer. See Figure I-11. It is freely available as a download from the Internet. Opera was developed in Norway. It includes an integrated search tool, e-mail client, contact manager, and instant messaging. Opera is an advertising-supported package so it contains built-in advertising windows. If you register the software for a fee, you can remove the advertising window. Opera has a multi-window interface; you can surf more than one site at a time with just one instance of the browser open.

- **Middleware:** Middleware is intelligent software that prioritizes packets on the Internet. It is the "glue" that binds together major applications and negotiates communications between them. The largest market of middleware is business-to-business. IBM is one of the leading developers of middleware.

- **Internet2:** A collection of about 150 universities is working together with high-tech corporations and some government agencies to build the next generation of the Internet. The driving force behind this project is the fact that the Internet, while stable and effective, is open to all, uncontrollable, and

basically unwieldy. Ironically, while this is the major advantage for most users of the Internet, it is proving to be a difficult environment for the originators of the Internet, researchers. Internet2 researchers are performing experiments using new and existing resources.

- **Future of XML: XML** (Extensible Markup Language) is the future of Web development. XML is a meta language in that lets you design your own markup. It is used to describe the structure of data. XML is being used in Web development, particularly handheld Web access. See Figure I-12.

- **Domain name Registry Services: ICANN (Internet Corporation for Assigned Names and Numbers)** is the nonprofit corporation that was assigned the responsibility for IP addresses and domain name system management. In November 2000, ICANN selected seven new top-level domains (TLD) for specific purposes, including .biz to help alleviate the load on the .com domain names and .info for information Web sites (www.icann.org/tlds). VeriSign Global Registry Services maintains the directory of millions of Web addresses and is responsible for the infrastructure that propagates this information throughout the Internet. Currently VeriSign Global Registry is the exclusive provider of registry services to .com, .net, and .org. As the Web continues to grow and change so too will Verisign Global Registry Services. In May 2001, ICANN announced and the Department of Commerce approved that the new .info and .biz top-level domain name extensions will be made available. At the moment, the trend is to consider .info as an unrestricted TLD, and .biz as a restricted TLD open for commercial and business purposes.

B2B: Business to Business: E-commerce has generated whole industry businesses that help other businesses do business, in particular, over the Web. Having a vast store of content is great, but it's useless if those who need the content can't find it or don't look in the right places for it. To meet that need, more and more businesses are specializing in providing the conduits for B2B (Business-to-Business) network content. This allows businesses to package and deliver content, and users to select and receive it automatically.

Music Trends and the Net: Napster was the pioneer in providing music through peer-to-peer networking, which allowed users who logged onto the Napster site to download the Napster software and then access MP3 files. Napster encountered legal difficulties when the courts determined they were infringing on intellectual property. Napster became a pivotal point in discussions regarding regulating the Web. Other file swapping services on the net include Limewire and BearShare.

MusicNet and MP3.com are subscription services that include features that resemble Napster's file-swapping service.

MusicNet, is a joint venture with AOL Time Warner, Bertelsmann and EMI Group. They plan to let music fans search for, then download or stream, a broad range of music owned by those three labels. These songs could be download from other MusicNet subscribers, as people would on Napster, as well as from central servers.

But there are key differences between the new music subscription services and Napster's file swapping. Only music that has been authorized by the labels will be available to trade.

Personalization technology: Today's Web applications include personalization technology, which allows for e-mail marketing and customized content. Personalization technology is built around collaborative filtering and rules-based matching capabilities. Personalization technology means if you buy a book on gardening from Amazon.com, you probably will start getting marketing materials from egarden.com, or some other Internet garden store. Personalization technology was developed and perfected by the dot-coms and e-commerce industries.

FIGURE I-11: *Opera, the Browser*

FIGURE I-12: *XML Web services*

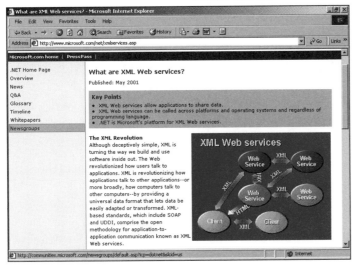

Exploring evolving trends in . . .
Productivity Software

Productivity software is defined as software that gets the job done. The basic categories of productivity software include document production, graphics database, spreadsheet, presentation graphics, and Web development. This lesson looks towards the future of productivity software—not only exciting new applications and new features to existing products, but also the ways products are delivered.

DETAILS

Speech recognition technologies: It is now becoming closer to reality to be able to speak to digital devices and have your words translated into digital code that is "understood" by your computer. Leaders in the field of speech recognition technology include Dragon Systems Dragon Naturally Speaking (NatSpeak) and IBM ViaVoice. See Figure I-13. The speech recognition development companies are working in conjunction with productivity software developers so that after "training" your computer to understand your voice and customize the application dictionary you can dictate words into documents, numbers into spreadsheets, and data into databases. These systems also work with handheld recording devices for the medical and legal professions. Hardware requirements are a simple microphone and soundcard.

Corporate productivity software: Software is available that automates just about every corporate administrative function. Activities such as filling out purchase requisitions, accessing human resource information, booking and approving travel, and expense reporting and tracking, are examples of how corporate productivity software can automate corporate tasks. Employees can track expenses and log hours using personal digital assistants and then transfer the data to computers.

Office productivity: Recent advances in database, word processing, presentation graphics, e-mail client, scheduling, and spreadsheet technologies include greater integration with the Web, and greater potential for collaboration. New features include; adding compressed MP3 files into slide shows, publishing slide shows as Macromedia Flash for the Web, compatibility with open standards including HTML with cascading style sheets, and support for XML and SGML for document files. These features make it easy to create Web pages using these programs, and to integrate Web applications with the files. The leading office productivity suites are Microsoft Office XP, Lotus SmartSuite, and Corel WordPerfect Office.

Graphics and imaging software: With digital cameras, photo printers, and paper becoming affordable and easy to use, digital cameras are capturing the hearts and imaginations of the consumers. Digital cameras are also changing the way many businesses capture and process their images. Real estate professionals, artists, law enforcement officials, medical professionals, and educators, are implementing digital cameras. Web sites for storing and sharing photographs continue to evolve including www.ofoto.com and www.kodak.com. New products continue to come out for digital cinema, digital imaging, and video editing.

eBooks: Adobe and Microsoft are the leading software publishers working with content developers to create eBooks. eBooks provide portable, on demand books that are downloaded from the Internet. Advances in type technology, such as Adobe Cooltype and Microsoft ClearType, improve text resolution. The software makes it easier to read the content on a computer display because of the improved text display. Adobe Acrobat eBook Reader and Microsoft Reader are provided free from the Internet and enable you to read ebooks directly on your notebook or desktop computer. See Figure I-14.

Web-based Application Service Providers (ASPs): The traditional model for purchasing software in a box off a shelf in an Office business center (whether it be an online retailer or a physical store) is changing. Many software publishers are turning to the Web as a delivery system.

Clients no longer have their software on servers in their companies, instead, ASPs charge customers via a service contract, or a pay-per-use deal, depending on the service software. Clients are sometimes subject to advertising banners in exchange for the service. Juno uses this model to provide Internet service. Some retailers provide limited free Internet access and E-mail in exchange for getting you to their Web sites. Hotmail is a free Web-based e-mail service through MSN.com.

The advantages to this system include the ability to automatically have the most recent version of software and any fixes to known bugs. However, hosted applications have some disadvantages. They work only when you're connected to the Internet. If you lose the connection, you are no longer able to access the application. Performance depends on the speed of the connection; therefore, high-speed connections are required. If the ASP has problems, you may find you cannot use the application at a critical moment, even if your computer is working perfectly.

With the Internet as the primary channel to promote and interact with potential employees, Web-based software automates the online recruiting process. These applications support requisition creation and approval and automate job postings, as well as, applicant review and hiring.

FIGURE I-13: *Speech recognition systems*

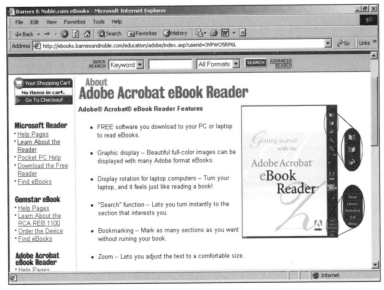

FIGURE I-14: *Ebook software*

Exploring evolving trends in ...
Leisure technology

Sony, Microsoft, and Nintendo are the leading console game developers. Where does the personal computer end and the personal gaming system begin? A video game system is a highly specialized computer. You can buy software games that play quite adequately on your desktop computer as well as for existing game systems. Why spend the extra money for a whole new system? What is it that these new consoles can do that your PC can't do? The newest game consoles are sporting Internet connectivity to change the way we will access and play. Online connections and hard drives with large storage capacities are changing the nature of game software. Rather than buying a game in a box in the form of a CD, or cartridge (or even floppy) that goes "stale" and ultimately gathers dust on a shelf, publishers will be able to provide "episodic content" over time through online connections. Leisure technologies also include advances in television. There are new computer-based technologies that will change television, as we know it. This lesson explores recent trends in gaming and other leisure technologies. As you explore these trends, think about how these systems will change the way we live and play.

DETAILS

- **PCs as TVs:** Sony Electronics' Vaio desktop computer includes a DVD drive and TV tuner along with built-in recording technology. The Vaio Digital Studio PC features a Giga Pocket Personal Video Recorder and allows consumers to watch TV programs streamed from cable or other analog sources onto the monitor and to record home videos or TV programs onto the hard drive.

- **Media terminals:** A medial terminal is a consumer product that can record TV programs, play games, and connect to the Internet. The device is based on a typical X86 processor and the Linux operating system. Nokia teamed up with the Linux gaming company Loki Software to strengthen its initiative to build an open-source home-entertainment platform. Nokia's blueprint for home-entertainment systems is called the "Open-Standards Terminal project."

- **Personal TV Service:** A personal TV Service, such as TiVo, is a computer-based system that allows you to control how and when you watch television. See Figure I-15. TiVo powers a digital video recorder and works with every TV system.

It is a subscription based-service that automatically records programs that you specify every time they are on. With TiVo, you are specifying events or programs not time slots, which is what you specify with traditional video recording. Because TiVo is computer-based, you can pause, rewind, and instantly replay live TV. Hughes, Phillips, and Sony provide the digital video recorders required for this service.

- **HDTV:** A new television system that gives you more information and a better quality image on your television screen. There are both digital and analog versions of HDTV. HDTV uses a wider aspect ratio that gives you more of a movie screen shape than the original television. **Digital Television (DTV)** is the transmission of pure digital television signals, along with the reception and display of those signals on a digital TV set. The digital signals might be broadcast over the air or transmitted by a cable or satellite system to your home. In your home, a decoder receives the signal and uses it, in digital form, to directly drive your digital TV set. Microsoft's new console, the XBox, will be the first video game system to completely support HDTV. See Figure I-16.

Video game basics: A video game console differs from a computer in that there are no compatibility issues, and the game is designed to easily connect to an entertainment system (stereo and TV). Video games basically have the following components: user control interface, CPU, RAM, operating system, storage medium for games (CD ROM, cartridge, or DVD), video output, audio output, and power supply.

Set-top box controllers: Many set-top box devices, those devices that sit on top of your television to access services that display through the television, have begun to use IBM's STBP (Set-Top Box Peripheral) chip technology. IBM is working with MontaVista Software Inc. Their version of Linux, Hat Linux 2.0, is planned to bring Linux into set-top boxes. The platform will support interactive television services as well as Internet access.

FIGURE I-15: *TiVo*

FIGURE I-16: *Xbox*

What are the implications of the UCITA software law?

UCITA (Uniform Computer Information Transactions Act) was drafted by the Chicago-based National Conference of Commissioners on Uniform State Laws (NCCUSL) and sent to all 50 states for their consideration as part of an effort to develop uniform commercial laws easing interstate commerce. In essence, this law is intended to govern all contracts involving computer software and information that you get electronically. It would apply to software, multimedia products, computer data and data-bases, online information, and any software product. This includes software from CDs, Web sites, and file transfers. It extends to cover software that is in computers, computer peripherals, and soft-ware that is in most every consumer electronics product today (televisions, cars, cell phones.)The UCITA grants new rights to software and information publishers. Essentially, it says that by default, the software developer or distributor is liable for flaws in the program, but allows a shrink-wrap license to override the default.

Proponents of UCITA include the Software and Information Industry Association (SIAA). Proponents hope that with rules more tailored to software, the warranties would come to be more commonly used rather than being routinely disclaimed. Proponents like that UCITA provides for the licensor or supplier to pay return costs if the terms are rejected. Proponents also like that UCITA mandates that warranties in mass-market licenses be made available for review.

Opponents include large corporations, the Free Software Foundation, Consumers Union, and the Association for Computing Machinery (ACM). Opponents claim that UCITA would have a negative effect on consumers. The Free Software Union claims that UCITA will threaten the free software community, and hold liable individuals rather than big companies for software standards.

The rules set forth in UCITA have significant opposition from consumer groups and many corporate users. The opponents, who set up a group called Americans for Fair Electronic Commerce Transactions, claim that UCITA is too favorable to software vendors. For example, they charge that the law would give vendors the ability to limit their liability, prohibit reverse-engineering, and shut down software remotely in some instances. But UCITA backers argue that the measure has been misunderstood and erroneously maligned, and they say corporate users would still be free to negotiate their own contract terms.

Opponents of UCITA say the laws are so restrictive that some large companies feel their business practices will have to change dramatically to stay in compliance with the new law. Everytime new software is acquired or installed, it would require an attorney or expert review to be sure the process was in compliance.

In order for UCITA to become law, it must be ratified by each state through the state's legislature. Several states have adopted the law including Maryland and Virginia.

Has the time come for UCITA? Can the differences cited by the opponents and the proponents be hammered out to create a compromise that is satisfactory to all? Is the UCITA forward thinking enough to address the issues of tomorrow that are surfacing today as a result of trends in technology?

1. Research the UCITA. What is it all about? What is the current status of the UCITA? What is the status in your state? Based on your findings, do you support the act? If so, explain why. If not, explain why not.

2. If UCITA is not the answer, what is? Research other proposals that address technology issues of today. Identify one to study in more detail. Write a brief summary of your research. Include responses to these questions: What is the purpose of the proposal? Who supports it? Why? Who opposes it? Why? Summarize your opinion of the proposal based on your research.

3. There are many organizations that are interested in policy-making as it relates to technology today and tomorrow. Research several of these organizations—a good starting point is the Electronic Frontier Foundation (EFF), the IEEE (I triple E), and the W3C. Review the mission statement and goals of each organization you research. Make a chart to help compare the organizations. Summarize your findings. Are these organizations working toward similar goals or cross-purposes? Do these organizations support or oppose UCITA?

End of Unit Exercises

STUDY TIPS

1. Review all of the bold-face terms in this unit to get an understanding of current terminology. Write your own definition or statement for each term. Use online resources to explore terms in more detail.

2. Look at the objectives list on the unit opener. Without referring to the lesson itself, write about one trend discussed for that lesson. Write additional questions you have about that trend and resources where you might find information.

3. Create a three column chart for each lesson. List the trends mentioned in each lesson in column 1. In column 2 record the status of the trend, e.g., is having impact in that technology sector, is no longer a player in that technology sector, has had its day but is now replaced by [name trend that has supplanted the one named in column 1]. In column 3 write your reaction to the status of the trend, e.g., to be expected, disappointing – but it never caught the imagination of the consumer, and so on.

4. Have you heard of trends not mentioned in this unit? For example, the lesson on processors mentions Intel's Pentium 4 and Transmeta's Crusoe chips. Have these been replaced by other more powerful chips? What trends have you heard about not mentioned in this unit? Write a brief description of three. Provide sources.

5. What are the various ways in which you access and use the Internet? What devices are you currently using to log on and access Web sites? What other features of the Internet (discussion groups, forums, e-mail) do you use? Make a list of the various devices that you use. Which browsers or software are you using on each of the devices?

6. How do you spend your leisure time? Do you take advantage of the new computer and Internet-based leisure technologies? Are you currently using a gaming console that was an upgrade from a previous version? What role, if any, does the Internet have in gaming activities? If so, which one? Do you believe the Internet enhances the games? If you were developing a game, which technologies would you take advantage of and why?

7. Do you use productivity software? Is this a new venue of productivity or an upgrade from a previous edition? If an upgrade, what enhancements have you noticed? How would you rank and rate the new features? Was it worth the upgrade? Would you like to see additional features built in that are not currently included with the software that you use? If this is a new product for you, what is your overall impresssion of the software?

8. Log onto the Internet and go to www.wlana.org. The site is a source for the Wireless Networking Industries Information. Review the site for any new standards and advances in wireless technology.

SELECT THE BEST ANSWER

1. Which of the following is not a feature you would want to find in a multipurpose PC?
   a. flat-panel display
   b. wireless keyboard
   c. wireless mouse
   d. dynamic speakers

2. ASP stands for
   a. Application Standards Protocol
   b. Application Service Provider
   c. Accessible Standards Protocol
   d. Adobe PostScript

3. Usage models for Bluetooth technology include
   a. A bridge to the Internet
   b. Interactive conference
   c. Wireless headset for mobile phone or computer
   d. Medical research technology

4. Palm and Handspring are companies that specialize in
   a. XML development
   b. Wireless connectivity
   c. Handheld devices
   d. B2B services

5. The Crusoe chip was developed by

a. AMD

b. Transmeta

c. Intel

d. Palm

6. One innovative trend of several productivity packages is

a. Spell-checking capability

b. Speech recognition technology

c. Multi-user capability

d. Personalization technology

7. The average size of a hard disk on a standard new desktop computer is

a. 100GB

b. 1GB

c. 1MB

d. 1MHz

8. CompactFlash and SmartMedia cards are examples of

a. Random Access Memory

b. Hard disk drives

c. Digital cameras

d. Flash memory

9. The main advantage to creating a wireless LAN is

a. increasing the speed of transmission over wired systems

b. overcoming the limitations of the cable or wire

c. increased security

d. greater broadband

10. Which of the following is not a browser?

a. Netscape Navigator

b. Windows XP

c. Opera

d. Internet Explorer

11. Software that provides advances in type technology to facilitate eBooks is

a. IBM ViaVoice

b. Ebookware

c. Dragon NatSpeak

d. Microsoft ClearType

12. The new top-level domain being offered for businesses is

a. .bix

b. .biz

c. .com

d. .buz

13. Xbox is a

a. gaming system developed by Microsoft

b. portable computer developed by Sony

c. cell phone

d. PDA

14. TiVo is a

a. form of digital television

b. subscription-based service for recording television

c. gaming console

d. operating system

INDEPENDENT CHALLENGE 1

It is your job as an office manager in a new startup company to select the package that will be used by your employees. The company creates artistic gift baskets to be delivered to local area residents. Your offices are in a new four story office building in a commercial office park off a major highway. The building is wired with network cable and you are renting 1000 square feet on one floor. You rely on local artisans to supply the items and work closely with manufacturers and other suppliers to put the baskets together. Your advertising is mostly local, although you have a new Web site and are planning to expand your client base.

1. The three leading office suites are Corel WordPerfect, Microsoft Office, and Lotus SmartSuite. Which package is best for you? Create a chart of features for each, and list which ones are most important and why.

2. Create a list of the types of software you will need to install and have available to get the company up and running. Explain the purpose of each.

3. What computers will you purchase? Components? Will they be standalone or networked? If networked, explain any special considerations.

4. What e-mail client will you select and why? Research available packages.

5. Write a report detailing your plan for implementing the software in the company.

INDEPENDENT CHALLENGE 2

How have PC components changed over time? Did the first computer look similar to the current offering by computer companies? As with automobiles, the basic appearance of a desktop computer has not changed. You still have the keyboard, the CPU, and the monitor or display device. Accessories have improved and expanded. The general consumer first used the mouse in 1983 on the Apple Lisa computer. What have been some other developments and major changes to the computer?

1. Research the history of the desktop computer for major developments and historic moments in personal computers.

2. Include photos from the Web, if you can find them, of the TRS-80, early external modems, early mice, and dot-matrix printers.

3. What technological development do you think is the most significant? Why? What new technologies do you think will be major driving forces in the way PCs look, feel, and work?

INDEPENDENT CHALLENGE 3

Electronic game consoles are a fast growing consumer market. You have to create a marketing campaign for a new console that your company MyCoolGAM2 is creating.

1. Research the current markets and trends in electronic gaming and prepare a statement that compares the top sellers.

2. List the top-selling games, and if they are marketed across platforms.

3. Draw a set of plans that lists the features that you would including in your gaming console. Name the device and list the price and ways consumers can buy and access games designed for your system.

4. Which strategies are in use to market the new console you are creating?

5. Create a poster that sells your new product.

INDEPENDENT CHALLENGE 4

Net appliances are the fast growth area. Perhaps because they help you turn your exiting TV into an interactive device through the Internet. Perhaps because they allow new gaming consoles to sport Internet connectivity. What are the net appliances available and how are they used?

1. Log onto the Internet and use your favorite search engine to research net appliances.

2. Create a list of new products that have net connectivity.

3. Print out any Web pages that show images of new appliances.

4. Are net appliances a big portion of the market?

5. Write a summary report detailing your findings.

INDEPENDENT CHALLENGE 5

The Internet was visualized and made a reality by pioneers. People such as Vannevar Bush, J.C.R. Licklider, Larry Roberts, and Tim Berners-Lee, have all had instrumental roles in shaping the Internet. Who are the Internet pioneers? What contributions did they make?

1. Log onto the Internet. Use your favorite search engine and the key phrase "Internet Pioneers." Follow links to several pioneers and read briefly about them.

2. Select one pioneer to research in more depth. Prepare a short paper on your findings. Be sure to include information about the individual's contribution to the Internet.

3. Discuss whether the contribution was viewed as a trend – a passing fancy, or an innovation when it was originally conceived.

4. Discuss what pieces had to be in place to make the innovation a reality.

5. Conclude your report with a brief statement about what surprised you the most as you researched Internet Pioneers.

6. If class reports are to be given, organize the reports to be presented in sequential order, based on Internet contributions. After all the presentations have been made, discuss which contributions were dependent on other Internet pioneer contributions and why.

The Web site shown in Figure I-17 is announcing the new .biz Internet domain. The page is most likely quite different by now but Neulevel is registering .biz domains for companies around the world. Log onto the Internet and search for sites that have the .biz domain. Did you find that leading companies who registered under .com also have the .biz domain? For example, do you get to the same site if you type www.microsoft.com and www.microsoft.biz? What new features is Neulevel offering at their site? What are the requirements and procedures for registering .biz URLs. Write a short paper on your findings.

FIGURE I-17

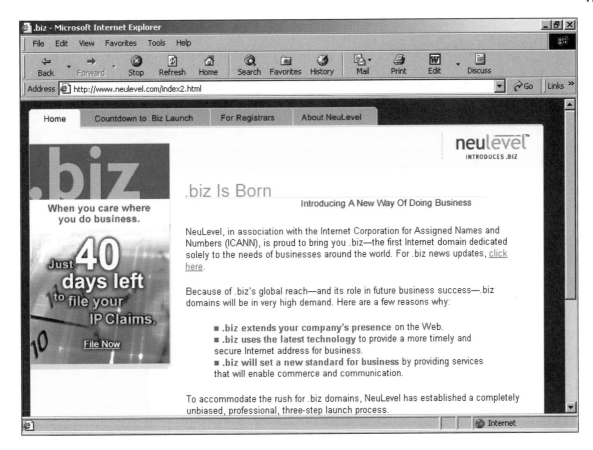

VISUAL WORKSHOP

The Web site show in Figure I-18 is from the Napster Web site—www.napster.com . Napster pioneered peer-to-peer file sharing over the Web world-wide and was sued by the record industry over copyright infringement when the global community used it to swap music files at incredible rates. Since the court ruling, Napster has had to modify its software to exclude all titles that the copyright holders want blocked. Other file sharing sites, such as Limewire and BearShare, are operating and not restricting access. Unlike Napster, these do not use a central server. Connect to the Internet and go to the Napster site. Research the court ruling and find out how Napster was affected by the ruling and what they are doing about it. Find out what Napster is doing to promote new music on the Internet. Go to www.limewire.com. Research the Gnutella file sharing network technology. Go to www.bearshare.com and research file sharing on that site. Compare and contrast the similarities and differences among Limewire, Bearshare, and Napster. Write a brief paper discussing what you found.

FIGURE I-18

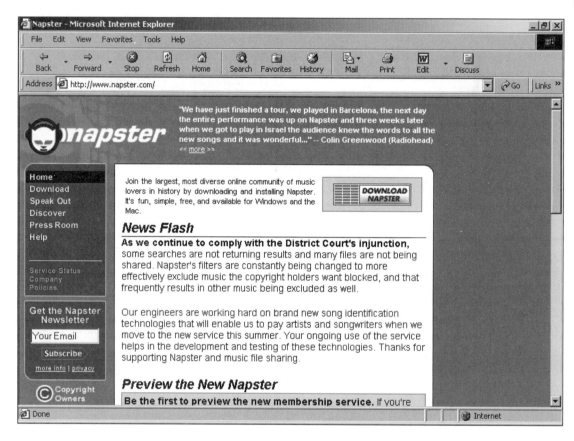

Bonus Issues and Up-to-Dates

Computer technology is constantly changing and ever evolving. Buying a computer is similar to buying a car—outdated as soon as you buy it. That is, as soon as you take the computer out of the box or drive the car off the lot, your purchase has already lost a good portion of its retail value. That's why it is important to remember, that like a car, you are buying a computer for its functionality. Since computers affect almost all aspects of daily life, you should know about general trends and significant developments in computer technology. But what defines significant? Sometimes an innovation that seems significant one year has minor impact on society or business and is gone within months, and sometimes a development that is barely noticed at first turns out to lead the way for technological advances for years to come. The lessons and exercises in this unit cover issues and topics that signal current trends for technology in our society.

Regardless of how cognizant you are of computers in your world, it is becoming increasingly more essential that you have some level of computer skills in order to "make it" in the world today. Some people have access to the best, newest, fastest, and coolest computers, networks, gadgets, and telephones in the world; other people have limited or no access. This gap, or digital divide, is one factor that defines economic opportunity for people in our information age.

The **digital divide** is defined as the difference in rates of access to computers and the Internet among different demographic groups. With the explosion of the Internet and the technology that drives the information age, forward-thinking social reformers recognized early on the potential for a divide between the "haves" and the "have nots." Not-for-profit organizations, such as the Benton Foundation, which produces and coordinates the Digital Divide Network (www.digitaldividenetwork.org), Digital Partners (www.digitaldivide.org), and government agencies, such as the Commerce Department's National Telecommunications and Information Administration (NTIA) (www.ntia.doc.gov and www.digitaldivide.gov), design studies to help them analyze the causes and effects of the digital divide. These studies have been conducted for the past few decades.

Time and again the research findings show that those with limited or no access find themselves on the bottom rungs of the job training and educational opportunity ladders, which leads to much lower standards of living and underscores problems connected with the digital divide. Individuals without Internet access do not have access to the assortment of opportunities advertised on the Web. On yet another level, Internet access is not enough; those individuals who do not have the technology skills needed to apply for such jobs are also denied economic opportunities.

But who is being left behind as a result of the digital divide? Even though there has been tremendous growth in the number of personal computers in households and Internet access among the population, certain demographic groups have been left behind. The studies show minority groups including the physically challenged are most likely to be affected by the digital divide. People who can access the Internet from home (as opposed to from public institutions such as libraries and schools) and have access to computers at home generally are able to spend more time and therefore benefit more from the technology. Studies continue to show that populations with lower incomes and education levels have Internet use rates much lower than national averages.

One of the factors contributing to the digital divide, according to the studies, is the rate of deployment for broadband technology. The research shows that if the technology for Internet access is focused primarily in urban markets by businesses that seek to gain the most return for their investment, it leaves the rural populations in the digital dark. How do we as a nation move toward "digital inclusion?" And is it important that we do so?

As part of his commencement speech June 5, 1998, at MIT, President Clinton made the following comment:

"Until every child has a computer in the classroom and the skills to use it ... until every student can tap the enormous resources of the Internet ... until every high-tech company can find skilled workers to fill its high-wage jobs ... America will miss the full promise of the Information Age."

There have been efforts both nationally and internationally to bridge the digital divide. These efforts have concentrated on concrete ways to address the concerns raised by the digital divide and to move toward "digital inclusion." Government incentives such as E-rate, which is a program created as part of the Telecommunications Act of 1996, provide discounts on telecommunications services and equipment to all K-12 public and private schools and libraries.

The Federal Universal Service Fund Surcharge that you probably see on your phone bill each month was mandated in The Telecommunications Act of 1996. As stated in the Telecommunications Act of 1996, the goals of Universal Service are to: "promote the availability of quality services at just, reasonable, and affordable rates; increase access to advanced telecommunications services throughout the Nation; advance the availability of such services to all consumers, including those in low-income, rural, insular, and high-cost areas at rates that are reasonably comparable to those charged in urban areas. In addition, the 1996 Act states that all providers of telecommunications services should contribute to Federal Universal Service in some equitable and nondiscriminatory manner; there should be specific, predictable, and sufficient Federal and State mechanisms to preserve and advance universal service; all schools, classrooms, health care providers, and libraries should, generally, have access to advanced telecommunications services; and, finally, that the Federal-State Joint Board and the Commission should determine those other principles that, consistent with the 1996 Act, are necessary to protect the public interest.

Research findings reported in 2000 by agencies such as the U.S. Department of Education and the Digital Divide indicate that the digital divide is narrowing. How far have we as a nation come in bridging the digital divide? Have we narrowed the gap at all, or is there more to the digital divide than access and technology skills?

EXPAND THE IDEAS

1. Is there a solution to the digital divide? Connect to the Internet and use your favorite search engine to search on the key phrase "digital divide." Among the sites you should find is the Digital Divide Web site at www.digitaldivide.gov. This site includes links to articles and research studies that address the digital divide. Review the findings for two studies or articles. Write a short paper summarizing two studies or articles. In your conclusion, comment on how you feel the digital divide affects our society and what we as a society should do about it, if anything.

2. Could you live without computers? Computers are ubiquitous beyond the obvious applications, such as using your word processor to write a report, as you come in contact with them during the course of your day in simple activities, such as shopping in a supermarket or getting cash from your bank's ATM machine. Create a log to track your daily activities that involve computers. Keep the log for one week. At the end of the week, write a summary of any surprises or insights you have as to how computers affect your life.

3. Is there a digital divide in your community? Create a survey that will determine Internet access and computer ownership among people that you know. The survey should consist of between 5-10 questions. You want to find out, within a chosen sector, who owns a computer, if they own more than one, what they use the computer for, if they have Internet access, and if they access the Internet from their home or elsewhere. Be sure to survey at least 20 people. The survey should be anonymous but include demographic information. Compile the results of your survey into a chart and write a short summary explaining your findings.

Up-to-Date: Pricing computers

It seems that as soon as you purchase a computer and as soon as you get your computer home and out of the box, a more powerful one supercedes the model you bought. In fact, the one with more memory, more features, and more "bells and whistles" probably costs the same as the one you bought. Even more frustrating and upsetting, perhaps, is that the price of the one you bought seems to plummet as soon as you buy it. There is no way to keep up with this fast-paced industry. At some point you need to "jump into the river" and buy your computer or upgrade an existing one. When you do this, you need to know that the one you buy is capable of doing the work you need to do.

Figure 1 shows a Web site for a popular Internet-based computer retailer. The desktop computers shown in the figure feature the Intel Pentium 4 processor. Prices are listed at the time this book was written.

FIGURE 1: *Pricing a computer*

1. Log onto the Internet, then use your favorite search engine to research online computer retailers.

2. List four online retailers and print a copy of the page showing their main desktop computers for sale. Find their low-end models and their high-end models.

3. Attempt to locate the computers shown in the figure or find ones with similar features. Create a chart showing price/feature comparisons.

4. Write a short summary answering the following questions:

   • Where you able to find the computers shown in the figure for sale?

   • How have prices changed?

   • What features do newer models offer?

Issue: What's all the fuss about open source development?

To understand the fuss, you need to understand that open source development is the development and use of free software. **Open source development** means that the source code for a software package or operating system (OS) is freely available. Developers who use the source code for other projects often suggest changes to the original source code to fix bugs or provide improvements. These 'fixes' are then incorporated into the code so that all users have access to them. As the saying goes, "many hands make light work," but in the case of open source development projects, some would say, "many programmers make for a stronger source code."

So what's all the fuss about? The word "free" in the definition should give a clue as to part of the fuss. Commercial companies spend a tremendous amount of money on research and development of software. Commercial companies are generally not open to the idea of the development and use of free software—their goal is to make money. But the Internet has opened the door for open source development and there are some companies who are embracing it—and still making money. Examples of open source development projects include Netscape Navigator, Linux, Apache, and Darwin.

Netscape is a leading proponent of open source development. It pioneered the distribution of software online when it freely offered Netscape Navigator over the Internet. Just a few years later, Netscape became the first commercial company to make its source code for Netscape Communicator free for modifications. Netscape has been both praised and criticized for its role in the open source development strategy.

Linux, developed under the **GNU General Public License**, is a free UNIX-type operating system that was originally developed by Linus Torvalds. The source code for Linux is distributed freely. Even though the source code is free, the applications that are developed under Linux are not. Linux is available in several formats called distributions. These are distributed for no charge by developers either by File Transfer Protocol (FTP) or for a nominal fee by CD. The Linux tools and utilities that are available include Linux applications for Administration, Multimedia, Graphics, system development, scientific applications, communications, and graphics.

Versions of the Microsoft operating systems have gone from MS-DOS in 1980 to Windows XP in 2001. Microsoft, to date, has not made source code for its OS available to developers. Since the beginning of the PC revolution, Microsoft's operating systems have dominated the markets. Why should Microsoft share its source code? After all, the operating system code is the intellectual property that is so highly coveted by Microsoft and is the foundation of its success.

Why is access to the OS source code so important to software developers? Remember the OS is what makes the software sing, so to speak. Software must be compatible with the OS to work. If Microsoft keeps its source code for its OS to itself, then it can dominate the market not only in the OS market, but in the applications market as well. For example, when the Internet Explorer browser was incorporated into Windows, it generated a firestorm of controversy. Because Microsoft had integrated the browser into the OS, it virtually excluded all third party competition.

Again, Microsoft is generating controversy with this release of Windows XP because of the new features that will be included with the operating system. Windows XP has a long list of new features: an Internet firewall, an integrated media player with CD-burning and DVD-playback features, remote access tools, movie-making and photo-editing software, wireless capabilities, broadband networking, and Internet messaging. Most of this functionality is already available as separate software packages published and marketed by other companies including Adobe Systems, Apple Computer, AOL Time Warner, Corel, RealNetworks, and Symantec. The question is: Will consumers simply purchase the Windows XP operating system and not buy software from third-party developers even if the functionality in the Windows XP is not as good as the add-on software? If Microsoft practiced open source development strategies, would their Windows XP end product be different? To date, Microsoft practices a closed source development strategy.

Linux is an open source development project and its success is surprising many Microsoft users. For example, Linux has been making inroads into the personal digital assistant (PDA) markets. In addition, several large corporations, that have traditionally used Windows NT servers to handle various computing tasks, are moving their tasks onto IBM mainframe computers running Linux. In fact, IBM has been boosting its support for Linux by launching new UNIX servers that make bringing Linux into large corporate systems easy. Major software developers have created alliances with Linux and are developing their applications to run under the Linux system. Corel, for example, has versions of WordPerfect and CorelDraw for Linux.

Linux creates an interesting dilemma for the Microsoft developers, who have always resisted and been able to avoid the need to release the source code. Will the unexpected early success of Linux lead Microsoft to rethink their development model? It is possible that Microsoft will begin to release and reveal the source code of some of its products? Will the open source development model continue to evolve? Will it include other software areas?

EXPAND THE IDEAS

1. Is the open source approach to software distribution the way to go? What is the GNU General Public License? You can find out more about open source principles and licensing by going to www.opensource.org and www.fsf.org. Research arguments for and against the open source development model and open source licensing. Write a brief paper on how you think it will affect the software development market in the future.

2. What is the history of DOS and what ever happened to OS2? What is the history of Windows and how was the controversy over Internet Explorer resolved? Log onto the Internet or use your library resources to write a brief two-page paper on the history of operating systems for personal computers. New developments in hardware generated the need for new operating systems. Be sure to include a short summary of OS2 and why it did not receive a wide audience. Be sure to include information about the competing operating systems that were available at the time. Include a summary of the types of features that each operating system offered.

3. So where are the Linux-based applications now? Linux-based applications are making inroads into commercial markets. Research existing products that use Linux as the operating system. Write a short paper explaining how open source development strategies have worked for Linux. Then provide details about the current products based on Linux, and include what features of Linux are used in the products.

Operating systems are not unique to the PC and mainframe markets. Apple Computer Company has been developing operating systems for its computers since the early days of the Apple II computer. While the PC market has its share of versions from MS DOS to Windows XP, the Apple Computer Company has developed its share of operating systems. Apple Computer Company is using open source projects to allow developers to enhance and customize Apple software. MAC OS X 10.0 is based on **Darwin**, which is the core of the MAC OS X. The source code for Darwin is freely available through Apple's public source projects. Figure 2 shows the latest Mac OS.

FIGURE 2: *Mac OS*

1. Log onto the Internet, then use your favorite search engine to research Mac OS. You might start by going to the Apple Computer Company Web site.

2. Click the link for Mac OS and research the various features that it supports. Write a brief list of the features and explain each one.

3. Notice the advertisement statement in Figure 2: "The power of UNIX with the simplicity and elegance of Macintosh." What does this mean?

4. Research the history of the Mac OS. What new features does this OS have over the previous version?

The productivity software that a company chooses is the driving force behind its entire information technology operation. Which package you buy for your home or educational use is the basis for your communications, writing, and collaboration. On the surface, many productivity packages look much the same: Microsoft Word, Lotus WordPro, or Corel WordPerfect; Lotus SmartSuite or Microsoft Office; Notes or Exchange. Is there really any difference between these packages? Does it really matter which one you use? Talk to users of each software package and you will find that there are distinct differences among the software packages.

Could it get any more confusing? YES. In addition to software packages most computer users are already familiar with, there are new emerging categories of software such as e-commerce software, B2B collaborative software, e-procurement systems software, and corporate productivity software. Making the decision as to which productivity software to get for your personal or business use is a difficult one. In addition to the type of software, recent developments in how software is distributed have added a new dimension to the problem.

Traditionally, software has been viewed as a product and marketed as a product. As such, when it came to acquiring software, you had to think about two options: should you buy it or should you rent it? Either way, the end result would be a packaged software product that you would have to install and upgrade as new versions of the software became available.

Another way of thinking about software is as a service, rather than as a product to be purchased, installed, and updated by the user. When software is provided as a service, the application resides on the supplier's Web site, not on the end user's computer. The end user obtains the use of an application through an **application service provider (ASP).** Initial ASPs offered the use of applications free of charge and the cost was absorbed by advertisers on the site. More and more, ASPs are charging users, generally via a subscription, perhaps as a prearranged contract, or on a fee-per-use basis, to use software via a Web site.

Steve Ballmer, CEO of Microsoft, stated, "In three to four years, high speed broadband communications will be available everywhere. The notion of software as a packaged product will disappear. That's a fact." Why is high-speed broadband communications the key to changing how software is made available to end users? Because high speed broadband communications provides quick and easy access to the Internet, which is a critical component of Web-hosted applications. In order for the ASP model to work, users will need very fast connections to the Internet because they are working with software off a Web site, rather than off their computers.

You might have already used an ASP and not even known it. For example, Hotmail.com is an ASP that provides e-mail application service to its clients. Users who use Hotmail work entirely off the Web; the applications are not on their computers at all. Another example of an ASP includes vendors who provide Web site development application services to clients. If you search for ASPs on the Web, you will quickly find that there are almost 1000 applications available (see www.aspisland.com).

One factor to consider before buying, renting, or subscribing through an ASP is the upgrade factor. With new versions of productivity software coming out every two years, how do you know whether or not the latest version has the enhancements that you need or will use? How do you know if the cost both in time and money is worth the upgrade? If you are currently using a version of software that meets your needs and the publisher releases an upgrade, should you upgrade? Software upgrade releases, which are typically based on two-year cycles, are as sure as the tides. Buying an upgrade may require additional hardware purchases and certainly investments in training, however, software upgrades often have many benefits. For example, new software suites, such as Microsoft Office and Corel WordPerfect Office, include expanded Web collaboration and integration that may be vital to your business.

Major manufacturers of productivity software are taking a long hard look at their traditional method of distributing software as a product and the Web-hosted model of becoming ASPs. For example, Microsoft has included new ways to deploy their Office software to individual buyers as well as corporations. Lotus SmartSuite is offered by subscription and rental. How can you know what's the best way to go?

The key to making appropriate decisions is having an arsenal of knowledge about the current trends and offerings. The resources are there for the research, and you have to know what your needs are and which path will best meet those needs.

EXPAND THE IDEAS

1. What's this about renting software? Buying off the shelf may be a thing of the past if Steve Ballmer's words come true. Research developments and options for acquiring software through lease arrangements or over the Internet, and write a short paper on your findings.

2. Research ASPs. Then create a graphic organizer, such as a concept web, a chart, or any visual representation that will provide an overview of what an ASP is and how it works. Be prepared to present your graphic organizer to the class, and to provide additional information or explanation not shown in the graphic organizer.

3. Research new or emerging software packages, such as those mentioned in this issue. Identify at least three to explore in more detail. Create a chart that provides essential information about each software package. Think about what functionality you might need, and write a summary as to which package would be most suited to your productivity software needs. Discuss whether you would purchase the software as a product or a service.

Up-to-Date: Speech-enabled technology

Office XP, the latest offering from Microsoft, promises to revolutionize the way your office does business. Lotus makes similar claims about its Millennium Edition. What are the new technologies available for you in these productivity packages? Improved Web collaboration features certainly are timely. Another new feature that spans all these offerings is speech-enabled technology. This technology is being incorporated into software packages, specifically productivity packages. Microsoft and IBM (ViaVoice technology) along with many other companies are making tremendous inroads in research and development. Apple Computer Company uses Apple's Speech Recognition and Speech Synthesis Technologies—see Figure 3. Can you picture yourself sitting at a desk talking to your computer? What about a busy office of people sitting in close proximity speaking to their computers? Would this work?

FIGURE 3: *Speech recognition technology*

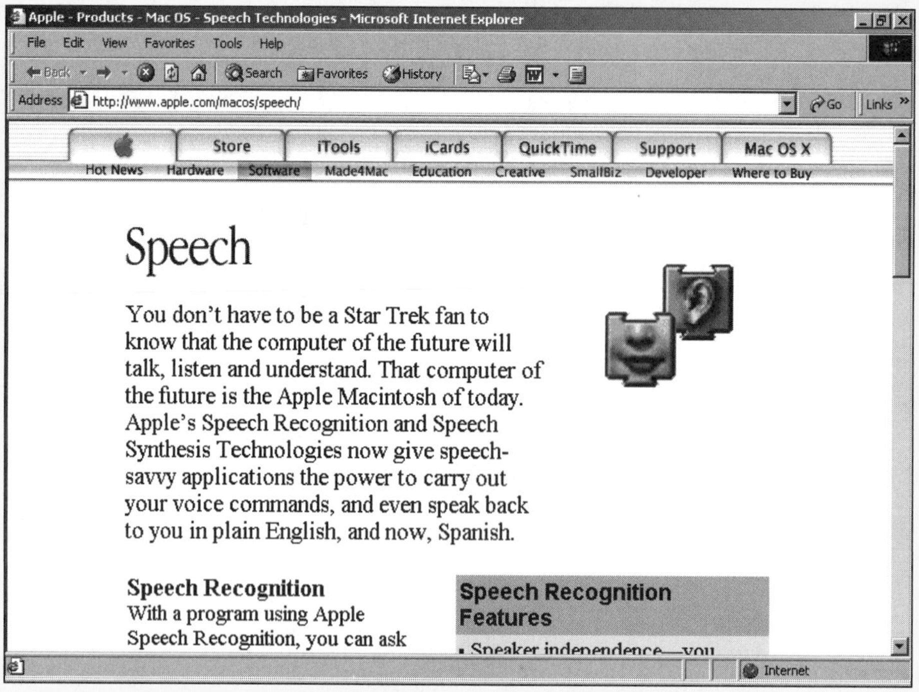

1. Log onto the Internet, then use your favorite search engine to research speech technology for productivity software. Explain how speech technology is being used in productivity software.

2. What features of Office XP and Lotus SmartSuite incorporate speech technology? How are they the same, and how do they differ?

3. Speech technology is a very "hot topic." Research developments in speech technology and write a brief paper on the types of software that would benefit from a speech component. What are the drawbacks and benefits to a speech-enabled software package?

Issue: Is a paperless society a possibility?

Databases containing more than a terabyte—that is, one trillion bytes—are more and more common as companies begin to keep their data online, stored on hard disk drives, where the information can be readily accessed. Individuals are also accumulating data at alarming rates—consider all the e-mail, audio CDs, and digital photographs an average consumer who owns a computer might have!

Now that our world has all this information, where and how are we going to store it?

Traditionally the answer was paper. If you wanted a backup of a document, you made a copy—sometimes in triplicate, for safekeeping. Today, people are generating enormous amounts of information at record rates for individuals, businesses, governments, and educational institutions. Consider all the data created with the constant flow of credit card transactions, legal proceedings, medical procedures, research in all areas, manufacturing, retail and inventory transactions, government and education proceedings, newspapers and writings, and digital images that are being collected by satellites or even digital cameras.

Some individuals insist that a paper copy is the only safe way to go. But imagine if all the data being generated today was committed to paper. Businesses would soon find themselves drowning in a sea of paper that would become more and more unmanageable and inaccessible as the data continued to grow. Some visionaries see us moving to a paperless society where everything is stored electronically or optically, or using some new medium yet to be discovered.

Advances in magnetic storage technologies have fueled the storage fires. Imagine just a few short years ago when a 10 MB hard disk drive seemed more than anyone could want or use; now a fairly inexpensive 10 GB drive comes standard with most home computers. Disk/Trend (www.disktrend.com) a Mountain View, CA-based market research firm that tracks the industry, reports, "The race to deliver even higher capacities and very competitive prices has been tough on disk drive manufacturers' profits, but it's been a good deal for the industry's customers. By 2002, the overall average price per megabyte for all disk drives is projected to be 0.3 cents."

Virtually anything can be stored digitally these days, even if the original object was not created digitally. But is this necessarily a good idea? What problems are associated with a paperless society? Storage medium, length of storage time issues, retrieval of information issues, confidentiality and accessibility of information issues, and ownership issues are all concerns related to digital storage. For example, how long should digital information be stored? Paper records tend to be discarded after they are no longer of value or they deteriorate beyond recognition. Whether or not digitally stored information deteriorates is yet unknown. So who will decide how long digital information should be stored? Because data is so easily accessible will there need to be regulations about data storage?

There really are two storage issues, the technology for short-term data storage, storing data that has to be accessible on a regular basis, and the technology for longer-term storage, storing records that may or may not need to be accessed at all, but certainly not on a regular basis.

What is currently available for short-term data storage? Recent developments in the data storage industry include **Network-centric** computing where data is stored on central servers. Optical storage devices have made advances to support the growth in storage requirements. DVD-RAM jukeboxes include up to 200 disks including DVDs, CDs, and DVD-RAMS that hold upwards of a terabyte of data. IBM has made advances in storage technology with their MicroDrive that can store over 1 GB of data on a hard disk the size of an American quarter.

Remote online storage is a trend that addresses the needs of the new mobile society. With remote devices proliferating our economy and businesses, the need for secure remote storage that can be accessed and organized online by any Internet-enabled device is inevitable. These devices provide a way for remote workers to connect to an Internet-based service, or use a standard Internet account to exchange data with the corporate back-up server. While online storage services are flexible, they can become expensive if you use them to back-up all the PCs on your network. The current online storage applications work best as a supplement to traditional back-up approaches.

Products like Xdrive Express—a Windows desktop application—display online storage space as a drive icon in Windows Explorer. Xdrive Technologies, a storage services provider, leases its 17.7 terabytes of managed storage capacity. Similar companies that provide storage services include FreeDrive, i-Drive, Driveway, My Docs Online, FreeWebspace.net, and NBCi Sharehouse.

How to store your data is just the beginning of the storage dilemma. Retrieval of stored data is another variable in the storage equation. If you cannot retrieve your stored data, you have nothing and your data is lost. Obsolescence of hardware is a serious concern. Without the hardware to retrieve the information (or music), the data is lost and not 'stored' even though the physical media may still exist.

Storage of digital data is an evolving field. Will society ever become a truly paperless society? Only time will tell; what do you think?

EXPAND THE IDEAS

1. The issue touches briefly on advantages and disadvantages of a paperless society. Use your favorite search engine and the key phrase "paperless society" to investigate the pros and cons of a world without paper. Write a brief research paper detailing your findings. In your conclusion, state your position on a paperless society. Be sure your resources support your position.

2. What are the leading trends in remote online storage? If you were planning to take advantage of mobile computing, how would you envision using remote storage? Research the recent trends in online storage and retrieval and write a short paper on the new developments. Be sure to include the advantages and disadvantages for each online storage and retrieval system you investigate.

3. How does a DVD Jukebox work? What are the principles behind the technology? What can you determine about changes in data storage and retrieval over the last few decades? What data does it store, play, retrieve and what is it best used for?

Up-to-Date: Holographic storage—the future in data storage

If you thought a holograph was just the image of Princess Leia saying "Obi-Wan Kenobi, you are my only hope," think again. Holographic storage devices are in development as a means to respond to the growing need for large data storage. Holographic technologies promise data retrieval speeds far exceeding magnetic or optical storage, as well as capacities far beyond anything currently available. Researchers are working to make this technology an affordable reality. Figure 4 shows a Web page from the IBM Science and Technology Center at Almaden that researches holographic technologies.

FIGURE 4: *Holographic storage*

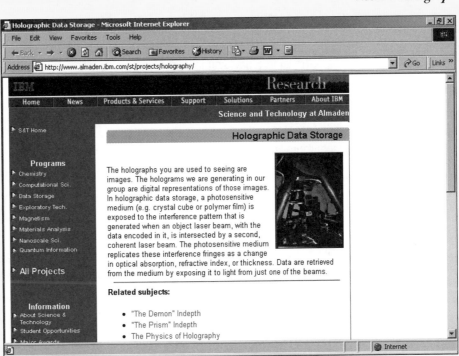

1. Use your favorite search engine to find and read about Holographic Storage. For example, you can read the feature article in the May 2000 edition of Scientific American (www.sciam.com). Write a brief summary of the article, and, based on what you read, explain the basics of how holographic memory works.

2. Research the current trends in holographic development. Are there any existing applications? How far has the technology come? What companies are working to develop these technologies? How far are we from using holocubes for data storage?

3. Write a scenario that includes the requirements and applications for holographic storage. Under what circumstances do you think such technologies would be useful, and what types of data do you think would best take advantage of this new technology?

Issue: How is the consumer affected by the "Processor Wars?"

All chips are not made equal. They have different specifications and are intended for different purposes. Controversy arises when chips don't work as intended, or contain components that not all users want. You may remember the controversy that swirled around Intel's Pentium III chip after it was first released. Intel had designed the Pentium III to maximize the performance of playing games over the Internet. Intel also assigned a processor serial number to every Pentium III. Analyzed individually, both of these factors sound reasonable. Taken together, however, controversy boiled over as privacy rights groups realized that their computers could be identified via their processor serial number by software controllers over the Internet. As a result of the controversy, Intel provided a utility program that could be downloaded by users who wanted more control over their processor serial numbers.

In addition to controversy, Intel processors have also had their competitors. Competitors, such as AMD and Transmeta, are heating up the processing wars. For example, AMD is a leading competitor to Intel and offers a complete line of processors, including, the newest 900MHz Duron processor. Transmeta Corporation developed and is selling the Crusoe Processor for mobile computing.

What do "processor wars" mean to the consumer? Each time a processor manufacturer delivers a new and improved processor to the market, the competitors step up to the plate to try and beat the specs of the latest and greatest. Advantages include faster processor with improved functionality, and prices on "outdated" processors being lowered as new processors become available. Disadvantages include initial cost of newer processors, as well as waiting for software to "catch up" and take advantage of the improved functionality.

Typically, however, you don't go to a store and buy a processor, instead you buy a PC that has a processor in it. Before purchasing your PC, it is worth your time to explore the processor features of each PC you consider buying. As a consumer, it is important to be aware of and stay on top of the "processor wars." If you do, your knowledge will help you get the best value for your money.

EXPAND THE IDEAS

1. Find out the latest in the processor wars. Use your favorite search engine and the key phrase "processor wars" to find articles about current developments in processors. Write a summary of your readings. Be sure your conclusion states your position on the following question: Are the processor wars a good thing for consumers?

2. Identify one manufacturer of processors, such as Intel. Create a time line that shows their next generation processor. Make notes regarding what new advances have been included in new-generation chips over the past generation chips.

Up-to-Date: Computing in the palm of your hand

Handheld computing is becoming the techno-gadget of choice among many people. Handheld computing power can be found in devices such as PDAs, digital cameras, mp3 players, modems, mobile Internet appliances, and cell phones.

When referring to the architecture of handhelds, you will find that there are many similarities to desktop or laptop computing. For example, like desktop and laptop computers, handhelds have RAM, batteries, operating systems, expansion slots, and processors. Figure 5 shows the home pages from Palm and Handspring, two leading companies in handheld computing.

FIGURE 5: *Handheld computing*

1. Log onto the Internet and use your favorite search engine to research two of the most recent products offered from each of the vendors shown in Figure 5. Create a comparison chart that lists the processor, amount of memory, and battery type for each model. Include any technical specifications. Write a summary statement to discuss your findings.

2. Palm and Handspring are not the only companies that offer handheld computing devices. Research other offerings and compare the architecture of the devices. Write a brief statement of your findings and create a comparison chart that details the other devices.

3. Compare the processor speed and technology in the most recent handhelds to the technology that is available on the most up-to-date PCs. Research historical data and compare it to the computing tasks of the time. Given the tasks that handhelds are being used for, do you see a time when the handhelds will need the processors and RAM of today's computers? Write a two-page paper explaining your findings.

E-mail is a pervasive part of many people's personal and professional lives. Personally, we use e-mail to stay connected with family and friends. Professionally, we use e-mail to correspond both internally with colleagues, and externally with clients and customers. In fact, in today's business environment, business correspondence, including communication among clients, internal staff, and freelancers or consultants, is conducted via e-mail. With the click of a button, an e-mail message and attached files can reach its recipient in a matter of moments. E-mail is definitely changing the way business gets done.

The first wave of e-mail required a computer and Internet or intranet connection. Initially these connections were over phone lines and required the use of a modem. As users recognized the power of e-mail, they demanded better and faster connections, which became possible through cable modems and T1 lines. This e-mail connectivity was better than phone modems and phone lines, but it still had its limitations. For one thing, your computer had to be physically connected to the medium that carried the e-mail message. Users demanded more mobility, and they are getting it through wireless communication.

Today, e-mail connectivity has joined the wireless world of communication. Numerous wireless e-mail solutions are available for business and personal use. Blackberry is one leading wireless e-mail provider. Blackberry provides wireless handhelds, as well as software and e-mail services. Handheld devices with monitor and keypad allow users to send and receive wireless e-mail messages. New high-speed wireless devices are available from equipment providers such as Qualcomm, Nokia, Ericsson, and Motorola. Wireless service is available from well-known communications carriers such as Sprint PCS, Nextel, and AT&T Wireless. A recent study conducted by Cahners In-Stat Group, a market research firm, predicts that "about 1.5 billion wireless-enabled phones, handheld computers, and other devices will be in use by 2004." *[Source: CNET News.com, "Study: 1.3 billion wireless Web surfers by 2004."]*

In addition to the equipment and the service, advocates of wireless technology are pursuing the concept of one number/one user. This concept, referred to as **Enum**, means that a person could be reached on any number of devices–telephone, pager, e-mail, instant messenger, or any other form of electronic communication–simply by typing one number on the Internet. According to advocates for one number/one user, Enum (electronic number) technology is the next step in merging current Internet technology and phone technology. Of course, while one number/one user might simplify things for the end user, there are many questions to be answered. For example: What standard will be used for the numbering system? Who will provide the service? How will people be billed for the service? The answers to questions such as these are critical because huge revenues are at stake for both the businesses that provide the service, and those that lose their current customers to the new service. If Enum becomes the global standard, wireless communication will become even more pervasive.

How pervasive is wireless technology in our society? According to an article in CNET news.com, "Danish ornithologists say that birds, especially starlings, have begun incorporating the sound of a ringing cellular phone into their own songs. So far, reports of wireless warbling have been restricted to Copenhagen, where birds seem to favor Nokia's classic ring tone." *[Source: CNET news.com. "Birds sing a new tune in wireless era."]* But are birds singing a new tune the only impact wireless technology will have on society? What other issues need to be addressed?

How will wireless communication change how business is conducted? How will it change the relationship between employer and employee? Wireless communication is already having an impact on the way people work. More and more people are working at least part-time from a remote location such as a satellite office or a home office. As this becomes the emerging business model, employees are finding that being connected is a necessity, not just a nicety.

In a recent survey commissioned by Anderson Consulting, 83% of American workers who vacationed for seven or more days were in touch with their place of employment. *[Source: www.mobilevillage.com "Survey 8 of 10 Professionals Take the Office on Vacation."]* When questioned, many professionals respond that they would rather stay in touch than face a backlog when they return to work. For many, checking e-mail has become a vital part of their day's routine…it is the first thing they do in the morning and the last thing they do at night. Is this trend healthy? It used to be that you worked from 9 to 5 and when you left the office, you left your work behind. Now with wireless e-mail and other wireless technology becoming the standard, work can be with you 24 hours a day. Is wireless e-mail a positive trend for our society? You decide.

EXPAND THE IDEAS

1. Wireless e-mail raises many societal questions, such as privacy issues, employer expectations vs. employee responsibilities, and the impact on family life. Choose one societal issue impacted by wireless e-mail. Research the issue and write a paper presenting your findings. Use your research to help you answer the question: Is wireless e-mail all it is cracked up to be?

2. Create an informal survey regarding e-mail usage. Include questions that will help you understand how respondents use e-mail at work and at home. If they access work e-mail from home, what are their views on wireless e-mail—would they use it and why? Distribute your survey to 10 colleagues. Write a brief summary interpreting your findings.

3. What is the latest and greatest in wireless e-mail? Use your favorite search engine and the key phrase "wireless e-mail" to find out more about wireless e-mail products. Research three products and summarize your findings in a comparative chart. Write a brief statement indicating which, if any, product you would use and why.

Up-To-Date: Middleware

First there was hardware and software to research and understand. Now you are being told that there is something called "middleware" that you need to understand. What is middleware? **Middleware** is specialized networked services that are shared by applications and users. Middleware evolved to include a variety of technologies that support and integrate applications.

"Middleware was developed as a bridge to enable distributed applications to be built and still have the service of legacy applications. Anyone who is building enterprise systems today almost has to look at a middleware solution," explains Joe Conron, director of development at NasTel Technologies Inc. (www.nastel.com). Figure 6 shows a diagram at the Carnegie Mellon Software Engineering Institute's Web site that illustrates how middleware exists in a network.

FIGURE 6: *Middleware*

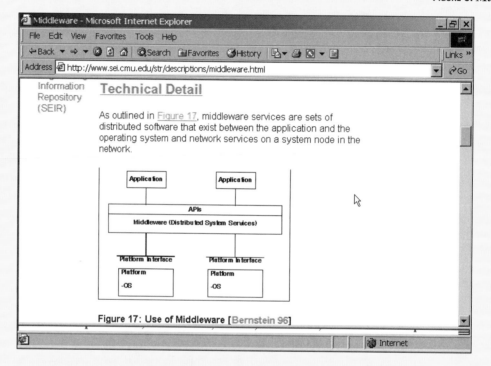

1. Log onto the Internet, then use your favorite search engine to research using the keyword "middleware." What new developments have been made for middleware applications?

2. Identify a list of companies that are creating middleware applications. Create a chart of all companies involved in research and development. Include the most recent offerings in middleware for each company.

3. Go to the Carnegie Mellon Software Engineering Web site and find the pages for middleware (www.sei.cum.edu/str/descriptions/middleware.html). Answer the following questions:

   • What is the Distributed Computing Environment? Write a brief description.

   • What is Object Management Groups Common Object Request Broker Architecture (COBRA)?

   • What is the Software Technology Review (STR)?

Issue: Should the Internet be regulated?

Originally thought to be the truest venue for unregulated free expression, it seems that the Internet may fall under restrictions and regulations once thought impossible. With the advent of new technologies and some recent laws (both national and international), it seems possible that online regulation of content and expression may not only be possible but probable.

Those who favor Internet restrictions and monitoring do so for a variety of reasons. Governments feel pressure to regulate the Internet for similar reasons. In its communication "Illegal and harmful content on the Internet," the Commission of European Communities summarized reasons governments feel pressure to regulate the Internet as follows:

- national security (fear of terrorist activities, bomb-making instructions)
- protection of minors (from violence, pornography)
- protection of human dignity (from racial hatred or racial discrimination)
- economic security (protection against fraud)
- information security (malicious hacking)
- protection of privacy (unauthorized distribution of personal data such as medical records)
- protection of reputation (libel)
- intellectual property (unauthorized distribution of copyrighted works)
  [Source: http://www.drugtext.org/legal/eu/eucnet1.htm]

Those groups and governments who favor regulating the Internet will soon have sophisticated tracking programs to do just that. Such programs will be capable not only of stopping the transfer of selected content on the Web, but also capable of locating those users who work outside the regulations. In addition to regulating content, there are a variety of issues related to business conducted over the Internet that some groups feel need to be regulated.

Software programs currently exist that provide for Internet regulation by individuals, parents, or organizations. Programs such as CyberSitter can filter content to protect against unwanted content. Some parents, schools, and libraries find these programs a first step in regulating the Internet. The bigger issue remains should there be global regulation of the Internet.

There are many questions that must be answered before regulating the Internet fairly can become a reality. First, what would be the purpose of regulating the Internet? Presumably the purpose would be to address the concerns listed previously. Next, who would make up the regulations?

One of the challenges that faces those who believe the Internet should be regulated is the global aspect of the Internet. Each country and its government bring a different set of rules and a different cultural perspective to the Internet. These must all be understood and respected if regulation of the Internet is to succeed. Finally, who would monitor the Internet and enforce the regulations? Once again the global nature of the Internet makes this a difficult question to answer.

Even if the "right" answers to the above questions can be found, there are those who do not believe the Internet should be regulated, and who believe in the original premise of the Internet – free and open communication. Groups such as Electronic Frontier Foundation (EFF) and the American National Standards Institute (ANSI) are working with policy makers to ensure the Internet remains a venue for free and open communication. The EFF, for example, has as one of its goals to "...develop among policy-makers a better understanding of the issues underlying free and open telecommunications,..." *[Source: http://www.eff.org/abouteff.html#mission.]*

Some movement has already been made to regulate the Internet. For example, with the Internet quickly becoming the global marketplace, the Federal Trade Commission (FTC) in the United States has been implementing various regulations regarding protection of consumer privacy information. Internationally, governments are proposing legislation to regulate business dealings on the Internet by providing basic rules to ensure that transactions and contracts completed online have the same protections and guidelines as those done face-to-face or on paper. In addition, new laws are being considered regarding ways to collect taxes on the sales of goods that fall outside the jurisdiction of the states' ability to collect taxes. There has also been talk of charging and taxing Internet use. The Federal Communications Commission (FCC) has been in favor of lifting some of the existing telecommunications restrictions in order to bring high-speed Internet access into homes; however they are also debating what, if any, restrictions they should place on the content that is delivered.

All these ideas are contrary to the original premise of the Internet, which was developed to provide an open, unregulated, and free forum for the exchange of ideas. With the Internet moving into areas of commerce and education, however, are laws to regulate the Internet necessary?

EXPAND THE IDEAS

1. Log onto the Internet, then use your favorite search engine and the key phrase "regulate the Internet." Create a concept map of the key ideas related to regulating the Internet discovered in your research. Write a brief summary indicating your answer to the question: Should the Internet be regulated? Be sure to provide support through your research for your conclusion.

2. Is regulating the Internet a good idea? Consider such laws as the following that were passed by the U.S. Congress: The U.S. Communications Decency Act (1996) and the Child Online Privacy Protection Act (2000). Research these laws and summarize how they regulate the Internet, who is protected, and who monitors the regulations.

3. Will the new laws that are being introduced in the US and around the world hamper trade and e-commerce, or provide a secure and stable environment to promote and expand Internet trade and commerce? Research recent proposals and developments regarding e-commerce both in the US and around the world. Write a short paper on your findings. In your conclusion, state how the proposals regulate the Internet, and if you think the proposals will work or not work and why?

4. In the United States, the FCC regulates cable and broadcast television. If the Internet is provided via cable through televisions, does regulation fall within their jurisdiction? What are the issues and recent regulations? Write a short paper discussing your findings.

More than 180 universities in the United States and industry leaders and government agencies are developing Internet2 to create the next generation Internet. Just as the original Internet was a collaborative effort, so too is Internet2.

Could the Internet be outgrown already? Originally developed by and for educators, now many educators are finding that the Internet is being "clogged" by commercial interests and not offering the technology they need. Among the many exciting applications, Internet2 developers have plans for advanced digital laboratories where people can interact with high-definition images in real time. They want a leading edge network that can provide the connectivity for applications across the educational community. Already thousands of educational institutions have connected to the Internet2 backbone. Internet2 will be able to allow people to collaborate and access information in ways that the current Internet cannot handle. See Figure 7. What can Internet2 offer that is outside the abilities of the Internet?

FIGURE 7: *Internet2*

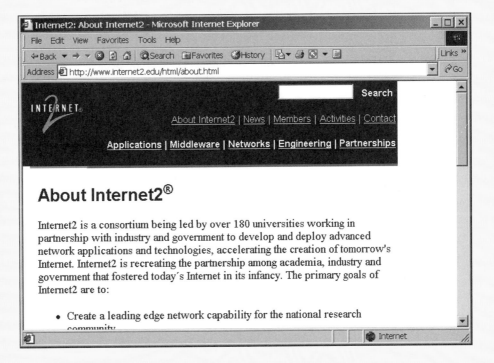

1. Log onto the Internet, then use your favorite search engine to find out more about Internet2. You might start at www.internet2.edu. Write a short paper on the goals of Internet2. Include information as to who is currently involved in development of Internet2.

2. Can you think of exciting applications that could be included in the Internet2 specs? Create a short list and explain how you would like to see Internet2 develop.

3. Be sure to browse through the Internet2 Web site to answer the following questions: What is Abilene? What is Ampath? Why is middleware important for Internet2?

The headlines in major papers keep hackers and their activities in the public eye. These stories detail how hackers have infiltrated a company's computer systems and Web sites and attacked valuable data, causing problems not only for the company, but for their customers as well. Whether the attackers intend to simply "look around," "steal information," or "damage data" doesn't really matter; it is still a breach of security and has to be eliminated. Headline stories tell tales of the many attempts to infiltrate and disrupt government Web sites, particularly the Department of Defense site and computers. The White House site has been hit, as has the Microsoft site.

These stories should serve as warnings to all of us. But many small and medium-size business owners probably choose to ignore these stories and their implications thinking attackers only look to large industry and sensitive government computers. Managers of these businesses often hide behind the false security of thinking no hacker is going to waste time breaking into their computer systems and their data; after all, what's there to find? They may also believe that their IT staff and other employees probably do not have enough computer knowledge or savvy to do damage, whether malicious and intentional, or accidental. What is not apparent is how simple it is for a disgruntled or bored employee to literally take down a computer system of an entire enterprise or business, causing data damage and raising questions about security.

Data security and control is a critical issue for all businesses because data is particularly vulnerable. Many businesses today are dependent upon their computer systems and networks for their entire business operation. Data is stored electronically. Business is conducted electronically. Users have expectations that information they submit will be secure. Sometimes damage to computer systems and data can result from a simple oversight. Employees can post their passwords using sticky notes on their computer, fail to change passwords, or make a critical change in their setup. All of these actions can result in data damage and loss of security. Sometimes damage to systems can be intentional or malicious.

In addition to being concerned about internal security—systems over which they have complete control, such as an internal LAN, businesses also have to be concerned about external security—systems over which they have less control, such as the Internet. Consider the Web-based e-market, which depends upon open access on the Internet. Security is always an issue on the Internet, as indicated by recent headlines about denial of service attacks on several major sites. A **denial of service attack** floods the bandwidth of the server with a high volume of illegitimate traffic rendering the server unable to process legitimate customer business. What safeguards should e-commerce businesses have in place to keep their operation safe? What safeguards should any business using a network have in place to keep their data secure?

Firewall technology provides a good measure of security for most businesses from breaches both from the inside and the outside. A **firewall** is a system that blocks Internet traffic based on specific criteria. So, in effect, you build a wall of security around your business. However, it has been shown that firewall technology is not very good at preventing viruses.

Is the choice of server a factor in your vulnerability? Less open systems with fewer points of entry and special service servers tend to be more tightly sealed. On the other side to that point there is some evidence that servers with many points of entry that a hacker can access are more open to attack. The problem is that these points of entry often create security holes that hackers can access. Since security holes make great headlines, businesses need to carefully evaluate their choice of server.

The World Wide Web (W3C) Consortium provides guidelines for users concerned about running a secure server. Current Web-based security systems are constantly being challenged and, therefore, are evolving.

Some businesses are using virtual LANs (VLANs) to streamline workgroups. A **VLAN** is a group of host computers on a local area network (LAN) that communicates as if they are physically connected using the same connection, even though they are on different LAN segments throughout a site. A VLAN is set up using logical LAN segments rather than physical LAN segments. This means that workstations do not have to be physically next to each other. VLANs allow network administrators to set up workgroups based on projects rather than location. Users can be added easily to VLAN workgroups and they do not have to be physically near one another. Once a workgroup completes its project, the VLAN can be reassigned to a new workgroup, or it can be reconfigured in other ways. As a result, VLANs provide more network flexibility than regular LANs. They also help manage the flow of traffic by channeling messages for a particular workgroup through a VLAN.

Another advancement in network systems are **virtual private networks (VPNs)**. A VPN is used to provide a secure connection over an otherwise insecure network, typically the Internet. An important part of a VPN is encryption. VPNs are generally less expensive than establishing and maintaining a private network over private lines. VPNs allow businesses to provide secure communications and connections over the Internet.

As network technologies continue to emerge, security will always be a factor. And at each twist and turn, businesses and consumers will find themselves asking, "How vulnerable is my business data?" The answer will impact the success or failure of the business.

EXPAND THE IDEAS

1. What are the concerns you should address when setting up an e-commerce site? Go to the World Wide Web Consortium site at www.w3.org and search on the key phrase "Web Security." Read through the list of FAQs regarding Web security. Summarize 10 main questions that you should address when setting up a Web server. The points should address a consumer's concern, "How safe is my data on your business site?"

2. Is there a firewall at the business or institution that you use? Or if you have a personal computer connected to the Internet, do you have a firewall set up? Do you believe these safeguards to be valuable? Write a brief paper explaining your position.

3. Have there been any denial of service attacks lately? What happened and what was the affect? Research denial of service attacks (you can find relevant information at www.cert.org). Why do you think people would sabotage sites like this?

Sen. Robert Bennett, R-Utah, a leading congressional evangelist on critical infrastructure protection issues, is proposing radical measures to defend our nation from cyberattacks. At issue is what foreign cyberattackers will aim for: the banking systems, power and transportation grids, or other targets that are dependent on computers. How much should government and business collaborate to set security initiatives? For example, what would happen if an attack shut down Fedwire, the Federal Reserve's fund transfer system? It could mean that no checks could be processed, and money could not be transferred from one account to another; in fact, it would mean no financial transactions could take place in the United States.

Emerging technologies include advances in encryption technology, as well as various security techniques. How we protect our data is of vital interest to governments and business interests.

FIGURE 8: *Data security*

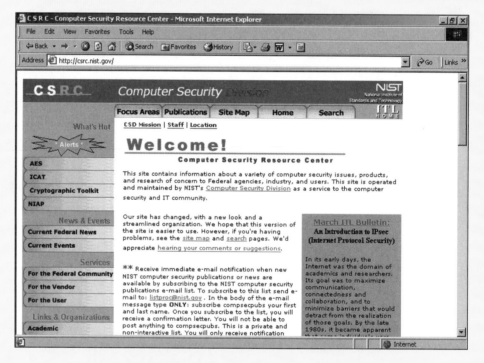

1. Log onto the Internet and go to the National Institute of Standards and Technology's Computer Security Division's Web site, www.csrc.nist.gov/nissc, which is shown in Figure 8. Take the time to browse the site. List the five focus areas and describe each one in a few short sentences.

2. What is the Advanced Encryption Standard? Who is developing it? What are the project goals? Write a brief definition and describe the project in a short paper.

3. Use your favorite search engine to research computers and national security. What are the advances and emerging technologies? What is being done in intrusion detections, firewall research, and incident response strategies?

A Buyer's Guide

Whether you are a first-time buyer or are upgrading your computer system, when the time comes to make your computer buying decision, you might find yourself overwhelmed by the vast amount of information available to you. There are thousands of computer advertisements in magazines and newspapers which list detailed technical specifications for their products. To get the best deal on a computer that meets your needs, you need to understand what these technical specifications mean and how they will affect your computing power. This Buyer's Guide will help you to organize your purchasing decisions. This guide also includes a worksheet that you can use to summarize your specifications for a computer and compare prices and features.

Deciding on a basic computer system

The first decision you should make is what basic configuration your new computer system should have. The first step is to establish the budget for your computer system, which will help you to exclude those system configurations that are too costly. Figure BG-1 shows a typical computer ad. You can't tell if this MicroPlus is a good deal unless you compare its specifications with those of computers from other vendors.

DETAILS

☞ Desktop or notebook: Will you be working from a single location or taking your computer with you to many locations? Choose a notebook if you plan to take your computer with you. Note, however, that notebooks cost more than a similarly configured desktop, so you will pay for portability.

☞ Network or stand-alone: Will you be working as part of a network or alone? Do you plan to tie into a network and take advantage of a central file server and microprocessor using your computer as a workstation? If you are setting up for a network, you need to purchase the network components, such as network interface cards (NICs) and cables.

☞ Platform—Macintosh or IBM-compatible PC: Evaluate the software available on both platforms to decide which better suits your needs. If you will be working closely with other people, decide whether you need to work on the same platform. The computer in the ad in Figure BG-1 is an IBM-compatible. It uses an Intel Pentium microprocessor.

☞ Case type: If you choose to buy a desktop, how much space is available for the computer? Towers can fit under a desk on the floor.

☞ Planning for expansion: The computer case includes openings, or "bays." An **external bay** provides an opening for installing devices such as a hard disk drive, floppy disk drive, Zip drive, removable hard disk drive, CD-ROM, and tape drive. An **internal bay** provides a mounting bracket to hold devices that do not need to be accessed from outside the system unit, such as a hard disk drive. A case with more bays provides you with greater expansion capability. To add peripheral devices such as a printer, scanner, or graphics tablet, your computer needs open **ports** or **expansion slots**.

FIGURE BG-1: *A typical computer ad*

MicroPlus Home PC XL550

MicroPlus award-winning computers offer strong performance at a reasonable price. Simply the fastest Windows machines you can buy. MicroPlus computers feature superior engineering, starting with a genuine Intel processor and a motherboard designed specifically to take advantage of the latest technological advancements. Of course, you are covered by the MicroPlus one-year, on-site parts and labor warranty.*

- ▶ Intel Pentium 550 MHz with 512K cache
- ▶ 128 MB SDRAM expandable to 384 MB
- ▶ 3.5" 1.44 MB floppy drive
- ▶ 13 GB Ultra ATA hard drive
- ▶ 40X variable CD-ROM drive
- ▶ Turtle Beach Montego Sound Blaster-compatible PCI sound card
- ▶ Stereo speakers
- ▶ 16 MB Diamond Viper AGP graphics card
- ▶ 56 K V.90 PCI data/fax modem
- ▶ 15" (13.8 vis) .26 dp monitor 1024 × 768 max. res
- ▶ 7-bay mid-tower case
- ▶ 2 USB, 1 parallel port
- ▶ Multifunction keyboard and mouse
- ▶ Windows 98
- ▶ Microsoft Office 2000
- ▶ MicroPlus Edutainment Pak

$1,499

*On-site service available for hardware only and only in the continental United States. Shipping and handling costs are not covered by warranty. All returns must be in original box and packaging. Shipping and handling costs are nonrefundable. Call for an RMA number. Prices and availability subject to change without notice.

A desktop computer typically includes one keyboard port, one mouse port, two USB ports, one parallel port, and two serial ports. The computer in the ad in Figure BG-1 has seven bays, two USB ports and one of which is a parallel port.

☞ Display device: The quality of the computer display depends on the features of the video display adapter and the capability of the monitor. Monitors are rated by their resolution capability as well as the size of the display screen. A typical desktop monitor can be 13",15", 17", 19", or 21". Prices increase with the size of the monitor. The monitor in the ad has a 15" screen with a viewable image size of 13.8". It also has a maximum resolution of 1024 × 768.

☞ Graphics card: A computer display system consists of a monitor and a **graphics card**, also called a video display adapter or video card. A graphics card is an expansion card that controls the signals that the computer sends to the monitor. Most computers include a graphics card, even if a monitor is not included. Graphics card specifications include the manufacturer, model, slot type, accelerator technology, and video memory capacity. The computer in the ad in Figure BG-1 has a 16 MB Diamond Viper AGP graphics card.

The clarity of a computer display depends on the quality of the monitor and the capability of the graphics card. Whether inserted in a PCI slot (slower to update the screen) or the AGP expansion slot (fastest graphics cards), most graphics cards use special graphics accelerator chips to boost performance. An **accelerated graphics card** can greatly increase the speed at which images are displayed.

Graphics cards carry their own memory circuitry, called **video memory**, which stores graphic images as they are processed and before they are displayed. The amount of memory on the card determines the maximum screen resolution and the color depth that can be sent to the display device. Today's video cards typically contain between 8 MB and 32 MB of video memory; the more video memory a card has, the more expensive it is.

Color depth refers to the number of colors that can be present on the screen at any one time. A 24-bit color depth is considered to be photographic quality and can display more than 16 million colors.

☞ Floppy disk drives: Most microcomputers today are configured with a single 3.5" floppy disk drive that reads from and writes to 1.44 MB disks. One 3.5" drive should be sufficient. The computer in the ad in Figure BG-1 has one 3.5" floppy disk drive. Many computers also include a 100 MB or 250 MB Zip drive as a low-cost add-on for backing up larger files.

☞ Hard disk drives: A hard disk drive (hard drive) is standard equipment on virtually every PC. Factors that influence hard drive performance and price include storage capacity, access time, and controller type.

Capacity is measured in gigabytes (GB). When you compare computer systems, the hard drive capacity should be a significant factor in your analysis. Most of today's computers are shipped with at least 10 GB of hard disk capacity.

Computer ads usually specify hard disk access time to give an indication of the drive performance. Access times between 6 ms and 11 ms are typical for today's microcomputer hard drives. Hard drive specifications also include a measure of speed in revolutions per minute (rpm). The faster a drive spins, the more quickly it can access data.

☞ Controller cards: A hard drive mechanism includes a circuit board called a **controller card** that positions the disk and read-write heads to locate data. Disk drives are categorized according to the type of controller cards they have. **EIDE** (Enhanced Integrated Device Electronics) and **Ultra ATA** (AT attachment) drives are essentially the same basic drive technology and feature high storage capacity and fast data transfer. Ultra ATA drives are twice as fast as their EIDE counterparts. **SCSI** (Small Computer System Interface) drives provide a slight performance advantage over EIDE drives and are recommended for high-performance microcomputer systems and minicomputers. Some computers feature DMA hard drives. **DMA** (direct memory access) is a companion technology that allows a computer to transfer data directly from a drive into RAM without intervention from the processor. The fastest drive action will occur when a computer has an Ultra ATA drive and that implements DMA data transfer. The computer in the ad in Figure BG-1 has a 13 GB Ultra ATA hard drive.

☞ CD and DVD drives: Many multimedia, game, educational, and reference applications are available only on CD-ROM or DVD disks. A CD-ROM or DVD drive gives your computer the capability to access these applications. Today, every microcomputer comes configured with a CD-ROM drive. DVD-ROM drives are typically included with more expensive computer systems. DVD-ROM drives read CD-ROM, CD-R, CD-RW, DVD-ROM, and DVD movie formats. A CD-ROM drive cannot read DVD-ROM or DVD movie formats.

The data transfer rate of the CD-ROM drive might be listed as 40X variable. This listing means that the data transfer rate of the CD-ROM varies between a minimum transfer rate of 2,500 KBps (17X) and a maximum speed of 6,0000 KBps (40X). Alternative terminology for 40X variable is 17–40X and 40X max. The computer in the ad has a 40x variable speed CD-ROM.

Determining your computer's architecture

Once you have established the basic configuration of your desired computer system, you need to think about the computer architecture. These technical specifications will ultimately determine your computing power.

DETAILS

☞ The microprocessor is the core component in a computer. Computer ads typically indicate the type of microprocessor, the company that manufactured the microprocessor, and the microprocessor's speed. Intel and AMD are currently the two major PC microprocessor manufacturers. Computers that contain Intel processors command higher prices than computers that contain other manufacturers' processors.

- AMD produces "work-alike" processors for PC-compatible processors. AMD processors offer manufacturers and customers an alternative to processors produced by Intel. AMD processors are generally less expensive than their Intel counterparts, but have many of the same features and capabilities of Intel processors.
- Intel also produces a "budget" processor called Celeron, which has a slightly less sophisticated architecture than Pentium models.
- AMD produces K6 and Athlon processors that compete directly with Intel's Pentium and Celeron processors. From a user's perspective, it is virtually impossible to find any operational differences between computers that use AMD processors and those with Intel processors.

If you want to run Macintosh software, select a computer with a 68000-series or PowerPC microprocessor. Until 1994, Macintosh computers contained a 68000-series microprocessor manufactured by Motorola. More recent models, called "Power Macs" contain a PowerPC microprocessor.

☞ When purchasing a processor, two components to consider are speed and cache capacity.

- Speed: Processor speed is a measure of clock rate, which is an indication of the number of instructions that can be processed per second. A computer with a 550 MHz processor would be faster than a computer with a 500 MHz processor if all other specifications for the two computers being compared were equal. Manufacturers charge a premium price for speed. For certain applications, such as 3-D games and desktop publishing, the fastest processor can be very desirable. Applications such as word processing and e-mail don't seem to benefit as much from accelerated clock speeds.
- Cache capacity: RAM cache is special high-speed circuitry that holds data just before the processor needs it. In theory, having a large cache area increases processing speed. Cache capacity is tied to the processor model. For example, a Celeron processor typically has 128 KB cache, whereas a Pentium III typically has a 512 KB cache.

Cache contributes to the speed of the chip and is often referred to in computer ads. The cache chip connects to the main processor by a dedicated high-speed bus and is often housed in the same chip carrier as the processor. With today's computer architecture, cache is not configurable.

- **Level 1 cache** (L1 cache) is built into the processor chip.
- **Level 2 cache** (L2 cache) is memory circuitry housed off the processor on a separate chip. Level 2 cache is much faster than RAM and almost as fast as cache built into the processor chip.

☞ Benchmark tests: A **benchmark test** is a set of standard processing tasks that measure the performance of computer hardware or software. You can use benchmark test results to compare the performance of two computers.

☞ RAM—requirements and cost: The amount of RAM a computer needs depends on the operating system and application software you plan to use. Today, RAM costs approximately $2.50 to $10 per megabyte. Your computer should have at least 32 MB of RAM, but additional memory modules can be added. Most computers come with at least 128 MB. Consumer advocates recommend that you get as much RAM as you can afford with your initial purchase. If a computer features SDRAM (synchronized dynamic RAM) technology, you can expect better performance from it than from computers with standard memory technology such as EDO and FPM.

LAB: buying a computer

BUYING A
COMPUTER

When buying from a mail-order or Internet computer vendor, consumers don't have an opportunity to take various computer models for a "test drive." They make their computer purchase decisions based solely on a list of specifications. Thus it is essential to understand the specifications in computer ads. In this lab, you will find out how to use a Shopping Glossary to interpret the specifications.

STEPS

1. Click the Steps button to learn how to use the Shopping Glossary. As you proceed through the Steps, answer all of the QuickCheck questions that appear. After you complete the Steps, you will see a QuickCheck Report. Follow the instructions on the screen to print this report.

2. Click the Explore button and read the ad for the Nevada Tech Systems computer in Ad 1. Use the Shopping Glossary to define the following terms:

   a. L2 cache

   b. SDRAM

   c. AGP

   d. Wavetable

   e. Zip

   f. V.90

3. In Explore, read the ads for the ZeePlus Value Pak and the ZeePlus Multimedia Pro computers. The two systems differ substantially in price. If you purchase the more expensive system, what additional features do you get?

4. In Explore, read the ad for the ZeePlus Multimedia Pro Computer (500 MHz) and the NP2 Super Systems Computer. What is the price difference between these two systems? What factors might account for this price difference?

5. In Explore, read the ads to find a notebook computer that's priced within $100 of the Nevada Tech Systems desktop computer. Make a list of the features that the desktop computer has, but the notebook computer lacks. Which one would you buy? Why?

6. Photocopy a computer ad from a recent issue of a computer magazine. On a separate sheet of paper, write each specification (for example, Intel Pentium III processor). For each specification, define each term (for example, Intel is a microprocessor manufacturer, Pentium is a type of microprocessor in the $\times 86$ family). Write out all acronyms (for example, RAM means "random access memory"). If you have difficulty with some of the terms and acronyms, click the Explore button and use the Shopping Glossary.

Additional resources

Before you make any computer-related purchasing decisions, | you might refer to the following InfoWebs. These InfoWebs are | your guide to print, film, television, and electronic resources.

WHICH CHIP?

BENCHMARKS

SOUND SYSTEMS

DISPLAY SYSTEMS

NOTEBOOKS

PCMCIA

PRINTERS

Reviewing notebook computers

Whether you purchase a desktop or notebook computer, the microprocessor will be critical in determining the computer's performance. If you decide to buy a notebook computer, however, you must make some additional decisions.

DETAILS

🔑 Notebook displays: Notebook computers do not use monitors that are big and heavy or that require too much electrical power to run on batteries. Instead, notebooks have flat panel liquid crystal displays. A **liquid crystal display** (LCD) uses a technically sophisticated method of passing light through a thin layer of liquid crystal cells to produce an image. The resulting flat panel screen is lightweight and compact.
- Many older notebooks have a **passive matrix screen**, sometimes referred to as a dual-scan screen. A passive matrix screen relies on timing to ensure that the liquid crystal cells are illuminated. As a result, the process of updating the screen image does not always keep up with moving images, and the display can appear blurred. Passive matrix technology is not suitable for multimedia applications that include animations and videos.
- An **active matrix screen**, also referred to as **TFT** (thin film transistor), is updated more rapidly and provides image quality similar to that of a monitor. Active matrix screens are essential for a crisp display of animation and video.

Notebook computer ads usually specify screen resolution as SVGA or XGA. **SVGA** (super video graphics array) is 800 × 600 resolution. **XGA** (extended graphics array) is 1024 × 768 resolution. The specified resolution might be the only resolution available, so be sure to ask a salesperson and check the specifications for the notebook computer carefully.

🔑 Port replicator: A **port replicator** is an inexpensive device that connects to a notebook computer by a bus connector plug. It contains a duplicate of the notebook computer's ports and makes it more convenient to connect and disconnect your notebook computer from devices, such as an external monitor, mouse, and keyboard. Port replicators do not include expansion slots and typically cannot be used to add a sound card or CD-ROM drive to your notebook computer.

🔑 External ports: Most notebook computers feature built-in ports to compensate for the limited user-installable expansion options. A notebook computer typically includes:
- One keyboard port for connecting an external keyboard
- One mouse port for connecting an external pointing device
- One graphics port for connecting an external monitor

  The advantage of an external monitor is the high-quality display. The disadvantage is that you need to disconnect the external monitor when you transport the computer.

- One parallel port for a printer or other parallel devices such as a scanner or external hard drive
- One USB port
- One serial port
- One infrared port for printers and PDAs that support wireless data transfer
- One audio-out port for external speakers or headphones
- One audio-in port for an external microphone

🔑 Expansion slot: A **PCMCIA** (Personal Computer Memory Card International Association) **slot** is a special type of expansion slot developed for notebook computers because they do not have enough space in the case to hold full-size expansion slots and cards. A PCMCIA slot is a small, external slot into which you can insert a **PCMCIA card**. See Figure BG-2.

🔑 PCMCIA cards: PCMCIA cards, also called PC cards, are credit-card-sized circuit boards that incorporate an expansion card and device. Some PCMCIA cards contain a modem, others contain memory expansion, and still others contain a hard disk drive. You can plug in and remove PCMCIA devices without turning the computer off, unlike desktop computer expansion cards. In this way, you can switch from one PCMCIA device to another without disrupting your work.

PCMCIA slots are categorized by size.

- Type I slots accept only the thinnest PCMCIA cards, such as memory expansion cards.
- Type II slots accept most of the popular PCMCIA cards—those that contain modems, sound cards, and network cards.
- Type III slots accept the thickest PCMCIA cards, which contain devices such as hard disk drives.

Many notebooks provide a multipurpose PCMCIA slot that will accept two Type I cards, two Type II cards, or one Type III card.

Docking station: A **docking station** is an additional expansion bus into which you plug your notebook computer. Notebook computer expansion devices tend to be more expensive than those for desktop computers, but it is possible to use desktop peripherals with notebook computers if you have a docking station or a port replicator. The notebook provides the processor and RAM. The docking station provides expansion slots for cards that will not fit into the notebook case. It allows you to purchase inexpensive expansion cards and peripherals designed for desktops, instead of the more expensive devices designed specifically for notebooks. When you use a docking station, you sacrifice portability, but gain the use of low-cost, powerful desktop peripherals.

Pointing device: Although a mouse is the standard pointing device used with desktop computers, it can be inconvenient to carry and use while traveling. Most notebook computers include an alternative pointing device. The three most popular options are a built-in trackball, a track point, and a touch pad.

Notebook power sources: Most notebook computers operate on power from either rechargeable batteries or a wall outlet. Because notebooks are designed for portability, the computing time provided by batteries is important and dependent on many factors. Fast processors, active matrix LCDs, and additional peripheral devices all demand significant power from notebook computer batteries. Notebook manufacturers have attempted to reduce the power consumption by building power-saving features into their computers. If you do not interact with the computer for a short time, these features automatically turn off the hard disk drive, LCD display, or even the processor. These devices are reactivated when you press a key or move the mouse.

- Most notebook computers use lithium ion batteries. Notebooks typically provide two to four hours of battery-powered operating time before the batteries need to be recharged.
- In addition, most notebook computers require an external AC adapter to plug into a wall outlet or to recharge the batteries. Some notebooks have eliminated the external adapter and require only a power cable to plug into a wall outlet. It is a good idea to use AC power whenever possible. The easiest way to extend the operating time of your notebook computer is to purchase extra batteries. Some notebooks allow you to swap batteries while the computer remains on; this process is called a **hot swap**.

Weight: Notebook computers can vary considerably in weight. Lighter notebooks are generally more expensive. Consider how often you will carry your computer to determine whether weight will be a factor in your purchasing decision.

Case to carry: Consider how you will carry your notebook computer and purchase a case that is well designed. The case should be well padded to protect the computer as well as provide the necessary compartments to store extra devices, power cords and cables, and any papers or notes you may carry.

Figure BG-2: *PCMCIA cards*

▶ To add a modem, network interface card, or hard disk to a notebook computer, plug in a PCMCIA card.

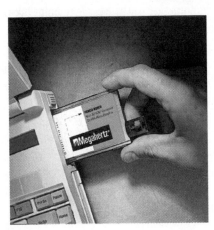

Selecting peripheral devices

Peripheral devices add functionality to your computer system by giving you different options for input, output, and storage. If your budget is limited, you do not have to include all of these devices when you buy your computer system. You can add any of them to your computer system later as your needs and budget permit.

DETAILS

- Pointing device: The computer mouse is the standard pointing device for desktop computers. You have several types from which to choose.
  - A serial mouse connects to your serial port.
  - A bus mouse connects directly to a bus port.
  - An infrared mouse does not connect to your computer with a cable. Instead, it uses infrared to transmit the movements and clicks to a receiver that plugs into the port on your computer.
  - A **scrolling mouse** helps alleviate wrist movements by providing a fixed mouse with a rolling ball and two buttons.

- Keyboards: Many desktop computers come equipped with a standard 104-key keyboard. Although most such computers include a standard keyboard and a mouse, you might want to consider alternative input devices. You can upgrade to other keyboards, including an ergonomically designed keyboard and a scrolling mouse.

- Printers: Printers are characterized as **dot matrix**, **ink-jet**, or **laser**. Occasionally a computer vendor offers a hardware bundle that includes a computer, printer, and software. More often, however, printers are sold separately so consumers can choose the quality, features, and price they want. Ink-jet and personal laser printers are most popular with today's consumers because they provide high-quality print on plain paper. Although color printers are available in each category, **color ink-jet printers** offer the best price-performance characteristics. Color laser printers are expensive, whereas color dot-matrix printers offer poor quality. When you purchase a printer, you should consider the following factors: resolution, color capability, print speed, printer cost, per-copy cost, and warranty.
  - Resolution: The quality of printed images and text depends on the printer's resolution—the density of the gridwork of dots that create an image. Printer resolution is measured by the number of dots it can print per linear inch, abbreviated **dpi**. Microcomputer printer resolutions vary from 60 dpi to 1,500 dpi.

- Color capability: Some printers are capable of printing in color, whereas others are limited to black, white, and shades of gray. If you have a printer that does not print color, then the colorful graphics and Web pages that you see on your computer screen will be printed as shades of gray.
- Print speed: Printer speeds are measured in terms of either pages per minute (ppm) or characters per second (cps).
- Printer cost: Microcomputer printers range in price from $100 to $5,000. Typically, more expensive printers provide higher resolution, faster printing speeds, and a high-capacity duty cycle. A **duty cycle** is an indication of the number of pages a printer can be expected to print per month without undue wear and tear on the machine.
- Per-copy cost: Printing requires ongoing costs for printer supplies, such as ribbons, ink cartridges, and toner. These costs vary with different types, brands, and models of printers. In comparative reviews, you might see these costs expressed as "per-copy costs" —the cost of printing a page with an average amount of text, graphics, and color.
- Warranty: Printers tend to be fairly reliable devices, but problems with circuit boards, paper-handling mechanisms, and print heads occur occasionally. Printer warranties typically cover mechanical and electronic problems, but require that you send the printer to a service center for repair.

  Multifunction printers use either laser or ink-jet technology to take the place of a variety of printing and communications devices, such as a computer printer, fax machine, answering machine, telephone, copier, and scanner.

- Sound cards: A basic computer sound system includes a sound card and a set of small speakers. The sound card circuitry for a notebook computer is often built into the motherboard, and the speakers are built into the case.

  A sound card converts the digital data in a sound file into analog signals for instrumental, vocal, and spoken sounds. In addition, a sound card lets you make your own recordings by converting analog sounds into digitized sound files that you can store on disk. To record your own sounds, you'll need to add a good-quality microphone to your sound system.

Typically, sound cards are manufactured by companies other than those that manufacture computers. Most multimedia software specifies the type of sound required.

☞ Most sound cards feature Sound Blaster compatibility and wavetable synthesis. **Wavetable synthesis** creates music by playing digitized sound samples of actual instruments. The size of the wavetable affects the resulting sound quality. The larger the wavetable, the more realistic the sound. Numbers such as 64, 128, or 512 in the sound card specification usually indicate the size of the wavetable.

☞ Speakers: A sound card outputs sound to speakers or earphones. As with any audio system, higher-quality speakers provide richer sound and enhanced volume. Speaker manufacturers such as Altec Lansing, Koss, Harmon/Kardon, and Yamaha are familiar names in the audio business.

☞ Modem: Many computer systems include a **modem** that transmits and receives data over phone lines to other computers. The baud rate identifies the transmission speed. Faster baud rates mean faster transmission; new systems typically come with a minimum 56.6 baud (kilobits per second) modem.

☞ Fax modems: A fax modem is a modem that includes fax capability. Such a device can send a document that is in the memory of your computer to any standard fax machine, where it appears in hard copy format, or to another fax modem to be printed later. Fax modems can also receive fax transmissions from standard fax machines or other fax modems.

☞ Scanner: A **scanner** reads images on a page and converts them to digital representation. It offers a fast way to convert images on paper to data that can be manipulated.

☞ Backup system: Depending on how much data you want to copy and how often you want to back up your hard disk, you may consider adding a tape backup system to your computer. Special high-capacity drives, such as Zip removable hard disk drives, provide removable storage. Table BG-1 compares the advantages and disadvantages of various backup media.

☞ Backup power systems: A surge protector protects your computer system against sudden fluctuations in power. A UPS (uninterruptible power supply) will protect your data if the power fails for a short time.

☞ Game accessories: For games that require motion input, consider purchasing a joy stick, flight yoke, or steering wheel, depending on the application.

TABLE BG-1: *Advantages and disadvantages of various backup media*

BACKUP MEDIUM	COSTS	ADVANTAGES	DISADVANTAGES
Floppy disks 1.44 MB	Drive: <$50 Disks (50): $10	Satisfactory for backing up a limited number of files.	Requires too many disks for a complete system backup.
Zip disks 250 MB	Drive: $199 Disks (5): $60	Reliable and especially useful for large data files.	Not practical for backing up all the programs and data on a large hard disk.
Removable hard disks 2 GB	Drive: $349 Disks (1): $125	Enough storage capacity for a full-system backup.	Potentially less reliable than floppy, Zip, or optical media.
CD-RW 650 MB	Drive: $349 Disks (1): $10	Reliable, with good storage capacity.	Slow, and not enough storage capacity for the entire contents of a large hard disk.
DVD-RAM 5 GB	Drive: $700 Disks (1): $40	Reliable, with enough capacity to back up the data typically stored on a hard disk.	Very expensive and slower than tape drives.
Tape 10 GB	Drive: $200 Tapes (1): $30	Low cost and high capacity.	Somewhat less reliable than optical media.
Paper 1 page	Drive: None Disks: Cheap	Inexpensive backup for documents.	Information must be digitized before being restored to disk. Cannot be used to back up programs.

Buying system and application software

You should also be aware of how the software market works and how to get the best deals. Refer to Table BG-2 for a summary of software.

TABLE B-2: *Categorizing software*

APPLICATION	USE TO	EXAMPLES
Software Category: Operating Systems		
Macintosh platform	Run the computer, manage files, allocate drive space, interact with peripheral devices.	Mac OS
PC platform	Run the computer, manage files, allocate drive space, interact with peripheral devices.	Windows 95, Windows 98, Windows NT, Windows NT Workstation, Windows 2000, Windows 2000 Professional
PCs, minicomputers, mainframe computers	Establish foundation technologies for networks and Web servers appropriate for servers and high-performance workstations.	UNIX and versions of UNIX, such as AIX from IBM and XENIX from Microsoft; ULTRIX from Digital Equipment Corporation; Linux, a variation of UNIX
Software Category: Document Production		
Word processing	Write and spell-check documents such as reports, letters, and marketing materials.	Microsoft Word, Corel WordPerfect, Lotus Word Pro
Desktop publishing	Enhance the format and appearance of documents such as newsletters, brochures, newspapers, magazines, and books through sophisticated graphic design features.	QuarkXPress, Adobe PageMaker, Corel Ventura, Microsoft Publisher
Web authoring	Design and develop Web pages that you can publish on the Internet.	Claris Home Page, SoftQuad HoTMetaL, Macromedia DreamWeaver, Microsoft FrontPage
Software Category: Graphics		
Graphics	Create, edit, and manipulate images.	Adobe Illustrator, CorelDraw, Micrografx Picture Publisher, Paintshop Pro
Paint	Create and edit bitmap images. Bitmaps are stored as a series of colored dots.	Microsoft Paint
Photo editing	Enhance and manipulate photographs by modifying contrast, brightness, and cropping, and by removing red-eye.	Adobe PhotoShop, Microsoft PhotoDraw
Vector graphics 3-D graphics	Create diagrams, corporate logos, and schematics. Represent a three-dimensional object by covering a wire frame with a surface color and texture.	AutoCAD MetaCreations BRYCE
Software Category: Presentation		
Presentation	Combine text, graphics, animation, and sound into a series of electronic slides.	Microsoft PowerPoint, Lotus Freelance Graphics

APPLICATION	USE TO	EXAMPLES
Software Category: Spreadsheet and Statistical		
Spreadsheet	Perform calculations based on numbers and formulas; transform data into graphs.	Microsoft Excel, Lotus 1-2-3
Statistical	Analyze large sets of data to discover relationships and patterns. Summarize survey results, experiment results, and test scores to help visualize and explore trends.	SPSS, JMP, Data Desk
Mathematical modeling	Solve a wide range of math, science, and engineering problems.	MathCad, Mathematica
Software Category: Data Management		
File management	Work with simple lists of information such as holiday card addresses.	Microsoft Works
Database	Manage a database, which is a collection of related files, to store, find, organize, update, and report information stored in more than one file.	For personal computers: Microsoft Access, Lotus Approach, Claris FileMaker Pro For mainframe databases: Oracle, IBM DB2
Software Category: Information and Reference		
Information and reference	Access information on a wide array of topics, such as general encyclopedias, medical references, and map software.	Microsoft Encarta, Groliers Encyclopedia, Compton's Encyclopedia, Britannica's CD
Software Category: Accounting and Finance		
Personal finance	Help track monetary transactions, bank accounts, credit card transactions, and bills as well as monitor investments; also support online banking.	Microsoft Money, Intuit Quicken
Small business	Track invoices, accounts, customer data, purchasing history, payroll, and inventory functions.	Peachtree Complete Accounting, Intuit QuickBooks, Best!Ware M.Y.O.B.
Software Category: Connectivity		
Communications	Dial your connection. Built into most microcomputer operating systems and often classified as a system utility.	Windows Dial-Up Network
Browser	View Web pages and navigates links on the Internet.	Netscape Navigator, Microsoft Internet Explorer
Remote control	Establish a connection between two computers, such as one in your home and one in your office; use the keyboard of one to control the other.	Symantec pcANYWHERE, Traveling Software LapLink
E-mail	Send and receive e-mail messages over the Internet; manage your computer mailbox.	Microsoft Outlook Express, Netscape Communicator, Lotus Notes, Qualcomm's Eudora
Software Category: Education and Training		
Education, edutainment	Learn and practice new skills, languages; prepare for standardized tests; play while learning.	Learning Company Reader Rabbit, Math Rabbit
Software Category: Entertainment		
Action, adventure, role playing, puzzles, simulations, strategy	Play games such as simulations, toys, and leisure fun. Often features 3-D graphics to play and interact with the environment.	Duke Nukem, Doom, Diablo, ToomRaider, SimCity, NASCAR Racing; also stand-alone Nintendo, Sony PlayStation

Finding purchasing and user support

As with any major purchase, you need reliable support before and after you purchase your computer system. You need to keep up with changes in technology and in the computer industry. For example, the announcement of a new operating system or a news article about a computer company downsizing could affect your purchasing decisions. After you make your purchase, you continue to need service and support from the vendor or manufacturer.

DETAILS

☞ Computer publications: Computer publications provide information on computers, computing, and the computer industry.

- Computer magazines generally target users of both personal and business computers. Articles focus on product evaluations, product comparisons, and practical tips for installing hardware and using software. These magazines are full of product advertisements that are useful if you want to keep informed about the latest products available for your computer.
- Computer industry trade journals target computer professionals, rather than consumers. Computer trade journals, such as *InfoWorld* and *Computer Reseller News*, focus on company profiles, product announcements, and sales techniques.
- Computing journals offer an academic perspective on computers and computing issues. Such journals focus on research in computing. These academic journals rarely advertise hardware and software products, because it might appear that advertisers could influence the content of articles. An article in a computing journal is usually "refereed"—that is, it is evaluated by a committee of experts who determine whether the article is original and based on sound research techniques.

☞ Internet sites: Internet sites are an excellent source of information about the computer industry and computer products. Several computer magazines and trade journals, as well as many computer companies, have Internet sites. Here you can usually find product specifications, product announcements, sales literature, technical support forums, and pricing information.

☞ Television: Television shows about computers provide hardware and software reviews, tips, and computer industry news for new and experienced users. Most of these shows are carried on cable TV.

☞ Industry analysts: Journalists and columnists alike monitor computer industry trends, evaluate industry events, and make predictions about what the trends seem to indicate. Computer analysts range from professional financial analysts who report in *The Wall Street Journal* and *Forbes Magazine* to "rumor-central" analysts who spark up the back pages of trade journals and computer magazines with the latest gossip about new computer products.

☞ Vendor and manufacturer support: As part of your purchasing decision, you want to know what sort of support and service you can expect from the vendor and from the manufacturer. You should look specifically at the following:

- Warranty and guarantee: Computer systems are major investments. Does the manufacturer provide reasonable guarantees on the equipment? Most computers come with a one-year parts and labor warranty. Also consider the reputation of the manufacturer and vendor.
- Local repair: Find out if you can expect in your home. If you need a component repaired, will the system be repaired locally? Do you have to send it out? Who pays shipping? These costs can be significant. Do you get a replacement while you wait for the system or part to be repaired? Some manufacturers provide an instant exchange program for components, giving you a refurbished unit in exchange for yours.
- Telephone support: If you have a problem and need to call the manufacturer or vendor, does it have a local or toll-free number? You don't want to add significant costs in phone expenses to your computer system. What is the typical waiting time for a technical support person?

Organize Your Findings: A Buyer's Guide Summary

CONSIDERATIONS	NOTES
Basic computer system	
Desktop or notebook?	
Platform: Macintosh or IBM-compatible PC?	
Case type: tower, desktop?	
Display device	
Computer architecture	
Network or stand-alone?	
Which microprocessor?	
What clock speed?	
How much RAM?	
Include RAM cache?	
Expansion cards	
Special considerations for notebook computers	
Display	
External monitor	
PCMCIA slot	
Weight	
Power source/battery type	
Mouse type	
Docking station	
Carrying case	
Peripheral devices	
Pointing device	
Printer	
Scanner	
Modem	
Fax modem	
Backup system	
Surge protector/UPS	
CD-ROM /DVD	
Sound card/speakers	
Floppy disk drive/Zip disk drive	
System and application software and storage	
Operating system	
Software bundles	
Hard disk	
Internet service	
Internet Service Provider	
Web browsers	

Comparing computers: buyer's specification worksheet

Before you make a decision, shop around to collect information on pricing, features, and support. See Figure BG-3. You can find comparative pricing at Web-based "price-quote" sites. Although you might be tempted to buy the computer with the lowest price and best features, don't forget to consider the warranty and the quality of the support you are likely to get from the vendor.

DETAILS

☞ When you use a price-quote site, be aware that some of these sites search only those merchants that have paid to participate.

FIGURE BG-3: *Comparative shopping feature list*

Comparative Shopping Feature List

- **Manufacturer:** _____
- **Model:** _____
- **Price:** _____
- Processor model: _____
- Processor speed: _____
- Cache capacity: _____
- RAM capacity: _____
- Hard disk drive capacity: _____
- Hard disk drive type and speed: _____
- CD/DVD drive speed: _____
- Zip drive included: _____
- Modem speed: _____
- Sound card model: _____

- Speaker description: _____
- Graphics card slot type (desktop only): _____
- Graphics card accelerator features: _____
- Graphics card video RAM capacity: _____
- Display type (LCD/CRT): _____
- Display screen size and dot pitch: _____
- Type of pointing device: _____
- Number and type of expansion ports: _____
- Number and type of expansion slots: _____
- Overall weight (notebook only): _____
- Battery operating time (notebook only): _____
- Operating system version: _____
- Bundled software (list): _____

Service and support

- What is the warranty period? _____ years
- Does the warranty cover parts and labor? ❏ Yes ❏ No
- Does the vendor have a good reputation for service? ❏ Yes ❏ No
- Are technical support hours adequate? ❏ Yes ❏ No
- Toll-free number for technical support? ❏ Yes ❏ No
- Can I contact technical support without waiting on hold for a long time? ❏ Yes ❏ No
- Are technical support people knowledgeable? ❏ Yes ❏ No

- Can I get my computer fixed in an acceptable time period? ❏ Yes ❏ No
- Are the costs and procedures for fixing the computer acceptable? ❏ Yes ❏ No
- Are other users satisfied with this brand and model of computer? ❏ Yes ❏ No
- Is the vendor likely to stay in business? ❏ Yes ❏ No
- Are the computer parts and components standard? ❏ Yes ❏ No

Working in the computer industry

The $290 billion computer industry employs more than 1.5 million people. Over the past 50 years, it has created jobs that never before existed and financial opportunities for those with motivation, creative ideas, and technical skills. Since 1970, high-tech business has produced more than 7,000 millionaires and more than a dozen billionaires. According to the U.S. Bureau of Labor Statistics, computer and data-processing services are projected to be the third fastest growing industry; systems analysts, computer engineers, and data-processing equipment repairers are expected to be among the 30 fastest growing occupations between now and 2005. Not everyone who uses a computer is employed in the computer industry, however. For a clear picture of computer jobs, it is useful to consider three categories.

DETAILS

☞ Computer industry categories: These categories can be somewhat loosely defined as computer-specific jobs, computer-related jobs, and computer-use jobs.

- **Computer-specific jobs**—such as computer programming, chip design, and Webmaster—would not exist without computers.
- **Computer-related jobs**, on the other hand, are variations of more generic jobs that you might find in any industry. For example, jobs in computer sales, high-tech recruiting, and graphics design are similar to sales, recruiting, and design jobs in the automobile or medical industries.
- **Computer-use jobs** require the use of computers to accomplish tasks in fields other than computing. Writers, reporters, accountants, retail clerks, medical technicians, auto mechanics, and many others use computers in the course of their everyday job activities.

Of these three categories, computer-specific jobs require the most preparation and will appeal to those who like working with, learning about, and thinking about computers.

☞ Educational requirements for computer-specific jobs: Jobs for people who design and develop computer hardware and software require a high degree of training and skill. A college degree is required for virtually any of these jobs, and many require a master's degree or doctorate. Most colleges offer degrees in computer engineering, computer science, and information systems that provide good qualifications for computer-specific jobs.

☞ Working conditions for computer-specific jobs: Graduates with computer engineering, computer science, and information systems degrees generally work in a comfortable office or laboratory environment. Many high-tech companies offer employee-friendly working conditions that include child care, flexible hours, and the opportunity to telecommute. As in any industry, the exact nature of the job will depend on the company and the particular projects that are in the works.

☞ Salaries for computer-specific jobs: In the computer industry, as in most industries, management positions command the highest salaries and salary levels increase with experience. Salaries vary by geographic location. In the Northeast and on the West Coast, salaries tend to be higher than in the Southeast, Midwest, Southwest, and Canada.

☞ Preparing for a computer career: Education and experience are the keys to gaining a challenging computer job with good potential for advancement. In addition to a degree in computer science, computer engineering, or information systems, think about how you can get on-the-job experience through internships, military service, government-sponsored training programs, or work-study programs. Owning your own computer, installing software, and troubleshooting provide good basic experience and familiarity with mass-market computing standards. You might pick up additional experience from projects sponsored by clubs and organizations. The three largest computer organizations in North America are the Association for Computing Machinery (ACM), the Association of Information Technology Professionals (AITP), and the Institute of Electrical and Electronics Engineers–Computer Society (IEEE-CS).

- Certification training: The Institute for Certification of Computing Professionals (ICCP) has a regular schedule of comprehensive exams for computer jobs, such as computer programming, systems analysis, and network management. If you are considering a career in computer network management, it might be worthwhile to complete the test for Novell NetWare, Microsoft MCSE, or Microsoft NT certification. MOUS (Microsoft Office User Specialist) certification for application software such as Microsoft Word, Excel, PowerPoint, and Access is also available.

- Use technology to find a job: The first step in your job search should be to realistically assess your qualifications and needs. Several excellent books and Web sites can provide information to help in your assessment. Your qualifications include your computer skills, educational background, previous work experience, communications skills, and personality. By comparing your qualifications with the requirements for a job, you can assess your chances of being hired. Your needs include your preferred geographical location, working conditions, corporate lifestyle, and salary. By comparing your needs with the information you discover about a prospective employer, you can assess your chances of enjoying a job once you've been hired.

- Researching the job market on the Internet: In 1999, an estimated one out of every three employers in North America used the Internet for recruiting. Popular Web-based "want ads" post descriptions of job openings. Usually the employers pay for these postings, so access is free to prospective employees. Web sites include general information about jobs, employment outlook, and salaries in computer-industry jobs. Because the salaries for most jobs are vaguely stated as "commensurate with experience," it is useful to discover what you're worth by studying Web-based salary reports.

- Preparing a résumé: You will need to prepare a résumé with your career goals, experience, skills, and education. Some career counselors suggest that high-tech candidates should not follow many of the rules delineated in traditional résumé guidebooks. Instead, your résumé should focus on demonstrating your technical savvy without appearing overly "packaged." For example, dot-matrix printing is hard to read and old-fashioned. By contrast, unless you're applying for a job as a Web site or graphical designer, you don't want your resume to look like an advertisement in a magazine. Remember that corporate cultures differ, so use your word processor to tailor your resume to the corporate culture of each prospective employer.

- Contact prospective employers: The standard procedure for mailing letters of application and résumés remains valid even in this age of high technology. Many companies, however, will accept résumés by fax or e-mail to reduce the time it takes to process applicants. Include your e-mail address on your application materials. You can also post your résumé on a placement Web site, where it can be viewed by corporate recruiters. Some of these Web sites charge a small fee for posting résumés; others are free. In addition, you can post your résumé on your personal Web page, if you have one. This approach can be particularly effective if you design these pages, because posting your Web pages allows you to showcase technical skills that are applicable to the job you're seeking.

Glossary

3G: Third Generation ► The standard for the next generation of wireless devices that will combine voice and Internet into portable wireless appliances operating with greater bandwidth

68000-series microprocessors ► A type of microprocessor used in Macintosh computers until 1994

Absolute reference ► In a spreadsheet formula, a reference that never changes when the user inserts rows or columns or copies or moves formulas in the spreadsheet

Accelerated graphics cards ► Graphics cards that use special graphics chips to boost performance

Access time ► The average time it takes a computer to locate data on the storage medium and read it

Accumulator ► In the arithmetic logic unit, the component that temporarily holds the result of an arithmetic or logical operation

Active matrix screen ► On a notebook computer, a display screen that utilizes thin film transistor technology to improve speed at which the screen updates the images and the overall quality of the image

ActiveX controls ► Software that adds processing and interactive capabilities to Web pages

Address ► In spreadsheet terminology, the location of a cell, derived from its column and row location

Address lines ► In data transport terminology, the components of the data bus that carry the location of the data being transported, to help the computer find the data that it needs to process

Algorithm ► A set of steps for carrying out a task

Analog device ► A device in which continuously varying data is processed as a continuous stream of varying information

Antivirus program ► See Virus detection program

Application server ► A computer that runs application software and forwards the results of processing to workstations, as requested

Application software ► Computer programs that help the user carry out a specific type of task (word processing, database management, etc.)

Application service provider (ASP) ► Vendors who charge users, generally via a subscription, perhaps as a prearranged contract or on a fee-per-use basis, to use software via a Web site

Application-specific filename extension ► A filename extension that is associated with a specific application and indicates which application was used to create the file

Archiving ► The process of moving data off a primary storage device onto a secondary storage device (such as a backup tape), for permanent storage

Arithmetic logic unit (ALU) ► The part of the central processing unit that performs arithmetic and logical operations

Artificial intelligence (AI) ► The ability of a machine to simulate or surpass intelligent human behavior

ASCII ► American Standard Code for Information Interchange, the data representation code most commonly used on microcomputers

Asynchronous discussion ► In Internet terminology, a discussion in which participants are not online at the same time

Asynchronous Transfer Mode (ATM) ► The small, constant packets allow ATM based on transferring data in packets of a fixed size; the packet is small compared with older technologies equipment to transmit different types of data over the same line, without interfering with one another

Attachment ► A file that is sent through an e-mail system along with an e-mail message

Auditing ► In spreadsheet terminology, testing in order to verify the accuracy of data and formulas

Authentication ► The process of ensuring that a message has been sent by the person who claims to have sent it

Available Bit Rate (ABR) ► provides a guaranteed minimum capacity but allows data to be bursted when the network allows. ATM packets take a fixed route, rather than TCP/IP where each packet can take different routes to the destination

.biz ► A restricted top level domain open for commercial and business purposes for the Web

Backup ► The process of making duplicate copies of data

Backup software ► Computer programs designed to manage hard disk backup to tapes or disks

Bandwidth ► The transmission capacity of a communications channel

Batch file ► A series of operating system commands used to automate tasks

Bays ► Openings in the computer system unit case that allow for the installation of peripherals

Benchmark ► A standard test that measures computer speed for word-processing, graphics, spreadsheet, and database tasks

Binary number system ► Number system used by digital computers to represent data using two digits, 0 and 1 (base 2)

Biometrics ► A method of personal identification that bases identification on a unique physical characteristic, such as a fingerprint

Bit ► The smallest unit of information in a computer system, consisting of a 1 or a 0 that represents data (abbreviation of binary digit)

Bitmap display ► (Also called graphics display) A form of display in which the monitor screen is divided into a matrix of small dots called pixels

Bitmapped image ► An image that is displayed and stored as a collection of individual pixels

Boilerplate ► Standard paragraphs used to create a new document

Block ► (Also called text blocks) Section text in a document that can be cut, copied, or moved

Block operation ► Operation that can be performed on a text block such as cutting, moving, or deleting text within a document

Bluetooth wireless technology ► An open specification for low-cost, personal area network connection among mobile computers, mobile phones and other devices; the Bluetooth wireless technology specification provides secure, radio-based transmission of data and voice; developed by the Bluetooth Special Interest Group - this group was founded in 1998 to define an industry-wide specification for connecting personal and business mobile devices

Bookmarks ► (Also called favorites) A list of your favorite sites, so you can link directly to them instead of entering a URL on the Web; stored as a list on a user's computer by means of Web browser software

Boot process ► The sequence of events that occurs within the computer system between the time the user starts the computer and the time it is ready to process commands

Boot sector viruses ► Computer viruses that infect the system files a user's computer relies on every time it is started up

Bus ► The component of a microcomputer motherboard that transports data between other components on the board

Bus topology ► Network topology that provides a common or shared communications pathway; typically used by cable TV companies

Business software ► Computer programs that help organizations to efficiently accomplish routine professional and clerical tasks

Button ► An area of the screen containing a three-dimensional image (usually square or rectangular) that can be pressed with the mouse pointer to activate a function

Byte ► An eight-bit unit of information, usually representing one character (a letter, punctuation mark, space, or numeral)

Cache ► (Also called RAM cache or cache memory) Special high-speed memory that gives the CPU more rapid access to data

Capacitor ► Electronic circuit component that stores an electrical charge; in binary code, a charged capacitor represents an "on" bit, and a discharged one represents an "off" bit

CD-R (compact disc-recordable) ► Compact discs on which the user can write data

CD-ROM (compact disc read-only memory) ► A high-capacity, optical storage medium

CD-ROM drive ► A storage device that uses laser technology to read data from a CD-ROM

CD-RW (compact disc-rewritable) ► Compact discs on which the user can write data and then change the data using special phase change technology

Cell ► In spreadsheet terminology, the intersection of a column and a row

Cell reference ► A letter/number combination that indicates the position of a cell in a spreadsheet

Central processing unit (CPU) ► The main control unit in a computer, consisting of circuitry that executes instructions to process data

Character ► A letter, numeral, space, punctuation mark, or other symbol, consisting of one byte of information

Character data ► Letters, symbols, or numerals that will not be used in arithmetic operations (name, social security number, etc.)

Character-based display ► Method of display in which the monitor screen is divided into a grid of rectangles, each of which can display a single character from the standard character set

Chat group ► A discussion in which a group of people communicate online simultaneously

Chip ► See Integrated circuit

Client/server architecture ▸ A network architecture in which processing is split between workstations (clients) and the server

Cluster ▸ (1) A group of sectors on a storage disk

Cluster ▸ (2) A group of workstations that share a server or group of servers. They can share work and provide back-ups in case of failures of any of the connected servers.

CMOS memory (complementary metal oxide semiconductor) ▸ A type of semiconductor that holds data and requires very little power to retain its contents

Coaxial cable ▸ A type of cable in which a center wire is surrounded by a grounded shield of braided wire; typically used to send cable television signals; used in connecting nodes on a network with silver BNC connectors on both ends

Columns ▸ In document production terminology, newspaper-style layout of paragraphs of text; in spreadsheet terminology, a vertical arrangement of items within a grid

Color depth ▸ The number of colors that can be present on the screen at any one time

Command ▸ An instruction that the user inputs into the computer to tell it to carry out a task

Command-line user interface ▸ An interface that requires the user to type in commands

Commercial software ▸ Software produced by manufacturers to be sold to consumers

Communication medium ▸ The hardware that carries one or more communications channels and provides a link between transmitting and receiving devices

Communications protocol ▸ A set of rules that ensures the orderly and accurate transmission and reception of data

Communications software ▸ Computer programs that interact with a computer's modem to dial up and establish a connection with a remote computer

Compatible ▸ In computer terminology, able to operate using the same format, commands, or languages

Competitive upgrade ▸ A special price offered to consumers who switch from one company's software product to the new version of the competitor's products

Complex instruction set computer (CISC) ▸ A computer based on a CPU with a lengthy, intricate set of instructions that take several clock cycles to execute

Compression software ▸ Software that effectively reduces the size of text and BMP files, such as WinZip and PKZip

Computer ▸ A device that accepts input, processes data, and produces output

Computer literacy ▸ The basic understanding of what a computer is, what it does, and why computers are important to your society

Computer network ▸ A collection of computers and related devices, connected in a way that allows them to share data, hardware, and software

Computer program ▸ A set of detailed, step-by-step instructions that tells a computer how to solve a problem or carry out a task

Computer programming language ▸ A standardized set of specific English-like phrases or predefined instructions used for writing computer programs

Computer system ▸ A collection of hardware, peripheral devices, and software connected in a way that allows a user to input, process, store, and output data

Computer virus ▸ A program designed to attach itself to a file, reproduce, and spread from one file to another, destroying data, displaying an irritating message, or otherwise disrupting computer operations

Computer-assisted instruction ▸ The use of computers to teach concepts, reinforce lecture presentations, deliver information, and test mastery of material

Computer-based tutorials ▸ On-screen displays of step-by-step instructions

Concordance ▸ An alphabetized list of works in a document and the frequency with which each word appears, used to perform literary analysis

Concurrent-use license ▸ Legal permission for an organization to use a certain number of copies of a software program at the same time

Connectivity software ▸ Computer programs that connect a computer to a local computer network or to the Internet and provide the user with tools to access the information it offers

Connection speed ▸ The maximum sped at which your modem can communicate with the modems maintained by your ISP

Constant Bit Rate (CBR) ▸ A fixed bit rate so that data is sent in a steady stream

Control unit ▸ The part of the ALU that directs and coordinates processing

Controller ▸ A circuit board in a hard drive that positions the disk and read-write heads to locate data

Controller card ▸ A circuit board that plugs into an expansion slot in the computer and provides the I/O circuitry for a peripheral device

Cookie ▸ In Internet technology, a message sent from a Web server to your browser and stored on your hard disk that records what data your computer is accessing and what data is requested during a session

Copy Disk ▸ A utility program that duplicates an entire floppy disk

Copy utility ▸ A program that copies one or more files

Copyright ▸ A form of legal protection that grants certain exclusive rights to the author of a program or the owner of the copyright

Copyright Act ▸ Laws that protect copyright; Sections 106 and 117 of the 1980 U.S Copyright Act states under what circumstance you can and cannot legally copy copyright software

Copyright infringement ▸ A violation of the exclusive right of a creator to a copyrighted work

Copyright notices ▸ Words or symbols used to inform the public that a work is copyrighted (after 1976, such notices were no longer required to preserve copyright)

CPU ▸ See Central processing unit

Cryptography ▸ The science of encoding and decoding information

Cursor ▸ A symbol that marks the user's place on the screen and shows where typing will appear

Cyberspace ▸ A term coined in 1984 by writer William Gibson to describe a computer-generated conceptual environment shared among computers; it has come to refer to the interconnected communication networks across the Web

Cylinder ▸ A vertical stack of tracks on a hard disk

Cypherpunks ▸ Individuals who campaign against the government's desire to eavesdrop on private digital communications, which they view as a threat to personal freedom

Cyphertext ▸ Encrypted plaintext

Darwin ▸ The core of the MAC OS X; the source code for Darwin is freely available through Apple's public source projects

Data ▸ The words, numbers, and graphics that describe people, events, things and ideas

Data access software ▸ The interface used to search for information in a database

Data bus ▸ An electronic pathway or circuit by means of which data travels from one location to another within a computer

Data file ▸ A file containing words, numbers, and/or pictures that the user can view, edit, save, send, and/or print

Data lines ▸ The wires in the data bus that carry the signals that represent data

Data management software ▸ Computer programs that help the user store, find, update, organize, and report information

Data security ▸ Techniques that provide protection for data

Database ▸ A collection of information stored on one or more computers

Database software ▸ (Also called database management software) Computer programs that provide tools for manipulating information stored in a database

Decryption ▸ The process of decoding data

Dedicated file server ▸ A file server devoted solely to the task of distributing resources to workstations

Default drive ▸ The drive that a computer system will attempt to read from or write to unless an alternate drive is specified

Defragmentation utility ▸ A tool used to rearrange the files on a disk so that they are stored in contiguous clusters

Dense Wave Division Multiplexing (DWDM) ▸ A fiber optic transmission technique that employ light wavelengths to transmit data parallel by bit or serial by character; DWDM provides multiple channels over fiber optics using different wavelengths of light

Desktop metaphor ▸ A graphical interface in which the icons resemble items commonly found in an office

Desktop microcomputer ▸ A computer that is built around a single microprocessor chip and is small enough to fit on a desk

Desktop publishing software ▸ Computer programs that combine graphics and word-processing tools to allow the user to create documents

Desktop video ▸ Images that are captured by a digital video camera or have been converted into digital format from a video tape

Device driver ▸ The software that provides the computer with the means to control a peripheral device

Device letter ▸ Used to identify storage devices or drives, usually followed by a colon

Dialog box ▸ A type of on-screen display, in the form of a window, that provides options associated with a command

Dial-up connection ▸ A connection that uses a phone line to establish a temporary Internet connection

Dial-up networking ▸ The use of a phone connection to access a network server

Differential backup ▸ A copy of all the files that have changed since the last full backup of a disk

Digital animation ▸ Video that is created "from scratch" with the help of computers, not footage of real objects

Digital camera ▸ A camera that records an image in such a way that special digitizing software and hardware can convert the image into a signal that the computer can store and transmit

Digital certificate ▸ A security method that identifies the author of an ActiveX control

Digital device ▸ A device that works with discrete numbers or digits

Digital divide ▸ The difference in rates of access to computers and the Internet among different demographic groups.

Digital signature ▸ An electronic method of signing a message, to assist in authentication

Digital video ▸ Video and animation that is based on footage from real objects

Digitized sound files ▸ Sound recordings that have been converted into a form that can be stored on a computer disk

Digitizing ▸ The process of converting videos or continuous sound or images into a format that can be stored on a computer disk

Direct access ▸ (Also called random access) The ability of a drive to move to any sector of a disk

Direct source input device ▸ A device that collects data directly from a document or object such as a bar code reader

Directory ▸ A list of files contained on a computer disk

Discussion group ▸ Online communications involving multiple participants sharing views on a specific issue or topic

Disk cache ▸ Part of RAM used to temporarily hold information read from a disk, speeding up processing

Disk density ▸ The size of the magnetic particles on the disk surface

Distribution disks ▸ Disks on which computer software is supplied to users

Distribution right ▸ The exclusive right to distribute copies or recordings of a copyrighted work to the public

Docking station ▸ An expansion bus into which the user can plug a notebook computer

Document production software ▸ Computer programs that assist the user in composing, editing, designing, and printing documents

Domain name ▸ An identifying name by which host computers on the Internet are familiarly known (for example, cocacola.com)

Domain name system ▸ The numeric system of assigning Internet Protocol (IP) addresses to host computers on the Internet

DOS ▸ Disk Operating System

DOS prompt ▸ A symbol indicating that DOS is ready to accept a command

Dot matrix printer ▸ A printer that creates characters and graphics by striking an inked ribbon with small wires called "pins," generating a fine pattern of dots

Dot pitch ▸ A measure of image clarity

Double-click ▸ To click the mouse button twice in rapid succession

Double-density (DD) disk ▸ A type of floppy disk that increased the density of data that could be stored to 360 KB, which was twice the density of the previous generation of disks

Double-sided disk (DS) ▸ A floppy disk that stores data on both the top and bottom sides of the disk

Downloading ▸ The process of transferring a copy of a file from a remote computer to another computer's disk drive

Downwardly compatible ▸ In reference to operating systems, able to use application software designed for earlier versions of the operating system, but not those designed for later versions

Drag, Dragging ▸ Placing the mouse pointer over an object, holding down the mouse button, moving the mouse pointer to a new location, and releasing the mouse button, in order to move an object to a new location

Drive hub ▸ The component of the floppy disk that the disk drive engages in order to rotate the disk

Drive spindle ▸ The component of the hard drive that supports one or more hard disk platters

Drop-down list ▸ A list of options that is displayed when the user clicks an arrow button

Dual-pipeline architecture ▸ A type of microprocessor chip design in which the chip can execute two instructions at one time

DVD disk (digital video disk) ▸ A variation of CD-ROM technology, a high-capacity optical disk designed to store full-length movies

DVD drive ▸ Storage device that uses laser technology to read DVD disks

DVD-ROM ▸ Storage technology ideally suited for distributing large multimedia applications such as games, encyclopedias, maps, and telephone number databases

DVD-RW ▸ Storage technology that makes it possible to write data on DVD disk by using phase change technology similar to CD-RW

EBCDIC (extended binary-coded decimal interchange code) ▸ A method by which digital computers represent character data

E-commerce ▸ Buying products and services by means of the Internet, encompasses online shopping, applies to innovative auction sites, and includes stock trading; many Web hosting services and portal sites offer an e-commerce enabled Web site

Education and training software ▸ Computer programs that help the user learn and perfect new skills

Edutainment software ▸ Computer programs that combine elements of game software and education software

EIDE (enhanced integrated device electronics) ▸ A type of drive that features high storage capacity and fast data transfer

Electronic mail (e-mail) ▸ Correspondence sent from one person to another electronically

Electronic mail system ▸ The hardware and software that collect and deliver e-mail messages

Electronic publishing ▸ The manipulation, storage, and transmission of electronic documents by means of electronic media or telecommunications services

E-mail address ▸ A person's network user ID, an @ symbol, and the name of his or her e-mail server

E-mail attachment ▸ A file such as a document, worksheet, or graphic that travels through the e-mail system along with the e-mail message

E-mail message ▸ A typed message or image sent electronically from one user to another

E-mail software ▸ Computer programs that manage the user's computer mailbox

E-mail system ▸ The hardware and software that collects and delivers e-mail messages

E-mail server software ▸ The software on the network server that controls the flow of e-mail

E-mail client software ▸ The software on a workstation that helps each user read, compose, send, and delete messages

E-mail servers ▸ The computers that store and forward e-mail

Encryption ▸ The process of scrambling or hiding information so that it cannot be understood without the key necessary to change it back into its original form

Enum (electronic number) ▸ The technology that would enable a person to be reached on any number of devices – telephone, pager, email, instant messenger, or any other form of electronic communication – simply by typing one number on the Internet

Error message ▸ A statement that appears on the computer screen, indicating that the user has made a mistake

Exabyte ▸ A quintillion (1018) bytes

Executable file ▸ A file that contains the instructions that tell a compute how to perform a specific task

Expansion board ▸ See Expansion card

Expansion bus ▸ The segment of the data bus that transports data between RAM and peripheral devices

Expansion card ▸ (Also called controller card) A circuit board that plugs into an expansion slot in the computer and provides the I/O circuitry for a peripheral device

Expansion port ▸ A socket on the expansion card into which the user plugs a cable from a peripheral device, allowing data to pass between the computer and the peripheral device

Expansion slot ▸ A socket into which the user can plug a small circuit board called an expansion card

Export data ▸ Move or copy data from one application program to import it for use in another application program

External bay ▸ An opening in the computer case that allows the user to install a device that must be accessed from outside the case

FAT (file allocation table) ▸ The file structure used by DOS to store information on disks

Fiber-optic cable ▸ A bundle of extremely thin tubes of glass; each tube, called an optical fiber; usually consists of a strong inner support wire; multiple strands of optical fiber, each covered by a plastic insulator; and a tough outer covering

File ▸ A named collection of program instructions or data that exists on a storage medium such as a hard disk, floppy disk, CD-ROM, or DVD

File management software ▸ Computer programs that help the user organize records, find records that match specific criteria, and print lists based on the information contained in records

File specification ▸ A combination of the drive letter, subdirectory, and filename and extension that identifies a file

Filename ▸ A unique set of letters and numbers that identifies a file

Filename extension ▸ A set of three letters and/or numbers added to the end of a filename to assist in identifying the nature of the file

Filenaming conventions ▸ Specific rules followed in establishing a filename (for example, file.doc to indicate that a file is a document)

Firewall ▸ A system that blocks Internet traffic based on specific criteria

Flash memory ▸ A solid state (no moving parts) easy and fast storage device used for digital cameras, video games, and computer BIOS chips

Flat-faced monitors ▸ Have less glare and images have a more realistic flatter appearance, however, they are more expensive and some believe that the square monitors have an edge in sharpness; resolution for flat-faced monitors should be at least 1024×768, but many of these monitors display 1280×1024.

Floppy disk ▸ A portable magnetic storage medium

Floppy disk drive ▸ A storage device that writes data on and reads data from floppy disks

Folder ▸ A subdirectory (a subdivision of a directory)

Font ▸ A typeface or style of lettering

Footer ▸ Text that appears in the bottom margin of each page of a document

Formula ▸ A combination of numbers and symbols that tells the computer how to use the contents of cells in calculations

Fragmented ▸ When data in a file is stored in noncontiguous clusters

Frame ▸ An outline or boundary, frequently defining a box; a predefined area into which text or graphics may be placed

Freeware ▸ Software that the creator has either committed to the public domain or has elected to allow users to copy, use, and distribute without compensation

Free-form database ▸ A loosely structured collection of information, usually stored as documents rather than as records

FTP (File Transfer Protocol) server ▸ A computer that maintains a collection of data that can be transferred over the Internet

FTP client software ▸ Special software that allows a user to upload files

Full backup ▸ A copy of all the files on a disk

Function keys ▸ The keys numbered F1 through F12 and located at the top of the computer keyboard that activate program-specific commands

Fuzzy logic ▸ A method of logic that allows a computer to express and process statements that incorporate ambiguity

Gateway ▶ An electronic link that connects one e-mail system to other e-mail systems

GB ▶ See Gigabyte

Generic filename extension ▶ A filename extension that indicates the type of data that a file contains, but does not tell the user which software application was used to create the file

Genetic algorithms ▶ Rules of inference that adapt and develop in a manner imitating the processes of Darwinian evolution

Generic filename extension ▶ A filename extension that indicates the general type of data contained in the file, usually means you can open it with one of many application software packages

Gigabyte (GB) ▶ Approximately one billion bytes

Grammar checker ▶ Feature of most word processors used to coach and correct sentence structure and word usage

Graffiti ▶ A digital shorthand that converts movement on the screen into text used to enter data with a stylus into a PDA

Graphical object ▶ A small picture on the computer screen that the user can manipulate using a mouse or other input device

Graphical user interface ▶ (GUI) Images on the screen that provide the user with a means of accessing program features and functions by means of a mouse or other input device

Graphics ▶ Visual images such as pictures and illustrations

Graphics card ▶ (Also called a video display adapter or video card) An expansion card used to connect a monitor and a computer, to allow the computer to send visual information to the monitor

Graphics software ▶ Computer programs that help the user create, edit, and manipulate images

Graphing software ▶ Computer programs that transform complex data into a visual format,

Groupware ▶ Software that provides ways for multiple users to collaborate on a project, usually through a pool of data that can be shared by members of the workgroup

Hackers ▶ (Also called crackers or cyberpunks) Vandals who damage, destroy, alter, and/or steal data

Hard disk ▶ One or more hard disk platters and their associated read-write heads (often used synonymously with hard disk drive)

Hard disk drive ▶ An electronic storage device containing a nonremovable disk platter

Hard disk platter ▶ The component of the hard disk drive on which data is stored, a flat, rigid disk made of aluminum or glass and coated with a magnetic oxide

Hardware ▶ The electric, electronic, and mechanical devices used for processing data (See also specific hardware)

Hardware redundancy ▶ Maintaining equipment that duplicates the functions of equipment critical to computing activities

Hash function ▶ An algorithm used in creating a digital signature

Head ▶ The part of an HTML document that specifies the title that appears on the title bar of a Web browser when a Web page is displayed

Head crash ▶ A collision between the read-write head and the surface of the hard disk platter, resulting in damage to some of the data on the disk

Header ▶ Text that appears in the top margin of each page of a document

Header label ▶ An initial component of a record stored on magnetic tape, which signals the beginning of a file

High-density (HD) disk ▶ A floppy disk that can store more data than a double-density disk

Hierarchy ▶ An organization of things that are ranked one above the other

Home page ▶ The first page that comes up when a Web site is accessed; it identifies the site and contains links to other pages at the site

Horizontal market software ▶ Any computer program that can be used by many different kinds of businesses

Host computer ▶ A central minicomputer or mainframe to which multiple terminals are attached; all processing takes place on the host computer; in Internet terminology, any computer connected to the Internet

Hotsync ▶ A device that attaches through cable connection to a computer for synchronizing data between a personal digital assistant and the computer

HTML (Hypertext Markup Language) document ▶ A document that contains special instructions that tell a Web browser how to display the text, graphics, and background of a Web page

HTML authoring tools ▶ Software that facilitates the creation of Web pages by means of word-processor style interfaces

HTML tags ▶ The instructions used by an HTML document to display information to a Web browser

HTTP (HyperText Transfer Protocol) ▶ An identifier that appears at the beginning of each Web page URL

Hypermedia ▶ A type of multimedia hypertext that involves graphics, sound, and video, as well as text

Hypertext ▶ In multimedia computer applications, a component in which documents are linked to each other

Hypertext index ▶ A screen-based menu that allows the user to access information in specific categories by clicking a hypertext link

.info ▶ A new unrestricted top level domain for the Web

I/O (Input/Output) ▶ The collection of data for the microprocessor to manipulate, and the transportation of the results to display, print, or storage devices

IC ▶ See Integrated circuit

ICANN (Internet Corporation for Assigned Named and Numbers) ▶ The non-profit corporation that was assigned the responsibility for IP addresses and domain name system management.

Icon ▶ A small picture on a computer screen that represents an object

IEEE Standard 802. 11b ▶ Establishes wireless network speed, which can reach up to 11Mbps (depending on distance from base unit) and lets your laptop hook up to your Ethernet wirelessly

Importing ▶ The process by which a program reads and translates data from another source

Incremental backup ▶ A copy of the files that have changed since the last backup

Inference engine ▶ A program that directs a computer to evaluate facts according to a specific set of rules, in order to solve problems, make decisions, or direct actions

Information ▶ The words, numbers, and graphics used as the basis for human actions and decisions

Information and reference software ▶ Computer programs that provide the user with a collection of information and the means to access that information

Infrared transmissions ▶ Communications networks that use a frequency range just below the visible light spectrum to transport data

Ink-jet printer ▶ A printer that creates characters and graphics by spraying ink onto paper

In-line spell checker ▶ A program that shows the user spelling errors, as the user types

In-place multimedia technology ▶ An Internet multimedia technology that plays a media element as part of a Web page

Input device ▶ A tool that gathers input and translates it into a form that the computer can process

Insertion point ▶ A flashing vertical bar that appears on the screen, indicating where the user can begin entering text

Installation process ▶ In reference to software, the process by which programs and data are copied to the hard disk of a computer system

Instruction cycle ▶ The process by which a computer executes a single instruction

Instruction pointer ▶ The location where the RAM address of an instruction is kept

Instruction register ▶ A location in memory where the control unit puts an instruction retrieved from RAM

Instruction set ▶ The list of instructions that a CPU carries out

Integrated circuit (IC) ▶ (Also called chips and microchips) A thin slice of crystal containing microscopic circuit elements such as transistors, wires, capacitors, and resistors (See also Microprocessors)

Internal bay ▶ A location inside the system unit case where devices that do not need to be accessed from outside the case can be installed

Internet ▶ A collection of local, regional, national and international computer networks that are linked together to exchange data and distribute processing tasks

Internet backbone ▶ The group of major Internet communication links

Internet communications software ▶ Computer programs that allow a computer to transmit and receive data using the Internet TCP/IP communications protocol

Internet mail address ▶ An identifier, consisting of a user ID and the user's mail server domain name, required to send e-mail over the Internet

Internet Relay Chat (IRC) ▶ The technology that makes text chat possible

Internet service provider (ISP) ▶ A company that provides Internet access to businesses, organizations, and individuals

Internetwork or internet ▶ Two or more connected networks

InterNIC (Internet Network Information Center) ▶ The organization that processes requests for IP addresses and domain names

Internet traffic ▶ The number of bytes transmitted from one Internet host computer to another

Intranet ▶ An infrastructure using Web technology that businesses use for internal communication

IP address ▶ A set of four numbers between 0 and 255 that are separated by periods that creates a unique identifying number assigned to each computer connected to the Internet

Java ▶ A programming language developed for Web applications

Java applets ▶ Small programs that add processing and interactive capabilities to Web pages

Java scripts ▶ Special programs that create animation, moving text, or other creative interfaces that enhance Web pages

Jaz disk drive ▶ A high capacity disk drive with removable disks used for backup

Justification ▶ Defines how letters and words are spaced across each line

Key length ▶ The number of characters that make up a key

Keyboard ▶ An arrangement of letter, number, and special function keys that acts as the primary input device to the computer

Keyboard shortcut ▶ A combination of keys that allows the user to activate a program function without clicking a series of menu options

Keyword search engine ▶ A means of accessing data about a particular subject, by searching for a significant word relevant to that subject

Kilobyte (KB) ▶ Approximately one thousand bytes

Laser printer ▶ A printer that uses laser-based technology, similar to that used by photocopiers, to produce text and graphics

LAN (local area network) ▶ Defined as a group of computers and associated devices that share a common communications line, such as a cable, and share the resources of a single processor or server within a small geographic area, such as an office building or school

LCD projection panel ▶ A device placed on an overhead projector to produce a large display of information shown on a computer screen

Level 2 cache ▶ In the Pentium Pro, memory circuitry housed off the processor on a separate chip

License ▶ The right to use software in return for the payment of a fee

Links ▶ (Also called hypertext links or hyperlinks) Underlined areas of text that allow users to jump between hypertext documents

Linux ▶ A free Unix-type operating system that was originally developed by Linus Torvalds under the GNU General Public License; the source code for Linux is distributed freely and has been available to anyone who wants it

Liquid crystal display (LCD) ▶ A type of flat panel computer screen, commonly found on notebook computers, in which light passes through a thin layer of liquid crystal cells, to produce an image

Local resources ▶ The peripherals such as a hard drive, software, data, and printer attached to an individual user's workstation on a network

Locked file ▶ Status of a file that is being used by one user on a network that keeps other users on the network from accessing it

Low-earth orbit (LEO) ▶ Orbit for many recent telecommunications satellites— about 1,000 miles above the earth; LEO satellites do not stay in the same location above the earth

Logic bomb ▶ A computer program that is triggered by the appearance or disappearance of specific data

Logical storage ▶ A conceptual model of the way data is stored

Mac OS Macintosh operating system ▶ A GUI-interface-based operating system developed by Apple Computer, Inc.

Macro virus ▶ A computer virus that infects documents such as those created with a word processor

Magnetic storage ▶ The recording of data onto disks or tape by magnetizing particles of an oxide-based surface coating

Magnetic surface ▶ The oxide-based surface coating of a magnetic storage disk or tape

Mail client software ▶ The software on a workstation that helps a user read, compose, send, and delete e-mail messages

Mail merge ▶ A software application that automates the process of producing customized documents such as letters

Mail server software ▶ The software on the network server that controls the flow of e-mail

Mailbox ▶ A term for the area on a host computer or network server where e-mail is stored

Main board ▶ See Motherboard

Mainframes ▶ Large, fast computers generally used by businesses or the government to provide centralized storage processing and management for large amounts of data

Mapping ▶ In network terminology, assigning a drive letter to a network server disk drive

Marketing tiers ▶ Categories of companies that market or sell computer hardware or software

Marketing outlets ▶ (Also called marketing channels) The means by which hardware and software are sold, include computer retail stores, mail order suppliers, value added resellers (VARs), and manufacturer direct sales

Mean time between failures (MTBF) ▶ A measurement of reliability that is applied to computer components

Media player ▶ Software that is provided with Windows and that includes controls to start, stop, and rewind media file types such as sound files with .wav extensions and videos with .avi extensions

Megabyte (MB) ▶ Approximately one million bytes

Megahertz (MHz) ▶ Millions of cycles per second; a measurement of the speed at which a computer can execute an instruction

Memory ▶ The area in a computer that holds data waiting to be processed

Menu ▶ A list of commands or options

Menu bar ▶ A list of menu titles

Menu item ▶ (Also called a menu option) A choice listed on a menu

Microcomputer ▶ (Also called a personal computer, or PC) A small computer incorporating a single microprocessor chip

Microprocessor ▶ The component of a microcomputer motherboard that contains the circuitry that performs arithmetic and logical operations

Microsoft Windows 3.1 ▶ An operating system that provides a GUI interface

Microwave ▶ An electromagnetic wave with a frequency of at least 1 gigahertz (GHz); data converted into microwaves can be sent over a microwave link

Microwave transmissions ▶ A method of sending data converted to microwaves through a high-frequency signal from a transmitting station to a receiving station that cannot be more than 25 or 30 miles away

Middleware ▶ Specialized networked services that are shared by applications and users, middleware evolved to include a variety of technologies that support and integrate applications

MIDI (musical instrument digital interface) sound ▶ Sound encoded by one of two MIDI standards, FM synthesis or wave table synthesis

Millisecond (ms) ▶ A thousandth of a second

Minicomputer ▶ A midrange computer, which is more powerful than a microcomputer that can carry out processing tasks for many users simultaneously

Modem ▶ A device that sends and receives data to and from computers over telephone lines

Modem card ▶ An interface card used to connect a computer to the telephone system in order to transport data from one computer to another over phone lines

Monitor ▶ A display device that forms an image by converting electrical signals from the computer into points of colored light on the screen

Motherboard ▶ The circuit board in the computer that houses the chips that control the processing functions

Mouse ▶ An input device and pointer that allows the user to manipulate objects on the screen

Multimedia ▶ An integrated collection of computer-based media, including text, graphics, sound, animation, photo images, and video

Multimedia encyclopedia ▶ Encyclopedia on CD-ROM that can include text, graphics, sound, animation, photo images, and video

Multimedia overlay technology ▶ An Internet multimedia technology that adds a separate window in which multimedia elements appear

Multiple-user license ▶ Legal permission for more than one than one person to use a particular software package

Multitasking ▶ Running two or more programs at the same time

Mylar disk ▶ Material used in manufacturing magnetic storage media

Natural language ▶ A language spoken by human beings as opposed to an artificially constructed language such as machine language

Natural selection ▶ A process in which species become better adapted to their environment over time

NetBIOS/NetBEUI (NetBIOS Extended User Interface) ▶ A Microsoft network protocol, shipped with the Windows operating system

Network ▶ A group of connected computers that allow users to share information

Network access points (NAPs) ▶ Communication links for Internet data interconnect at several points called network access points so data can travel between network service providers

Network administrator ▶ (Also called network supervisor) The person responsible for setting up user accounts and maintaining a network

Network cables ▶ The hardware that provides the physical connections or communications channels for the computers in a network

Network-centric computing ▶ Data is stored on central servers

Network client software ▶ Programs that are installed on the local hard drive of each workstation and act as a device driver for the network interface card

Network Drives ▶ Drives that are directly connected to your LAN and are accessible from all computers on the LAN

Network hardware ▶ The equipment that directs the flow of data over the network cables

Network hub ▶ A device that joins communication lines together on most of today's networks

Network interface card (NIC) ▶ A small circuit board that is designed to plug into an expansion slot on a computer motherboard that sends data from a workstation out over the network, and collects incoming data for the workstation; a notebook computer NIC is usually on a PCMCIA card

Network license ▶ Legal permission for the use of a software program by multiple users on a network

Network operating system (NOS) ▶ Programs designed to control the flow of data, maintain security, and keep track of accounts on a network

Network printer ▶ A printer on a network to which all network users can send output from their workstations

Network resources ▶ Peripherals and application software available to users through a central server on a network

Network server ▶ A computer connected to a network that "serves," or distributes, resources to the network users

Network server software ▶ Programs installed on a file server that control file access from the server hard drive, manage the print queue, and track user data such as IDs and passwords

Network service provider (NSP) ▶ A company that maintains a series of nationwide Internet links

Nondedicated file server (peer-to-peer architecture) ▶ A network computer that acts as both a server and a workstation

Notebook computer ▶ A small, lightweight portable computer

Numeric analysis software ▶ Computer programs that simplify the tasks of constructing and analyzing numeric models

Numeric data ▶ Numbers that represent quantities and can be used in arithmetic operations

Numeric keypad ▶ A calculator-style input device for entering numbers and arithmetic symbols

Office Suite ▶ A number of applications that are packaged and sold as a unit

Op code ▶ (short for operation code) A command word designating an operation, such as add, compare, or jump

Open source development ▸ The source code for a computer software package is freely available

Operand ▸ The part of an instruction that specifies the data, or the address of the data, on which the operation is to be performed

Operating system ▸ The software that controls the computer's use of its hardware resources, such as memory and disk storage space

Operator error ▸ A mistake made by a computer user

Optical storage ▸ A means of recording data in which the data is burned into the storage medium, using laser beams (See also CD-ROM disks)

Option buttons ▸ Buttons that allow the user to select one of two or more options in a dialog box

Organic light emitting diode (OLED) ▸ A low-energy display technology that allows brighter displays at lower costs

Orthogonal frequency division multiplexing (OFDM) ▸ A method of digital modulation in which a signal is split into several narrowband channels at different frequencies; currently, **OFDM** is used in European digital audio broadcast serves and is being considered for digital television transmission.

Outline feature ▸ A feature in some word processing programs that helps users develop a document as a hierarchy of headings and subheadings

Output ▸ The results produced by a computer (for example, reports, graphs, and music) (See also Input/output)

Output device ▸ A computer peripheral that displays, prints, or transfers the results of processing from the computer memory

Packet switching ▸ Technology that divides a message into smaller units called packets; each packet in one message is addressed to the same destination, but one packet can travel a different route over the network than other packets

Palm-top computer ▸ See Personal digital assistant

Parallel processing ▸ A technique by which two or more processors in a computer perform processing tasks simultaneously

Passive matrix screen ▸ A display found on older notebook computers

Password ▸ A special set of symbols used to restrict access to a user's computer

Payload ▸ The disruptive instructions delivered by a computer virus

PCMCIA (Personal Computer Memory Card International Association) cards ▸ Credit-card-sized circuit boards that consists of an expansion card and a built-in peripheral device

PCMCIA slot ▸ A small external expansion slot, found on notebook computers, into which a PCMCIA card can be inserted

Peer-to-peer architecture ▸ See Nondedicated file server

Pentium ▸ A recent Intel microprocessor in the x86 family

Pentium II ▸ A version of the Pentium Pro chip with added MMX technology, which is designed to speed up the execution of multimedia applications

Pentium Pro ▸ An Intel chip that is optimized for the 32-bit instruction set

Peripheral devices ▸ Components that expand the computer's input, output, and storage capabilities

Personal computers ▸ Microcomputers based on the architecture of the first IBM microcomputers

Personal digital assistant (PDA) ▸ (Also called a palm-top computer) A computer that is smaller and more portable than a notebook computer

Personal firewall software ▸ Computer programs that protect a computer from harmful Java applets and ActiveX controls

Personalization technology ▸ Today's Web applications include personalization technology, which allows for

e-mail marketing and customized content; personalization technology is built around collaborative filtering and rules-based matching capabilities

Phase change technology ▸ Technology that alters the crystal structure of a compact discs so the user can write data and then change the data on a CD-R, CD-RW, DVD-R, and DVD-RW

Physical storage ▸ The manner in which data is stored on a physical disk

Pipelining ▸ A technology that allows a processor to begin executing an instruction before completing the previous instruction

Pirated software ▸ Software that has been illegally copied, distributed, or modified

Pixels ▸ Small dots of light that compose the images displayed on the computer screen

Plaintext ▸ Data that has not been encrypted

Plotter ▸ A peripheral device that uses pens to draw an image on paper

Plug-and-Play ▸ A feature of some peripheral devices that allows them to be automatically installed by operating systems such as Windows 95

Point to Point Protocol (PPP) ▸ A version of TCP/IP software designed to handle Internet communications over dial-up connections

Pointer ▸ A symbol on the computer screen, usually shaped like an arrow, whose movement corresponds to the movement of the user's mouse

Pointing device ▸ An instrument such as a mouse, track-ball, or light pen, that allows the user to manipulate on-screen objects and select menu options

Polymorphic viruses ▸ Computer viruses that change, in order to avoid detection, after they infect a computer system

Port ▸ A socket on a computer into which a cable from a peripheral device can be plugged

Port replicator ▸ A device that connects to a notebook computer, by means of a bus connector plug, and contains a duplicate of the notebook computer's ports for connecting devices such as an external monitor, mouse, or keyboard

POST ▸ See Power-on self-test

Power failure ▸ A complete loss of power to the computer system

Power spike ▸ A sudden increase of power that lasts less than a millionth of a second

Power surge ▸ A sudden increase of power that lasts a few millionths of a second

Power strip ▸ A device that contains multiple outlets for power plugs like a surge strip, but does not contain the electronics necessary to filter out power spikes and surges

Power-on self-test (POST) ▸ A diagnostic process that runs during startup to check components of the computer such as the graphics card, RAM, keyboard, and disk drives

PowerPC microprocessor ▸ A microprocessor used in recent models of Macintosh computers that implements RISC architecture to provide faster performance

Presentation software ▸ Computer programs that provide the user with the tools to combine text, graphics, graphs, animation, and/or sound into a series of electronic displays that can be output as overhead transparencies, paper copies, or 35-millimeter slides

Pretty Good Privacy (PGP) ▸ A popular public key encryption system

Print job ▸ A file sent to the printer

Print queue ▸ A special holding area on a network server where files are stored until they are printed

Print server ▸ A server that stores files in a print queue, and sends each queued file to the network printer

Printed tutorial ▸ A book or manual that provides step-by-step lessons about computer hardware and software

Private key ▸ The key used to decrypt cyphertext in public-key cryptography

Process ▸ A systematic series of actions that a computer performs, in order to manipulate data

Productivity software ▸ Computer programs that help the user work more effectively

Productivity paradox ▸ A phenomenon described by economists that refers to the discrepancy between increasing technology and decreasing work productivity

Programs ▸ Instructions and associated data, stored in electronic format, that direct the computer to accomplish a task

Prompt ▸ A message displayed on the computer screen that asks for input from the user

Prompted dialog ▸ A simulated conversation between a user and a computer, in which the computer's responses consist of a series of prompts

Public domain ▸ A term used to indicate that the copyright on a work has expired and that it can be used or copied without fear of infringing the copyright

Public domain software ▸ Software that can be freely used by anyone, either because it has not been copyrighted, or because the author has made it available for public use

Public key ▸ The key used to encrypt plaintext in public-key cryptography

Public key encryption ▸ An encryption method that uses a pair of keys, a public key (known to everyone) that encrypts the message, and a private key (known only to the recipient) that decrypts it

Pull technology ▸ An Internet multimedia technology in which a Web browser is used to request Web pages and "pull" them into view on a user's computer screen

Push technology ▸ An Internet multimedia technology in which the user downloads special push plug-in software that allows a Web site to send the user information without a direct request having been received

QIC (quarter-inch cartridge) ▸ A cartridge tape that measures a quarter of an inch wide, and is used by microcomputer tape drives

Query by example (QBE) ▸ A type of database interface in which the user fills in a field with information related to the desired information, in order to initiate a search

Query language ▸ A set of command words that the user uses to direct the computer to create databases, locate information, sort records, and change the data in those records

RAID (Redundant Array of Independent Disks) ▸ Storage options that provide fault tolerance and increased performance; originally RAID was used for servers only, but now it can be used as disk storage; RAID comes in 9 levels.

RAM address ▸ An identifying value associated with each bank of capacitors that holds information in RAM

RAM cache ▸ See Cache

Random access ▸ See Direct access

Random access memory (RAM) ▸ Memory that temporarily holds data that is being processed

Readability formulas ▸ A feature in most grammar checkers that counts the number of words in each sentence and the number of syllables per word to determine the reading level of the passage being checked; helps the user to write at a level appropriate for a particular target audience

Read-only ▸ An indication that a computer can retrieve data from a storage medium such as a CD-ROM but cannot write new data onto it

Read-only memory (ROM) ► A set of chips containing permanent, nonchangeable instructions that help a computer prepare for processing tasks

Read-write head ► The component of a disk drive that magnetizes particles on the storage disk surface in order to encode data

Real-time clock ► In a computer system, a battery-powered clock chip that maintains the current date and time

Redundancy ► The storage of duplicate data in more than one location for protection against media failure

Reference manuals ► Books or online resources that describe the features of a hardware device or a software package

Register ► A region of high-speed memory in an electronic processing device, such as an ALU, used to hold data that is being processed

Remote control software ► Computer programs used to establish a connection, via modem, between two machines

Removable hard disks ► Hard disk cartridges that contain platters and read-write heads, and that can be removed from the hard drive

Resolution ► The number of dots per unit of measurement displayed by a computer monitor; the greater the number of dots, the higher the resolution

Ring topology ► Network topology that connects devices in a continuous loop—it is essentially a bus topology in which the ends of the bus are connected

RISC (Reduced instruction set computer) ► A microprocessor that uses a streamlined instruction set for more rapid and efficient processing

Risk management ► The process of weighing threats to computer data against the expendability of that data and the cost of protecting it

ROM BIOS ► A small set of basic input/output system instructions stored in ROM, which cause the system to load critical operating files when the user turns on the computer

Root directory ► The main directory of a disk

Router ► A computer found at each intersection on the Internet backbone that examines IP address of the incoming data and forwards the data towards its destination

Sampling rate ► The number of times per second that the sound is measured during the recording process, expressed in hertz (Hz)

Saving a file ► The process of storing data

Screen size ► The measurement in inches from one corner of the screen diagonally across to the opposite corner

Scanner ► A peripheral device that converts a page of text into or images into electronic format

Scrolling mouse ► A mouse that alleviates the wrist movement by providing a fixed mouse with a rolling ball and two buttons

Search and replace ► A feature of document production software that allows the user to automatically locate all instances of a particular word or phrase and substitute another word or phrase for it

Search engine ► An information-locating component of file management and database software

Search feature ► A feature of document production software that allows the user to automatically locate all the instances of a particular word or phrase

Secret key ► A sequence of numbers or characters used to produce cyphertext

Sectors ► Subdivisions of the tracks on a computer disk on which information is stored

Segmentation ► The division of a network into separate shared-media sub networks

Self-extracting file ► A single file that holds all the modules for the software package

Sequential access ► A form of data storage in which data is stored and read as a sequence of bytes along the length of a tape

Server ► A computer and software that make data available to other computers

Setup program ► Software that guides you through the installation of application software

Shareware ► Software that can be used free of charge for a limited evaluation period, after which it must be licensed

Shrink-wrap license ► A legal agreement printed on computer software packaging, which goes into effect when the package is opened

S-HTTP (Secure HTTP) ► A security protocol that encrypts data sent between your computer and a Web server, but does so one message at a time rather than by setting up an entire secure connection

Signature ► A unique series of bytes that can be used by a virus detection program to identify a known virus

Simulation software ► Computer programs that cause a computer to create a model of a situation, based on data input by the user

Single-user license ► A legal usage agreement limiting the use of a software program to one user at any given time

Site ► In Internet terminology, a computer with a domain name

Site license ► Legal permission for software to be used on any and all computers at a specific location

SLIP (Serial Line Internet Protocol) ► A version of TCP/IP software designed to handle Internet communications over dial-up connections

Software ► See Computer program

Software license ► A legal contract that defines the ways in which a user may use a computer program

Software package ► The disks containing a computer program and the supporting reference material

Software pirates ► Individuals who illegally copy, distribute, or modify software

Software publishers ► Companies that produce computer software

Sound card ► An interface card that gives the computer the ability to accept audio input from a microphone, play sound files stored on disks, and produce audio output through speakers or headphones

Source files ► Files that contain instructions that the computer must translate into a format that it can directly use, before executing them

Spin boxes ► Graphical user interface objects that let the user increase or decrease a number by clicking arrow buttons

Spreadsheet ► A numerical model or representation of a real situation, presented in the form of a table

Spreadsheet modeling ► Setting up numbers in a worksheet format to simulate a real-world situation

Spreadsheet software ► Computer programs that perform calculations on the basis of numbers and formulas supplied by the user and that produce output in the form of tables and graphs

SSL (Secure Sockets Layer) ► A security protocol that uses encryption to establish a secure connection between a computer and a Web server

Standalone computer ► A computer that is not connected to a network

Star topology ► A network topology where communication lines fan out from a central location and each line provides essentially a private link to a centralized hub; used to connect telephone lines to the phone company's switching station

Statistical software ► Computer programs that analyze large sets of data to discover patterns and relationships within them

Status screen ► A recognizable user interface characteristic of a particular software program

Storage ► The area in a computer where data is retained on a permanent basis

Storage capacity ► The maximum amount of data that can be recorded on a storage medium, usually measured in kilobytes, megabytes, or gigabytes

Storage device ► A mechanical apparatus that records data to and retrieves data from a storage medium

Storage media ► The physical materials used for long-term storage (for example, floppy disks)

Storage technology ► A term used to describe a storage device and the media it uses

Store-and-forward ► A technology such as e-mail, in which information is stored on a server and sent to a workstation when requested

Streaming media ► An internet multimedia technology that sends a small segment of a media file to a user's computer and begins to play it while the next segment is being sent

Street price ► The average discounted price for software

Structured database ► A file of information consisting of records and fields organized in a uniform format (for example, a library card catalogue)

Submenu ► The menu that appears after you make a selection from a menu that is arranged in a hierarchical structure

Supercomputer ► The fastest and most expensive type of computer, capable of processing one trillion instructions per second

Surge protector ► (Also called a surge strip or surge suppressor) A device that protects computer equipment from electrical spikes and surges

Syntax ► Specifications for the sequence and punctuation of command words, parameters, and switches

Syntax error ► See Error message

System clock ► A device in the computer that emits pulses to establish the timing for all system operations

Systems operator (sysop) ► The individual responsible for maintaining access to a computer system and for the integrity of all data stored on that system

System requirements ► Specifications for the operating system type and minimum hardware configuration necessary for a software product to work correctly

System resource ► Any part of a computer system, such as a disk drive, memory, or printer, that can be used by a computer program

System software ► Computer programs that help the computer carry out its basic operating tasks

System unit ► The case or box that contains the computer's power supply, storage devices, and the main circuit board with the computer's main processor and memory

Table ► Displays data in a grid of rows and columns

Tape backup ► A copy of data from a computer's hard disk, stored on magnetic tape and used to restore lost data

Tape cartridge ► A removable magnetic tape module, similar to a cassette tape

TCP/IP (Transport Control Protocol/Internet Protocol) ► A standard set of communication rules used by every computer that connects to the Internet

Telephone support ► A service offered over the phone by a hardware manufacturer or software publisher to customers who have questions about how to use a software or hardware product

Template ► A preformatted document into which you type text; can also have spreadsheet and database templates as well as templates for other applications

Terabyte ► 1,000,000,000,000 bytes

Terminal ► A device with a keyboard and a screen, used for input and output but not for processing

Terminal emulation software ► Programs that make it possible for a microcomputer to connect to a host computer and behave as if it were a terminal of the host computer

Text ► In spreadsheet terminology, words used for worksheet titles and for labels that identify columns and rows

TFT (thin film transistor) ► See Active matrix screen

Thesaurus ► Used to find descriptive words to clarify and enliven your writing by finding synonyms and antonyms

Time bomb ► A type of computer program that stays in a computer system undetected until it is triggered at a certain date or time

Time-sharing system ► A configuration in which terminals must share the host computer's processing time

Toggle key ► A key that switches a device back and forth between two modes

Top-level domains ► The major categories into which groups of computers on the Internet are divided

Topology ► The pattern of interconnections in a communications system; common topologies for networks are star, bus, and ring

Touch pad ► A touch-sensitive device that allows the user to control an on-screen pointer by running over the pad's surface

Tower case ► A vertically-oriented microcomputer case, usually placed on the floor to conserve desk space

Trackball ► A pointing device consisting of a ball that is rotated in a frame, in order to move a pointer around a computer screen

Tracks ► A series of concentric subdivisions created on a storage disk during the formatting process

Transfer rate ► The speed at which you can actually send and receive data

Transponder ► Used to send signals from a satellite

Trap door ► A special set of instructions, often created during development and testing, that allow an individual to bypass the normal security precautions and enter the system

Trojan horse ► A computer program that appears to perform one function while actually doing something else, such as inserting a virus into a computer system

Turing Test ► A test invented by Alan Turning in 1950 that would allow a computer to demonstrate its intelligence

Twisted-pair cable ► (Also called UTP) A type of cable in which two separate insulated strands of wire are twisted together

Uninterruptible power supply (UPS) ► A device containing a battery and other circuitry that provides a continuous supply of power to a computer system in the event of disruptions of power

UNIX operating system ► A multiuser, multitasking operating system developed by AT&T's Bell Laboratories in 1969 that is a foundation technology for networks and Web servers

Uploading ► The process of sending a copy of a file from a user's computer to a remote computer

Unspecified Bit Rate (UBR) ► For the transfer of ATM packets; doesn't guarantee any throughput levels

URL (Uniform Resource Locator) ► An Internet address used to access a Web page on the World Wide Web

Usenet server ► A computer that handles the exchange of comments among members of Internet discussion groups

User account ► A means of providing a user with access to network resources

User ID ► (Also called user name) A combination of letters and numbers that serves as a user's "call sign" or identification

User interface ► The means by which human beings interact with computers

User rights ► Rules that specify the directories and files that an individual user can access

Utilities ► A subcategory of system software designed to augment the operating system by providing ways for a computer user to control the allocation and use of hardware resources

Valid filename ► A filename that adheres to filenaming conventions

Value-added reseller (VAR) ► A company that combines commercially available products with additional hardware, software, and/or services to create a system designed to meet specific needs

Variable Bit Rate (VBR) ► A specified maximum throughput capacity but data is sent at even bit rates.

Vector graphics ► In graphics software terminology, images composed of lines and filled shapes

Version ► A new or totally redesigned product

Vertical market software ► Computer programs designed to meet the needs of a specific market segment or industry

Video card ► See Graphics card

Video conferencing ► A means of allowing two or more people or groups of people in separate locations to see and hear each other simultaneously

Viewable image size (vis) ► A measurement of the maximum image size that can be displayed on a monitor screen

Virtual Local Area Network (VLAN) ► A group of personal computers, servers and other network resources that are on physically different segments of a network but communicate as though they were on the same wire; a VLAN is a logical grouping rather than physical LAN segments

Virtual memory ► A computer's use of hard disk storage to simulate RAM during processing

virtual private networks (VPNs) ► VPNs are used to provide a secure connection over an otherwise insecure network, typically the Internet; an important part of a VPN is encryption; VPNs are generally less expensive than establishing and maintaining a private network over private lines; VPNs allow business to provide secure communications and connections over the Internet

Virus ► See Computer virus

Virus detection program ► (Also called antivirus program) Software that examines the files stored on a disk to determine if they are infected with a virus and, if necessary, disinfects the disk

vis ► See Viewable image size

Voice synthesis ► A translation of text into computer-generated speech

WAN (wide area network) ► Defined as a telecommunications network that is not limited by geographic boundaries; it is a broad telecommunications structure that includes public (shared user) networks; WANs may be privately owned or rented

Waveform ► A digital representation of sound

Wave table synthesis ► A MIDI standard that creates music by playing digitized sound samples of actual instruments

Web (Also called World Wide Web, WWW) ► A wide-area hypermedia information retrieval initiative on the Internet aiming to give universal access to a large universe of documents Web authoring software Computer programs that help the user design and develop customized Web pages that can be published electronically on the Internet

Web-based Application Service Providers (ASPs) ► Charge customers via a service contract, or a pay-per-use deal, depending on the service software for use of the software which stays on the Web server

Web browser software ► Computer programs (for example, Netscape Navigator and Microsoft Internet Explorer) that allow the user to view Web pages and that manage the links

Web server ► A computer that uses special software to transmit Web pages over the Internet

Webcast ► A continually changing stream of information broadcast over the Web by means of push technology

Web portal ► A Web site that provides a group of particular Web services, such as a search engine, e-mail access, chat rooms, and links to shopping, weather, news, and sports

What-if analysis ► The process of setting up a model in a spreadsheet and experimenting to see what happens when different values are entered

Wildcard character ► A symbol, such as an asterisk, used to represent a general group of characters

Window ► A visual representation of a work area in a GUI interface

Windows ► GUI-interface-based operating systems produced by Microsoft Corporation

Windows NT Workstation ► Workstation version of the Windows operating system produced by Microsoft Corporation

Windows 2000 Professional ► Workstation version of the Windows operating system produced by Microsoft Corporation

Wireless Application Protocol (WAP) ► A global open standard that gives mobile users access to the Internet through handheld devices

Wireless network ► A network that uses radio or infrared signals (instead of cables) to transmit data from one network device to another

Wizard ► A sequence of screens that direct the user through multistep tasks

Workstation ► High performance single-user microcomputer that would typically be used for advanced or high-end computing tasks

Word size ► The number of bits the CPU can manipulate at one time, which is dependent on the size of the registers in the CPU and on the number of data lines in the bus

Word wrap ► A feature of document production software that automatically moves the cursor to the beginning of the next line of text when it reaches the end of the current line

Word processing software ► Computer programs that assist the user in producing documents such as reports, letters, papers, and manuscripts

Workbook ► A combination of several worksheets created by a spreadsheet

Workflow software ► Programs that automate the process of electronically routing documents from one person to another, in a specified sequence and time frame

Worksheet ► An on-screen spreadsheet (See also Spreadsheet)

Workstation ► A computer connected to a local area network

Workstation installation ► A process in which some, but not all, of the program files from a program installed on a network server are copied to a workstation's local hard drive and the workstation's menu is updated

Worm ► A software program designed to enter a computer system, usually a network, through security "holes"

Write-protect window ► A latch in the upper right-hand corner of a floppy disk that, when open, makes the disk read-only

x86 family ► A series of Intel microprocessors commonly used in PCs (for example, 386 or 486 chips)

XML (Extensible Markup Language) ► A document format similar to HTML but it allows the Web page developer to define customized tags and produce custom effects not available with HTML.

Y2K (year 2000 time bomb) ► A time bomb that was unintentionally created by computer programmers when they wrote programs that use a two-digit, rather than four-digit, field for the year, with the result that computers would read the digits 00 as 1900 rather than as 2000

Zip disk drive ► A high-capacity floppy disk manufactured by Iomega Corporation, frequently used for backups

Index